THE **ROUGH GUIDE** TO
CULT FICTION

KT-448-056

CULT FICTION

Text editors Paul Simpson, Michaela Bushell, Helen Rodiss
Contributors Tom Bullough, Rob Ganley, Michelle de Larrabeiti,
Michael Hann, Roger Bardon, Mark Ellingham, Richard Koss, Hunter Slaton,
Damian Hall, Marcela Mora y Araujo, Paul Bradshaw, Kath Stathers,
Robert Jeffery, Richard Pendleton, Shaun Campbell, Victoria Williams,
Al Spicer, Dave Burton, Jess McAree, Marianne Gray, Ann Oliver,
Lesley Simpson, Jon Hotten, Nick Moore, Sergio Lopez, Eric Lithander
Graphic novels (except Tintin) Paul Gravett
Production Stephanie Jones, Ian Cranna, Kath Stathers
Picture editors Jenny Quiggin, Dominique Campbell, Lara Richards
Special Merit Department Emma Mercer, Mark Ellingham, Andrew Lockett, Simon
Kanter, Simon Bracken, Julia Bovis, Daniel May
Cover and Design Sharon O'Connor
Printed in Spain by Graphy Cems
Dedicated to Delmore Schwartz

Images supplied by: Cover Henry Cartier-Bresson/Magnum Photos
Back cover Sophie Bassouls/Corbis; Kim Stringfellow Spine New Directions Books
Inside covers Horst Tappe/Rue des Archives; Robert LaVigne
Inside Nicolas Tikhomiroff/Magnum Photos; Riber Hansson; Granada Sky
Broadcasting; Franklin McMahon/Corbis; Vinmag Archive; Sunset
Boulevard/Corbis; Joseph Scherschel/Time Life Pictures/Getty Images;
Keystone/Getty Images; Moviestore Collection; Cecil Stoughton, White House/John
Fitzgerald Kennedy Library; Everett Collection/Rex Features; Dennis
Stock/Magnum Photos; ©1997–1999 International Museum of Cartoon Art

Publishing Information
This edition published April 2005 was prepared by Haymarket Customer
Publishing for Rough Guides Ltd, 80 Strand, London WC2R ORL

Distributed by the Penguin Group
Penguin Books Ltd, 80 Strand, London WC2R ORL

No part of this book may be reproduced in any form without permission from the
publisher except for the quotation of brief passages in reviews

© Haymarket Customer Publishing 2005
A catalogue record for this book is available from the British Library
ISBN 1-84353-387-1
3   5   7   9   8   6   4   2

* The essential equipment of a cult author, as collected by William Burroughs

HAMPSHIRE COUNTY LIBRARY	
C013907727	
H J	17/01/2006
R809.3	£7.99
1843533871	

"The book was thick and red. It was almost thicker than it was wide, a thickness that somehow enhanced its bookishness. It was – to me aged 12 – quite clearly more of a book than most, if not all, of the paperbacks untidily stacked on the shelves of my father's study"

Will Self appreciates Catch-22
before he even reads the first page

WINCHESTER REFERENCE LIBRARY
81 NORTH WALLS WINCHESTER
Tel: 01962 826666
Fax: 01962 856615

THE BASICS

Google the words 'cult fiction' and you may unearth: a story about a religious sect suspected of coercion in Oxford; a compilation album from Virgin called **This Is The Return Of Cult Fiction** ("**North By Northwest**, **Taxi Driver** + 34 other cult and classic TV and film themes"); while one online forum kicked off with the plaintive cry: "Who has a definition of cult fiction for me? Is it a genre?"

Cult fiction is, of course, what this book is all about – its main aim is to introduce you to authors or novels that you might find intriguing, or to send you back to writers – and books – you already know for another look. With over **200 authors**, **30 graphic novelists**, **nearly 70 other novels** and one literary gent who defies categorisation (**Hergé**), this book is designed mainly to make you want to read more, although we hope you will be entertained along the way.

The term cult fiction implies lengthy and irrational devotion probably, though not necessarily, by an ardent minority, to an author or book. A work that is reread over and over. **Toby Litt**, the appropriately named British novelist, suggests that, in their purest form, cult books ought to have been out of print for ten years, although the title he nominates as his all-time cult book – **The Bible** – has never been unavailable in the last 400 years. He has a point, though, when he suggests that cult fiction can be dangerous. Think **J.D. Salinger**'s **The Catcher In The Rye**: a classic novel of protest against phonies and a sacred text for a surprising number of America's most famous assassins. Cult fiction moves people, often in unexpected ways. Thousands wanted to go on the road with **Jack Kerouac**, discuss mystic motorcycle maintenance with **Robert Pirsig** (cult fiction doesn't even need to be pure fiction), debate existentialism, and raincoats, with **Albert Camus** or pay simple (yet to the recipient, vaguely disturbing) homage to the likes of Salinger, **Thomas Pynchon** or **Gabriel Garcia Marquez**.

CULT FICTION

The quality of the writing is often beside the point. When we asked a colleague, who is also a novelist, whether **Marcel Proust** should be considered cult. He snorted indignantly: "Proust is not a cult writer He is a great writer!" Proust is reviewed in this book because being cult and being great are not mutually exclusive. But you can be a bad writer and cult too. **Truman Capote** had a point when he said Kerouac's work was "not writing, but typing", yet it is Kerouac's books, not his critic's, which seem to strike a recurring chord with the generations.

Being a cult author brings certain messianic burdens, which may be why so many (Salinger, Pynchon) have gone underground. **James Joyce**, so inspired **F. Scott Fitzgerald** that, on meeting his idol, the American novelist offered to throw himself out of the window to prove his dedication. Their mutual friend, Sylvia Beach, owned a copy of **The Great Gatsby** in which Fitzgerald had drawn himself kneeling before a haloed Joyce. The drawing was titled Festival Of St James.

For less impulsive souls cult worship may begin, and end, with the purchase of a cherished writer's complete works. Yet cultness is a fickle business. Nothing kills a literary cult quite as fast as being studied in classrooms, which is why you won't find **William Golding**'s **Lord Of The Flies**, widely seen as cult in the 1960s, here.

If the true cult book should be out of print for ten years, the truly cult author, ought to have written one seminal novel, behaved abominably in public and then died tragically young or, better still, vanished. Although the strategy is not infallible. In 1955, the American poet and short-story writer **Weldon Kees** abandoned his car near the Golden Gate Bridge in San Francisco and was never seen again. He was 21. His mysterious exit, however, failed to lead to a posthumous boom either in sales or reputation. Meanwhile, **Dylan Thomas** never wrote a serious amount of fiction (or anything, for that matter), but he lived up to the stereotype of how cult authors ought to (mis)behave. Not long before his death, as a guest in Cornwall, he ran out into a sunny field one morning sipping a local herbalist's champagne wine tonic and talking copiously. Then, he stopped suddenly and said: "Somebody's boring me – I think it's me."

"THE BOOK THAT MEANS MOST TO ME IS..."

Just for Rough Guides, actors, musos and authors reveal their literary tastes

Charlotte Rampling
I will read and reread **Ian McEwan**'s **Atonement**. I adore his books, they are so dark, so provocative.

Dougray Scott
The Cone Gatherers by **Robin Jenkins**. Set on an estate in Scotland, it is about a gamekeeper's descent into madness and two cone gatherers in the forest. It is about class issues, unexplained goodness and badness.

Kristin Scott-Thomas
Black Dogs by **Ian McEwan**. It's his usual dark stuff about dysfunctional family life, but unputdownable.

John Cale
Alain Robbe-Grillet's **Repetition**, because you can read and reread each page endlessly and you will always come up with something new in it.

Minnie Driver
Under Milk Wood, preferably read by **Richard Burton**, would be my dream entertainment.

Emily Mortimer
A Hero Of Our Times by **Mikhail Lermontov**. The protagonist Pechorin is cold, proud and dangerous, one of Russia's original anti-heroes. I like its daring, its descriptions of the Caucasus and its lurking mysticism.

Laurence Fishburne
Ishmael Reed's novel **Yellow Black Radio Broke Down**. You gotta read it.

Lynda La Plante
One of my all-time favourites is **The Bear Went Over The Mountain** by **William Kotzwinkle**. It is hilarious and ironic; a fable for adults, with special meaning for writers because it is about a writer who loses his precious manuscript and a bear who finds it,

reads it, likes it, changes the name on the front cover and sells it to a publisher, taking the literary world by storm.

Jeanne Moreau
The Reader by **Bernhard Schlink** is a compelling book about the Holocaust, very personal, very universal, about the redemptive power of understanding.

Miriam Margolyes
Little Dorritt by **Charles Dickens**. One of his dark books, it pulls you into his world and tears your heart. Written when his life was in turmoil, it shows in the bleakness of the relationships.

Oprah Winfrey
Toni Morrison's novel **Beloved**, a book about a mother's love, a ghost story, a spiritual quest. I felt this was part of the reason I was born.

Bert Kwouk
Catcher In The Rye by **J.D. Salinger** had a huge, subliminal effect on me. I was caught up by that age, that time. It's about an outsider and being an Oriental I could relate.

Kyle McLachan
Franz Kafka's **The Trial**. When I first read it I thought Josef K, the man in a nightmare tale at the mercy of authority, was a very hyper guy, a tenacious man driving himself for answers. Then I got to play him on film and found he was a little like Twin Peaks' Dale Cooper — an innocent drawn to darkness.

Gérard Depardieu
Anything by **Oscar Wilde**. **The Picture of Dorian Gray** is fantastic. Wilde is someone who carried the pain, the hypocrisy of the whole world.

Olivia Williams
Giuseppe di Lampedusa's **The Leopard**. I'm reading it for the fifth time.

7

CULT BIBLIOPHILIA

Time was when us cult bibliophiles had to seek out a small coterie of bookstores – places like **City Lights** in San Francisco, **Gotham Book Mart** in New York, or the late-lamented **Compendium** in London – to service our habit. But times have changed and these days you can do it all from home on the **web**: a less-random process that means foregoing the chance of a signed **Edward Gorey** postcard or a battered 1970s pulp paperback of **Paul Bowles** you happen upon in the dust, but which will likely provide a better hit rate for the novels you can't find in your local bookshop.

> "You have the idea and you put down what you want to say. Then get somebody to add commas, maybe fix the spelling. They have people who do that"
>
> Elmore Leonard

Your first stops online should be **Amazon** (amazon.com and amazon.co.uk) and its used-and-rare-books partner **Bibliofind** (bibliofind.com), and the awesome dealers emporium **Abebooks** (abebooks.com). The US and UK Amazon stores will provide access to pretty much everything that's new – bar the most arcane small presses – and Bibliofind and Amazon between them mop up just about every book dealer who bothers to have a presence online. If you are still struggling to find a rare, used title, try **usedbooksearch.co.uk** and **bookfinder.com**, or there's always **eBay** (ebay.com and ebay.co.uk), where the random and impulsive know no bounds.

Alternatively, if you have a particular field of interest, there's probably an online store where you can browse: for example, **Beatbooks** (www.beatbooks.com) for the Beat writers. And many of the best specialist stores maintain their own websites, where you can view recommendations or search. **City Lights** (citylights.com) will steer you through Dadaism, Situationism and Muckraking. The wonderful **Serendipity Books** in Berkeley (serendipitybooks.com) has catalogues to download on subjects ranging from **Robert Crumb** through to the first editions of 1,600 authors' first books.

What's maybe most difficult is buying original-language foreign editions. Start at the **European Bookshop** (europeanbookshop.com) or, for literature in French, **FNAC** (fnac.com). However, this isn't the richest area of the web, and it is, alas, a lot easier to buy a Bulgarian villa online than it is a Bulgarian novel.

THE AUTHORS

YOUR GUIDE TO THE GENRE BENDERS, BEATS,
GURUS, SINNERS, SURREALISTS, DRUNKS, JUNKIES,
POSTMODERNISTS AND DISAPPEARANCE ARTISTS BEHIND
THE WORLD'S MOST INTRIGUING FICTION

Woman "If I vacuum, will I disturb your writing?"

Charles Bukowski "Nothing can disturb my writing.
It's a disease"

THE AUTHORS

Fiction isn't dead, even if many of these authors are. **Xenophon**, an associate of **Socrates**, has been credited with writing what some say is the first novel, The Education Of Cyrus in 400BC. Xenophon was ,obviously ahead of his time because he also pioneered the noble art of horse whispering. Almost two-and-a-half millenia later, the art of fiction – novels, novella, short stories – is as alive as ever and there's no better proof than the semi-continuous debate: is fiction dead? If you have to ask, the answer's obvious – nobody holds seminars addressing the vital question: is the dodo dead? These writers have all, in their intriguing, surprising and often strange ways, contributed to that life force. Two of them – **Arthur Rimbaud** and **Allen Ginsberg** – are so cult they're included even though they haven't written any fiction.

KOBO ABE

"No man or woman is wooed by theory alone"

There is a slightly patronising tendency, even in literary criticism, to pair novelists who didn't write in one of the major European languages with Western equivalents. **Kobo Abe** (1924–1993) has suffered from this, being dubbed 'the Japanese **Kafka**' and compared, for his existentialism in some works, to **Camus**.

Yet, as **David Keffer** argues in a perceptive essay on the **Scriptorium** (modernword.com/scriptorium), the biggest influences on Abe may be his father (a doctor), and the fact that he studied medicine at Tokyo University. He never practised however, giving it up to join a literary group that aimed to apply surrealist techniques to Marxist ideology. But the surrealist/Marxist experiment never liberated his style, and Abe remained more interested in ideas than techniques: his prose can seem stiff today (especially if you've become acquainted with the Japanese novel through **Haruki Murakami**), with the emphasis on exposition rather than narrative, particularly in the early works.

His heroes were often scientists – he seemed to find their mind-set comforting – but he had the confidence to roam across such genres as sci-fi, mystery and the existential novel. If he learned you could not woo readers with theory, he did so by experiment, waxing philosophical and existential in novels like The Woman In The Dunes (filmed by **Hiroshi Teshigahara**) and gauging the reaction.

Abe's first novel – The Road Sign At The End Of The Street – was published in 1948. He won his first proper literary prize in 1951 with The Crime Of S. Karuma. His most fruitful period was between 1964, when his work first achieved international recognition, and 1979, when his existential satire Secret Rendezvous, about a man whose wife vanishes in an ambulance (a scenario later imagined by Hollywood scriptwriter **Larry Cohen**), was published. His most inviting work, for a new reader, may be The Ruined Map, a kind of mystery novel in which the detective loses his way and sense of self. In the 1970s he began to retreat from anything that might be deemed realism and, in works as strange as Secret Rendezvous, character and psychology are of little interest. But in novels like The Ruined Map he can leave the reader with a lingering, disquieting effect.

INFLUENCED BY Edgar Allan Poe; Kafka; Dostoevksy; Bertolt Brecht; Arthur Miller; Orwell; Camus.
INFLUENCE ON Hanada Kiyoteru (though he influenced Abe too).
ESSENTIAL READING **The Woman In The Dunes**; **The Ruined Map**.
FURTHER READING **The Box Man** is his funniest novel.

12

WALTER ABISH
Master of postmodern tomfoolery and other gimmicks

Private eyes have a gimmick, so why shouldn't novelists? There are so many of them, how else is the general public to tell them apart? German writer **Walter**

WALTER ABISH'S ALPHABET SOUP

Alphabetical Africa has 52 chapters, going from A to Z and then Z to A. Each chapter is meant to contain only words beginning with the letters of the alphabet up to whatever the chapter-heading letter is – so the fifth (and the forty-eighth) chapter (both E) only contain words beginning with A, B, C, D and E.

Despite being, as **John Updike** noted in his original review, a "ludicrously programmatic novel", Abish's debut still works but,

embarrassingly, neither Abish nor the copy editor noticed that he had broken his own rules. The first O chapter includes the rogue word 'promise' starting with a painfully premature P. In the second F chapter, an untimely I ('innovative') lets the side down and I, again, slips through the net twice in the second C chapter.

Pedantic nit-picking? Up to a point. But as Abish designed this rigorous exercise, he ought to live by it. Don't, though, let this put you off the novel.

THE AUTHORS

Abish (1931–) has a chest of drawers full of gimmicks – the most obvious being the triangular black eye-patch he sports in his author's photo. If that's not enough, in his first novel Alphabetical Africa he decided what letter the words in each chapter should start with by a bizarre alphabetical scheme (see box). He capped this with the short-story collection Minds Meet, in which **Proust** lives in Albuquerque in a tale called How A Comb Gives Fresh Meaning To The Hair. His most famous novel, How German Is It?, is a wonder which, in **John Updike**'s elegant phrase, harnessed "postmodern verbal tomfoolery to a thriller plot and a passionately distrustful concern with modern Germany."

Abish was born in Vienna, but his Jewish family fled to Shanghai in 1940 from where, in turn, they fled Maoism for Israel before settling in New York. In the 1970s his absurdist short stories were published in magazines. How German Is It? was his breakthrough. A classic work of metafiction, it never lets you forget you're reading a novel as it digs for Nazi traces under the glossy exterior of democratic, prosperous West Germany. It did not endear him to some Germans; one interviewer tried to force him to admit it was a "Jew's revenge".

Abish has been oddly quiet since; his major recent work has been his memoir, Double Vision. In 99: The New Meaning he rearranged fragments of words from authors, in a literary game that some relished but others dismissed as a misshapen jigsaw puzzle. His novel Eclipse Fever, set among the elite of Mexico City, was inevitably greeted with 'How Mexican Is It?' gags, but it lived up to his creed of, in his own words, "engaging the reader by withholding the familiar."

INFLUENCED BY Donald Barthelme; T.S. Eliot; Heidegger; Proust.

INFLUENCE ON Austrian novelist Bernard Cohen; Jim Lewis.

ESSENTIAL READING **How German Is It?**: vintage Abish yet very accessible.

FURTHER READING **Alphabetical Africa**; **Double Vision** – it reveals more about his failure to separate modern Germany from its past than he intended.

KATHY ACKER

Power, punk and porn

A random selection of the titles of the works of **Kathy Acker** (1947–1998) – Hannibal Lecter, My Father; I Dreamt I Was A Nymphomaniac; Pussy, King Of The Pirates – conveys her talent to shock, rebel and outrage. These all came masterfully together in her most famous work, Blood And Guts In High School. No respecter of critics, literary greats (she was famous for violent, pornographic pastiches of classics like Don Quixote), narrative (**William Burroughs**'s cut-up techniques were a favourite device) or the rules of language, Acker is a literary warrior princess, credited with inventing a new kind of feminist prose: aggressive, spartan, even primordial, yet intimately personal.

Born in New York, Acker never knew her father – sinister dads are a recurring theme for her – and fell out with her mother, supporting herself as an erotic dancer. Her first work, Politics, was published in 1972 when she was 25. With Blood And Guts she became notorious. Britain cherished her, but after **Harold Robbins** threatened to sue her in the British courts for plagiarising a sex scene, she fled to New York and then to California, where she took up body-building and taught literature to rich kids, while writing an amazing quantity of books, including the fine Empire Of The Senseless. Diagnosed with breast cancer in 1996, she died two years later; one of her last chores was interviewing the **Spice Girls**, advocates of a softer brand of Girl Power, for **The Guardian**.

> "Too much
> 'I used to be in
> a bad marriage,
> now I'm a
> happy lesbian,'
> not enough
> language"
>
> Kathy Acker on the flaws
> in much feminist fiction

There is, as **Brian Bowdrey** said of Pussy, King Of The Pirates, "something to offend everybody" in her fiction. Influenced by Burroughs, her stories, he notes, proceed "via perpetual revolution and terrorism." Some feminists have accused her of pandering to male sexual fantasies, while others have smothered her in theory. **Robert Lort** summed her up best: "Kathy was always out on her own, a strange girl blown out towards the thresholds of language and thought." Irreplaceable, not always easy to read, but seldom dull, Acker was too iconoclastic to join a movement in life or be adopted by one in death.

INFLUENCED BY Burroughs; Georges Bataille; Robbe-Grillet; Jean Genet; radical French philosopher Gilles Deleuze; the Black Mountain poets.

INFLUENCE ON Dennis Cooper; Dodie Bellamy.

ESSENTIAL READING If you like one Acker novel you'll like almost all of them. The reverse also applies. But **Blood And Guts**; **Empire Of The Senseless**; and **The Adult Life Of Toulouse Lautrec By Henri Toulouse Lautrec** stand out.

FURTHER READING **Bodies Of Work**: the theory behind the fiction.

DOUGLAS ADAMS

His prose often 'accidentally' hit on universal truths

The Hitchhiker's Guide To The Galaxy has sold over 14 million copies worldwide and, according to **The Guardian**, invented a new genre: "gently clever" comedy sci-fi. Not bad for an idea that came to its author as he lay drunk in a field in Innsbruck, Austria as a 19-year-old student.

Douglas Noel Adams (1952–2001) was born in Cambridge (a few months before another type of DNA, as he often joked), to a nurse and a theology teacher who divorced five years later. "I was a very disturbed child," he said, "twitchy and strange." He studied English at Cambridge, had an epiphanic hitchhiking trip around Europe and left university wanting "to be **John Cleese**". After a doomed co-writing experience with Monty Python's **Graham Chapman**, Adams had some success as a script writer/editor for Doctor Who before pitching his idea – a satirical blend of sci-fi and comedy – to BBC radio.

The plot chronicles the journey of Arthur Dent and alien Ford Prefect after Earth is destroyed to make way for a galactic freeway. The search for an answer to the meaning of life (it's 42, by the way) involves the comically implausible two-headed, three-armed Zaphod Beeblebrox and Marvin, a depressed, paranoid android. Adams has a unique grasp of glorious nonsense ("The ships hung in the sky, much the same way that bricks don't") that often 'accidentally' hit on universal truths. After the 1978 radio series won awards, Adams turned his idea into a novel. This was soon followed by The Restaurant At The End Of The Universe – an idea inspired by the **Procol Harum** song Grand Hotel – Life, The

Douglas Adams, possibly the only man ever to know why the answer is 42

Universe And Everything and, in 1984, So Long, And Thanks For All The Fish, the last book written to meet commercial demand and it showed. "I really shouldn't have written [it]… it wasn't really from the heart," he admitted.

Adams was famously non-prolific. He struggled with writer's block, once saying, "I love deadlines. I love the whooshing noise they make as they go by," and it was eight years before the final book, Mostly Harmless, was finished. Adams's other work often gets overlooked, yet Dirk Gently's Holistic Detective Agency and the sequel The Long Dark Tea-Time Of The Soul are full of comic ingenuity.

Adams suffered a fatal heart attack at 49. The posthumous Salmon Of Doubt is a collection of his articles, plus everything left on his desk, including chapters of a new Dirk Gently novel he had realised would better befit Arthur Dent and friends.

INFLUENCED BY P.G. Wodehouse, who he once called the "Lewis Carroll of the 20th century"; Dickens; Jane Austen; Kurt Vonnegut; Ruth Rendell; the scientist Richard Dawkins; Monty Python.

INFLUENCE ON Terry Pratchett; Neil Gaiman; **Red Dwarf**; **Men In Black**.

ESSENTIAL READING **The Ultimate Hitchhiker's Guide To The Galaxy**.

FURTHER READING **Dirk Gently's Holistic Detective Agency**; **The Meaning Of Liff** – a quirky, funny, alternative dictionary.

NELSON ALGREN

Social realist who walked, and wrote, on the wild side

Nelson Algren (1909–1981) believed lost souls "sometimes develop into greater human beings than those who have never been lost." Algren lost himself, in the Deep South in the Great Depression where, in 1933, he wrote his first short story So Help Me in a derelict petrol station.

Algren grew up in a poor part of Detroit. His grandfather was a Swedish convert to Judaism and his mother owned a candy store. **Simone de Beauvoir**, who had an affair with him and fictionalised him as Lewis Bogan in her novel The Mandarins, regarded him as an example of that "classic American species, the self-made leftist writer." Convinced it was a writer's job to shine a light on the world's darkest places, his natural subjects were, "drunks, pimps, prostitutes, freaks, drug addicts, prize fighters, corrupt politicians and hoodlums." He admitted he "never believed in writing directly from my imagination" and,

Admirable Nelson

THE AUTHORS

though his novels are powerful and crafted rather than mere reportage, they can be overwhelmed by his need to tell. **Richard Wright**, when asked his opinion about an Algren novel, said: "I think some plot would not hurt at all, Nelson."

Although he is famous for such novels as The Man With The Golden Arm (a tale about a heroin addict adapted by **Otto Preminger** for the cinema) and Walk On The Wild Side, which gave **Lou Reed** a song title, his reputation began to slide in the late 1950s as his work dried up, his simple-minded radicalism and an indisputable strain of misogyny (he privately referred to Beauvoir as "Mme Utter Drivelau") counting against him. The business of living like an American writer, which, in Algren's view, meant experiencing as much as possible, (especially if it involved drinking, womanising and gambling) began to take over from the work. After Walk On The Wild Side appeared in 1956, his next novel, The Devil's Stocking, wasn't published until 1983, two years after his death.

Algren is, possibly unfairly, less revered than writers like **Dashiell Hammett** who stuck closer to a specific genre. After his death a street in Chicago, where he lived for years, was named in his honour and then renamed after protests, summing up the ambivalence with which his work is viewed today.

INFLUENCED BY Stephen Crane; Jack London; Theodore Dreiser; John Dos Passos; John Steinbeck.

17

INFLUENCE ON Joseph Heller; Kurt Vonnegut; Russell Banks; Hubert Selby Jr; you can see echoes of Algren in Pynchon.

ESSENTIAL READING His best, flawed, work is **Walk On The Wild Side** – a poetic, picaresque novel that swings with an American beat.

FURTHER READING **The Man With The Golden Arm** is his next best; the biography by Bettina Drew – **A Life On The Wild Side** – is a good read.

RICHARD ALLEN

The Charles Dickens of skinheads

James Moffat (1922–1993) was a Canadian-born writer who once published a magazine about bowling and who, under sundry pseudonyms, wrote hack fiction (westerns, children's stories, mysteries). In 1970 he was asked, because he was so versatile and prolific, to write a book for the **New English Library** about skinheads, the white working-class youths whose thuggery seemed, to some, an authentic cry of alienation and, to others, the decline of Western civilisation.

Allen's first novel, Skinhead, uneasily combined self-righteous fascist rhetoric, nihilist indifference and the shocked voice of reason. But it succeeded with its authentic portrayal of Joe Hawkins, the 16-year-old gangster convinced the Cockneys had lost control of their patch, London, and whose life of rape,

CULT FICTION

drink and hooliganism ends in a kind of triumph when he is jailed for beating a cop – a punishment which, he gloats, makes him king of the skinheads.

After that sold a million, the formula stayed pretty constant for 17 other novels – seven with the words 'skin' or 'skinhead' in the title. Allen brought to the task an enthusiasm for research, speed – he once completed a novel in less than week –

narrative drive and pulp flair. The opening line of *Suedehead* is masterful: "As he stood in the dock, Joe Hawkins considered his situation with utter detachment." Yet the author, uncomfortable with charges he encouraged violence, later blamed: "leniency in courtrooms, catering to fads by mercenary-minded rag-trade merchants, a soft-peddling attitude by politicians who look for teenage votes and an overwhelming pandering by the media."

Rediscovered in his seventies, Allen was planning a sequel, *Skinhead Return*, when years of writing at short notice aided by tobacco and booze finally caught up with him. He died in 1993.

INFLUENCED BY Pulp fiction; Harold Robbins.

INFLUENCE ON His success led to a plethora of books like Bill Buford's **Among The Thugs**, in which intellectual types slummed it with violent oiks.

ESSENTIAL READING **Skinhead** and **Suedehead** stand apart.

FURTHER READING As Trudi Maxwell, Allen wrote the compellingly dire **Diary Of A Female Wrestler**: unforgettably, ludicrously bad.

THE FASTEST TYPEWRITER IN THE EAST

Michael Avallone's parents were prolific – he was one of 17 children – and so was he. As a hack of all trades, Avallone (1925–1999) wrote 62 novels under his own name, 20 erotic spy stories about a hero called Rod Damon (his nickname: 'capitalism's favourite tool') under a pseudonym and countless novelisations of such TV shows as The Partridge Family.

Avallone gloried in the title **The Fastest Typewriter In The East** and once claimed to have written a 1,500-word story in 20 minutes and a novel in a day and a half.

Yet this New Yorker got very feisty if anyone accused him of being a hack. He feuded with **Stephen King**, accusing the famous author of stealing his ideas. King wasn't, though, inspired by the punning titling style (Turn The Other Sheik) of a writer who had almost as many aliases (**Troy Conway**, **Jeanne-Anne dePre**, **Dora Highland**) as novels, but who was most appropriately known as **The King Of Cheese**.

From bright young thing to Smarty Anus, but where next?

Martin Amis (1949–) found fame as a comic novelist with his first book, The Rachel Papers, when he was 24. Like his father **Kingsley**'s first novel Lucky Jim, it won the Somerset Maugham Award. While father and son both satirised society in their day, stylistically they are worlds apart. Martin was postmodernist from the off – his narrators always self-conscious of the fact they're telling a story – and his cleverness annoyed Kingsley, as did his son's "terrible compulsive vividness… a constant demonstrating of his command of English."

Born in Oxford, Martin spent much of his childhood in Swansea. Educated at more than a dozen schools, including spells in New Jersey and Majorca, he salvaged his secondary education at a 'crammer' and then won a formal First in English at Oxford. The Rachel Papers, exploring the rubric of teenage sex, was published while he was editorial assistant at the **Times Literary Supplement**. In his second novel, Dead Babies, a group of wealthy young hedonists (including a murdering nihilist psychopath) descend on a country house owned by a sex- and dentistry-obsessed dwarf, for a weekend of orgies and drug-fuelled debauchery. As a satire on the sexual and chemical excess of the 1970s, it's outstanding.

By the early 1980s Amis had become the hard-drinking, chain-smoking enfant terrible of British fiction, inviting praise and criticism in equal measure. Fellow author **Julian Barnes** declared him "the finest prose stylist now writing in English", while **Private Eye** named him Smarty Anus for his flights of purple prose. His fourth novel, Money, is widely considered his best, a satire on the greed of Thatcherism and Reaganism, in which inarticulate narrator and filmmaker John Self has a massive appetite for alcohol and pornography and worships money. There is a cameo from novelist Martin Amis and, as ever, Amis humiliates the narrator constantly. The book was a turning point for the author: "It is about tiring of being single; it is about the fear that childlessness will condemn you to childishness," he wrote in his memoir Experience. He married on the day Money was published and his first son was born four months later.

After Money Amis seemed to aspire to gravitas, political and intellectual: he wrote of his dread of nuclear war (Einstein's Monsters), fear of the planet dying (London Fields) and the Holocaust (Time's Arrow). He had a rough ride in the mid-1990s. A very public divorce was followed by a second marriage to an American heiress and he ditched his agent **Pat Kavanagh**, wife of his best friend Julian Barnes. Barnes's friendship-ending letter ended: "Fuck off." He spent much of his £500,000 advance for The Information on high-profile dentistry. When the book came out, his enemies gleefully accused him of hubris, others of sexism (to be fair, his male characters are usually odious too). Bewildered by the hostility, Amis was told by an American academic: "It's just that people hate you."

As well as documenting all this in Experience, he paints a touching portrait of his relationship with his father: "My father never encouraged me to write… he praised me less often than he publicly dispraised me; but it worked." Experience might be a candid account of his life (with a few too many digressions to ponder his cousin's fate in the horrific **Fred West** murders), but his comic riffing is as brilliant as ever: he starts the book recalling a conversation he had with his father: "If two tigers jumped on a blue whale, could they kill it?"

INFLUENCED BY Saul Bellow; Nabokov; Amis senior.

INFLUENCE ON Will Self; Julian Barnes.

ESSENTIAL READING **Money**; **Dead Babies**.

FURTHER READING **Experience**, for an insight into his obsessions.

MIGUEL ANGEL ASTURIAS

The Guatemalan man of many parts: novelist, surrealist, diplomat

Miguel Angel Asturias (1899–1974) was the first and clearest exponent of an authentically Latin American novel, one that was no longer merely an offspring of the European tradition.

A native of Guatemala, he was a founding member of the Universidad Popular de Guatemala in 1922, where he helped teach local workers to read. That same year he graduated as a lawyer and published his thesis The Indian's Social Problem, an essay widely regarded as racist but an early indication of a theme he would frequently return to throughout his life.

In 1924 he travelled to London to study, and later that year moved to Paris, where he met **James Joyce**, **André Breton**, **Picasso** and poet **Pablo Neruda**, among others. Asturias was excited by surrealism's suggestion that the world can be changed with ideas. Interest in 'primitive cultures' was also fashionable in 1920s Paris; there were courses in Mayan culture at the Ecole Pratique des Hautes Etudes. It was through the eyes of Europe that Asturias rediscovered America. In an article in 1927, in an apparent U-turn from his earlier thesis, he wrote, "Our disdain and our ignorance of our own culture borders on the criminal."

After embarking on a Spanish translation of the Popol Vuh – The Sacred Book Of Ancient Mayas he wrote Legends Of Guatemala, in which he described Guatemala's natural world, recreating a magical, mythical world using texts of the Mayan tradition. "In these I laid out my devotion to my small homeland, to my small corner of volcanoes, of lakes, of mountains, of clouds, of birds," he said.

Asturias's two most famous works, The President and Men Of Maize, were published in 1946 and 1949, although Asturias had completed The President in 1932 and both books contain sections that had been published as stories over the years. With these books Asturias laid bare a tormented political and social reality. The President tells the tale of a Latin American dictator; in Men Of Maize Mayan myths are accentuated in a conflict between the sacred and the profane, the Indian and the white man. (Asturias's son, Rodrigo, became a figurehead in Guatemalan politics, leading the guerrillas under the assumed name of **Gaspar Ilom**, the ideological character in Men Of Maize.)

In the 1940s Asturias became more detached from literature and more involved in diplomacy, but found time to write his famous banana trilogy, attacking the exploitative policies of the United Fruit company, and Weekend In Guatemala, stories fictionalising the American intervention that toppled a centre-left government in Guatemala. In the 1960s his fiction gained international acclaim. In 1962 The President won the William Faulkner Foundation prize for best Latin American novel and in 1967 (by which time he was Guatemalan ambassador to France) he won the **Nobel Prize** for Literature.

> "Just remember how many writers down the ages have written to entertain, and who remembers them now?"
>
> Miguel Angel Asturias, in his Nobel Prize speech

21

INFLUENCED BY Pablo Neruda; José Vasconcelos; **Popol Vuh – The Sacred Book Of Ancient Mayas**.

INFLUENCE ON Gabriel García Márquez; Mario Vargas Llosa.

ESSENTIAL READING **The President**; **Men Of Maize**.

FURTHER READING **Legends Of Guatemala**.

PAUL AUSTER

What a difference a coincidence makes

In The Red Notebook, a collection of interviews, reflections and experiences, **Paul Auster** (1947–) recounts his disappointment as an eight-year-old at not getting New York Giants baseball star **Willie Mays**'s autograph because he didn't have a pencil. "After that I started carrying a pencil with me wherever I went," Auster writes. "If there's a pencil in your pocket, there's a good chance that one day you'll feel tempted to start using it." This idea that chance encounters change a person's life is his trademark. Coincidences are "the mechanics of reality".

Auster was born in Newark, New Jersey. He wanted to be a writer from an early age and started two novels – In The Country Of Last Things and Moon Palace – at college, but admits that they were too ambitious and he turned to poetry. His published work includes poems, essays, novels, screenplays and translations.

One of his early works of prose, The Invention Of Solitude, explores fatherhood, including his own grief at the sudden death of his father. Although he denies that the book is autobiographical, it is an extremely personal account, a tactic echoed through much of Auster's later fiction. His first meeting with his second wife, writer **Siri Hustvedt**, in 1981, is used in Leviathan when Peter meets Iris (Siri in reverse), and the events in The New York Trilogy centre on his favourite theme of coincidence and are littered with autobiographical references.

The first story in the trilogy, City Of Glass, unravels from an incident in 1980 when Auster received two phone calls from a man asking for the Pinkerton Agency. Both times Auster told the man he had the wrong number, but then got to thinking: what if he hadn't corrected the caller? In the story, the hero Daniel Quinn is a crime writer whose fiction becomes reality when he goes along with the calls, only the caller is looking for an investigator named Paul Auster.

More recently Auster has turned his hand to film. He wrote the screenplay for Smoke based on his story called Auggie Wren's Christmas Story. One of the characters – a novelist played by **William Hurt** – is called Paul Benjamin, Auster's pseudonym. In 1998 he made his solo directorial debut with Lulu On The Bridge, starring **Harvey Keitel**, **Mira Sorvino** and **Willem Dafoe**. Love of film infuses – some would say prolongs the agony of – The Book Of Illusions, one of Auster's darkest novels, which some critics declared his best ever.

Auster has been called a mystery writer, but his novels are not whodunnit capers: it's rather that he uses the form of detective novels to explore the subjects he finds fascinating – the natures of identity and chance. In The Red Notebook he tells the story of a friend who went into labour while watching an **Audrey Hepburn** film on TV. Three years later, and due to give birth again, she turned on the TV to find the same film at the exact point where she had had to leave it three years before. Later that day she gave birth to her second daughter. As Auster said, "Reality is a great deal more mysterious than we ever give it credit for."

INFLUENCED BY Kafka; Beckett; Cervantes's **Don Quixote**; Nathanael Hawthorne; Herman Melville; Tolstoy; Dostoevsky.

INFLUENCE ON Australian novelist Rupert Thompson.

ESSENTIAL READING **The New York Trilogy**; **The Invention Of Solitude**.

FURTHER READING **Hand To Mouth**, the autobiography of his early years.

J.G. BALLARD

"This author is beyond psychiatric help. Do not publish!"

The world is a strange place in the novels of **J.G. Ballard** (1930–). Since arriving in England, aged 16, he's struggled with "…the density of light, the angle of light, the temperature, the cloud cover, a thousand and one social constructs… there is still an underlying strangeness for me about the English landscape."

The son of an English businessman in Shanghai, he and his family were interned in a civilian prison camp for nearly three years after the bombing of Pearl Harbour in 1941 and the invasion of China by Japan. Forty years later he published the semi-autobiographical Empire Of The Sun, a moving book in which a boy finds peace and security amid the malnutrition and violence of life in the camp, and protection from the horror of the war outside. These experiences surely lie at the root of all of Ballard's literary obsessions: the individual's relation to a violent physical and social landscape.

From his early years writing sci-fi in the 1960s, Ballard's thoughts have dwelt on the future. He was excited by the space age, youth countercultures, drug explosions, the power of TV and its effect on media and communications. Many of his early works deal with the chaos of a dying planet. The best of these include The Drowned World, which takes place in a primal swampland of lagoons, and The Crystal World, where the planet is slowly turning into a lifeless mineral sculpture. In the midst of this period came the beautiful Vermilion Sands, a

The seer of Shepperton: J.G. Ballard in his ordinary semi-detached home

collection of stories about enchantresses that contains some of his finest writing.

In the 1970s Ballard's fiction acquired a darker edge, often set in empty stretches of motorway, concrete flyovers, suburbia, airfields or Pacific islands. The Atrocity Exhibition (pulped for a story called Why I Want To Fuck Ronald Reagan, which predicted the Great Communicator's rise to the White House) is a disturbing satire on laboratory-obsessed researchers who are crashing pigs into concrete blocks or showing pornography to disturbed housewives. "The psychopathic should be preserved as a nature reserve, a last refuge for a certain kind of human freedom," he says. "It should be treasured because the imagination is an endangered species."

Ballard's most infamous novel, Crash – in which the characters take sexual pleasure from the aftermath of car crashes – prompted one editor to declare Ballard was beyond psychiatric help. Another editor of the book supposedly locked it away at night for fear young colleagues might read it and be traumatised. A recurring theme is the idea of inner space: the place where the most terrifying alien landscapes are to be found – in the author's mind. Compared to, say, **William Burroughs**, and in striking contrast to his fictional world, Ballard has spent his adult life relatively quietly, in the town of Shepperton, Middlesex.

"People used to come to this little suburban house expecting a miasma of drug addiction and perversion of every conceivable kind," he says. "Instead they found this easy-going man playing with his golden retriever and bringing up a family of happy young children. I used to find this a mystery myself. I would sit down at my desk and start writing about mutilation and perversion."

INFLUENCED BY J.B. Priestley; sci-fi; Burroughs; Graham Greene.

INFLUENCE ON William Gibson; Will Self.

ESSENTIAL READING **Crash**; **Vermilion Sands** for sheer quality; **The Atrocity Exhibition** – with Ballard's own footnotes.

FURTHER READING **The Unlimited Dream Company**; **Cocaine Nights**.

JOHN FRANKLIN BARDIN

Alcoholism, madness and mayhem – and that's the life, not the novels

In an era when much fiction is tediously attached to an ism, there's an appealing directness about **John Franklin Bardin** (1916–1981), who declared: "To me there is no distinction between the mystery novel and the novel, only between good books and bad books." Bardin would bring his own sensibility to the mystery genre. In The Deadly Percheron (a percheron is a breed of carthorse), the psychiatrist hero meets a patient with red hibiscus in his hair who is connected to dwarves, spends some time in a tumble dryer and has to assume the identity of a Coney Island café-worker. As the **New York Times** said, "this story of murder, mayhem and hideous torture will hold your attention to the last."

Bardin was born in Cincinatti, but after losing all his family by the time he reached his teens (his mother was a paranoid schizophrenic; madness, and the fear of it, would be one of his favourite themes), he moved to New York. There he worked in advertising, journalism and PR, as well as teaching creative writing. His fiction – ten novels in all – never strayed too far from noirish thriller/mystery territory but he came up with some fine, original variations on familiar themes. In The Last Of Philip Banter a drunken, womanising amnesiac is driven to destruction with murder ending – rather than starting – the book. In The Case Against Butterfly a model describes her own murder – but was she hallucinating?

These themes infuse novels that are powerful, paranoid and surreal. **Patricia Highsmith** noted of Devil Take The Blue Fly: "Those who can take it will read in horror. And they will not forget very soon" – which applies to all of Bardin's best work. His serious novels, such as Christmas Comes But Once A Year, were not as good and in some of his mysteries the reader has to swallow some implausibility, but his best novels are an exciting ride.

INFLUENCED BY Edgar Allan Poe; Eric Ambler; Graham Greene; Patricia Highsmith.

INFLUENCE ON Cornwell Woolrich; Jim Fusilli.

ESSENTIAL READING **The Deadly Percheron**; **Devil Take The Blue Fly**.

FURTHER READING Published pseudonymously, **A Shroud For Grandmama** was praised by noir novelist Dorothy B. Hughes as a graceful gothic horror.

> "The words 'I love you,' spoken on a sun-streaked terrace during a joyous day, can cement a betrayal"
>
> John Franklin Bardin in The Last Of Philip Banter

25

JOHN BARTH

The doyen of postmodernism, who offers no answers and no solace either

There are few better examples of the dangers of taking writers' pronouncements too seriously than **John Barth** (1930–). In 1967 Barth wrote a famous essay called The Literature Of Exhaustion. In 1979 he seemed to rebut his own words with another essay, The Literature Of Replenishment. Replenished, exhausted, postmodernist, non-postmodernist, Barth is an easy writer to theorise about but a hard one to categorise. For all his intellectual pyrotechnics, cerebral puzzles and symbolic cross-referencing, he sets most of his fiction, in a charmingly old-fashioned way, in the Tidewater region of Maryland where he grew up.

Barth sprang to fame with novels that were, as **Malcolm Bradbury** noted, "concerned, in 1950s fashion, with existential crises in an absurd world." But from Giles Goat-Boy his fiction became more self-examining and wilfully self-conscious, a trend that peaked artistically with Chimera, which won the 1972 National Book Award. In his next work, the almost unreadable Letters, characters from his previous novels write to him, justifying themselves. Then, in three novels set mostly in boats on Chesapeake Bay – Sabbatical, The Tidewater Tales and The Last Voyage Of Somebody The Sailor – he turned to matters of life, death, sex, love, meaning and fiction. **Robert Towers**, having read the last of these three, concluded wistfully: "One sometimes feels with Barth that the soul of a computer whizz-kid is embedded within the mind of a novelist."

Gore Vidal is no fan, arguing that Barth's promise as a "traditional cracker-barrelly sort of American writer" has been smothered by reading too much Novel Theory and, perhaps, by the obligation every American novelist has to be great – by creating their own world. After one Barth epic, Vidal moaned: "As the weary eyes flick from sentence to sentence, one starts willing the author to be good." Yet admirers applaud his desire to find the story beyond the generation of creativity. Barth's challenges – form, structure and length – for the reader are matched by the compensations – his erudition, his humour and an epic sense of adventure.

JOSEPH McELROY

A serious meta-man, **Joseph McElroy** (1930–) is more purist than **Barth** as a metafiction writer. He doesn't try to convince you it's all a game. For him, this storytelling business could, if you take it far enough, lead to the heart of the matter. This may be why he hasn't acquired the following of Barth or **Robert Coover**. But if you're seriously into the metafiction business you could try Plus, a sci-fi-inspired novel that is best described as a bildungsroman about a disembodied human brain.

INFLUENCED BY Nabokov; Borges; Saul Bellow; Pynchon; Italo Calvino; Donald Barthelme; Cervantes.

INFLUENCE ON Don DeLillo; Richard Powers; David Foster Wallace.

ESSENTIAL READING **The Tidewater Tales; Chimera**.

FURTHER READING **The Floating Opera**, which decides suicide is pointless.

DONALD BARTHELME

A fragmentary genius

Fiction can be too big for its own good. Many novelists, especially in America, engage in the literary equivalent of an arms race, in which each new work is designed to detonate over as large an area as possible. In contrast, art historian **Donald Barthelme** (1931–1989) declared, "Fragments are the only form I trust."

And it is his beautifully judged, perfectly pitched short stories – Sadness, Some Of Us Had Been Threatening Our Friend Colly – that are treasured the most. The fact that critics have compared him to **Kafka**, **Ronald Firbank**, **Borges** and the humorist **S.J. Perelman** may, on the one hand, pay tribute to the quality of his work but, on the other, doesn't really help to describe the work itself.

Barthelme was happy to make theoretical statements (but just as happy for them to be ignored) and once suggested collage – the technique used to sublime effect in **T.S. Eliot**'s The Waste Land, to which he often alludes – and cut-and-paste were pre-eminent tools for today's writers. In one of his more inspired cut-and-paste jobs he took Snow White to New York's East Village and retold it as a ménage à huit. Some, notably **Dale Peck**, have called his tales "reductive cardboard constructions", yet Barthelme makes the reader feel surprisingly at home in his fictional world which, for all his playfulness, is a sad place.

INFLUENCED BY John Dos Passos; Robbe-Grillet; Borges; Eugene Ionesco; Italo Calvino; Beckett; T.S. Eliot.

INFLUENCE ON His work is, alas, in need of re-evaluation.

ESSENTIAL READING **Sixty Stories** is the best place to start.

FURTHER READING His novella **The Dead Father**, in which a talking statue-carcass is dragged across America, won even Gore Vidal round.

GEORGES BATAILLE

The uses of effrontery

The Observer, reviewing an 'intellectual biography' of **Georges Bataille** (1897–1962), summed up the problem he poses in its opening line: "His obsessions were human sacrifice, surreal porn and monkey-ogling, but what were his faults?"

The French are obliged to take Bataille seriously, especially as he is French. Yet critic **Peter Conrad** is surely right when he says: "Bataille adopted extreme positions in a spirit of zany, cunning frivolity. As a surrealist, he understood the uses of effrontery and is best understood as a subversive intellectual comedian."

With a case like Bataille, the temptation is always to blame the parents, and the fact that his mother tried, unsuccessfully, to kill herself several times, while his father was blinded and paralysed by syphilis before dying in 1915, must have affected young Georges. It is tempting to see his acts of outrage as a prescription for the illness and depression that intermittently plagued him. It can, you feel, be no coincidence that when his first wife remarried, she wed a psychoanalyst.

Too much of a loose cannon for the surrealists – **André Breton** expelled him – Bataille is chiefly of interest as a writer of erotic fiction (though as a journal founder he discovered **Jacques Derrida** and **Roland Barthes**). His unholy trilogy

– *The Story Of the Eye*, *Blue Of Noon* and *The Abbott C* – was every bit as odd as you would expect from a man whose favourite set of photographs, pored over at intervals throughout his life, show a Chinese soldier, stoned on opium, being lengthily dismembered. *The Story Of Eye* is an exploration of taboos – involving eggs, eyeballs removed from corpses and wardrobes – so single-minded it makes $9^1/_2$ *Weeks* seem as explicit as a **Jane Austen** novel. In *Blue Of Noon*, Bataille's lovers copulate in a graveyard and watch a Hitler Youth band play marching songs. To give Bataille his due, he was never satisfied with the usual debauchery.

For **Milan Kundera**, Bataille's philosophical erotica stands up better than the more prosaic sexual confessions of many other authors. "How dated **Lawrence** seems, or even **Henry Miller** with his lyricism of obscenity. Yet certain erotic passages of Bataille have made a lasting impression on me." His strength as a writer may be that no one, not even the **Marquis de Sade**, has ever seen things quite like Bataille – or had the courage and sheer gall to commit such a vision to print.

INFLUENCED BY Nietzsche; Marquis de Sade.

INFLUENCE ON Barthes; Derrida; Michel Foucault; Philippe Sollers.

ESSENTIAL READING **The Story Of An Eye** is the best of the unholy trilogy.

FURTHER READING **Erotism: Death And Sensuality** – these musings on his pet subjects is a bracing read.

HEINRICH BÖLL

The horror and the hope

If the work of **Heinrich Böll** (1917–1985) is discussed, the conversation often runs along familiar lines: "**Nobel Prize** winner… moral disintegration… social conscience…" But Böll is not just an important novelist, he's a compelling one.

True, Böll was one of several German novelists who hovered over the newly reconstituted West Germany like doctors, trying to diagnose why a country that was outwardly so healthy could be so dead inside. But as his titles suggest – *The Lost Honour Of Katharina Blum*, *Group Portrait With A Lady*, *Billiards At Half-Past Nine* – he brings to his social novels some tactics from pulp fiction. His most famous novel, in which *Blum* is destroyed by the media, starts with her telling the police she's murdered someone. In *Group Portrait With A Lady* documentary-making techniques are applied to a powerful story in which the narrator's detachment breaks down as the lady's life becomes ever more painful.

Böll's criticism of German society was informed by his Catholic faith and by his life. He had refused to join the Hitler Youth, served six years as a private corporal on the eastern and western fronts, was wounded four times (losing all his toes through frostbite) and emerged to find, in his view, a nation where too many people blamed a diabolical leader, the times or peer pressure for Nazism.

His first novels were collectively known as '**Trummerliteratur**' – the literature of the rubble – and his very first, The Silent Angel, published posthumously, was rejected as too gloomy – or too heavily symbolic – by his publisher. But works such as The Train Was On Time were too powerful to ignore, and by the 1950s he had an international reputation. In the 1960s and 1970s his style broadened. His best novels were brilliantly ironic exposés of hypocrisy and a nation's amnesia, and especially prized in eastern Europe. When **Aleksandr Solzhenitsyn** was expelled from the USSR in 1974, he took refuge with Böll.

Böll shares obvious concerns with **Günter Grass**, yet some have compared his irony, seriousness of purpose, Catholic faith and stylistic polish to **Graham Greene**. The crucial difference is that Böll is as conscious of the hope as of the horror. When his hero in The Clown says, "Strangely enough, I like the kind to which I belong: people," he could be speaking for Böll. If anything, Böll was braver than Greene in his fiction, satirising terrorism in Safety Net in the very decade the German media had been transfixed by the **Baader-Meinhof Gang**.

29

INFLUENCED BY James Joyce (especially **The Dubliners**); Robert Musil.

INFLUENCE ON Michelle Richmond, American novelist; Richard Paul Russo.

ESSENTIAL READING **The Lost Honour Of Katharina Blum**; **Group Portrait With A Lady**.

FURTHER READING **The Stories Of Heinrich Böll** show his gift for humour.

JORGE LUIS BORGES

The blind visionary

Argentinian Jorge Luis Borges (1899–1986) was fascinated by Western metaphysics, from the Greeks to **Bertrand Russell**'s positivism, and by Christian, Hebrew and Hindu theology. He said of his own work: "I am neither a thinker nor a moraliser. Simply a man of words who reflects in his writing his own confusion and the respectable system of confusions we call philosophy."

Borges was brought up bilingual (his maternal grandmother was English). He learned to read in English before Spanish and translated **Oscar Wilde**'s The Happy Prince when he was nine. He wrote poems and essays, but it is his mastery of the short story that elevated the latter to a perfection seldom seen before or since. He was one of the most important writers of his century, pioneering a new form of literary expression: essay fiction. In his essays and short stories he explores historical characters and events and weaves fantastical, fictitious attributes into them. His concern with time, mortality and identity are both universal and deeply subjective; his subject is the workings of the mind itself.

Between 1914 and 1918 Borges lived in Geneva, where he finished high school, and then moved to Spain where he became involved with the ultraist movement in poetry, later joking that the main ideals of ultraism were to be "enemies of rhyme". In 1921 he returned to Buenos Aires and rediscovered his city. He became interested in the traditional southern neighborhoods, the tango and knife fights… all themes that appear in his first book of poems, Fervor De Buenos Aires. By 1925 he was considered one of the main leaders of the literary vanguard. Tired of ultraism, between 1930 and 1950 he produced Historia Universal De La Infamia, Ficciones and El Aleph, some of the most remarkable fiction of the century with a fantastical and magical narrative.

Much of his best work, written in the 1940s, was not translated into English until the 1960s. He won many honours, including an OBE, but never the Nobel Prize (though **Luis Buñuel** says he talked about it obsessively). Borges, who suffered from progressive blindness, combined his writing with a job at the National Library and a professorship at Buenos Aires University. He stayed away from politics, but as an Anglophile he memorably described the Falklands conflict as "two bald men fighting over a comb." Erudite, intellectual, metaphysical, full of puzzles and games, his fiction has been pored over like sacred texts by other novelists. Borges would probably be amused. As he warned an admirer: "I am decidedly monotonous."

INFLUENCED BY Leopoldo Lugones; Robert Louis Stevenson; Schopenhauer; Joseph Conrad; Herman Melville; Lewis Carroll; H.G. Wells; Cervantes.

INFLUENCE ON Italo Calvino; Carlos Fuentes; Umberto Eco; John Barth.

ESSENTIAL READING **Fictions**; **The Aleph**.

FURTHER READING **Historia Universal De La Infamia**.

JANE BOWLES

Wrote very little, but with a unique voice

Few writers of any note have written, or published, less than **Jane Bowles** (1917–1973). "Ambivalence was her natural element," wrote her husband **Paul** (see below). "To be obliged to make a decision filled her with anguish." Her literary debut, the novel Two Serious Ladies, appeared in 1943, and she felt crushed by the apparent lack of attention. She resolved, Paul says, to create something "completely different" but only wrote a few further short stories and one play. But what writing it is. Comic, sad, farcical and moving, it has dialogue that makes you laugh out loud and applaud. And Two Serious Ladies is, to a small body of enthusiasts, one of the key works of 20th-century fiction.

The book is loosely based on Jane's honeymoon with Paul in Central America and Paris. The couple split, briefly, in France, and a year later Jane, who'd previously only had relationships with women, declared their sexual life should cease. From then on both Jane and Paul resumed their homosexual affiliations, while remaining devoted companions. In the novel Mr and Mrs Copperfield go off to Panama, and Mr Copperfield presses his wife to go off to the jungle. She prefers to remain with a local prostitute and the couple part. "I hope this day has not been spoiled," Mrs Copperfield says. And if this seems a strange central core for a novel, consider how it begins, with the other serious lady of the title, Miss Goering, at age 13, playing a weird religious game called 'I Forgive You For All Your Sins'. The novel is such fun that you never for a moment suspect you are in the midst of the avant-garde.

> "The farther a man follows the rainbow, the harder it is for him to get back to the life which he left starving like an old dog"
>
> Jane Bowles, poetic as ever in Plain Pleasures

With her play In The Summer House the writing seems more obviously at the edge. It is impossible to summarise: a play of poetic relationships, with a murder and a romance, mysterious yet funny. And that is almost the extent of Jane Bowles's work. Her only other substantial stories are A Guatemalan Idyll, originally a section from Two Serious Ladies which Paul suggested cutting, and Camp Cataract, a very odd tale of a woman plotting escape from her unconsciously incestuous sister. Of the remainder, the story Everything Is Nice stands out. It is almost the only one Jane set in Morocco and concerns a Western woman who goes to live with Muslim friends. It is partly autobiographical, for in Tangier, Jane set up home with Cherifa, a market trader. Paul contended that Cherifa enacted dark magic on Jane, that precipitated the stroke in 1957 from which she never fully recovered. After the stroke Jane wrote only fragments, and spent her last years at a nuns' hospice in Malaga.

INFLUENCED BY Nobody.

INFLUENCE ON Too little.

ESSENTIAL READING My Sister's Hand In Mine: The Collected Works Of Jane Bowles has pretty much all there is.

FURTHER READING Millicent Dillon's A Little Original Sin is a fine biography.

CULT FICTION

PAUL BOWLES

Paul Bowles (1910–1999) was one of America's most outstanding prose stylists. His style was not so much old-fashioned as classic, resonating like music. But then Bowles was first a musician. He studied under **Aaron Copland**, with whom he travelled to Tangier, Morocco, where he later made his home.

Bowles was a prodigy. An only child – he claimed not to have seen another child until he was eight – he grew up in New York State, before setting out as a teenager to visit **Gertrude Stein** in Paris. He had submitted poems to Stein, which she had published, but when he arrived she suggested his talent lay elsewhere. For a time that meant music, and through the 1930s and 1940s he scored music for **Tennessee Williams** plays. In 1937 he married the writer **Jane Auer** (see above) and began to turn his attentions towards prose. He became the **Herald Tribune**'s music critic and translated **Jean-Paul Sartre**'s play Huis Clos, giving it the memorably Bowlesian title No Exit. Then at the end of the war, after a trip to North Africa, he wrote The Sheltering Sky. Published in 1949, it was an American bestseller, a novel that punctuated its time, with its story of a disaffected American couple adrift in an unknowable culture.

Settled in Tangier, although travelling often and living for a time on an island off the Sri Lankan coast, Bowles produced an amazing amount of work in the 1950s, including the short-story collection The Delicate Prey and the novels Let It Come Down and The Spider's House. But the end of the decade brought tragedy, when Jane had a stroke, from which she never recovered. Although she was an active lesbian and Paul had homosexual relationships with, among others, Moroccan painter **Ahmed Yacoubi**, the Bowles's marriage was important to each of them. They lived in flats one above the other in Tangier until Jane fell ill.

From the 1960s until his death Paul was an archetypal cult author, sought out in Tangier by the **Beats** (**William Burroughs** became a friend) and a succession of would-be writers. His cult status perhaps lay with the disappearance of his books from the mainstream. Only one more novel appeared, Up Above The World, and although Bowles produced a string of short stories, and translations of Moroccan storytellers such as **Mohammed Mrabet**, he published with small presses, notably City Lights and Black Sparrow Press.

The stories stand as a unique product of Bowles's life in Tangier, **Poe**-like in their disquiet and dread, with brutal episodes of alienation and violence (in A Distant Episode a professor is kidnapped by nomads who cut out his tongue and make him perform as a clown). But most often the stories have the brilliant quality of dreams, in which, as **Gore Vidal** put it, "nothing and everything happens." They explore myth and magic (in Allal a boy changes identity with a snake), sorcery and the effects of hashish (notably in the collection A Hundred

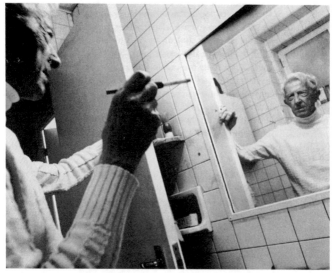

Is this a cigarette holder I see before me? Paul Bowles reflects on life in Tangier

Camels In The Courtyard). They describe the physical world with precision, yet leave characters only loosely delineated, through their speech and actions. They are, simply, not like other 20th-century literature.

INFLUENCED BY Moroccan storytellers, notably Mohammed Mrabet.

INFLUENCE ON Burroughs; Ian McEwan (early stories); Thomas McGuane.

ESSENTIAL READING **The Sheltering Sky**; but don't ignore **The Spider's House**, one of the best political novels ever written.

FURTHER READING **The Stories Of Paul Bowles**, the complete Ecco edition, 2001. For converts, his autobiography **Without Stopping** is compelling.

KAY BOYLE

The lost member of the lost generation

History hasn't been particularly kind to **Kay Boyle** (1902–1992). As a writer she was probably too versatile and too prolific for the good of her own reputation. Yet she was, in her day, hailed as the best of her generation by such judges as **Ezra Pound**, **William Carlos Williams** and **Katherine Anne Porter**.

Born in St Paul, Minnesota, she started writing fiction in her father's garage, moving to New York to become a freelance writer. In 1923 she followed her husband, a French engineering student, to Paris for what was intended to be a summer vacation but became a 19-year sojourn. Boyle liked France, suggesting that, unlike America, it wouldn't imprison leaders like **Eugene V. Debs** for the crime of socialism. France wasn't just politically liberating. In 1929 she signed a manifesto (along with the American poet **Hart Crane**) called The Revolution Of The Word, which used **James Joyce**'s Finnegans Wake as a blueprint for the future of literature. It's not clear how consistently she applied its 12 rules in her own work though her first novel, Process, certainly bears its imprint.

She became attached to another literary grouping, the **Lost Generation**, a catch-all phrase for a group of American authors who fled America for France in the 1920s. Most memoirs of this set focus on who got drunk with whom and when, but Boyle was more committed politically than **Hemingway** or **F. Scott Fitzgerald**. In 1936 she wrote Death Of A Man, attacking a creed, Nazism, that many Americans were not then even aware of. She paid the price for such commitment when she returned to the US with her third husband, the marvellously named **Baron Joseph von Franckenstein**. He lost his job after the war thanks to pressure from **McCarthy** witch-hunters; she was sacked by **The New Yorker** and blacklisted by other magazines. Radicalised by the experience, Boyle became a political activist, joined San Francisco academia and, in her mid-seventies, stopped writing.

Although she published 14 novels (most of which are out of print), it is in her short stories – notably Astronomer's Wife, Episode and Wedding Day – that her interest in literary technique, bold use of language, moral dilemmas and psychological insight find best expression. Her short novel The Crazy Hunter was hailed as "close to perfection" by **Katherine Anne Porter**.

INFLUENCED BY James Joyce; Ezra Pound.

INFLUENCE ON Louise Erdrich; Marge Piercy.

ESSENTIAL READING **Fifty Stories** is a decent collection, prefaced by Erdrich.

FURTHER READING For some aficionados her only great novel is **Monday Night**, a tale of an alcoholic writer on the edge.

LEIGH BRACKETT

A pulp princess, New Wave godmother and Hollywood hired hand

Howard Hawks was looking for someone gifted – and cheap – to make a screenplay out of **Raymond Chandler**'s The Big Sleep. After reading a hard-boiled novel called No Good For A Corpse, he decided to hire the author **Leigh Brackett** (1915–1978), but was shocked to realise he had hired a woman.

Brackett had been writing since infancy, making her initial mark with such swashbuckling space sagas as The Dragon Queen Of Jupiter. She wrote for such magazines as **Planet Stories** in the 1940s, but intrigued by a new kind of pulp fiction, the hard-boiled crime novel, created No Good For A Corpse.

She was in demand for the next 40 years, especially after she (with **William Faulkner**) made The Big Sleep a smash. She later wrote scripts for El Dorado (her favourite – until Hawks changed the sad ending), The Long Goodbye (the panned **Robert Altman** film of the Chandler novel, now recognised as a classic) and just before her death, a draft for The Empire Strikes Back. Her most notable novels are The Long Tomorrow, a serious allegory about a fascist America; The Tiger Among Us, a tale of vigilante justice; and I Feel Bad Killing You, published in 1944, which anticipates the brutal force of **Mickey Spillane** (though it's better written.)

> "Any resemblance between this movie and Chandler's novel is not only coincidental, it's libellous"
>
> A typical review for The Long Goodbye

Today, Brackett is chiefly treasured for her film work and her sci-fi tales that inspired **George Lucas**. Sci-fi novelist **Michael Moorcock** says the heroes of her space operas were cowboys, often aware of some moral transgression that everyone – but themselves – had forgiven. But it is the tone of these stories which, Moorcock says, sets them apart – "she brought the spare, laconic prose and psychically wounded heroes of **Hemingway**, **Hammett** and **Chandler** into sci-fi pulp." To Moorcock, and others, she is one of the "true godmothers of the New Wave".

35

INFLUENCED BY Edgar Rice Burroughs; Robert Howard; C.L. Moore; Ray Bradbury; Hammett; Chandler.

INFLUENCE ON Ray Bradbury (he and Brackett used to read each other's stories when they started out); Moorcock; George Lucas.

ESSENTIAL READING **Martian Quest: The Early Brackett** collects the best of her early pulp sci-fi; **The Long Tomorrow**.

FURTHER READING Try **Jirel Of Joiry**, a swashbuckling swordplay epic by Catherine L. Moore, the woman who inspired Brackett to write sci-fi.

RICHARD BRAUTIGAN

The Beat who made trout fishing cool – for a while

Richard Brautigan (1935–1984) would probably have remained among the ranks of the minor **Beat** poets, had he not caught the countercultural wave of

1960s San Francisco with his surreal, pastoral classic, Trout Fishing In America. Famously, the cover shows Brautigan in front of a statue of **Benjamin Franklin**: every bit the hippie icon with his moustache, shaggy hair and little round glasses.

Brautigan was born in Tacoma, Washington, and brought up in poverty by his mother, a hard-drinking waitress with a string of abusive lovers. He almost never talked about his childhood, but one story relates that, in the early 1940s, he and his half-sister Barbara were kept tethered to a bedpost in Great Falls, Montana – fed sporadically by one of their many 'stepfathers'.

At high school in Eugene, Oregon, Brautigan was a solitary boy devoted to the work of **William Carlos Williams** and **Emily Dickinson**. He published his first poem, The Light, in 1952 but, on graduation, his writing grew increasingly troubled and he was sectioned for three months in the state hospital, where he was given electric-shock therapy and diagnosed as a paranoid schizophrenic.

On his release in 1955, Brautigan settled in San Francisco where he tried to publish a novel, The God Of The Martians, often slept rough and associated with such Beats as **Kenneth Rexroth**, **Gary Snyder** and **Allen Ginsberg**. He

Surreal trout fisherman

married **Virginia Alder** in 1957 and, while shy and awkward, he was soon recognised as one of the leading young San Francisco poets, joining the Dharma Committee group of artists and writers and publishing three experimental collections somewhere between poetry and prose.

It was not until 1961, while on a camping holiday with his wife and one-year-old daughter in Idaho, that Brautigan first attempted prose proper, writing an early draft of Trout Fishing on a battered portable typewriter. When Virginia left him the following year for one of his best friends, he sank his devastation into his work and began what became his first, fragmentary novel – A Confederate General In Big Sur – the story of a beatnik with a keen interest in hallucinogenic drugs wandering around the San Francisco and Big Sur area.

Although it was well received – **Auberon Waugh** described it as "five thousand times better than **Kerouac**" – Brautigan failed to achieve true success until Trout Fishing In America was published in 1967. It caught the spirit of the moment perfectly, with its 47 amorphous passages about a man, his wife and child escaping the stress of the city to explore rural America. It is a weird book but very funny and lyrical, and has sold two million copies.

The following few years saw Brautigan publish In Watermelon Sugar, the poetry collections The Pill Versus The Springhill Mine Disaster and Please

Plant This Book – a folder of seed packets with poems printed on the sides – and an excellent book of short stories, Revenge Of The Lawn, which had been serialised in **Rolling Stone**. But suffering from insomnia, paranoia and alcoholism, and with a growing fascination with firearms, he struggled to recreate the vibrancy of his first three novels in The Hawkline Monster and the sado-masochistic Willard And His Bowling Trophies. He had a brief revival of spirits after visiting Tokyo in 1976, where he met his second wife, **Akiko Nishizawa Yoshimura**.

Brautigan's last novel, So The Wind Won't Blow It All Away, sold less than 15,000 copies and was mauled or ignored by critics. Alone and depressed, he shot himself on 14 September 1984, while looking out to sea. It was almost six weeks before his body was discovered.

INFLUENCED BY Hemingway; Emily Dickinson; William Carlos Williams.

INFLUENCE ON Alan Gullette; T.K. Splake.

ESSENTIAL READING **Trout Fishing In America**.

FURTHER READING **You Can't Catch Death** by Ianthe Brautigan is a moving account of the author's relationship with her father.

HAROLD BRODKEY

One of American literature's great vanishing acts

Some 20th-century novelists, especially American ones, became as famous for not writing as for writing. **Harold Brodkey** (1930–1996) is one of these. After his collection of stories First Love And Other Sorrows came out in 1957, readers had to wait 28 years for his next work, Women And Angels.

After the acclaim that greeted his debut, Brodkey had declared his follow-up would be a novel called A Party For Animals. Instead, he spent most of the next 30 years publishing short stories, usually in **The New Yorker**, which formed pieces of the mammoth autobiographical novel that was published in 1991 as The Runaway Soul and greeted with respectful, puzzled, reviews. Ironically, Stories In An Almost Classical Mode, which contained some of the same material in a more accessible form, is now recognised as Brodkey's finest work.

As you might expect from a writer whose chief outlet was **The New Yorker**, Brodkey's style became increasingly nuanced. He slowed down time to a point where even **Proust** might have snapped his madeleine in two with impatience, once taking 30 pages, in a story called Innocence, to describe his efforts to give his girlfriend an orgasm. But his masterpieces are so finely honed, the idiosyncratic prose style so melodic, that most readers can't help but be entranced.

Brodkey's comeback didn't last long. Five years after his one-and-only novel was published he died of an AIDS-related illness, his final struggle captured in the haunting, egomaniacal The Wild Darkness: The Story Of My Death. Asked if he ever read other fiction while writing his own, Brodkey said he didn't because "to discover – to rediscover – that others see and speak differently is an assault somewhat like being manhandled and interrogated by a foreign policeman who insists that you explain yourself to him although he knows little or nothing about the kind of man you are." That captures Brodkey as well as anything he wrote.

INFLUENCED BY William Blake; Proust; James Joyce.

INFLUENCE ON Michael Cunningham.

ESSENTIAL READING **Stories In An Almost Classical Mode**.

FURTHER READING **The Wild Darkness**, harrowing yet gripping.

CHARLES BUKOWSKI

The Bard of booze and broads, whose finest creation was his own legend

Defining where mythology ends and reality begins is nearly impossible when it comes to **Charles Bukowski** (1920–1994). Legends of the man's crawl from the gutter to become the darling of the literary underground tell of a down-and-out drunk, yo-yoing between dead-end jobs until critical acclaim and regular cheques turned him into the poet laureate of Skid Row. **Jean-Paul Sartre** called him "America's greatest poet".

Yet there are troubling inconsistencies in the Bukowski chronology – claims that the hard-drinking womaniser of legend may actually have been, for much of his life, a conscientious employee who handled liquor poorly and craved monogamy. In his later years he drove a BMW, listened to **Mahler** and rubbed shoulders with Hollywood glitterati.

The reality of Bukowski's life is crucial to his legacy. Much of his fiction featured his thinly disguised alter ego Henry Chinaski, and the central themes of his work were the lack of honesty among his fellow poets and his need to share every hangover or disastrous sexual experience with his audience. Pockmarked, grotesquely ugly (by his own admission) and lacking even the most basic social skills, Bukowski still retained a faith of sorts in humanity, and most of his work, while outwardly morbid, is profoundly uplifting.

The often-brutal humour displayed in the novels Women and Post Office, where Chinaski struggles to maintain jobs and relationships as his mental and physical health deteriorate, is made all the more powerful by the stark, simple language of Bukowski's prose. His colloquial style and powerful metaphors recall the simplicity of **Ernest Hemingway** – with whom Bukowski enjoyed a love-hate relationship – but also frequently push the boundaries of taste and have led to his being unfairly labelled a 'dirty' or misogynistic writer. "An artist is someone who says a hard thing in a simple way," he claimed.

Bukowski had more in common with the **Beats**, much as he detested **Jack Kerouac** and **Allen Ginsberg**, than with Hemingway. His alternative worldview may have stretched no further than hiding from society by typing, drunk and bitter, in his filthy room, but Bukowski's rejection of literary and societal convention made him an underground icon. After years of moving from city to city, taking on menial jobs, fighting in bars and cohabiting with loose women, he finally found stability working for the Post Office and began writing poems and short stories to some acclaim in small, underground magazines.

After 11 years in the job, and his first alcohol-induced near-death experience when "blood poured out of my mouth and ass", he decided, "I have one of two choices – stay in the Post Office and go crazy… or stay out here and play at writer and starve. I have decided to starve."

A sympathetic publisher – **John Martin** of Black Sparrow Press – offered him $100 a month for life. Post Office, Bukowski's first novel, was a success, especially in Europe. Embellished or not, Chinaski's daily struggle with back-breaking mail bags and worsening health is a vision of a mundane, borderline existence that has never been bettered. It is the desperate, tortured truth **Knut Hamsun** tried to find in Hunger, only funnier, grubbier and a lot more explicit.

The best of his prolific output of short stories, poems and newspaper columns were collected in Notes Of A Dirty Old Man, but his imagination grew wilder as his success and reputation increased. Later collections like The Most Beautiful Woman In Town see Chinaski belatedly living something approaching a high life, taking advantage of the women who had once shunned him and travelling America to open for rock acts and read his poetry. But drink was the only stable factor in Bukowski's life: "When you drank, the world was still out there," he wrote, "but for the moment it didn't have you by the throat."

The movie Barfly, in which Chinaski was portrayed by **Mickey Rourke**, increased Bukowski's stock still further. He inspired an unlikely devotion among those who discovered his work, but remained a jobbing writer to the end, firing off dozens of poems every day even when told he would die within weeks. "If I die," he wrote, "I hope to go with my head on that typewriter. It's my battlefield."

INFLUENCED BY Céline; John Fante; Hemingway.

INFLUENCE ON Jonathan Ames; Henry Rollins; Tom Waits.

ESSENTIAL READING **Women**; **Post Office**; **Factotum**.

FURTHER READING In **Ham On Rye** Bukowski looks at his early years; **Notes Of A Dirty Old Man** is an amusing collection of columns.

THE SEXPLOITATION BUSINESS

Since pen first met paper, sex has been a pre-eminent inspiration for writers of everything from science fiction to satire. Yet 'erotic writing' – a catch-all term that allows many explicit novels to be conveniently placed on out-of-reach shelves – has long been denied literary merit. Worse still, writers who dabble in eroticism to any degree – **Henry Miller**, **Charles Bukowski**, **Erica Jong** – are forever tainted as 'dirty' no matter how broad their wider oeuvre. Here we look back at a few literary milestones in this awkward genre.

The Song Of Solomon

This Old Testament book, while far from scandalously explicit, has long presented interpretative problems for the church. Solomon is a lengthy love poem with both male and female narratives and no mention of God. It starts: "How I wish you would kiss me passionately/For your lovemaking is more delightful than wine." The book is usually seen as a mutual appreciation between Solomon and his new bride, but other explanations abound, notably that it details a love triangle between Solomon, his wife and a shepherd.

John Wilmot

The **Earl of Rochester** (1647–1680) can be seen as a later version of Roman poet **Catullus**, using his wealth to fund a playboy lifestyle that spawned plenty of erotic verse and several plays. Most of his work was released anonymously as pamphlets, but it still created a stir. "Her nimble tongue, love's lesser lightning, played/Within my mouth, and to my thoughts conveyed/Swift orders that I should prepare to throw/The all-dissolving thunderbolt

below," reads one poem. **Samuel Johnson**, Wilmot's biographer, said "he lived worthless and useless, and blazed out his youth and health in lavish voluptuousness." He was lucky to be free at all, after one of his verses about **King Charles** found its way to the monarch: "Restless, he rolls about from whore to whore/A merry monarch, scandalous and poor." His life is the subject of a planned **Johnny Depp/John Malkovich** movie.

Octave Mirbeau

By the turn of the 20th century, the bar had been raised far further. **Octave Mirbeau** (1848–1917) was a French anarchist and art critic whose book The Torture Garden remains a sado-masochistic classic (not to a mention a well-written piece of literature). Mirbeau's tale sees an inhibited civil servant being taken to China by an Englishwoman who delights in Oriental methods of torturing prisoners. Blasted as "the most sickening work of art of the 19th century", The Torture Garden has points to make about societal and moral values, but few could see beyond the graphic images of group sex and bondage. As the protagonist proclaims: "I realised that the very thing that held me to her was the frightful rottenness of her soul."

Henry Miller

Mirbeau's work was never banned, unlike that of **Henry Miller** (1891–1980), proving that any sexual practice is acceptable in print, as long as none of the anatomical parts involved are referred to by name. Miller's liberal language saw Tropic Of Cancer (1934) absent from US bookstores for almost 30 years, but he proved in his Rosy Crucifixion trilogy (Sexus, Plexus and Nexus) that he was more than a pornographer: "Obscenity, like sex, has its natural, rightful place in literature, as in life, and it will never be obliterated, no matter what laws are passed," he said. The books, which follow Miller as a young, struggling artist in 1930s Paris, are notable for delightful, free-flowing monologues, showing Miller as a writer who loved to wring every last drop from the English language. Miller did, though, write an explicit pornographic novel, Opus Pistorum, to pay debts. His mistress was identified as **Anaïs Nin** who, in her diaries Henry And June, revealed she was also having sex with his wife.

The Story Of O

One of the final boundaries in sexual literature was for a female writer to come to the fore. **Anne Desclos**, as **Pauline Reage**, filled the void with 1957's The Story Of O, a notorious tale of a female photographer who submits absolutely to her rich, older lover. Desclos wrote it to impress her boyfriend, but among its literary fans was **Graham Greene**.

Fear Of Flying

Erica Jong (1942–) achieved similar notoriety with a more cerebral approach to female sexuality in Fear Of Flying, a tale of a bored housewife who finds spiritual enlightenment via sudden rampant promiscuity. The book was savaged (but sold well), partly for Jong's liberal use of the newly-coined 'zipless fuck' – "…zipless because when you came together zippers fell away like rose petals…"

MIKHAIL BULGAKOV

A doctor writes

"Am I conceivable in the USSR?" asked **Mikhail Bulgakov** (1891–1940) in his famous 1930 letter to the Soviet government. A satirist in the tradition of **Gogol**, Bulgakov existed in opposition to a state that allowed no opposition. Although his masterpiece, The Master And Margarita, is one of the best Russian novels of the 20th century, he lived for the most part in poverty, fear and relative obscurity.

The son of a professor at the Kiev Theological Academy in Ukraine, Bulgakov qualified as a doctor in 1916, and for 18 months he practised in the remote province of Smolensk – a period of great hardship leading to morphine addiction, later described in A Country Doctor's Notebook.

With the end of World War I and the start of the Russian civil war, he returned to Kiev to work as a field doctor – his brothers had joined the anti-communist White Army.

He fictionalised his war-time experiences in The White Guard, the story of a middle-class family who consider the Bolsheviks "worse than anything on earth". As the book progresses, the family comes to despise the Tsarists equally.

The book caused a storm on publication because of its depiction of non-proletarian characters as ordinary, loving human beings. Bizarrely, the dramatised version was one of **Josef Stalin**'s favourite plays.

41

In late 1919, after a serious illness, Bulgakov abandoned medicine and became a journalist in the Caucasus, where he began to write plays and short stories. In 1921 he settled in Moscow and wrote a collection of stories, Diaboliad, and the novellas The Fatal Eggs and The Heart Of A Dog. In these years his style changed from a taut lyricism to grotesque magical realism. In The Heart Of A Dog a professor transplants a criminal's pituitary gland and testicles into a stray dog, transforming it into a heavy-drinking half-dog, half-human who perfectly suits Soviet society.

Many of these books remained unpublished for decades. During his lifetime Bulgakov was mainly known as a playwright: in 1928 three of his plays were running

Satan's cat in The Master And Margarita is Begemot – hippopotamus in Russian

simultaneously in Moscow. The critics, however, were savage, declaring Bulgakov "untalented, toothless and quite wretched", and in 1929 every one of his plays and books was banned. He began The Master And Margarita in 1928 and was still dictating revisions on his deathbed in 1940; it wasn't published until 1967. It is an immense and deeply ambiguous novel, a study of good and evil in three strands. Bizarre and hilarious, it embraces the complexity of the world, and its only unambiguous opinion is reserved for the vain, greedy, selfish citizens of Moscow, who are unable to accept that their version of truth might be wrong.

As a result of his 1930 letter to the government, **Stalin** phoned Bulgakov and appointed him assistant director at the Moscow Arts Theatre. During the 1930s he continued to write plays, adapted several classics for the stage and began a theatrical novel Black Snow, but in 1939 he lost his eyesight and died the following year of a hereditary kidney disease. He remained controversial after death, regarded as un-Soviet, only being properly re-evaluated in the 1980s.

INFLUENCED BY Gogol; Dostoevsky; Alexander Pushkin; Dickens.

INFLUENCE ON Russian sci-fi writer Arkady Strugatsky; Victor Pelevin; Salman Rushdie.

ESSENTIAL READING **The Master And Margarita**.

FURTHER READING **The Heart Of A Dog**, **The White Guard** and Vitaly Shentalinsky's **The KGB's Literary Archive**, which contains extracts from Bulgakov's long-lost diary and discusses his persecution by the secret police.

WILLIAM S. BURROUGHS

The Invisible Man who experimented with drugs and language

William Seward Burroughs (1914–1997) was born into an affluent midwest American family he could never fit into. By the time of his birth his father had already sold most of his stock in the Burroughs Corporation (set up by William's grandfather, who invented the adding machine), but the family were still wealthy enough to fund William Junior's drug habit after he graduated from Harvard.

For Burroughs, drug addiction was a lifestyle choice. He first decided to smoke opium after he experienced nightmares at boarding school and the school nurse told him smoking opium would give him sweet dreams. In the late 1930s he moved to New York especially to hunt out its underground drug and crime culture. Here he met **Herbert Huncke** (who initially mistook him for an FBI agent), from whom he learned the art of rolling drunks and picking pockets. Hunke introduced Burroughs to morphine ("That's very interesting indeed" was Burrough's response to his first hit) and to three Columbia University students: **Allen Ginsberg**, **Jack Kerouac** and his future wife **Joan Vollmer Adams** (with whom the homosexual Burroughs would have a son).

43

Burroughs was much older than his new friends, who were all turning to writing, and under their influence Burroughs followed suit. Junky, his drug autobiography, was published as a pulp paperback in 1953. "Every word is autobiographical and every word is fiction," Burroughs explained to **Tennessee Williams**. A similar autobiography about his sexuality, Queer, written at the same time, was rejected as obscene (it wasn't published until 1985).

By 1954 Burroughs was living in Tangier, after having accidentally shot his wife Joan in the head, doing what he called their "**William Tell** act" after a heavy day's drinking. Devastated, Burroughs turned to writing more intensely: "the death of Joan brought me in contact with… the Ugly Spirit and manoeuvred me into a lifelong struggle, in which I have had no choice except to write my way out."

In Tangiers, Burroughs met **Jane and Paul Bowles** and **Brion Gysin**. Kerouac and Ginsberg later joined Burroughs in Tangier, where he earned his nickname 'El Hombre Invisible' as he skulked through the back alleys in search of sex and drugs. Burroughs was working on a series of bizarre, experimental stories that ignored contemporary narrative structure and form. Kerouac and Ginsberg helped type up the work which, at Kerouac's suggestion, became Naked Lunch.

It was so-named because it tells things like they really are, the "moment when everyone sees what is on the end of every fork", (although it was sold to his publisher with the more salacious and fabricated explanation that the title was a euphemism for sex in the afternoon).

Naked Lunch made Burroughs an underground celebrity. **Norman Mailer** hailed him as "the only American writer who may conceivably be possessed by genius." Burroughs probably preferred **Samuel Beckett**'s simple praise: "He's a writer." Not everyone was so impressed. The novel was prosecuted for obscenity and was printed in Italy, where the non-English speaking printers returned the stories in random order, an order Burroughs retained as he believed the reader could start anywhere in the book. It won the court case, which opened the door for such works as **Henry Miller**'s Tropic Of Cancer to be published in the US.

Gysin introduced Burroughs to a discovery he had made of creating texts by cutting up newspapers and slicing them together randomly. Burroughs soon saw the scope for more literary experimentation, comparing his new technique to **T.S. Eliot**'s The Waste Land, which he considered the "first great cut-up collage". A trilogy of cut-up novels was completed by 1964.

When Burroughs returned to the US in 1974 he continued to work prolifically – writing Cities Of The Red Night, That Place Of Dead Roads and The Western Lands – and became a cultural and artistic icon. His praises were sung by **Mick Jagger**, **Frank Zappa**, **Patti Smith** and **David Bowie** (who used his cut-up technique for his lyrics; Burroughs said of him: "He's very calculating, he knows where he wants to be and how to get there"). He became an honorary godfather to the New York wave of punk and coined the term heavy metal (in his novel The Soft Machine). The influential psychedelic band **Soft Machine** and the jazz-influenced **Steely Dan** both took their names from his work. In 1992 **Kurt Cobain** released an album, The Priest They Called Him, in which he plays guitar under the writer's spoken voice. Burroughs also recorded with **Laurie Anderson, John Cale** and New York multi-instrumentalist **Bill Laswell**, among others.

BOOKS BILL LIKED

Dune **Frank Herbert**
Fury **Hal Kuttner**
The Star Virus **Barrington Bailey**
Three To Conquer **Eric Frank Russell**
The Snows Of Kilimanjaro **Ernest Hemingway**
The Time Machine **H.G. Wells**
The Waste Land **T.S. Eliot**

Burroughs's misogyny ("Women are a perfect curse"), his juvenile fascination with guns (often lovingly described) and some of his dafter ideas (**Simon Bolivar**, Burroughs said, didn't free South America because he spoke Spanish and not a liberating language like Chinese) have all to be considered in any rounded assessment. He is still a resounding force in art, literature and music but

El Hombre Invisible captured in a rare moment of visibility

he continues to have his critics, who call him overrated and overexposed, with ideas that were more influential in their conception than their execution.

INFLUENCED BY Denton Welch; Paul Bowles; James Joyce; F. Scott Fitzgerald.

INFLUENCE ON William Gibson; J.G. Ballard; Michael Moorcock; Will Self.

ESSENTIAL READING **Naked Lunch**; **The Western Lands**.

FURTHER READING **The Adding Machine**, a collection of Burroughs's fiction and non-fiction that introduces his thought.

CULT FICTION
JAMES M. CAIN

A poet of sex, greed and murder

Harold Strauss, reviewing The Postman Always Rings Twice in the **New York Times** in 1934, had no doubt as to why the novel was so successful: "Cain can get down to primary impulses of greed and sex in fewer words than any writer we know of." Some reviews are so apt and to the point that they cry out to be carved on the writer's tombstone. Sadly, the author **James M. Cain** (1892–1977) exhausted both the critics' and the public's enthusiasm. **Raymond Chandler**, who adapted Cain's Double Indemnity for the movie, even sneered that the author was just a "**Proust** in greasy overalls," while **Hemingway** accused him of bad taste.

For a man whose powerful pulp fiction influenced **Camus** and who was dubbed the 'American **Zola**', Cain is oddly neglected. The charge that he was a fake doesn't really stick. He brought to his novels the directness of a newspaper reporter. His economical first-person narration avoids moral judgements, though the regularity with which his male characters were used by stronger women may have had something to do with the regularity with which Cain paid for expensive divorce settlements. His best novels – Postman, Double Indemnity, Mildred Pierce (all becoming classic Hollywood movies) – were published between 1934 and 1941. After this, although he continued writing fiction (including the under-rated historical novel Past All Dishonour), he lost the power that had attracted people like Camus and the Italian filmmaker **Luchino Visconti**. The point at which he mislaid the plot is probably the 1943 novel Serenade, in which the narrator is a male opera singer, sacramental wine is used in iguana stew and some dodgy ideas about homosexuality are presented. In his final years he was preoccupied not by greed and sex, but by **Shakespeare**'s sonnets and classical music. A strange fate for a man the critic **Edmund Wilson** had called "a poet of the tabloid murder."

> "I write of the wish that comes true – for some reason a terrifying concept"
>
> James M. Cain on the method in his badness

INFLUENCED BY H.L. Mencken; Horace McCoy.

INFLUENCE ON Camus; Chandler; Norman Mailer; Cornwell Woolrich; Horace McCoy; James Ellroy; Michael Moorcock.

ESSENTIAL READING If you can find it, Picador's omnibus **Five Great Novels** has the three stand-outs, plus **The Butterfly** and **Love's Lovely Counterfeit**. If not, **The Postman Always Ring Twice** and **Double Indemnity**.

FURTHER READING Cain's personal favourite, **The Moth**, is set in the Baltimore he knew as a reporter.

The fabulous fabulist

Italo Calvino (1923–1985) coaxed and cajoled fiction into new and unexpected possibilities. With its fabulist aura and metafictional sensibility, his work explored the art of narrative while meditating on subjective perception. If that makes him sound dull, it is only fair to add that he can, and probably will, entertain you while he goes about such business.

The son of botanists, Calvino came of age in the anti-Fascist resistance during World War II. His first novel The Path To The Nest Of Spiders drew on his experiences as a partisan; its neo-realism is characteristic of early postwar Italian fiction and film. Yet he was soon bored with realism (and communism) and his writing took on surreal, if allegorical, strains. The most notable of his 1950s works, The Baron In The Trees, details the escapades of a young 18th-century nobleman who seeks freedom from society by spending his life up trees.

In the 1960s Calvino applied some of the **Oulipo** (see **Raymond Queneau**) school's formalist matrices to his fiction, notably in The Castle Of Crossed Destinies, whose speechless characters recount their often overlapping tales through a Tarot deck. He also dabbled in science fiction with Cosmicomics, a series of mathematical short stories. His imaginative power is best displayed in Invisible Cities. Based on **Marco Polo**'s descriptions of the cities of **Kublai Khan**'s vast empire that the emperor never saw, it imagines underground cities, cities resembling carpets draped from the sky and spider-web cities suspended between mountains. Consummate, playful, intelligent, it established him internationally.

"A classic," Calvino said, "is a book that has never finished saying what it has to say," – a book like If On A Winter's Night A Traveller. In his masterpiece of metafiction, two people read a book called If On A Winter's Night A Traveller, which consists of ten different shorter fictions, parodying fictive styles that keep breaking off. The conjuring trick works because, as his friend **Gore Vidal** joked, he worked so hard on his fiction his name ought to have been Italian Calvinist.

INFLUENCED BY Oulipo; Nabokov; Roland Barthes; Borges; Ludovico Ariosto.
INFLUENCE ON Stanislaw Lem; Georges Perec; Milorad Pavic; Jonathan Lethem.
ESSENTIAL READING **Invisible Cities**; **If On A Winter's Night A Traveller**.
FURTHER READING **The Baron In The Trees**.

ALBERT CAMUS

A rebel with a cause and a certain style

It's too easy to forget that **Albert Camus** (1913–1960), existentialist icon, spare-time philosopher, Resistance hero, goalkeeper, friend – and antagonist – of

Jean-Paul Sartre, could actually write. He created one of Western literature's most famous opening lines for The Outsider ("Mother died today…") yet that novel, his most celebrated and most studied, is probably inferior as a work of art to his last, vastly under-rated work, The Fall, in which fiction's most stylish existentialist turns his elegant irony on everything, including himself, to reach the almost Christian conclusion that we must recognise our own inadequacies to achieve grace.

The Outsider with its portrait of a man on trial not for a murder he committed but for his way of life, is a classic novel of alienation, complete with some nifty epigraphs. Such trials were, as Camus sensed and **Kafka** had suggested, to become commonplace in dictatorships and democracies; the

novel also owes a debt to **James M. Cain**'s The Postman Always Rings Twice. The unnoticed irony in the work is that the hero Mersault does not mourn his mother's death, whereas Camus would later be tried by left-wing opinion for putting his mother, who (like him) grew up French in Algeria, before the justice of the African colony's case for independence. For Camus, who had seemed to personify the idea of universal justice, his life, like his character's, was used against him.

His novel The Plague catches the horror of France's Nazi occupation with an allegorical plague of rats. Those three novels apart, Camus left behind the pained short-stories Exile And The Kingdom, two treatises – The Myth Of Sisyphus and The Rebel – and his notebooks, which **Robert Kennedy** constantly reread. In one entry, he meets a man at a party and realises that as they're talking the man's eyes are flickering around the room. Camus notes simply: "Womaniser." It's written with contempt, even though he was one himself.

But then, as in the Algerian controversy, Camus is full of contradictions. He was a man who, in his time, was famed for his intellect, yet today is as valued for his image – hunched shoulders, turned-up raincoat, cigarette elegantly dangling from a lip, more private eye than philosopher prince – and for the small body of unusual fiction he left behind. Death, in the car crash he had absurdly predicted, made him almost as much of an icon in the 1960s and 1970s as **James Dean**.

INFLUENCED BY Sartre; James M. Cain; Nietzsche; St Augustine; Dostoevsky.

INFLUENCE ON Alexander Trocchi; William Golding (his novel **Free Fall** is an answer to Camus's **The Fall**); T. Coraghessan Boyle.

ESSENTIAL READING **The Outsider**; **The Fall** – the latter, apart from its other delights, is a triumph of the rarely used second-person narrative.

FURTHER READING His **Selected Essays And Notebooks**.

JIM CARROLL

Sex, drugs and basketball

Jim Carroll (1951–) grew up on the tough streets of working-class Manhattan. Inspired by **Kerouac**, he kept a diary from the age of 12, but published his poetry before the autobiographical The Basketball Diaries because he didn't want to be tagged a 'street writer'. The Diaries, an instant cult classic (later filmed starring **Leonardo DiCaprio**), details his coming of age from 1963 to 1966 – full of drug addiction, hustling, sex and basketball – in street language and graphic imagery.

Carroll won a scholarship to the Manhattan high school where he became a basketball star, before turning his back on the sport for drugs and to write. He immersed himself in the social circles of **William Burroughs**, **Allen Ginsberg** and **Andy Warhol**, writing for **Rolling Stone** and the **Paris Review** while hooked on heroin, amphetamines and barbiturates. Many of these experiences went into Forced Entries, a kind of sequel to The Basketball Diaries covering Carroll's life from 1970 to 1972. "A lot of them were 'forced' in the sense that they were painful to write," says Carroll, who admits to being not entirely sure of the years they cover.

Inspired by his friend **Patti Smith**, he formed The Jim Carroll Band in the late 1970s and recorded three albums. The best is the first, Catholic Boy, with its near-hit People Who Died, an emotional roll-call of the victims of drugs. Carroll then returned to prose and, with such titles as The Book Of Nods and Fear Of Dreaming, to poetry.

Carroll's published prose focuses on himself, steering away from plot twists and imagined characters. The real source material was too good: "All my prose has been autobiographical." He is thought to have been writing two fictional novels for a decade or so, provisionally entitled The Petting Zoo and Stigma.

INFLUENCED BY Ginsberg; Burroughs; Hunter S. Thompson.

INFLUENCE ON Nick McDonnell.

ESSENTIAL READING **The Basketball Diaries**.

FURTHER READING **Forced Entries**, recommended by Burroughs.

LEWIS CARROLL

"The proper definition of a man is an animal that writes letters"

This logical mathematician created some of the greatest characters in literature and wrote the kind of mind-bending fiction often attributed to habitual drug

The White Rabbit memorial in Llandudno, where Carroll first told Alice his tale

use, though he never touched them. The writing of **Lewis Carroll** (1832–1898) is packed with philosophical metaphors and cryptic wit. His Alice books have been inspected for all kinds of meaning – Freudian, political, satirical – and even been searched for anagrams to see if he is a potential **Jack the Ripper**. He isn't.

Born **Charles Lutwidge Dodgson**, he was the third of 11 children. He attended Rugby school and gained a first in mathematics at Christ Church, Oxford. Like his father, he was ordained as a deacon, in 1861, but he worked mainly as a Christ Church lecturer. When writing for the magazine **The Train**, he signed himself 'BB'. The editor, **Edmund Yates**, asked Dodgson for a full pseudonym and, out of four, Yates chose Lewis Carroll. Dodgson had created the name by Latinising and transposing his first names.

Shortly after, he took the first of three boat trips that would inspire his most famous work. On 4 July 1862, entertaining **Alice Liddell** and the other daughters of the Dean of Christ Church, he began telling what he then called Alice's Adventures Under Ground. He didn't start to write anything down until a few months later, and after two years it was long enough to be published. Enlisting an illustrator, **John Tenniel** from **Punch**, he produced 2,000 copies of Alice's Adventures In Wonderland at his own expense. **Queen Victoria** enjoyed it so much she asked that his next book be dedicated to her. She perhaps didn't expect it to be An Elementary Treatise On Determinants.

Much gossip and myth surround Carroll's character and fondness for young girls. He once entered what he thought was a children's party on hands and knees, pretending to be a bear – only to find he had the wrong address and was in a women's reformers meeting. Certainly the Liddell family were offended when the 31-year-old Dodgson suggested he might later marry the then 11-year-old Alice. Experimenting, he also photographed naked girls, with parental permission, stopping in 1880 in the face of growing disapproval.

Carroll's desire to amuse children inspired such works as Through The Looking Glass, The Hunting Of The Snark, Sylvie And Bruno and Sylvie And Bruno Concluded – all with his trademark nonsense, confusion and impossibilities. But it's the likes of Alice ("the least sentimental most real child character in children's literature," says A.S. Byatt), the Mad Hatter and the Cheshire Cat who have ensured that, over a century on, his influence is seen in films like Dogma, the music of John Lennon and Jefferson Airplane and a raft of parodies and computer games.

> "I would like to have the energy to write about battling with the NHS, but I haven't. I write overblown purple prose, so what?"
>
> Angela Carter explains her approach to fiction

51

INFLUENCED BY Edward Lear; the philosopher Leibniz; George MacDonald; Jonathan Swift's satires also play with space and time.

INFLUENCE ON Borges; Nabokov; Oscar Wilde; Flannery O'Connor; Jeff Noon (Alice is the prime suspect in the 'jigsaw murders' in his **Automated Alice**); Hunter S. Thompson (the song **White Rabbit** appears in one of **Fear And Loathing**'s drug sequences); J.K. Rowling (the hippogriff in **Prisoner Of Azkaban** is reminiscent of Carroll's gryphon).

ESSENTIAL READING **Alice's Adventures In Wonderland**.

FURTHER READING **Through The Looking Glass**; Karoline Leach's **Lewis Carroll: In The Shadow Of The Dreamchild** reassesses the Carroll myths.

ANGELA CARTER

When realistic fiction is too much like hard work, invent...

So many of the labels used to describe **Angela Carter** (1940–1992) – be it magic realism or postmodern – cannot do justice to the dazzling cocktail of her work. She is postmodern because of her acknowledgement of the influence of such questioners of myth and language as **Barthes** and **Foucault**. Yet her questioning encompassed class, gender, sexuality and identity – nothing was sacred. Her rich array of ingredients include parody, allegory, the body, family, art, music, theatre, music hall, cinema, comedy, wordplay and vulgarity.

The daughter of a Scottish journalist and a Yorkshire mother, Carter was born in Eastbourne but spent the war years with her maternal grandmother in Yorkshire. After school she followed her father into journalism, working for the **Croydon Advertiser**, until she escaped by marrying **Paul Carter** at the age of 20.

Carter famously described herself as being "in the demythologising business". Her first novel Shadow Dance, a detective story whose hedonistic protagonist presents the reader with an examination of sexuality, was written while Carter was studying English at Bristol University. Her third, Several Perceptions, won the £500 **Somerset Maugham Award**, enabling Carter – who had left her husband – to travel to Japan with a lover. She later settled in south London with her new partner and had a son at 43.

Carter's brand of socialism and feminism has distinguished her fiction from that of contemporary female novelists. "I've got nothing against realism," she said. "I'd really like to have had the guts and energy to be able to write about… people having battles with the DHSS… but I haven't, I've done other things. I'm an arty person, OK? I write overblown, purple, self-indulgent prose – so fucking what?"

In 1979 she gained wider recognition. Beginning to be studied in academia, she published The Sadeian Woman, An Exercise In Cultural History and The Bloody Chamber, a retelling of classic fairy tales. Her version of Little Red Riding Hood became the **Neil Jordan** movie The Company Of Wolves, for which she also wrote the script. In her telling, it is a tale of sexual awakening where the girl is not a victim, but brazenly confident in her ability to charm the wolf ("The girl burst out laughing. She knew she was nobody's meat") and therefore survive.

Her later works Nights At The Circus and Wise Children are both enchanting and often paired because they are set in the world of entertainment and narrated by exuberant female Cockney performers. In the former, Fevvers is a high-wire artist (or 'aerialiste' as she prefers to be called) with real wings. In Wise Children, twin Dora Chance is born on the "wrong side of the blanket" into a **Shakespearean** acting dynasty The Hazards. It was Carter's last book and her funniest, celebrating the Chance sisters as exemplars of the pleasures of life, whose philosophy is summed up in Dora's final sentence, "What a joy it is to dance and sing!"

INFLUENCED BY Virginia Woolf; Georges Bataille; Simone de Beauvoir; Gabriel García Márquez; Jean-Luc Godard; Edgar Allan Poe; Marquis De Sade; the Brothers Grimm.

INFLUENCE ON Jeanette Winterson; Marina Warner; Robert Coover.

ESSENTIAL READING **Nights At The Circus**; **Wise Children**.

FURTHER READING **Several Perceptions**; **The Bloody Chamber**.

The American Chekhov

Raymond Carver (1938–1988) crammed two full lifespans into his 50 short years, mastered and revitalised the short story and is a continuing source of comfort and inspiration to authors who, as he did, "get a little nervous in earshot of sombre discussion about 'formal innovation' in writing."

Carver began writing partly to escape the hell of being married and a father before his 20th birthday. In 1958 he moved his family from Washington state to Paradise, California, to study under **John Gardner**, and for the next 30 years, until his death, his life was punctuated by bankruptcies, bouts of drinking, troubled personal relationships and the struggle to write.

The family lived hand-to-mouth throughout the 1960s. Carver worked as an advertising director, writing sporadically and drinking heavily, until 1970 when, in quick succession, he won an award for his poetry, had his first book Winter Insomnia published and was made redundant with a big enough pay-off and benefits to write for almost a year. Backed by support from **Gordon Lish** at **Esquire** magazine, Carver became visiting lecturer in creative writing at the University of California in Santa Cruz.

> "I don't fire up the prose, I just tell it straight and don't fool around with it"
>
> Raymond Carver's thoughts on his style

With his ultra-lean, pared-down style, Carver was lazily classed as a minimalist – a label he hated, "it smacks of smallness of vision and execution." If anything, he was a precisionist. He rewrote each of his short stories many times: The Bath, for example, exists in three different versions. Gardner famously advised Carver to use 15 words instead of 25; Lish instructed him to use 5 in place of 15.

By the end of 1974 Carver abandoned academia to concentrate on his second bankruptcy and drinking. He spent two years writing almost nothing, barely noticing the publication of his third book of poetry nor that of his first major short-story collection, Will You Please Be Quiet, Please? By January 1977 he had been admitted to hospital four times in as many months: alcohol was killing him and alienating him from his family.

Carver quit drinking, sold the family home, was reunited with his wife Maryann and soon the books began to flow. Well enough to attend a writers' conference in Dallas, he met the poet **Tess Gallagher**, while Maryann, realising that a sober Carver was not the man she had married, left him for good. Carver later married Gallagher and moved to New York as an established author and Professor of English at Syracuse University. Another award gave him the means to leave work and oversee the publication of his third collection of short stories,

Cathedral. Four years later he developed lung cancer; he died in 1988 while working on a last book of poems.

Carver was a poet of working-class life, drawing on his own experiences of the Pacific Northwest and awarding blue-collar guys and hard-working girls the dignity of their labour by recording it as literature. Aware of his good fortune in being allowed a second chance at life, he saw each new day as "pure gravy". **Robert Altman**'s Short Cuts, based on Carver's stories, is a fitting film tribute to the man's fictional legacy.

INFLUENCED BY Ezra Pound; Stephen Crane; Hemingway.

INFLUENCE ON Chuck Kinder; Martyn Bedford; Larry Brown; Susan Minot; Todd Zuniga; Kim McLarin; Jonathan Ames; Jay McInerney.

ESSENTIAL READING **Will You Please Be Quiet, Please?**; **Cathedral**.

FURTHER READING **Furious Seasons And Other Stories**.

LOUIS-FERDINAND CÉLINE

"The more one is hated, the happier one is"

With an unflinching nihilism and inspired misanthropy, **Louis-Ferdinand Céline** (1894–1961) produced two autobiographical novels, Journey To The End Of The Night and Death On The Installment Plan, in which he vomited forth his revulsion for 1930s society. Though later writings verge on the unreadable and his reputation has been tainted by charges of Nazi collaboration, the grim humour, innovative syntax, use of street slang and sheer narrative energy of his first two works have assured them a devoted following.

Louis-Ferdinand Destouches was raised in Paris, in a flat over the shopping arcade where his mother had a lace store. After an education that included stints in Germany and England, he enlisted in the army in 1912, suffering serious injuries in World War I – a crippled arm and headaches that plagued him all his life – but also winning a medal of honour. His subsequent employers included the French passport office in London, a West African lumber company and the League of Nations, which sent him to work as a doctor in Africa, Canada, the US and Cuba.

Under the pseudonym Céline, he drew on his work at a Paris clinic in Journey To The End Of The Night. From the brutal trenches and the lonely jungle to the miserable factories of Detroit and a cynical medical practice in the Paris slums, he tracks his antihero Bardamu through a world where human sentiment is a sham; love is dismissed as "the infinite placed within the reach of poodles."

Céline's writing embraced underworld slang and popular references that unfortunately lose much in translation (and even more in time). It was also punctuated by innumerable ellipses that did not so much derail trains of

Carver invented his own fictional country as surely as Faulkner or Hemingway

thought… as pause… then recharge them with renewed bursts of phlegm. This style is more pronounced in Death On The Installment Plan, which retraces Bardamu's early years. The teenage perspective gives its nihilism a breezier, Catcher In The Rye-accent, but the author, who once claimed: "The more one is hated, I find, the happier one is," still imbued the work with customary venom.

In 1937 Céline penned the pamphlet Bagatelles Pour Un Massacre, warning of a Jewish conspiracy to trigger world war. He shared his violent anti-Semitism and loathing of bourgeois society with the Nazis, but seems to have detested them too – once dismissing **Hitler** as a Jew. Certainly he had friends who collaborated, and after the liberation of France he had to flee, first to Berlin, then Denmark. This journey was recounted in his trilogy Castle To Castle, North and Rigadoon, a horrific diet of paranoia and madness only the most loyal of Céline readers can stomach. Imprisoned in Denmark, he was convicted, in absentia, of collaboration but allowed to return home in 1951 for the last decade of his life.

INFLUENCED BY Parisian slang; Rimbaud.

INFLUENCE ON Henry Miller; Joseph Heller; Kurt Vonnegut; Bukowski; Burroughs.

ESSENTIAL READING **Journey To The End Of The Night**; **Death On The Installment Plan**.

FURTHER READING **The Golden Age of Louis-Ferdinand Céline** by Nicholas Hewitt; **Céline And The Politics Of Difference**.

RAYMOND CHANDLER

He could make you imagine a bishop kicking a hole in a stained-glass window

He only invented one protagonist he, or anybody else, cared about; his plots had holes the size of Moose Malloy's fists and his female characters could be so cardboard they would have been blown over by a gust of Philip Marlowe's whiskey-sodden breath. Yet somehow **Raymond Chandler**'s work is imprinted so powerfully on the public mind that we spot a parody after half a sentence.

Chandler (1888–1959) failed at a lot of things – clerking, poetry, journalism, the oil business – before he turned in depressed desolation to writing pulp fiction and a story called Blackmailers Don't Shoot when he was 44. Writing at Chandler's speed – five stories a year – was never going to keep him in whiskey, so he wrote a novel, The Big Sleep, starring a lone, tough-guy private detective called Philip Marlowe (see page 321). He wrote six Marlowe novels – the finest being Farewell My Lovely and the bitter, melancholy The Long Goodbye.

His archetypes have since become clichés, but it's the language as much as the character or plots, that keeps his best novels fresh; a gift that doesn't begin and end with punchlines about women with figures that could make bishops kick holes in stained-glass windows. The larger implausibilities are matched by smaller notes of truth – the shabbiness of an apartment, the seediness of a crooked doctor, the grim, mundane horror of a corpse. Without this, some of his plots would look as conspicuous as, say, a tarantula on a slice of angel cake. It didn't harm his cause either that he was prepared to heed his own advice on plots and, when in doubt, have a character walk through the door with a gun.

Chandler was on top form for 14 years, from The Big Sleep to The Long Goodbye. You can feel him tiring of his hero in Playback, published a year before his death, in which the more blatant sex scenes are a lame attempt to compete with **Mickey Spillane**'s crudities. That doesn't matter much, because he gave us three of the best pulp crime novels of the 20th century and the most famous fictional detective since Hercule Poirot. Any appreciation of Chandler's art has to acknowledge the chauffeur – the one who dies in The Big Sleep. Asked who had murdered him, Chandler said simply: "Oh him – I forgot about him."

INFLUENCED BY Hammett; F. Scott Fitzgerald.

INFLUENCE ON Ross Macdonald; James Ellroy; James Hadley Chase; Spillane.

ESSENTIAL READING **Farewell My Lovely** and **The Long Goodbye** push the private-eye novel into a kind of social history.

FURTHER READING If you've exhausted Chandler's fiction try Ross Macdonald's **Archer** novels: his mysteries often prove to be family tragedies.

CHANDLER'S ZEN DISCIPLE

At a distinct tangent to **Raymond Chandler**, yet influenced by him, are the Amsterdam detective novels of **Janwillem van der Wetering**.

Starting with Outsider In Amsterdam, the novels combine a sure grasp of police procedure (the author was a reserve policeman in the Dutch capital when he was writing this), a subtly atmospheric sense of place and three unusual heroes: detective sergeant Gripstra, adjutant de Gier and their boss, the arthritic, suffering, philosophical Commissaris.

Van der Wetering spent time in a Japanese Buddhist monastery – recalled in his memoir The Empty Mirror – and brings a quirky Zen sensibility to this most traditional of genres, but many of his later novels upset traditionalists and critics with what some saw as their incoherence and implausibility.

Often in van der Wetering's work, the hunt for clues and suspects is replaced by a psychological battle as the cops try to break the criminal. The Maine Massacre, in which the Commissaris has to consider his own sister as a potential murder suspect, is a late, amusing masterpiece.

CULT FICTION

ARTHUR C. CLARKE

The man who invented the future

Arthur Charles Clarke (1917–) is a grand master of science fiction with a rigorous training in science fact, who has shown a clear-eyed appreciation of what the future ought to hold for the next six decades. The world has recognised his genius, naming an asteroid **4923 Clarke** after him, calling the geostationary orbit of satellites **The Clarke Orbit** and christening a dinosaur, discovered in Inverloch, Australia, **Serendipaceratops arthurcclarkei.**

Born in Minehead, Somerset, the young Clarke was a keen amateur astronomer with a voracious appetite for pulp sci-fi, a hunger for hard facts and the limitless universe of the imagination that have stayed with him. In World War II he worked on the RAF's ultra-secret RADAR system, augmenting his pay by selling science-fiction pieces to magazines. He was still in the air force when, in **Wireless World** in 1945, he predicted geostationary satellites and their role in telecommunications. After the war and a first-class degree in maths and physics, Clarke turned to writing full-time. In 1956 he moved to his present home in Colombo, Sri Lanka, where his imagination was given full rein and he began producing reams of short stories and pronouncements on the future. His early collection Tales From The White Hart presented almost-feasible Earth-based technology in easy pieces, framed as a collection of tall stories told in the pub of the book's title.

Clarke forecast brainwave technology that could record and play back sensual experiences (noting it would only become widespread if pornographers were involved), and in his novel The Fountains Of Paradise he described a space elevator that is now being considered as a replacement for the space shuttle. He was also behind one of the 20th century's finest, most enigmatic films, 2001: A Space Odyssey, which has its roots in his short story The Sentinel, written in 1948 for a BBC competition (it failed to make the shortlist). Clarke worked on set with director **Stanley Kubrick** on the script and has said: "If you understand 2001 completely, we failed. We wanted to raise far more questions than we answered." It certainly had the desired effect on **Rock Hudson**, who walked out of the premiere saying, "Will someone tell me what the hell this is about?" One of several sequels, 2010 was also filmed with Clarke appearing as a man feeding pigeons from a bench outside the White House.

Clarke's output has been prodigious. Apart from the sequels to 2001, it includes the Rama novels, a tome of short stories and two volumes of autobiography. In 2004 he was working on a novel about Fermat's theorem and the CIA – a long way from the "bug-eyed monsters threatening nubile maidens" stories he read as a child.

INFLUENCED BY Classic US pulp-fiction magazines such as **Astounding Tales.**

INFLUENCE ON Innumerable sci-fi short-story tyros.

ESSENTIAL READING **Tales From The White Hart**; **2001: A Space Odyssey**; **Rendezvous With Rama**.

FURTHER READING **Greetings, Carbon-Based Bipeds**, his best non-fiction.

JEAN COCTEAU

Like a true poet he did not bother to be poetical

Jean Cocteau (1889–1963) made his name when he was 20 with the volume of poems Aladdin's Lamp, but he was a versatile chap and became a celebrated novelist, playwright, film director, essayist, painter, set designer and actor. Although he thought of himself first and foremost as a poet, he took the view that prose and other art forms could be poeticised. "A true poet does not bother to be poetical. Nor does a nursery gardener scent his roses," he once said.

Cocteau was born to a wealthy family on the outskirts of Paris. When he was nine, his father, an amateur painter, killed himself. At 15 he was expelled from school and ran away to Marseilles, where he lived in the red-light district under a false name until the police found him and returned him to his uncle's care.

After Aladdin's Lamp Cocteau was known in artistic circles as the '**Frivolous Prince**', which was the title of a volume of poems he published aged 21. After writing a libretto for a ballet, he wrote the prose fantasy Le Potomak about a creature caged in an aquarium. In World War I he served as an ambulance driver, where his experiences infused his poetry. Afterwards, he worked with **Picasso** and **Erik Satie** on the ballet Parade and when Le Potomak finally appeared in 1919, his reputation as a writer was established.

His psychological novel Thomas The Imposter followed, but the death of his protégé, a precocious young novelist **Raymond Radiguet**, from typhoid, drove Cocteau to opium addiction. It was during his recovery that he wrote his most important novel, Les Enfants Terribles, which follows three children through to early adulthood in a tale with an atmosphere of incest and bohemia.

In the 1930s and 1940s Cocteau turned to filmmaking, the first being The Blood Of A Poet and the best Beauty And The Beast. He also wrote plays, his greatest The Infernal Machine was based on **Sophocles**'s Oedipus Rex. As **W.H. Auden** said, "To enclose the collected works of Cocteau, one would need not a bookshelf but a warehouse." Later still he tried acting and painting, had a facelift and took to wearing leather trousers and a matador's cape. Legend has it that on learning of his friend **Edith Piaf**'s death in 1963, he said, "Ah, Piaf's dead. I can die too," and promptly died of a heart attack.

Cocteau, whose works reflect the influences of Surrealism, psychoanalysis, Cubism and Catholicism, has enjoyed a strange posthumous fame as one of the alleged leaders of a secret order devoted to Christ's bloodline, immortalised in The Holy Blood And The Holy Grail and The Da Vinci Code.

INFLUENCED BY Picasso; Radiguet; opium.

INFLUENCE ON Jean Genet; underground film; Julio Cortázar.

ESSENTIAL READING **Les Enfants Terribles**: Cocteau's most famous novel popularised a cliché and anticipates Ian McEwan's **The Cement Garden**.

FURTHER READING **Opium**, Cocteau was crushed by the death of Radiguet and the effects of the drug: this is his tale of rehab.

JONATHAN COE

Coe looks back in anger and humour

He's angry, funny, daft as Dickens...

If you're British and were born around 1960, odds are that when you first read Birmingham-born **Jonathan Coe** (1961–) you thought: that's the novel I always planned to write. For Coe's talent is to delineate a time and its issues, serve up a cast of believable and farcical characters, give it a postmodern shake-up and from time to time turn the angry political satire dial up to 11. Yet for all his mad twists and turns of character, for all his **Dickensian** disregard for psychological plotting, you truly care what happens to Coe's people and even his country. There's both anger and love in his novels.

Coe had three unpublished works piling up under his desk before The Accidental Woman was published in 1987. It took a couple more – A Touch Of Love and The Dwarves Of Death – plus two film-star biographies before he got into his stride with What A Carve Up! But the apprenticeship paid off.

For British readers What A Carve Up! defines the 1980s and nails the whole shitty world of **Thatcherism**, which destroyed manufacturing industry, turned farms into concentration camps, and made arms-dealing respectable. These are all targets of Coe's ire, exemplified by a family of stunning ruthlessness, whose trail of human victims makes you weep. All of which might suggest a left-wing earnestness. Not a bit of it. With this book, Coe staked a claim to being one of the funniest British writers since **Wodehouse** or **Waugh**. Funny and postmodern to boot, it mixes realism with all manner of (often film-influenced) set-pieces, not least a spoof Theatre Of Blood-style denouement, in which the author joyously kills off his enemies.

It was a tough act to follow and The House Of Sleep was perhaps inevitably a smaller book, substituting panoramic political intents with an exploration of gender, sleep and dysfunction. However, The Rotters' Club was a triumphant return to expectation: the difficult third album (well, the sixth) that found a new subject – the 1970s of Coe's schooldays – and engaged it full on. The satire was bent more this time to storytelling, as a more realistic cast appeared, fleshed out in all their achingly embarrassing adolescent traits. And the form of the novel, again, was effortlessly daring (to the reader at least): a book that starts and halts twice, leaving its ends untied, and which rounds off, in an act that doesn't seem altogether wilful, with a 15,000-word sentence. The world and characters Coe created in The Rotters' Club were returned to life 20 years on in The Closed Circle, a novel that breaks down almost exactly into two halves: first – terrific, second – contrived, pretty awful. It was disappointing for Coe's following, who latched on to the book with an eagerness akin to his hero Ben Trotter awaiting the latest album from the Hatfields, way back when.

Coe's following, incidentally, is in both Britain and Europe pleasingly mass market – a sign that a cult writer, with apparent disregard for lit fashions, can certainly cut it alongside the gold-embossed covers.

INFLUENCED BY P.G. Wodehouse; Alisdair Gray; B.S. Johnson.

INFLUENCE ON Not yet, but give him time.

ESSENTIAL READING **What A Carve Up!**; **The Rotters' Club**.

FURTHER READING **The House Of Sleep** and his biography of **B.S. Johnson**.

LEONARD COHEN

"I don't know anything about people – that's why I wanted to be a novelist"

Long before **Leonard Cohen** (1934–) became famous for songs so miserable the music press felt obliged to dub him **Laughing Len**, he could have been **Michael Ondaatje**. Indeed, if he had pursued his literary ambitions, we might never have had The English Patient, the world possibly not ready to greet two unshaven, sensitive poet-novelists from Canada at the same time.

But Cohen, a Jewish boy who felt an outsider growing up in Catholic Montreal, gave up poetry and novels in the 1960s for songs in which he challenged himself, and his listeners, to slit their wrists, confessed to a fling with **Janis Joplin** ("She told me again she preferred handsome men/But for me she would make an exception") and suggested the Nazis were overthrown by the power of music. At the time the career move was no sure thing, as he was blessed with a voice even **Bob Dylan** fans thought lacked musicality.

His subsequent career makes his two published novels – The Favourite Game and Beautiful Losers – hard to judge now. His first manuscript, Beauty At Close Quarters, has never been published, even in uncut form. The Favourite Game is a fiercely imagined, deeply Jewish, funny novel in which poet Lawrence Breavman relates hi

ROCK STARS IN THEIR OWN WRITE

The history of modern music is littered with those who believed their own hype and made the leap from stage to page.

John Lennon's nonsense verse and invented words owed a lot to **Lewis Carroll** and **James Joyce**, yet In His Own Write and A Spaniard In The Works still sold over 100,000 copies. Meanwhile, in An American Prayer, **Jim Morrison** leaned on the Romantic tradition of poetry. The year Morrison died, **Bob Dylan** published Tarantula, a free-form book-length poem.

In the 1980s the biblical lyrics and furious instrumentation of **Nick Cave** (below) attracted a cult following eager to devour an anthology of lyrics and plays, King Ink. Critical acclaim followed with the **Faulkneresque** And The Ass Saw The Angel, a story of smalltown murder told by a deaf mute that is one of the best rock star-penned works of fiction.

Cave collaborator **Lydia Lunch** mixes performing with writing, including the comic Toxic Gumbo. And the equally brutal

Henry Rollins formed a publishing company to release his own work 2:13:61 (his birthdate), the first in a stream of books he has produced.

Musicians who have proved more successful as authors include 'Jewish Cowboy' and country crooner **Kinky Friedman**, who started writing mystery books in the 1980s. He's now penned over 15 about a black-humoured former country singer that turned private eye called, er… Kinky Friedman.

Even Britpop spawned an acclaimed storyteller. **Louise Werner**, former frontwoman of **Sleeper**, has written two comic novels: Goodnight Steve McQueen and The Big Blind.

The crossover of writers (often an introverted breed) is less common, but **Leonard Cohen** and **Patti Smith** both entered music as published poets.

Stephen King, **Amy Tan** and **Matt Groening** belong to a rock group called the **Rock Bottom Remainders**, "hailed by critics as having one of the world's highest ratios of noise to talent."

62

history and, in a prescient glimpse of postmodernism, imagines himself as a character in his own autobiography. The flaws – a certain, possibly chemically induced, repetition – are compensated for by the unusual metaphors that make Cohen's lyrics so distinctive. The first edition failed to sell 1,000 copies in the UK and North America.

Beautiful Losers sounds like the title of a Cohen album but it was, Ondaatje noted in 1970, "the funniest novel to appear in a long time," taking the idea of "sex as religious liberation" to a level so absurd it kills it. Manic, sensational, savage: it is, as critic **T.F. Rigelhof** notes, driven by the "tantric sex practices, amphetamine overdoses, obsessions with the songs of **Ray Charles** that fed its composition." There's a surprising political sub-text here, with an anarchist separatist Quebecois as a main character. Cohen says he might return to fiction, it's just that songs make money faster.

INFLUENCED BY The **Bible**; Stephen Vizinczey, friend and author of **In Praise Of Older Women**; Saul Bellow, especially **Herzog**.

INFLUENCE ON Iain Rankin admits his world view has been influenced by Cohen's songs; Tom Robbins has penned his sleeve notes.

ESSENTIAL READING Try both novels.

FURTHER READING Vizinczey's **In Praise Of Older Women** offers an interesting parallel in time and place to Cohen's fiction.

COLETTE

The 20th-century marketing dream

Widely regarded as 'the first woman who wrote as a woman', **Colette** (1873–1954) wrote from the heart, delving into her childhood and adult experiences to focus on the often controversial themes of love, female sexuality, a woman's battle for independence and, less controversially, cats.

Born **Sidonie-Gabrielle Colette**, in the rural Burgundian village of Saint-Sauveur-en Puisaye, Colette grew up surrounded by nature, pets and books. At 20 she was married to writer and critic **Henri Gauthier-Villars**, 15 years her senior. For all his frequent infidelities, he pushed Colette into writing, asking her to write about her childhood experiences but to make it "spicy", reportedly locking her in a room until she had produced enough pages. His harsh methods worked: the four Claudine novels, released under Villars's pen name **Willy** turned Colette (although she could never get her name rightfully restored to the books) into a literary celebrity and an early 20th-century marketing dream. The novels detailed the improper adventures of a teenage girl and included such spice as lesbian relationships and, in Claudine Married, voyeurism. The novels' success led to a play, Claudine perfume, cosmetics, clothing and even cigars. Colette's immediate response to such success was to free herself from the shackles of her philandering husband and support herself as a music-hall performer. Throughout her life Colette instigated a series of firsts, beginning with her stage performances: she was the first woman to bare her breasts on stage (it was only one but it still caused a stir) and the first to simulate stage copulation, her risqué mime causing a riot at the **Moulin Rouge**.

Such incidences, lesbian dalliances and an affair with her stepson, would have engulfed many writers, but her refreshing frankness and prolific output (over 50 books and numerous short stories) meant she was still seen as a novelist. Whether writing about the bond of a mother and daughter – La Maison De Claudine and Sido; the aches of love – Cheri; or female sexuality – Le Képi; Colette employed an almost biographical tone, acutely observing the trials, tribulations, aspirations and joys of being a woman. Despite two failed marriages she found love for a third and final time with **Maurice Goudaket**, whom she married in 1935. The marriage lasted until her death in 1954, when she became the first and (still only) woman to be given a state funeral in France.

INFLUENCED BY Guy de Maupassant.

INFLUENCE ON Simone de Beauvoir's **The Second Sex**; the late Françoise Sagan, was considered Colette's literary heir.

ESSENTIAL READING The **Claudine** novels; **The Pure And The Impure**, considered by Colette to be her best work.

FURTHER READING **The Vagabond**, regarded by some critics as her best.

SIR ARTHUR CONAN DOYLE

Money matters... or how Sherlock Holmes lived twice

Sir Arthur Conan Doyle (1859–1930) is synonymous with an iconic detective, yet he achieved so much that the creation of Sherlock Holmes could almost be a footnote. He wrote prolifically, threw himself into politics, medicine, sport, the military and even solved the odd crime. He was an early espouser of spiritualism, science-fiction, body building and skiing in Switzerland. He pushed for a Channel tunnel and metal helmets for soldiers and conceived the life jacket.

One of ten children, **Arthur Ignatius Conan Doyle** was born in Edinburgh into a rich Irish-Catholic family. Apart from his father Charles (institutionalised for epilepsy and alcoholism), the Conan Doyles were an artistic bunch. Arthur's uncle drew covers for **Punch** and his mother had a gift for storytelling. After the usual boarding-school bigotry and brutality, he studied medicine in Edinburgh and met **Dr Joseph Bell**, a master of observation, logic and diagnosis. **Chamber Journal**

Colette never believed in the 'tidy desk, tidy mind' school of office management

published Conan Doyle's first story, The Mystery Of Sasassa Valley, in 1879.

Graduated, married and living in Portsmouth, his new practice gave him plenty of time for writing and in 1888 the **Beeton's Christmas Annual** carried A Study Of Scarlet. Conan Doyle's love-hate relationship with the king crime-solver Sherlock Holmes had begun. He craved respect as a serious writer, but felt overshadowed by the detective stories. Five years after creating him, Conan Doyle felt he had to kill him off. When The Final Problem was the final word on Holmes, 20,000 readers cancelled their subscriptions to **The Strand** magazine.

In 1900 Conan Doyle was desperate to enlist for the Boer War, even at a rotund 40. Rejected, he enrolled as a doctor. On his return he wrote the 500-page Great Boer War, a 'masterpiece' of military scholarship, then failed to get elected to parliament. Recuperating from both setbacks in Devon, he found the inspiration for his next novel: Dartmoor. Rather than resuscitate the popular detective, The Hound Of The Baskervilles was billed as an "untold adventure" and became a worldwide sensation.

In 1902 Conan Doyle was knighted by **Edward VII** (thought also to be a Holmes fan). Maybe the king had a word, because Conan Doyle resurrected the detective in The Return Of Sherlock Holmes. Conan Doyle's wife died in July 1906 and he recovered from depression by solving a miscarriage of justice and marrying, in 1907, **Jean Leckie**, a relative of **Rob Roy**. Despite the success of Professor Challenger in the sci-fi classic The Lost World, Conan Doyle still needed Holmes to pay bills, so came The Speckled Band and The Valley Of Fear.

At the start of World War I Conan Doyle, now 55, tried to enlist again, when snubbed he wrote to the War Office suggesting sailors wear "inflatable rubber belts". **Winston Churchill** wrote back thanking him for his ideas.

With six members of his family, including a son, lost to the war, Conan Doyle's fascination with the afterlife grew. He made his faith in spiritualism public, but was mocked by the press. To fund his travelling "psychic crusades", he returned to his typewriter in 1926 to write 12 more Holmes adventures. His touring continued until he was diagnosed with angina pectoris in 1929. He died a year later, bequeathing the world an immense catalogue of literature, many other legacies and one legendary sleuth puffing away on his pipe at 221b Baker Street. Just for the record, Holmes never, ever said, "Elementary, my dear Watson."

INFLUENCED BY Herman Melville; Edgar Allan Poe; Bret Harte; Dr Joseph Bell.

INFLUENCE ON Michael Crichton and legions of crime writers.

ESSENTIAL READING **The Hound Of The Baskervilles; The Adventures Of Sherlock Holmes**.

FURTHER READING **The White Company**, his best historical novel.

RICHARD CONDON

High entertainment, low comedy and middlebrow intrigue

Richard Condon (1915–1996) was probably too prolific for his own good. If he had published only his best-known titles – The Manchurian Candidate, Winter Kills, Prizzi's Honour – he might be better read. Yet his 26 novels include too many works like Mile High: slick, satirical, yet unsatisfying.

At his best, Condon writes as if he is mining the secrets of American history in the last half of the 20th century. He didn't start writing until his forties, spending 20 years in PR in Hollywood. The experience of hype stood him in good stead when he came to write about his pet subject, American politics, although his standout political novels – The Manchurian Candidate and Winter Kills have both been misunderstood. In the former, the mechanics of the brainwashed assassin, memorably retold in **John Frankenheimer**'s film, seemed to prefigure the murders of both Kennedy brothers. As **Greil Marcus** noted, "It was an unusual success, a bestseller and a cult book, casual reading for the public and the subject of hushed conversations among sophisticates: could it happen here?" Yet, the novel also highlights the phoniness of **McCarthyite** über-patriotism. In Winter

Kills, Condon revisits the **JFK** assassination, underlining the contradiction between the increasingly liberal president and the machine, presided over by corrupt **Joe Kennedy** and built with the aid of the Mafia, that elected him.

As good as Prizzi's Honour is, nothing matches those two, though An Infinity Of Mirrors, about Nazi leader **Reinhard Heydrich**, was praised by **Philip K. Dick**, who said: "He had the guts to get in the face of Heydrich and imagine along those lines." Condon had the confidence to write the unthinkable and was a master of that rare fictional tactic, heavy sarcasm. He summed up his motto as a novelist: "When you don't know the truth, the worst you can imagine is bound to be close." Had he written The Da Vinci Code it would have sold half as many copies – and been four times as readable.

INFLUENCED BY Stendhal; Aldous Huxley; Ian Fleming.

INFLUENCE ON Charles McCarry; thrillers with political-social trappings.

ESSENTIAL READING **The Manchurian Candidate**; **Winter Kills**; **An Infinity Of Mirrors**.

FURTHER READING The **Prizzi** hit-man novels.

CLARENCE COOPER JR

Young, gifted and addicted

Critics called him "the black **William Burroughs**", "one of the most under-rated writers in America", and claimed "not even **Nelson Algren** burns with this intensity". Unfortunately for **Clarence Cooper Jr** (1934–1978), these things were mostly said after he had died penniless in New York City.

Cooper was a writer of obvious gifts and even more obvious self-destructive tendencies. When his first novel The Scene, detailing the exploits of a pimp-pusher, was published in 1961, Cooper had to enjoy the reviews in prison. Born in Detroit, he worked as an editor for the **Chicago Messenger**, but by the end of the 1950s, heroin was working him – as it would for the rest of his life.

Unlike some black American novelists, notably **James Baldwin**, Cooper did not aim for political influence. His bleak, incendiary novels offer no easy solutions and little hope, reflecting the ruthless brutality of their milieu. **Harlan Ellison**, the short-story writer who edited some of Cooper's 1960s novels that were first printed in slash-and-crash paperback editions, recalled: "I knew he was an incredibly talented writer, but getting readers to listen was another story."

In the heyday of the civil-rights struggle and **Kennedy** presidency, many Americans, even black Americans, wanted to believe progress was being made and Cooper's novels, dealing with contract killers, bank robbers, drugs, prison inmates, drugs, poverty and more drugs kicked against a national hope. It didn't matter that Cooper was an innovative stylist – The Farm, his last novel, relates a desperate junkie's quest for love and redemption in prison, showing the influence of **Dante's** Inferno. Dismayed by The Farm's failure, Cooper continued drifting in and out of jail but never wrote another novel.

INFLUENCED BY Iceberg Slim; Burroughs; Hubert Selby Jr; heroin.

INFLUENCE ON Gary Philips, novelist and graphic novelist; you can hear echoes of Cooper's **Weed** in Walter Mosley's novels.

ESSENTIAL READING **The Farm**, hailed by one critic as "the lion's testicles".

FURTHER READING **Black!**, three classic novellas delivered with the authority of someone who's lived there and fears he might die there.

DENNIS COOPER

The writer who can put romance into gore

> "Make the actual act of evil visible, and give it a bunch of facets so that you can actually look at it and experience it. You're seduced"
>
> Dennis Cooper explains his fictional drives

"I'll say this once," says **Dennis Cooper** (1953–) in Guide, "I'm extremely fucked up." Cooper's five-novel cycle – Closer, Frisk, Try, Guide and Period – is a study in obsessive sexual pathology, focusing on the sexual and physical abuse of young men in stomach-turning detail, but with a detachment and a pulse that scarcely quickens its beat. No wonder **Bret Easton Ellis** has called Cooper "the last literary outlaw in mainstream American fiction."

Cooper resolved to write his fantasies when, aged 12, he was fascinated and aroused by a story of three boys who were raped and mutilated near his home. He doesn't blame his alcoholic mother for terrorising him, but says, "I cut my family off emotionally when I was 16." He found inspiration in the punk scene of the 1970s and founded his own publishers, interviewing punk stars and publishing poetry in the magazine **Little Caesar Press**. A decade later he moved to Amsterdam, became a music critic and idolised **Rimbaud**. From his first short stories, he has dwelled on sex, murder, worship and torture. Beautiful young boys are cut up and raped – in fantasies Cooper has felt compelled to communicate; a conviction endorsed by **William Burroughs**: "The writer cannot pull back from what he finds because it shocks or upsets him, because he fears the disapproval of the reader."

While in Amsterdam, Cooper wrote Closer, a book inspired by an image of Mickey Mouse carved into the back of a young boy. With the publication of Period he claimed finally to have worked his fantasies out of his system. "I used to use a lot of drugs, I used to be crazy, and I'm not any more. I'm not as sexual… It was psychosis to write about it, but when I wrote it, I did believe it." Underpinning the action is the search for love and affection amid the ongoing abuse: men break down the objects of their desire to understand why they have a hold over them, mutilating one another to somehow get closer, more intimate. For all the horror, Cooper can hardly be accused of glamorising violence. His characters are inarticulate, but we balk at their mistreatment and sympathise as they try to escape their suffering.

INFLUENCED BY Burroughs; Jean Genet; Bret Easton Ellis.

INFLUENCE ON Poppy Z. Brite.

ESSENTIAL READING **Closer**.

FURTHER READING **Wrong: Stories** – "from my crazy, drugged-out days."

ROBERT COOVER

More than a perfect parodist

It is not entirely the fault of **Robert Coover** (1932–) that his books can be found on courses entitled 'Parodistic Intertextuality And Intermediality In Postmodern Fiction'. He may have toyed with hypertext, be adept at deconstructing myth, mythmaking, story and storytelling but, at his peak, as in the great political novel The Public Burning, his fiction is fired with urgency and anger.

His first novel The Origins Of The Brunists is surprisingly straightforward, focusing on an apocalyptic Christian sect; only the language and grim world-view hint at fiction to come. In his most popular work The Universal Baseball Association, Inc., J. Henry Waugh, Prop., a lonely man runs a baseball league in his imagination. In Pricksongs & Descants every story is a vivid metafiction. In one tale, a husband walks across a room to his wife's bed, but by the time he arrives, she's been dead three weeks and cops are hammering down the door.

His grim fantasia The Public Burning sees the deaths of **Ethel** and **Julius Rosenberg**, executed as traitors at the height of America's Cold War paranoia in the 1950s, presented by **Cecil B. De Mille** in Times Square as a public spectacle. By exploring the fiction we call public history, Coover's imaginative reconstruction brings him back to social reality. Such scope makes his misanthropic, misogynistic tendencies easier to bear. In smaller canvases, like Gerald's Party, proceedings can turn ugly or dull despite the postmodernist brilliance. Spanking The Maid suffers similar problems. Admirers acclaim the parody, yet the fact tha the Amazon.com page on the book once offered spanking and punishment merchandise suggests such work may be taken literally.

INFLUENCED BY Beckett; James Joyce; Angela Carter; Roland Barthes; John Hawkes.
INFLUENCE ON T. Coraghessan Boyle; Rick Moody.
ESSENTIAL READING **The Public Burning**; **Pricksongs & Descants**.
FURTHER READING **The Universal Baseball Association Inc**.

JULIO CORTÁZAR

The anti-novelist from Buenos Aires

Julio Cortázar (1914–1984) was born in Belgium, but his Argentinian diplomat parents returned to their homeland when he was four years old. Although his most internationally acclaimed novel Hopscotch was only published in 1963, by which time he was almost 50, he was already widely considered one of the finest short-story writers in the Spanish language.

His earlier stories, bordering on science-fiction, are full of monsters and freaks, often denoted by the made-up words that characterise much of his writing. By the time his most celebrated collection, Bestiary, was published in 1951, he had acquired a more subtle psychological approach. A middle-class intellectual, Cortázar hated the anti-intellectual, anti-bourgeois attack of **Peronism**; his opposition is most evident in short stories like Raided House. Driven to self-imposed exile in Paris in 1951, he worked as a translator for Unesco while honing his writing. He found a voice rooted in the narrative traditions of the River Plate – Argentinian and Uruguayan, urban, cultured and metropolitan with humour and

fantasy. Twin passions for boxing and jazz permeated his work and his 1964 story El Perseguidor was based on the life of sax player **Charlie Parker**.

Cortázar believed writing should facilitate freedom, not limit it with aesthetic and formal considerations, and was attracted to the romanticism of **Keats** (on whom he wrote a 600-page study), the existentialism of **Rimbaud** and the Surrealism of **Cocteau**, inspired by reading Opium in one sitting.

He broke with conventional style and language in Hopscotch, his structurally innovative, self-proclaimed "anti-novel". Like most of his post-exile works, it is permeated by duality – the action divided between a Buenos Aires he hadn't seen for 15 years and a Paris where expatriate artists try to cope with displacement. He has made a surprising impact on films. **Antonioni**'s Blow Up was based on his Las Babas Del Diablo (Cortázar had a cameo as a homeless man), while La Autopista Del Sur inspired **Jean-Luc Godard**'s Week End.

He later developed an enthusiasm for communism, particularly the Cuban variety and for post-Sandinista Nicaragua, rueing his virulent opposition to Argentina's populist experiment, given the brutal dictatorships that followed.

INFLUENCED BY Cocteau; Borges; Edgar Allan Poe; Keats; James Joyce; Jules Verne; Rainer Maria Rilke.

INFLUENCE ON Carlos Fuentes; Gabriel García Márquez.

ESSENTIAL READING **Hopscotch**.

FURTHER READING **Bestiary**.

DOUGLAS COUPLAND

Spokesman for a generation, but was it X, Y or Z?

Few authors have their fingers on the pulse of popular culture quite as firmly as **Douglas Coupland** (1961–). With his first novel, Generation X: Tales For An Accelerated Culture, he defined a generation – the novel has often been called The Catcher In The Rye of his times. He has always denied having coined the phrase **Generation X**, but his novel of disillusioned twentysomethings trying to find their place in society has made him something of a spokesperson for it.

Born on a Canadian military base in Germany, Coupland grew up in Vancouver and graduated in sculpture. He completed a course in business science, fine art and industrial design in Japan in 1986 and worked as a sculptor – even holding a successful exhibition – and a journalist before becoming an author. So far he has written ten works of fiction (his latest, Eleanor Rigby, appeared in late 2004) and many books of non-fiction.

Coupland's subject matter has changed, but his fiction remains concerned with the culture in which he lives. His fourth novel Microserfs examines geek culture in the Silicon Valley boom, while Hey Nostradamus! centres on a Columbine-style high-school massacre. Alienation is central to many of Coupland's novels. In Miss Wyoming he examines society's fascination with celebrities, while All Families Are Psychotic has one of the most dysfunctional families in contemporary fiction, although it turns surprisingly gooey at the end.

He has been criticised for his weak plots and characters, but for those who have grown up in the era he writes about, his pop-culture references and quirky sensibility make him a chronicler of the age. His weaker novels cry out to be edited and made less flippant, but on form he creates a world in which it is disturbingly easy to recognise friends, family members and even oneself.

INFLUENCED BY Truman Capote; Joan Didion; Andy Warhol; John O'Hara.
INFLUENCE ON British novelist Jon McGregor; Po Bronson.
ESSENTIAL READING **Generation X**.
FURTHER READING **Microserfs**.

HARRY CREWS

Harry has seen all he needs of hell

Harry Crews (1935–) is as famous for his life as his fiction. He's been knocked out cold by a spectator while reporting on a dogfight, escorted **Sean Penn** and **Madonna** to a **Mike Tyson** fight and, at the age of five, had to lie in bed for weeks until the muscles in his leg stopped contracting. When he was 21 months old, his father died of a heart attack. When he was six, he fell up to his neck in a pot of boiling water. When he was 17, he volunteered to fight in Korea.

No surprise then that Crews's novels aren't gentle comedies of manners or abstruse works of postmodernism. That said, in Where Does One Go When There's No Place Left To Go? he is kidnapped by his own characters. He did, later, have the grace to apologise, admitting "I don't admire that shit."

The title All We Need Of Hell sums up his fiction. He comes from Georgia and is invariably compared to **Carson McCullers** and **Flannery O' Connor**, but his novels are stranger than such a synthesis might suggest. Crews doesn't like his characters to be called rednecks – he prefers 'grits', but his novels run the risk of affirming the Yankee prejudices about dumb Southerners he is rebelling against. In Car, a man promises to eat a car down to the last bolt; in The Gypsy Curse a man walks on his hands, his withered legs strapped to his backside, while in his debut The Gospel Singer sex-crazed missionaries take a bow. But then Crews might argue, as **Fay Weldon** suggested in her **New York Times** review, "the aberrant, the deviant, the desperate, the murderous and suicidal have become normal enough – we need our writers to make sense of them."

His childhood woes are reflected in his fiction – his obsession with freaks and their opposite, the physical perfection of the women bodybuilders in Body. And he admits that "the smell of blood" on his books can be a little too strong. He is in danger, as **Salon** noted, of being typecast as a connoisseur of ruin. But at his lucid best, his novels have real depth, while even the weakest are invariably enlivened by his expansive and eccentric supporting cast of characters.

INFLUENCED BY Norman Mailer; Graham Greene; Flannery O' Connor.

INFLUENCE ON Madonna; Michael Connelly; Lydia Lunch, the leader of Teenage Jesus and the Jerks, who founded a band named **Harry Crews**.

ESSENTIAL READING **The Gospel Singer**.

FURTHER READING **Car**; **The Knock-Out Punch**.

JAMES CRUMLEY

"The bastard son of Raymond Chandler"

When **James Crumley** (1939–) gave his friend and mentor **Richard Yates** some of his early stories to read, he recalled, "Dick had little to say, just scratched his head and suggested a rewrite." Subsequent reviewers have been much kinder. **Kinky Friedman** called him "an American poet" who "does not merely reflect our culture, but subverts it," while **George Pellecanos** declared: "James Crumley's The Last Good Kiss has to be the finest detective novel written in my lifetime."

Crumley was born in Texas and served three years in Vietnam, experience reflected in his first novel One To Count Cadence. But it was as a crime writer that he acquired a cult following, creating two marvellously idiosyncratic characters, investigator Milo Mogradovitch, whose favourite things include peppermint schnapps and cocaine, and ex-army spy and anti-hero C.W. Sughrue, both at least partly autobiographical.

Crumley calls himself a "bastard son of **Raymond Chandler**" yet his novels are more than mere mysteries. Whodunnits are the hook for him to explore character, language, the landscape and mythology of the American West and the effects of 20th-century wars on American individualism. Male friendships, whiskey and guns all have a role to play. The characters zing, the epigrams bite and the prose has a restless vitality. Aficionados may hate the thought, but he might need a decent Hollywood adaptation to make that big breakthrough.

INFLUENCED BY Chandler; Joseph Conrad; Ross Macdonald; James Ellroy.

INFLUENCE ON Crime novelists James Lincoln Warren and Natsuo Kirino.

ESSENTIAL READING **The Last Good Kiss**, from the immortal opening: "When I finally caught up with Abraham Trahearne, he was drinking beer with an alcoholic bulldog named Fireball Roberts in a ramshackle joint just outside of Sonoma, California, drinking the heart right out of a fine spring afternoon."

FURTHER READING **The Mexican Tree Duck**.

CULT FICTION

SAMUEL R. DELANY

The James Joyce of sci-fi and fantasy

If science fiction has escaped from the literary ghetto, it is thanks to such writers as **Samuel R. Delany** (1942–), an ambitious autodidact responsible, among other things, for Hogg, invariably referred to as the most offensive novel ever written – the kind of label to make an author proud. Still, critics have said nicer things about him. California State University's **David Samuelson** says: "If **H.G. Wells** is the **William Shakespeare** of science fiction, Delany is its **James Joyce**." As befits a cult author, Delany, probably the first major black sci-fi writer, has been both inter-galactically acclaimed and, at times, seriously out of print. In the mid-1990s some of his rarer books were changing hands for $60 or more.

His canvas is both broader and more limited than the sci-fi tag suggests.

"The forgetful old man, who walks with a cane and stutters when not reading a prepared text, just isn't that interesting"

Samuel R. Delany deflects literary stalkers

Broader because he has touched on pornography, linguistic theory, swashbuckling in space and the emotional subtleties of sado-masochism; and narrower because he says: "I think of myself as quintessentially a New York writer." New York, where he was born, raised and resides (among his contributions to community life, he founded **Gay Fathers Of The Upper West Side** in the 1980s), is a constant source of inspiration. The wrecked city in Dhalgren was inspired by 1970s Harlem, especially the 130th Street ghost town, while the socially complex sex of Stars In My Pocket Like Grains Of Sand reflected, he says, "the sexual variety you find all over New York." Delany's partner **Denis Rickett** was homeless for six years before he met the author, and the city's homeless were the models for the strange cast of The Mad Man.

Eclectic, ambitious yet heartfelt, his novels have included such differing triumphs as: Nova, his bid to do for the space swashbuckler what Moby Dick did for seafaring fiction; Hogg, an inside look at rape, pederasty and other kinds of sexual excess, written in the 1970s but unpublishable until the mid-1990s; and The Mad Man, in which a young African-American scholar finds love with a homeless redneck. Among the minor puzzles in his fiction are a fondness for characters who bite their nails (he admits the men he fancied most when he was on the prowl bit their nails) and only have one shoe (the significance of this is still debated).

INFLUENCED BY James Joyce; Thomas M. Disch; Michael Perkins.

INFLUENCE ON William Gibson; R.E.M.; Kathy Acker; Joanna Russ.

ESSENTIAL READING **Hogg**, if you've got the stomach for it; **Dhalgren**; **Nova**; and his **Nevèryon** archeological fantasy series.

FURTHER READING **The Motion Of Light In Water** is a moving account of Delany's life in the early 1960s.

DON DELILLO

A novelist in pursuit of greatness, a poet of paranoia, his subject is America

Obsessive, intelligent and funny, master of language **Don DeLillo** (1936–) would like you to love him for his mind. He has written some of America's most original, visionary and intelligent fiction since World War II. Underworld, his mammoth novel of history, is a conscious bid for greatness and delivers on the promise he showed back in 1972 with his American football/nuclear-war novel End Zone.

With the acclaim, though, comes a few caveats. His most superbly realised character is probably **Marguerite Oswald**, the mother of **JFK**'s alleged assassin, in his superb novel Libra. It is not illegal for a novelist of DeLillo's gifts to reimagine real people rather than create his own great characters, but it is unusual.

For some, there is something a little too considered about DeLillo's work, as if he had sat down with a blank sheet of paper, jotted down a few conclusions about the state of American society and the direction the novel is heading in and crafted his fiction to suit. He has, in his novels, touched on all the themes (the JFK assassination, the **Rat Pack**, **Hitler**, **Elvis**, religious cults, terrorists, chemical spills, the movies) you would expect of a novelist who set out to be cult by sheer force of will. This approach is at its most bankrupt in Running Dogs, which reads as if he has set himself the exercise of combining Hitler and pornography in one novel. Yet he can move the reader, as he shows in small scenes, such as the father in White Noise admitting the closest he comes to a religious experience is watching his child sleep.

Those caveats qualify DeLillo's greatness, rather than undermine it. His main interest, he says, is in "trying to write beautifully clear language" and he usually succeeds. What he lacks in character construction, he makes up for in scene construction. Even a weaker novel, like Mao II, leaves you with dazzling images. And his books teem with ideas. At his best – Underworld, Libra, most of White Noise and the under-rated The Names – he creates a world that will rattle around your head for days, weeks, months, years. And, as **Jay McInerney** says, "Because he is so deadly serious, it is not said often enough that he is tremendously funny."

INFLUENCED BY Pynchon; Burroughs; Norman Mailer; William Gaddis; Joan Didion; J.G. Ballard (the car crash seminars in **White Noise** are reminiscent of Ballard's **Crash**); Robert Stone.

CULT FICTION

INFLUENCE ON David Foster Wallace; Richard Powers; Jonathan Franzen.

ESSENTIAL READING **Underworld**, the 50-page recreation of a famous baseball game between the Brooklyn Dodgers and the New York Giants is his finest writing; **Libra**, a classic recreation, and **White Noise**, his funniest.

FURTHER READING **The Names**, too genre-bound, too loose for some, is a sinister, haunting tale of a cult that murders people with the wrong initials.

PHILIP K. DICK

Hollywood's favourite hyper-paranoid yet visionary, pulp-fiction hack

Philip Kindred Dick (1928–1982) was one of a gifted generation of American authors who, by embracing drugs as an aid to the imagination, wrenched science fiction from the hands of little green men and chisel-jawed heroes.

After a brief stint at the University of California, Dick sold his first story in 1952 and wrote for a living, more or less full-time, from then on, selling his first novel in 1955. Writing meant a precarious hand-to-mouth existence. Only in 1963, when he won the **Hugo Award** for The Man In The High Castle, did he begin to be recognised. The book led to his being called a genius by aficionados of the wilder edges of science fiction. But publishers saw the genre as the lowest form of culture and paid its authors the lowest rates; despite many awards and a prolific output, Dick was in financial trouble for most of his working life.

Dick changed the sci-fi genre profoundly. His work is typically set in a grubby corner of an uncomfortable part of the universe, and most of his characters belong to the blue-collar class of the future. By moving away from shiny space-worlds populated by happy supermen he made his stories easier to believe. By ignoring ray guns and rockets he was able to concentrate on problems of the human (or alien) condition, the nature of reality, moral issues and the infinity of subtly different alternate universes that a single changed step in the past might

have created. The fragile realities he wrote about were populated by spies, aliens and robots, with whole worlds sometimes revealed to be nothing more than hallucinations.

Dick was an early advocate of the California counterculture, digging the **Beats** in the late 1950s, experimenting with drugs, hanging out with American communists and vocally opposing the Vietnam war. Not surprisingly, the FBI opened a file on him. The pressures of work, drugs and the Feds' surveillance would have been enough to push many creative minds beyond their limits and Dick had what sounds like a psychotic episode in 1974, triggered, according to legend, by an amulet worn by a pharmaceutical delivery clerk. He noticed it while signing for a batch of painkillers to help deal with a toothache and was plunged into a series of strange visions that continued for weeks.

He later referred to this period as 2-3-74, short for February and March of 1974, describing visions of laser beams and geometric patterns, with occasional brief pictures of **Jesus Christ** and ancient Rome. Refusing to accept these as drug-induced, he began to talk about his previous life as Thomas, a Christian persecuted by Romans in the first century, and claimed he had been contacted by a god-entity called Zebra or most often Valis (Vast Active Living Intelligence System), which he later suggested was a satellite communicating with people on Earth. For the rest of his life, Dick's grip on reality was shaky. He began to question his own sanity and doubted the existence of 'reality'. He scribbled his nights away, channelling the amphetamine-driven whirling of his brain into The Exegesis, a journal of 8,000 pages and more than a million words. He grew increasingly paranoid, fearful of the FBI and KGB, and died of a stroke in 1982.

Several of Dick's stories have been filmed, but most are so loosely based on his intricate plots as to be of minimal interest to his fans. Notable exceptions are **Ridley Scott**'s Blade Runner, Total Recall and Minority Report.

INFLUENCED BY Classical literature; Nathanael West; James Joyce; Robert Heinlein; A.E. van Vogt.

INFLUENCE ON Cyberpunk; William Gibson; Ursula Le Guin, who likened him to Borges.

ESSENTIAL READING **The Man In The High Castle**; **Do Androids Dream Of Electric Sheep?**; **The Minority Report And Other Stories**.

FURTHER READING **Nick And The Glimmung** (for children).

BRET EASTON ELLIS

Brilliant satirist or passing fad?

Forget the murder, rape and mutilation – the biggest controversy surrounding the work of **Bret Easton Ellis** (1964–) concerns its literary merit. Does this millionaire's son reflect our disposable culture, or help create it? Is this writer, obsessed with cataloguing celebrities, brand names and pop culture, little more than a passing fad? Is the stark, scatter-gun effect of American Psycho and Less Than Zero the work of a limited author masking his flaws or a brilliant satirist?

Few modern writers have caused such division, and the nature of Ellis's career has only fuelled his detractors. The son of a wealthy property developer, he grew up in a particularly affluent area of Los Angeles before attending an exclusive college in Vermont. His debut novel Less Than Zero, published while he was 20 (and still a student), set the template for the rest of his work, cataloguing endless drug-taking and promiscuity among wealthy, disaffected young Californians. Like most of Ellis's creations, they have empty and ultimately disturbing lives, though their characters are never fully developed and the plot meanders.

Something in Ellis's work tapped into the literary zeitgeist. While many critics dismissed him as an "MTV writer", jumping from scene to scene, trying to grab the reader's attention with name-dropping or pointless sensationalism, others felt his style perfectly parodied the vacuous lives he was portraying and provided a fresh, highly original voice in a stale literary landscape. The Rules Of Attraction was less acclaimed, exploring a college love triangle through diary accounts.

Ellis might have been just another bright young thing had it not been for American Psycho. This notorious book made headlines before it was published – Simon & Schuster cancelled the writer's contract and refused to release it, and when it did see the light of day the **Washington Post** called it "the literary equivalent of a snuff flick." Ellis received death threats and various women's groups organised protests. He called it "basically almost a feminist tract."

American Psycho is every bit as gruesome as its reputation suggests, but is also intelligently crafted and full of impact. Ellis pushed the ideas in his first two novels to the limit, with his yuppie anti-hero Patrick Bateman callously murdering and debasing friends, acquaintances and prostitutes. The contrast between the high fashion, glitzy parties and high finance and the unspeakable acts committed behind closed doors was a stark commentary on contemporary America. The novel is shocking, yet full of dark humour – the killings are juxtaposed with a straight-faced critique of the 1980s music of **Phil Collins**, **Whitney Houston** and **Huey Lewis**. Many of the book's devices (endless list-making, cold narrative detachment and an ambiguous ending that throws the tale into question) have dominated much of the decade's writing.

The Informers was a tamer series of vignettes on, yes, bored young Americans. But Ellis returned to the dark side for Glamorama, an epic satirical thriller. It begins by examining the ultimately empty day-to-day life of a young male model, but quickly becomes a tale of intrigue, torture and international terrorism that showcases Ellis's love of big ideas and crafty contrasts. This glorious return to form markedly failed to inspire or incite critics or readers.

INFLUENCED BY Joan Didion; Truman Capote; Gertrude Stein.

INFLUENCE ON Will Self; Jay McInerney.

ESSENTIAL READING **American Psycho**; **Glamorama**.

FURTHER READING **Less Than Zero**.

Visionary genius, versatile storyteller and professional contrarian

On his first – and last – day as a **Walt Disney** writer, **Harlan Ellison** (1934–) suggested Disney make a porno movie. He did more than suggest it – acting out scenes in the voices of favourite Disney characters, not realising that **Roy Disney** and various studio heads were sitting at a nearby table. Ellison has also allegedly had to sign a non-aggression pact with a critic he may have assaulted and has, since the 1970s, been working on a third anthology of sci-fi stories, The Last Dangerous Visions, which, due to its continued failure to appear, is one of the great lost books of American publishing.

> "Bernard Berenson once said, 'Consistency requires you to be as ignorant today as you were a year ago'"
>
> Harlan Ellison, waxing philosophically online

Yet Ellison's achievements in the field some call 'speculative fiction' are immense. As editor and writer, he has pushed back the genre's boundaries, incorporating the influence of the **Beats**, **Kafka** and **Edgar Allan Poe**. Apart from the sci-fi series he has been involved with – Star Trek, The Outer Limits, Babylon 5 – his reputation rests on such seminal short stories as I Have No Mouth And I Must Scream, in which the last remaining humans are trapped inside a super-computer that saved them, only to make them suffer forever.

Born into what he claimed was the only Jewish family in Painesville, Ohio, Ellison drifted as a young man before finding a niche, in the 1950s, selling sci-fi stories to pulp magazines. He has now written over 1,000 short stories, becoming one of America's most prolific and best exponents of the form. Once dubbed the 20th-century **Lewis Carroll**, Ellison has written stories in bookshops in the world's major cities, edited a monthly comic book, endured four disastrous marriages (he is now enjoying one happy one) and used a pseudonym, **Cordwainer Bird**, if he felt unduly messed around on a project.

His friend **Isaac Asimov** admitted that Ellison was often too abrasive for his own good, noting "it is simply terrible that he should be embroiled and enmeshed in matters which really have nothing to do with his writing." There is something reminiscent of Humboldt, the semi-fictional crazed writer in **Saul Bellow**'s novel, in the way his antics have begun to distract from his work. This is a pity because in a four-page story like The Boulevard Of Broken Dreams, about a man haunted by visions of dead Nazi war criminals, he can terrify and haunt. Nor is his prowess restricted to sci-fi. **Dorothy Parker**, reading his Memos From Purgatory, based on research with a New York street gang, called him a "good, clean, honest writer," while **Greil Marcus** has called Spider Kiss one of the finest rock novels ever. Not that Ellison himself would be impressed by such praise – he once declared being a plumber was a nobler art than being a writer.

INFLUENCED BY Kafka; Edgar Allan Poe; Theodore Sturgeon; the Beats; Gerald Kersh; Borges.

INFLUENCE ON Bruce Sterling (Ellison financed his tuition); Stephen King; Neil Gaiman; Allan Steele; **Battlestar Galactica**.

ESSENTIAL READING **"Repent Harlequin!" Said The Ticktockman**; **Slippage** (which includes his acclaimed Christopher Columbus story); and **I Have No Mouth And I Must Scream**.

FURTHER READING **Spider Kiss**; **Memos From Purgatory**.

JAMES ELLROY

The self-proclaimed "Mad Dog of American crime fiction"

Many authors write from the heart, but few delve as deeply as **James Ellroy** (1948–), his worst demons laid bare in his novels. He admits his work is dark, but denies he has a tortured psyche, once saying in his inimitable non-PC way, "French interviewers insist I must be in terrible pain to write these dark, awful books. I say no, you don't get it, Froggy – I'm having a blast."

Lee Earle Ellroy was born in Los Angeles to **Armand Ellroy** (a former manager of **Rita Hayworth**), whose final words to his son were "Try to pick up every waitress who serves you", and **Geneva 'Jean' Hilliker**, a buxom red-headed nurse who brought home a stream of 'uncles' after her divorce. Mother and son lived in the low-rent LA suburb of El Monte until, on 21 June 1958, Jean left the Desert Inn bar with a mystery man and was found the next morning strangled to death. Her murder remains unsolved by the LAPD and unresolved in her son's mind. The crime permeates much of his work. Jean is found in varying degrees in all his novels but particularly in Clandestine, The Black Dahlia and My Dark Places.

Ellroy sums up what happened next: "Boy's mother murdered. Boy's life shattered. Boy grows up homeless alcoholic jailbird. Jailbird cleans up and writes his way to salvation. Jailbird becomes Mad Dog of American crime fiction." His mother's murder gave Ellroy his subject (and first-hand experience available to few writers), but his father provided inspiration, introducing his son to The Hardy Boys, The Fugitive and **Jack Webb**'s The Badge: A History Of The LAPD.

His first novel, Brown's Requiem, is a brisk, well-imagined noir mystery in the manner of **Dashiell Hammett** and **Raymond Chandler**. But even this early work is, as he says, "peopled with every type of human scum". Autobiographical themes recur in Ellroy's novels (note the repeated derision of women-beaters), but his characters, he says, are not self-projections: "My heroes are white Anglo-Saxon male heterosexuals, who express the attitudes of their times in the language of their times."

Ellroy brings rare venom to his fiction. At best, he writes slickly-plotted, noirish crime novels that offer the salacious, sensational secrets you would expect from a scandal mag like the one he spoofs in LA Confidential, served up with some of the best dialogue this side of a **Billy Wilder** script, allied to a grim, cynical view of the human race and American society. Characters such as Buzz Meeks (fixer-cum-bagman to both gangster **Mickey Cohen** and **Howard Hughes** in The Big Nowhere) and Dudley Smith (the corrupt, racist police chief of LA Confidential) are vividly portrayed, warts, charisma and all.

Six years after his debut, Ellroy wrote The Black Dahlia, a fictional account of the 1947 murder of Hollywood starlet **Elizabeth Short**. It's classic Ellroy, the book he had always wanted to write, although featuring less of his famous machine-gun style dialogue. Ellroy first heard of Short in 1959, a year after his own mother's death, and the similarities between the two cases ensured that neither woman escaped his memory.

The man nicknamed Demon Dog (after a poem he wrote about a dog whose sex organs glow in the dark) has, **Ian Rankin** believes, revitalised crime fiction: "He invented this incredible staccato, edgy style that provides extraordinary pace and dialogue. And in White Jazz he essentially invents a language. That book is crime fiction's Ulysses." If LA symbolises America in many of his novels, he has now turned to America itself, bringing a cold cynical eye to the **Kennedy** era in American Tabloid and his bitter late masterpiece The Cold Six Thousand.

INFLUENCED BY Hammett; Chandler, although Ellroy came to hate what he called Chandler's "shitbird cops out to fuck the disenfranchised" schtick; ex-LAPD officer-turned-writer, Joseph Wambaugh (**The Onion Field**); TV series **The Fugitive**.

INFLUENCE ON John Ridley; Michael Connelly; James Lee Burke; Ian Rankin.

ESSENTIAL READING The LA quartet (**The Black Dahlia**, **The Big Nowhere**, **LA Confidential** and **White Jazz**) is a triumph of criminal social history.

FURTHER READING For an under-rated writer, not as sensationalist as Ellroy but just as knowing about America's dark places, try George V. Higgins, starting with **The Friends Of Eddie Coyle**.

CULT FICTION

JOHN FANTE

John Fante (1909–1983) is a beacon of hope for every unrecognised writer. Years of indifferent reviews, sluggish sales and the odd dollop of lavish praise had left this gifted author bitter in his Malibu home, writing B-movies – "the most disgusting job in Christ's kingdom." But a mention in a **Charles Bukowski** novel started a remarkable resurgence that led to his work being reissued, a new title received by an adoring literary public and the place among the American legends – **Nathanael West**, **Ernest Hemingway** – he believed he deserved. The tragedy was that Fante would enjoy so little of his belated recognition.

The books that made his name are a quartet of novels charting the lifelong struggles of Arturo Bandini, like Fante an angry, ambitious young Italian-American who moves to Los Angeles determined to become a writer. Instead he fights landlords, agents and publishers and is sidetracked by women and drink, all the while trying to rationalise his lowly position in the city and chasing the impossible dream of fame. The tales recall **Knut Hamsun**'s Hunger in their droll romanticising of a bleak existence, but Fante's language was more accessible, his scope greater and his use of symbolic imagery more imaginative. He caught youthful ambition and gleeful romanticism perfectly, but, like **J.D. Salinger**, was not afraid to crush his alter-ego's dreams. In an exquisitely disturbing passage in The Road To Los Angeles, Bandini massacres a group of crabs he imagines have mocked him, while railing against a world that has ignored him.

Fante often insisted his prose was better than Hemingway's, but by the end of World War II he had all but abandoned fiction and was drinking and gambling heavily while screenwriting. In 1978 he lost both legs and his eyesight to diabetes, but returned to prominence when Bukowski referenced him in Women and persuaded Black Sparrow Press to republish his work and to dust off The Road To Los Angeles.

Fante, dictating to his wife, completed the Bandini tales with Dreams Of Bunker Hill, but died in 1983 before his stock had risen to its present levels. But then, somehow, Bandini the success story wouldn't seem right. As his admirer, screenwriter and novelist **Cindra Wilson**, says, his consoling message to readers is: "Don't feel so bad. I was an even bigger jerk than you once."

INFLUENCED BY Knut Hamsun; Ring Lardner; critic and editor H.L. Mencken.

Better than Hemingway?

INFLUENCE ON Bukowski, who called Fante's

writing "a wild and enormous miracle"; the Beats; Chuck Palahniuk.

ESSENTIAL READING **The Bandini Quartet**.

FURTHER READING **West Of Rome** contains two fine novellas.

RONALD FIRBANK

The master of high camp

The work of **Ronald Firbank** (1886–1926), noted **Sir John Betjeman**, was "polished… like a jewelled and clockwork nightingale among London sparrows." **Evelyn Waugh** claimed that "from the fashionable chatter of his period, vapid and interminable, he has plucked, like tiny brilliant feathers from the breast of a bird, the particles of his design." In person, though, the critic **Matthew Hodgart** noted Firbank could be "excessively shy, elusive and drunken".

The elegance, the precision, the elaborateness and the social condescension of these tributes captures much of Firbank's art, although, as a homosexual writer who didn't want to share the same fate as his idol **Oscar Wilde**, he was a master of innuendo and, in the words of the **New York Review Of Books**, "the outstanding practitioner of high camp."

Arthur Annesley Ronald Firbank may have been the grandson of a Durham miner but, financed by the same grandparent's fortune acquired on the railways, he played the capricious aesthete to perfection. The most fantastic of all English dandies and decadents, Firbank was invariably seen at the Café Royal, sipping champagne, often laughing hysterically, a cover for his morbid nervousness.

A frail child, he was educated at home, converted to Roman Catholicism at Cambridge and spent much of his life travelling, socialising and writing a series of short stories and novels (his first novel, Vainglory, was published in 1915). Although one novel – Sorrow In Sunlight (in the UK, Prancing Nigger in the US) – had a serious theme (racial discrimination), that wasn't really Firbank's forte. His usual preoccupations were, as **Jocelyn Brooke** noted, "sex, religion and social grandeur" – by sex, Firbank often meant sexual frustration. He remained, almost deliberately, a minor writer, content to delight, divert, excavate the hidden homosexual meaning of almost everything and subvert. In Concerning The Eccentricities Of Cardinal Pirelli, his titular character's eccentricities include baptising dogs and chasing choirboys. In The Flower Beneath The Foot, set in a fictional Balkan kingdom, Mrs Bedley, who runs a library, complains of Firbank's Valmouth: "Was there ever a novel more coarse?"

Firbank was, as Brooke notes, a figure out of time. His mockery, allusions and irony would have been better understood back in the 1890s, yet his descriptions of social events prefigure **Anthony Powell**'s approach in A Dance To The Music Of Time, and his use of dialogue – he often used overlapping conversations without a 'he said' or a 'she said', as if they had been taped – would inspire **Evelyn Waugh**. Firbank was also one of the first English novelists to use cinematic narrative techniques, cutting in a way that we are used to today but which must, in 1915, have seemed faintly alarming. In other words, in a very Firbankian touch, he was a throwback who was ahead of his time.

INFLUENCED BY Belgian playwright/poet Maurice Maeterlinck; Aubrey Beardsley; Oscar Wilde (who appears thinly disguised in the one-act play on the theme of a gay-lesbian utopia **The Princess Zoubaroff**); Thomas Hardy.

INFLUENCE ON Evelyn Waugh; Ivy Compton-Burnett; Anthony Powell; Aldous Huxley; Mervyn Peake; Michael Moorcock; Allan Hollinghurst.

ESSENTIAL READING **Valmouth**; **Concerning The Eccentricities Of Cardinal Pirelli**.

FURTHER READING **The Flower Beneath The Foot**, which inspired Waugh's **Black Mischief**.

F. SCOTT FITZGERALD

A reckless genius who wrote like an angel

There's more to **F. Scott Fitzgerald** (1896–1940) than the Jazz Age, The Great Gatsby and alcoholism. If his biography proved his maxim that "There are no second acts in American lives," his work endures, intrigues and surprises.

The two most famous anecdotes about Fitzgerald both involve his friend and rival **Ernest Hemingway**, both told to Scott's discredit. In one, worried by his wife **Zelda**'s questioning of his manhood, he asks Hemingway to check the size of his penis. In the other, he tells Hemingway that the rich are different, only for Ernie to reply: "Yes, they have more money." You could argue that Hemingway's cynical, blunt response showed just the kind of literal-minded thick-headedness he

struggled to overcome as a writer. Relations between the two were never simple: **Dorothy Parker** recalls that Hemingway was once so desperate to distract attention when he saw his rival holding court at her party that he smashed a glass against the wall.

Fitzgerald lived an extravagant, reckless life until poverty, ill-health and the love of gossip columnist **Sheila Graham** caught up with him. He and his wife Zelda, lately a feminist icon, were almost as careless as Tom and Daisy in The Great Gatsby, his best novel. But unlike the Buchanans, the Fitzgeralds paid for their carelessness: Zelda with her sanity, Fitzgerald by not writing the novels his talent had always promised. When he died, Parker gave him the same epitaph Jay Gatsby had at his funeral: "Poor son of a bitch."

The idea that Fitzgerald was some kind of idiot savant, a poor master of his instinctive genius, lasts for about as long as it takes you to read the opening of his third novel The Great Gatsby. The novel, controlled by techniques he had learned from **Joseph Conrad**, lightly seasoned with the flavour of his idol **James Joyce**, was hailed by **T.S. Eliot**. Often interpreted solely in terms of the American Dream, Gatsby is much broader – and suggestive – than that. Fitzgerald hadn't read **Marx** at this point, but it's intriguing that Gatsby, waiting for his true love, is reading a book on economics, that Daisy's voice is full of money, that the mistress's nose bleeds over towels showing scenes of decadent Versailles…

Gatsby's long-delayed successor Tender Is The Night is a heartbreaking novel which, even in its fractured form, achieves what he had aspired for – a "wise and tragic sense of life." Some of his stories (especially The Diamond As Big As The Ritz) are masterpieces. His presence inspired **Budd Schulberg**'s fine novel The Disenchanted, a nightmarish account of a drunken weekend that captures Fitzgerald's recklessness and brilliance. He had, as **John O'Hara** noted, the arrogance of the truly gifted, never changing his style to suit fashion and once getting himself fired from a screenwriting job after writing a love scene in which the hero asks his panting heroine: "Tell me, who is your dentist?"

When he died in 1940 the prevailing reaction was surprise that he hadn't died long ago. Yet he is reread today partly because, as **Raymond Chandler** noted, "he had one of the rarest qualities in literature – charm, charm as **Keats** would have used it, not a matter of pretty writing style but a kind of subdued magic, controlled and exquisite, the sort of thing you get from good string quartettes."

INFLUENCED BY James Joyce; Joseph Conrad; Hemingway; Edmund Wilson.

INFLUENCE ON John O'Hara; Anthony Powell; Burroughs; Jay McInerney.

ESSENTIAL READING **The Great Gatsby**; **Tender Is The Night**.

FURTHER READING **The Last Tycoon**, even unfinished, was described by Anthony Burgess as "the best Hollywood novel we ever had."

JASPER FFORDE

He writes novels about novels that are novel

Jasper Fforde (1961–) is a conundrum. His novels are nonsense, as he freely admits, but they trade in some of the top characters in the literary canon and are about as postmodern as it gets. At times, the parallel Britain of his Thursday Next series appears to be a fabulous satire, an absurdist look at multinationals, pulp television, hypocritical politicians and aggressive foreign policy – only for it all to be levelled by a particularly daft passage about Miss Havisham and her rage-counselling sessions with the cast of Wuthering Heights.

The least scholarly member of an academic family, Fforde left school with an A-level in art to become a runner in the film industry. By the early 1990s his ambitions to direct had come to nothing and his passion for stories was increasingly diverted into writing – initially short stories, but then a novel about the death of Humpty Dumpty, Nursery Crime. He had completed five more novels and received 76 rejection letters before The Eyre Affair was finally picked up by Hodder. Conceived in 1988, it began as a noir London thriller but evolved into a bizarre Swindon fantasy with echoes of **Lewis Carroll**. The "differently moralled" Acheron Hades is kidnapping characters from classic novels so Thursday Next, a "literary detective" from Swindon, uses the Prose Portal invented by her uncle Mycroft to enter the world of fiction and stop him.

> "Visit Pete & Dave's dodo emporium – for the finest in re-engineered species."
>
> Jasper Fforde's website goes into merchandising

In Thursday's very English England literature is so popular there are **Henry Fielding** bubblegum cards, the Crimean War still rages, the country is led by **George Formby** and Wales is a separate socialist state. A post-1984 **Orwellian** satire? Fforde says he would never have thought of anything so erudite.

The books – like Fforde – have no pretensions. A performance of Richard III in The Eyre Affair involves the audience shouting and chanting along, even providing the actors, conjuring up the kind of ambience that might have inspired **Shakespeare**'s popularity originally. Fforde's influences are unimpeachable: **Carroll**'s Cheshire Cat is a librarian in The Well Of Lost Plots, the dodos and mundane Englishness recall **Douglas Adams** and the daft juggling with great cultural figures suggests **Monty Python**, even if the subplots, flashbacks, location changes and car chases have their roots in Fforde's film ambitions.

The series becomes darker and more satirical. The genetically re-engineered Neanderthals are tragic, enslaved foils to humanity. Something Rotten involves a book-burning, a would-be dictator – albeit one who has escaped from a self-published romantic novel – and swarms with Goliath apologists, all apologising unreservedly for anything you might mention.

The Fforde cult is edging now towards mainstream proportions. Children have been christened Thursday, several streets in Swindon have been named after his characters and it is possible to buy t-shirts, caps and mugs from his website. Fforde has secured a deal for his five unpublished Jack Spratt novels, beginning with Nursery Crime, which is, as he puts it, "the final vindication".

INFLUENCED BY Lewis Carroll; Douglas Adams; Kurt Vonnegut.

INFLUENCE ON Swindon council.

ESSENTIAL READING **The Eyre Affair** then, if you like it, just carry on…

FURTHER READING Fforde's website – **thursdaynext.com** – includes special features, deleted chapters and a 'making of' wordamentary.

DAVID FOSTER

Not to be confused with David Foster Wallace

"Owen Evans was found disembowelled in a urinal." **Annie Proulx** discovered Australian author **David Foster** (1944–) while thumbing through Dog Rock in a bookshop, and that was the first sentence her eyes fell on. Won over by his narrator, D'Arcy D'Oliveres, she praised Foster's "rich and complex language, intelligence and daring imagination."

D'Arcy D'Oliveres is the hero of Dog Rock: A Postal Pastoral and The Pale Blue Crochet Coathanger Cover, now published together as Dog Rock. He is an Eton-schooled English nobleman, the 15th Baron D'Oliveres, who has emigrated to Australia where he is a penniless postman, beekeeper and sometime detective. "Among the inhabitants of this wholly decent and typical Aussie town is a mass murderer so vile he could almost be a Welshman…" D'Arcy declares in Dog Rock.

D'Arcy, the funniest fictional curmudgeon in many a year, reappears in The Glade Within The Grove, an epic, multi-layered retelling of the classical myth of Attis, who emasculates himself for the love of the goddess Cybele and is reborn a woman. The story is transplanted to 20th-century Australia, when D'Arcy finds a discarded poem in a mailbag and investigates its story of a 1960s back-to-nature commune in a hidden forest, preoccupied by murder, sex, tree-worship and castration. The **Times Literary Supplement** said: "The work of the novel is done so well there can be no achievement beyond it." The flora and fauna of Foster's novels is so exotic he makes Australia seem a magical world of its own. His elaborate sentences can be hard to cope with, but the dialogue is brilliantly observed, while the breadth and depth of Foster's knowledge is stunning.

Foster was born in Katoomba, near Sydney, son of a vaudeville comedian and an actress. He studied inorganic chemistry to PhD level, then did post-doctoral work in Pennsylvania. He was also, for 20 years, a motorbike-riding drummer in various bands. He abandoned science in 1972 to write. Many of his novels are satirical. Moonlite meditates upon the purpose of life, and paradise lost and regained; Plumbum holds up a mirror to the music industry he knows so well. He's also written widely about black-white relations and Australia's place in the world.

The Glade won Foster the 1997 **Miles Franklin Award** (an Aussie 'Pulitzer'). "About time," he declared in his acceptance speech – he has always had prickly relations with the intelligentsia. The prize money meant he could write on; he had had to support his family as a postman and as a crewman on prawn trawlers. A tae kwon do black-belt, he is also deputy captain in the bush-fire brigade.

INFLUENCED BY Reviewers have found echoes of Saul Bellow, but each of Foster's novels could have been written by a different author.

INFLUENCE ON Annie Proulx – she also has a scientist's eye for minutiae.

ESSENTIAL READING **Dog Rock** and **In The New Country**, a lightweight, funnier alternative to **The Glade**.

FURTHER READING **Studs And Nogs**, essays on his wide-ranging interests.

JOHN FOWLES

He's gifted but you may feel life is too short

John Fowles (1926–) is one of the few authors who has simultaneously managed to top the bestselling list, wow critics and convince others he is a tedious show-off. His popularity stems from his ability to write gripping yarns that also raise deep philosophical questions and analyse the role of the author in the novel. His unpopularity stems from the crudity of some of his interpolations as author.

None of this would be readable without the epic atmospheres he conjures and his classic narrative prose (he's been called a postmodern **Thomas Hardy**). His language can be verbose (even an admiring reviewer of his Daniel Martin had to admit "it can sometimes wax extremely tedious"). Some fault him for his inability to provide a satisfactory ending; others see such ambiguity as a strength, warming to the way he enters his own novels as a narrator, commenting on the action or explaining how things might have been different.

Fowles was born in Leigh-on-Sea to conformist, conservative and, he found, stifling parents. He was headboy at school, where he says he used to "beat on average three or four boys a day." He was desperate to escape – something that might explain his work's preoccupation with the question of freedom.

His first novel, The Collector, examines the themes of obsession and illusion that recur in Fowles's work. It was followed in 1963 by The Magus, originally subtitled The Godgame. This layered story of a man staying on a Greek island, trying to discover if what he is experiencing is real or not, uses a mixture of magic, illusion, shifting realities, Greek mythology and elements from The Tempest. Fowles admitted later: "I was trying to tell a fable about the relationship between

John Fowles
The Magus

man and his conception of God and I hadn't the technique." Easy to read, harder to decipher, The Magus made Fowles a cult figure across American campuses. Others were less impressed. When asked if he would do anything differently were he to relive his life, **Kingsley Amis** answered, "Not read The Magus."

In The French Lieutenant's Woman Fowles is the 20th-century narrator of a 19th-century novel, interrupting the narrative to inform us about Victorian conventions, remind us how he doesn't know what is going to happen or tell us about the cracks in a Toby Jug the protagonist has just bought: "As I can testify, having bought it myself a year or two ago for a good deal more." The novel has alternate endings, supplied after Fowles's wife **Elizabeth** made him scrap a sentimental ending. Elizabeth was his editorial confidante, and when he stopped asking her advice, after the 1960s, his fiction weakened.

Certainly none of Fowles's later fiction reached the heights of his early work. Daniel Martin has more of a natural style and satisfactory 'proper' ending – though it takes a while to get to it (Fowles called it a "very long novel about Englishness"). Mantissa takes place in the mind of a novelist who is in hospital following a stroke, while A Maggot offers a rare combination of real-life 18th-century murder investigation and time-travelling aliens.

Fowles once said he has "no memory at all for novels, for their ideas, plots and characters. I could not even reconstitute my own with any accuracy if I were obliged to." (In an October 2003 interview in **The Guardian** he forgot the title of The Magus, referring to it as "that Greek book I wrote a long time ago.") With the shifting realities and illusionary games he plays on readers, we could be forgiven for feeling similarly forgetful after – or even while – reading some of his work.

INFLUENCED BY Thomas Hardy; Flaubert; Daniel Defoe; Alain-Fournier; Claire de Duras's 1824 novel **Ourika**, which he says was on his mind as he wrote **The French Lieutenant's Woman**.

INFLUENCE ON James W. Hall; Nelson DeMille; Paulo Coelho.

ESSENTIAL READING **The Magus**; **The French Lieutenant's Woman**.

FURTHER READING **Wormholes**: Fowles's intriguing essays and articles.

JANET FRAME

She definitely wasn't mad, but was she a genius?

Literature saved the mind of **Janet Frame** (1924–2004) not metaphorically, but horribly literally. By winning a New Zealand literary prize with her first book of fiction, The Lagoon And Other Stories, she convinced the superintendent of the hospital where she was a mental patient to cancel an operation that would have left her in a vegetative state. Later, after more incarcerations, some in London, she was given a piece of paper that declared that she was not schizophrenic. She later used this paper to rebut those who tried to explain her art by her 'madness'.

Frame may not have been mad but she was often sad. Her authorised biography Wrestling With The Angel says she and her sisters saw themselves as the **Brontës**. Born in Dunedin, her childhood was blighted by the absence of a father who worked on the railways and the deaths, by drowning, of two sisters. The weight of these burdens led to an emotional breakdown when she was 20.

Family traumas and mental hospitals, including some 200 electric shock treatments, fuelled her first novel Owls Do Cry. It is, as **Joanna Griffiths** noted in **The Observer**, a moot point how much of her fiction is actually fiction: her 1961 novel Faces In The Water was, Frame said, "simply a truthful account of some past experiences." Often in her novels, romantic visionaries pitted against a sterile society risk the dissolution of madness and death. In her later work her concerns become more universal, influenced by her travels and use of language, (at times, almost baroque). She wrote seven novels, two collections of short stories and a three-part autobiography, but it was only when **Jane Campion** filmed her memoirs Angel At My Table in 1990 that she was able to live off her royalties.

Frame has the emotional power to move readers, especially those who have suffered similar trials. The summary of her fiction by **Eve Auchincloss**, reviewing Frame's anthology The Reservoir and Snowman Snowman in the **New York Review Of Books** in 1963, still stands. Auchincloss called her: "a richly gifted writer in shaky control of her gifts; in fact, the gifts have the upper hand much of the time but when these pieces work, life's sad truths come smiling out of them."

INFLUENCED BY The Brontë sisters; Katherine Mansfield; Virginia Woolf; Frank Sargeson – the New Zealand short-story writer was so moved by her plight he gave her food and shelter for a year.

INFLUENCE ON Patrick White; crime novelist Chris Niles; emerging New Zealand writers like Tracey Slaughter.

ESSENTIAL READING **Owls Do Cry**; **Faces In The Water**.

FURTHER READING Her best work in her last two decades was probably her memoirs, now collected in one volume by The Women's Press.

JONATHAN FRANZEN

What the Dickens? A social novelist writes

Good job nobody told **Jonathan Franzen** (1959–) that the social novel is dead. If he had known we might never have had The Corrections, a novel whose quality is best illustrated by the paradox that, though one of the main characters slips into the parallel, unknown universe that is Parkinson's disease,

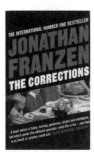

the reader is often left almost helpless with laughter.

In an essay for **Harpers** magazine in 1996, Franzen bemoaned the irrelevance of contemporary fiction. His novels – from The Twenty-Seventh City back in 1988 – have sought to make their own correction to fiction's course. The breakthrough success of The Corrections has been good for both Franzen and his cause. As he says, "After the much talked about postmoderns, a lot of us are looking again at character and, in particular, at family." Franzen's scope, sympathy, impatience and comic brio suggest that if **Charles Dickens** were alive today he would be writing novels like The Corrections and Strong Motions, a compelling novel of love, hate, geophysics, Marxism, anti-abortion and fanaticism.

Many contemporary novelists choose characters on the extremes, using them to shed light from the margins, but in The Corrections Franzen's family are central, plausible and sympathetic, and their lives touch the reader deeply – both through laughter and pain. Unlike, say, **Richard Ford**, whose novels of alienation can, in his default mode, feel as grey as prison walls, Franzen's crises are often hilarious, possibly because he brings the same energy to his language as he does to the task of weaving all the threads together in his novel.

For some he can, at times, come across as **Pynchon**-lite. Yet even that might not be such a bad thing – the world is full of novelists who try to impress with their erudition, the quality of their research or the sophistication of their experiments. It's refreshing, for once, to find a novelist who welcomes the reader in a novel that has, as **Blake Morrison** suggests, the satisfaction of serious soap opera. The hard bit, for Franzen, is that The Corrections looks like a tough act to follow.

> "Proust changed my life with books one, two and three. I'll read more of Moby Dick, but three Proust books may have to suffice"
>
> Jonathan Franzen on his heavyweight reading

INFLUENCED BY Pynchon; David Foster Wallace; Don DeLillo; Dickens; Henry Green; William Gaddis; Donald Antrim, especially his **Hundred Brothers**.

INFLUENCE ON The family novel – it's back.

ESSENTIAL READING **The Corrections**.

FURTHER READING **Strong Motion** and **The Twenty-Seventh City** are good, but very different to his breakthrough novel.

CULT FICTION
WILLIAM GADDIS

"A writer should be read and not heard"

Although he produced only four novels in 40 years, the sheer ambition and scope of **William Gaddis** (1922–1998) has earned him a pivotal place in postwar American fiction. Born in New York, he left Harvard University in his final year, working as a fact-checker at **The New Yorker** magazine and travelling in Europe, North Africa and Central America before returning to the US in 1951. His writing gleefully skewered the materialism of American society while probing the struggle of the artist with a compassion that was often heart-rending.

Sprawling across 950 pages, The Recognitions met critical and commercial rejection. Shifting voices and lurching into the occasional hallucination, the intensely allusive work traces the Faustian life of Wyatt Gwyon who is persuaded, by a philistine art dealer and an amoral critic, to forge Flemish masters.

Over the next 20 years, during which Gaddis worked as a corporate speech-writer, a job he hated, The Recognitions gradually acquired a devoted following. His next novel JR received the prestigious **National Book Award.** A radical departure, it is composed almost entirely of 'spoken' text, weaving dialogue, television and radio interjections and monologues both interior and drunken into a postmodern collage. With an incredible touch for the nuances of dialect, Gaddis chronicles the hilarious yet terrifying rise of a relentlessly grasping 11-year-old entrepreneur buying and selling out of a phone booth.

Gaddis's third novel, Carpenter's Gothic, is his most accessible and his darkest. Amid a maelstrom of religious demagoguery and political opportunism, a mysterious former CIA operative and one-time author returns home to assess his life but finds no sense of vindication. His final major work, A Frolic Of His Own, details a series of ridiculous lawsuits – including one brought by the book's hero against himself – that counterpoise notions of justice and of the law in a manner reminiscent of **Charles Dickens**'s Bleak House. His position as one of the great postmodern writers in the English language is confirmed by the astonishing – for such a low-profile novelist – number of times he has been referenced in the novels of **Joseph McElroy, Jack Kerouac, Don DeLillo, David Markson** and **Jonathan Franzen** (an email address used in The Corrections is exprof@gaddisfly.com).

INFLUENCED BY Above all T.S. Eliot; James Joyce; but not, according to Gaddis, Pynchon.

INFLUENCE ON William Gass; Don DeLillo; David Foster Wallace.

ESSENTIAL READING **The Recognitions**; **JR**.

FURTHER READING The William Gaddis essays **Rush For Second Place**.

Secrets, sex, S&M and philosophy

Mary Gaitskill (1954–) is the anti-**Helen Fielding**, her work concerned with people's isolation and failure to connect, often set in a world where conventional love is rarer than kinky sex. Her books are often shocking, with the realism she can add to scenes of S&M testament to both her talents as a writer and her intense connection with themes stemming from her own personal life. Gaitskill was once quoted as saying, "I think you could love somebody and want to piss in their mouth."

The Toronto-born daughter of a teacher and a social worker, Gaitskill's adolescence served as the blueprint for her later literary output. She was expelled from her boarding school and her parents placed her in a mental institute before she upped and left for the city, picking up work as a stripper, which she has described as "an interesting experience and often a pleasurable one."

Despite being surrounded by pimps and prostitutes, Gaitskill doesn't believe her background has any relevance to her writing, aside from teaching her "to examine the way people, including myself, create survival systems and psychological 'safe' places for themselves in unorthodox and sometimes

THE GADDIS, PYNCHON, TINASKY MYSTERY

In March 1955 **William Gaddis**'s The Recognitions, a novel whose major theme was mistaken identity, was published to poor sales and worse reviews. Two years later an actuary called **Christopher Carlisle Reid** quit his job and typed, mimeographed and sold a publication called **Newspaper**, in which he said The Recognitions was "the best novel ever written in America." In issues 12 and 13 of **Newspaper**, published five years later, **Graham Greene** penned a famously indignant article entitled **Fire The Bastards!** attacking the nation's critics.

So began a 40-year saga of secret identities and readers' letters that led to claims (by postal worker and **Beat** poet **Thomas Hawkins**) that Gaddis was really Greene. Later it was alleged that Greene, Gaddis and **Thomas Pynchon** were the same person. This charge was made in a series of letters attributed to one **Wanda Tinasky**, published in such august journals as the **Mendocino Commentary** and **Anderson Valley Advertiser** from 1983 to 1988.

These letters were, in turn, alleged to be written by Pynchon who, in 1997, had to phone **CNN** to deny his authorship. Further investigation (by **Don Foster**, who had outed **Joe Klein** as the anonymous author of Primary Colours) proved that most of the Tinasky letters (published in book form in 1996) were written by... Hawkins, who had accused Gaddis and Greene of being the same person back in 1963.

The affair, which might have been deemed irritatingly convoluted and far-fetched in a Pynchon or Gaddis novel, is one of the odder footnotes in the history of postwar American fiction.

apparently self-effacing ways." Leaving the world of stripping behind, Gaitskill opted for a more staid existence as a legal proof-reader and university student in Michigan. While at university, she won praise for a collection of short stories – The Woman Who Knew Judo And Other Stories – but it would take seven more years for her to become a published writer: Bad Behaviour, another collection of short stories, was issued in 1988. But while Gaitskill shares the same honesty in her language as **Bret Easton Ellis**, her books lie far away from his, populated with seamy underdogs, hustlers, pimps and thieves, as opposed to Ellis's greedy rich kids.

The novel Two Girls, Fat And Thin followed in 1991, developing what Gaitskill refers to as "confusion and violation with closeness." Despite initially appearing to be opposites of one another, the two girls of the title – one a thin ambitious journalist, the other a dowdy word-processor – are brought together through their appreciation of the philosophical movement of Anna Granite (read **Ayn Rand**), only to find that disturbing events in their pasts mean they are more alike than they first think. Harrowing but humorous in equal measure and featuring S&M sequences, rape and sexual abuse, this is one of the most emotionally challenging reads of recent times.

J.T. LEROY

Admitting that **Mary Gaitskill** is a "colossal influence", **J.T. Leroy** (1980–) has mined golden prose from a white-trash childhood. He achieved notoriety with his debut Sarah, published when he was 20, in which a 12-year-old boy sets out to become a truckstop whore. The acclaimed The Heart Is Deceitful In All Things followed, as did an assignment to script Elephant, the film about the Columbine school massacre. The only fear for fans of his fiction is that profiles in glossy mags, the adulation of celebs like **Madonna** and the temptation to write open letters to the **Olsen** twins for **Salon** might persuade J.T. (who already has a worryingly self-referential website) to take his eye off the ball.

94

Hollywood has now discovered her work: Secretary, **Steven Shainberg**'s 2002 movie of workplace S&M, was both a commercial and critical success.

INFLUENCED BY Nabokov, one of her favourite writers, in terms of his humour, language and fascination for more unusual, often deemed perverse, aspects of sex; Ayn Rand; Flannery O' Connor.

INFLUENCE ON J.T. Leroy (see box).

ESSENTIAL READING **Because They Want To** – Gaitskill's most recent collection of short stories isn't as raw as her earlier output, but shows her work, emotionally and in terms of language and humour, to be maturing.

FURTHER READING Check out Ayn Rand's **Philosophy, Who Needs It** for added insight into Gaitskill's characters in **Two Girls**.

The master of magic realism

In 1967 One Hundred Years Of Solitude made the name of its author, **Gabriel García Márquez** (1928–). Although success seemed to come overnight – the first print run of 8,000 sold out in a week – it had been a long time coming. García Márquez had published his first novel La Hojarasca 12 years previously to little acclaim. He worked on his breakthrough novel for 18 months, pawning his possessions and even his wife's hairdryer to send off the manuscript.

Born in the town of Aracataca in northern Colombia, García Márquez spent his first nine years with his grandparents, the deepest influence on his work. His grandfather had fought in Colombia's War of a Thousand Days – one of the country's many bloody civil wars – and his life had an epic quality. He allegedly fathered 16 children (three legitimately), shot a man in a duel, helped found Aracataca and heroically spoke out about a gruesome massacre of banana workers – stories familiar to anyone who has read García Márquez's fiction.

His grandmother was just as inspirational. Her family was from Colombia's Guajira peninsula, an area with a strong tradition of folk tales, ghost stories and supernatural happenings, and she provided the voice for his work. "The tone that I eventually used in One Hundred Years Of Solitude," he has said, "was based on the way my grandmother used to tell stories… I discovered that what I had to do was believe in them [the stories] myself and write them with the same expression with which my grandmother told them: with a brick face."

This combination of the fantastic and real is now known as magical realism and 'Gabo' is heralded as its founding father. Like many writers, he was a journalist – at one time he worked for **Prensa Latina**, a Cuban news agency, and his close friendship with **Fidel Castro** dates from this time. García Márquez has described himself as "really a journalist who happens to write some fiction on the side." This may sound outlandishly modest, but much of his fiction is based

on real events. For News Of A Kidnapping, an account of ten Colombian kidnappings, he interviewed surviving victims and their families, resulting in a powerful book, written with a rare mix of humanity and story-telling. Clandestine In Chile, his reimagining of an exiled film director's return to Chile in disguise, offers similar pleasures.

The **Nobel Prize** winner in 1982, he has published 11 books of fiction, the most celebrated being Love In The Time Of Cholera. A dazzling tale of unrequited love that lasts more than 50 years, it is built around the tale of his parents' courtship. His own courtship was

BEFORE AND AFTER MÁRQUEZ

Magic realism and the modern Latin American novel do not begin and end with **Gabriel García Márquez**, though he throws a huge shadow over both.

The tag 'founder of magic realism' has almost been copyrighted on behalf of **Alejo Carpentier**, the Cuban novelist whose works, notably The Kingdom Of The World, a marvellously compressed account of revolution in Haiti, anticipate García Márquez's richness of language, social concern, vivid imagery and narrative techniques.

Other gifted exponents of the form include **Isabelle Allende, Mario Vargas Llosa, Rudolfo Anaya, Salman Rushdie** and, before the term was even coined, **Franz Kafka**.

In South America there has been something of a backlash, with novelist **Alberto Fuguet** accusing García Márquez and co of cranking out fairytales. In 1996, he and a group of other writers launched McOndo, the title spinning off the kingdom in One Hundred Years Of Solitude, an anthology of stories offering less magic, more realism. This approach may lead to a global re-evaluation of Uruguayan novelist **Juan Carlos Onetti** (1909–1994). Politicised, pessimistic, drawn to some very seedy characters indeed, his novels, notably El Pozo, deserve to be much better known.

unconventional: he proposed to his wife when she was 13, but didn't marry her until 14 years later. His most recent publication is Living To Tell The Tale, the first instalment of his memoirs. You may find you prefer the stories in his novels.

INFLUENCED BY Kafka ("I didn't know anyone was allowed to write things like that"); Hemingway; James Joyce; Virginia Woolf; Faulkner's Yoknapatawpha gave him the inspiration for Macondo and Sophocles gave him the plot for **One Hundred Years Of Solitude**.

INFLUENCE ON Isabel Allende; Louis de Bernières (who described himself as a "Márquez parasite"); Salman Rushdie, to name but a few.

ESSENTIAL READING **One Hundred Years Of Solitude; Love In The Time Of Cholera**.

FURTHER READING **News Of A Kidnapping; Chronicle Of A Death Foretold** is vintage García Márquez, yet reads like a thriller paying a debt to Camus. His short fiction, notably **Strange Pilgrims**.

JEAN GENET

Choirboy, prostitute, thief, pop icon – just your average French literary life

"The Jean Genie, lives on his back… he's outrageous, he screams and he bawls," sang **David Bowie** in his song Jean Genie about the French novelist, playwright and poet **Jean Genet** (1910–1986). It's a good snapshot. Born in 1910, Genet trawled the Parisian underworld in his youth, committed his first theft while a choirboy and later lived as a male prostitute. At pains to construct an image of himself as the angelic thug, he was widely read and cultured, but was often jailed for stealing – mostly books and notably **Marcel Proust**'s work. While in jail, in 1942, he wrote The Man Condemned To Death, publishing it himself. A year later he met **Jean Cocteau**, who admired the poem but was shocked by the explicit gay content of Genet's novel Our Lady Of The Flowers. Despite his reservations, Cocteau helped find a publisher for it.

When Genet was arrested in May 1943, for stealing books, he faced a life sentence because of his recidivism. Cocteau told the judge Genet was the "greatest writer of the modern era" and his sentence was reduced to three months. In prison he wrote The Miracle Of The Rose, which was published in 1946. Three weeks after his release, Genet was again caught and jailed – for the same crime – and freed only after serious intervention by his supporters. It was the last time. By now he was a darling of such Left-Bank intellectuals as **Jean-Paul Sartre**, **Jacques Derrida** and **Michel Foucault**. In 1948 Sartre and Cocteau launched a petition signed by artists and intellectuals to win him a pardon – although he was still liable for two years in prison for past crimes.

Sartre widened Genet's literary acceptance with his 1952 book Saint Genet. The title alluded to Genet's view that he found triumph through humility, his suffering bringing him an almost saintly transcendence: "I am waiting for heaven to slam me in the face. Saintliness means making good use of pain. It's a way of forcing the Devil to be God," he wrote in The Thief's Journal.

All Genet's five novels drew on his childhood, reform school, bohemian wanderings in Paris and wartime experiences. In his fictional world, criminals were violent, treacherous yet somehow beautiful. Pimps were cowardly, transvestites were brave and crazy. Our Lady Of The Flowers describes a journey through the Parisian underworld. In The Miracle Of The Rose he focuses on his life in prison. After The Thief's Journal he fell into a depression and creative silence that lasted more than six years, but made a comeback with three great plays in the mid-1950s – The Balcony, The Blacks and The Screens.

Genet remained a vagabond until his death in 1986. He never owned a house, despite buying apartments for various lovers. His entire belongings could be carried in a suitcase, and he usually stayed in hotels near railway stations – that way, like all good criminals, he always had an escape route ready.

INFLUENCED BY Rimbaud; Sartre.

INFLUENCE ON Burroughs; Spanish novelist Juan Goytisolo.

ESSENTIAL READING His first and best novel **Our Lady Of The Flowers**.

FURTHER READING **Genet: A Biography** by Edmund White.

The man who imagined cyberspace and invented cyberpunk

William Ford Gibson (1948–) is credited with inventing the idea of cyberspace and, despite being a comparatively late arrival in the digital world, he is a very likely candidate for patron saint of the worldwide web.

He was born in Conway, South Carolina and was orphaned young – his father died when he was eight, his mother while he was a teenager away at school in Arizona. Mature beyond his age and reluctant to resettle with relations in Virginia, Gibson went travelling, met his wife Deborah in Vancouver and settled there in 1972. Some of his rougher edges smoothed by age and experience, Gibson settled down to study for his English degree.

Like most people his age in 1970s America, he knew something about traditional science fiction – TV shows, **Robert Heinlein** novels etc. He had even progressed to more experimental authors such as **William Burroughs**, **J.G. Ballard** and **Thomas Pynchon**. But it wasn't love of sci-fi that prompted him to sign up for a course in the genre: he needed a course to pad his credits. Set a short story instead of the usual term exam, Gibson produced Fragments Of A Hologram Rose, published in **Unearth** magazine. After being encouraged by author **John Shirley**, Gibson's second story was accepted by **OMNI** magazine, and cyberpunk – a term used by **Bruce Bethke** in a 1983 short story that defined a hip, new, futuristic style of sci-fi – was born.

After the worldwide success of his first novel Neuromancer, Gibson became renowned for his bleakly efficient, cybernetically assisted city The Sprawl, in which technology has made anonymity impossible, privacy rare and precious, and the idea of dropping off the system's screens terribly attractive.

With film producers competing for the rights (they finally went for $100,000, then unheard of for a first novel), Gibson was financially secure. He spent the rest of the 1980s writing the rest of a trilogy set in The Sprawl, but the public were

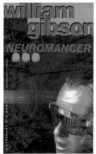

keen to see more, so 1986 saw the publication of Burning Chrome, a set of early short stories including Johnny Mnemonic, later filmed with **Keanu Reeves**.

The 1990s saw another trilogy starting with Virtual Light, based in and around The Bridge (a future society of outcasts and non-citizens living precarious existences mainly on the unused Golden Gate bridge). Set much earlier than the Neuromancer stories, this showed Gibson at his predictive best, describing a human society struggling desperately to cope with cybernetic 'advances'. In the new millennium he entered the mainstream bestseller lists at last: Pattern

Recognition explores the unpredictable consequences of technological progress on society, but is less immediately classifiable as sci-fi.

Gibson has a talent for peering into the near future – paradoxically more difficult than imagining aeons ahead – and is a gifted weaver of tales to warn of impending dystopia and disaster. In his worlds, the globalisation of society has become so entrenched that concepts of nationality are in decline.

INFLUENCED BY Hammett; Hemingway; James Joyce; Kafka; Ursula Le Guin; Pynchon; Susan Wood.

INFLUENCE ON Cyberpunk; **The X Files** (Gibson worked on two episodes).

ESSENTIAL READING **The Bridge Trilogy** (includes **Virtual Light**).

FURTHER READING **The Sprawl Trilogy** (includes **Neuromancer**).

ANDRÉ GIDE

"Please do not understand me too quickly"

André Gide (1869–1951) is a 'difficult' author, and one of the hardest to summarise. His works have attracted admiration, adulation, hatred, scandal and contempt in equal measure.

99

Gide was heavily influenced by his strict Calvinist mother. Her domineering, puritanical personality had a profound effect – at first in his rejection of her teaching and later in his obsession with the contradictions of religion, freedom and morality. Despite living what many consider an immoral life (he admitted to sexual relationships with young boys), Gide remained deeply religious. Near the end of his life he considered converting to Catholicism, despite having outraged the Catholic Church with his novel The Vatican Cellars and other works.

His most controversial, best-known work is The Immoralist, an examination of one man's rejection of morality and its consequences. Through Michel's narrative, we see Gide's struggle to free himself from his Calvinist upbringing – and the terrible results. The book is semi-autobiographical: like Michel, Gide discovered his homosexuality in North Africa. Like Michel, he rejected and mistreated his wife – **Madeleine**, who was his elder cousin and childhood sweetheart – and the novel can be seen as a first, subconscious draft of his final work, Madeleine, a harrowing admission of his poor treatment of her.

If The Immoralist examines the consequences of unrestrained physical impulse, Gide provided the antidote in Strait Is The Gate, his most overtly religious work, in which hero and heroine are denied happiness by their religious devotion. The heroine Alissa is a Christ-like figure who sacrifices her own and her partner's happiness to save both their souls. The tragedy derives from impulses the very opposite of Michel's, yet they produce the same results.

In all Gide's works, characters try to reconcile their own 'free' impulses with seemingly absolute dogma (of whatever variety) and fail. Moreover, they risk losing their own personalities in the process. The Counterfeiters is Gide's bleakest work in this vein. All the characters are deceiving themselves and others. Even the format is subversive, using a first-person narrative to give one particular point of view whose veracity is clearly undermined by the reader's perception of truths that appear darkly between the lines.

Gide published a huge body of work, including plays and translations – he was a brilliant linguist, also speaking German and English. In his life he scandalised friends and appalled society: much of his work openly challenges authority, particularly religious (La Symphonie Pastorale is a brilliant assertion of the victory of pagan human goodness over religious dogma). When he died the Vatican gave him the honour of forbidding Catholics to read any of his work. Yet Gide has much to say that appeals as strongly to us as it did to Edwardians.

INFLUENCED BY Oscar Wilde (meeting Wilde and Lord Alfred Douglas caused Gide to question his sexuality); Goethe; Jean-Jacques Rousseau.

INFLUENCE ON Sartre; Camus; André Malraux.

ESSENTIAL READING **The Immoralist; The Counterfeiters** (which has some of the atmosphere of **The Usual Suspects**); **Strait Is The Gate**.

FURTHER READING Much of Gide's intriguing work is still little known, such as **Isabelle**, a short first-person novella about a man who falls in love with a woman he hasn't met – only to be disappointed when they come face to face.

ALLEN GINSBERG

The Beat poet whose Howl resounded in fiction and pop culture

Unlike some of his **Beat** contemporaries, **Allen Ginsberg** (1926–1997) has remained relevant far beyond the 1950s. Howl And Other Poems shattered the world of contemporary American poetry with its drug-inspired visions and taboo homosexual fantasies, but it also introduced a truthfulness and honesty that resound to this day.

Ginsberg was born in Newark, New Jersey – the son of Louis, a teacher and published poet, and Naomi, a Communist and irrepressible nudist who was later hospitalised with paranoid schizophrenia. As a child he read such poets as **William Blake** and **Edgar Allan Poe**, and his first poem was published in the **Paterson Evening News** at the age of nine. Intending to become a labour lawyer, Ginsberg won a scholarship to Columbia University, New York, where he met **William Burroughs** and **Jack Kerouac**, who encouraged him to write. For two years he immersed himself in literature, crime and alcohol – a period that culminated in 1945 when he was suspended from Columbia and (partly in emulation of Kerouac) left to spend a year in the merchant marines.

On his return to Columbia, Ginsberg met and fell in (unrequited) love with **Neal Cassady** (see page 310). Although he came out publicly in 1946, Ginsberg was deeply depressed about his homosexuality and in 1949 volunteered to spend several months at the Columbia Psychiatric Institute, where he convinced himself he was heterosexual. This was a particularly troubled period for him: by 1947 his mother's condition had deteriorated so badly he was obliged to sign the papers to have her lobotomised.

Even as he forced himself into social and sexual conformity, Ginsberg struggled with a literary form to overthrow it. Inspired by Kerouac's experiments with "spontaneous bop prosody" and a life-changing vision of Blake reading Ah, Sunflower in 1948, he began to abandon rhyme and metre for a more instinctive form. But it was only after he met his lifelong (if far from monogamous) companion **Peter Orlovsky** in 1954 that he started work on Howl. A scream of pain, an elegy for 1940s bohemia and an invective against 1950s America, this was the first great piece of Beat literature – its sales boosted by an obscenity trial – and saw Ginsberg finally able to reject society's "fear of total feeling, really, total being." As the controversy raged, Ginsberg travelled to Morocco to see Burroughs, then Paris, where he began Kaddish, completed in New York in 1958. Written under the influence of morphine and amphetamines, it is a heartbreaking, incantatory account of his childhood, and particularly the horror and loneliness of his mother, who had died in 1956.

In 1959 Ginsberg took part in the first LSD experiments at Stanford University, California, signalling his emergence as a leading countercultural icon. During the 1960s he travelled widely, was expelled from Czechoslovakia and Cuba (partly for saying he thought Che Guevara was "cute"), coined the slogan 'Flower Power', participated in **Ken Kesey**'s Acid Tests, helped organise the 1967 Human Be-In in San Francisco and was arrested many times on marches against drug laws, nuclear weapons and the Vietnam war.

At this time his poetry – compiled in The Fall Of America: 1965-71 – took on a more meditative, ecological and directly political flavour, often improvised straight into a tape recorder. His Indian Journals describe the spiritual quest that led him eventually to adopt Buddhist vows. His experimental approach and political activism continued through the 1970s to the 1990s. He died of liver cancer, aged 70, surrounded by family and friends.

Ginsberg collaborated with musicians such as **Bob Dylan** (on whose lyrics he was a major influence), **The Clash** and **Philip Glass**, won numerous awards and remains more than just of historical interest today. His disciple **Camille Paglia** says his "hallucinatory imagery, incantatory rhythms and jazz syncopations are the ultimate operatic expression of 20th-century sexual and political radicalism." Just as inspirational is the fearlessness – and impartiality – of his political commitment to victims of oppression.

INFLUENCED BY William Blake; Walt Whitman; Kerouac; Burroughs.

INFLUENCE ON Bob Dylan; Spalding Gray; Vaclav Havel; Yevgeny Yevtushenko.

ESSENTIAL READING **Howl; Kaddish**.

FURTHER READING Ed Sanders's **The Poetry And Life Of Allen Ginsberg**.

NIKOLAI GOGOL

He wrote, he burned, he repented, he invented

Satirical but reactionary, fantastical but fanatically religious, **Nikolai Vasiliev Gogol** (1809–1852) is one of the strangest and most influential writers to have emerged from 19th-century Russia. His St Petersburg Tales – such as Diary Of A Madman and The Overcoat – gave birth to the ghostly, inhuman city of Crime And Punishment as well as the grotesque humour of the Soviet magical realists, while his masterpiece Dead Souls is arguably the first modern Russian novel. As **Dostoevsky** put it, "We all came out from under Gogol's Overcoat."

Gogol grew up on his family estate in Ukraine. His father was a gifted poet and playwright, but his mother – a pious Christian of the hell-fire variety – was the dominant influence. Although he showed little academic promise, he began to write poetry at school and in 1829, after taking up a minor government post in St Petersburg, he published his first work anonymously: the narrative poem Hans Küchelgarten, ridiculed by the critics.

In a pattern that became familiar, Gogol found and burned every available copy of Hans Küchelgarten and fled to Germany for three months. On his return he turned to prose, drawing on Ukrainian folklore for Evenings On A Farm Near Dikanka: a collection of stories in which God and the Devil participate directly in earthly affairs. The collection earned Gogol the friendship of **Alexander Pushkin**, who encouraged him to write a second volume (in 1832), as well as Mirgorod, which includes Taras Bulba – a brutal, epic tale about the 16th-century Cossack revolt against the Poles.

Populated with lunatics, drunks and petty bureaucrats, the St Petersburg Tales abandoned any direct divine or demonic explanation for their magical events. In The Nose (which was also Gogol's most prominent facial feature) the nose of a collegiate assessor decides on an independent existence and is seen about the city in the uniform of a civil councillor. In Diary Of A Madman an unimportant clerk overhears a pair of dogs talking about him, then realises that he is, in fact, the king of Spain. The use of these strange and supernatural devices makes for powerful satire, side-stepping the censors in a manner emulated by later Russian writers (notably **Mikhail Bulgakov**), and provide an insight into Gogol's highly religious mind; for him the inexplicable and transcendental were a part of ordinary life.

One unifying factor in Gogol's work is the danger surrounding sexuality. Even in his early stories love or desire for a woman normally leads to trouble, and in his comic plays The Inspector General and The Marriage an escape from marriage provides the happy ending. Similarly, the picaresque adventures of Chichikov in Dead Souls involve none of the bawdiness of, say, Tom Jones, and instead idealise reclusive male cohabitation. As a rigid Christian, Gogol seems to have been uneasy about sex in general, although the scattered information about his private life leaves little doubt that he was homosexual.

After The Inspector General was harshly criticised by conservatives, Gogol again fled to Europe, settling in Rome, where he remained for much of the rest of his life and where he wrote Dead Souls – employing a device involving the purchase of dead serfs to explore the estates of provincial Russia. Packed with social snobbery, surreally irrelevant detail and appalling peasant suffering, it appears to be a ruthless and beautifully crafted satire, although – to the distress of liberal aficionados – Gogol later refuted this view in Selected Passages From Correspondence With Friends, describing his writing as "sinful" and "useless" and, among other things, justifying slavery on Biblical grounds.

103

Gogol completed part two of Dead Souls, but burned the manuscript ten days before his death in 1852, leaving only fragments. Increasingly religious and irrational, he had fallen under the influence of a priest named **Father Konstantinovsky**, whose ascetic teachings led to Gogol's physical deterioration. He died in a frenzy – he refused to eat, had hot loaves applied to his person and leeches attached to his nose – shouting "A ladder! Bring me a ladder!" It was a scene straight out of his own fiction or from a nightmarish painting of **Hieronymus Bosch**, whose art, at times, seemed to mirror Gogol's fictional world.

INFLUENCED BY E.T.A. Hoffman; Alexander Pushkin; Walter Scott; Cervantes.

INFLUENCE ON Yevgeny Zamyatin; Mikhail Bulgakov; Dostoevsky.

ESSENTIAL READING **Dead Souls; Diary Of A Madman And Other Stories**.

FURTHER READING Nabokov's **Nikolai Gogol** is a suitable place to start.

CULT FICTION
DONALD GOINES

A king of black gangster fiction, **Donald Goines** (1936–1974) published his first novel, Dopefiend, in 1971. Three years – and 15 novels – later, he and his wife were shot to death for no apparent reason. He was just 37.

The career trajectories of cult writers are often accelerated journeys between glory and death, but Goines's day came and went faster than most. He might have sensed this because, released from prison for the last time in 1970, he kept up a ferocious schedule, writing in the morning and shooting heroin in the afternoon. For a writer who has drawn comparisons with such diverse authors as **Iceberg Slim**, **Ernest Hemingway** and **Jean-Jacques Rousseau**, Goines's work is remarkably consistent. Often strangely plotted, with writing that could be basic at times, his novels come with all the authority of having been lived. Remorseless, dramatic, at times sickeningly violent, yet sharp, Goines can be subtler than he is usually given credit for – in Black Gangster he is intriguingly ambivalent about black revolutionaries: his title character's black political agenda is a cover for his crimes. In the more political novels (written under the pseudonym **Al C. Clark**), chronicling the adventures of a black militant named Kenyatta (named after the first post-colonial president of Kenya), the battle lines were more simply drawn – the enemy being the white race. These novels drew on **Black Panther** rhetoric and anticipated some of the tactics of the **Black Muslims** as the hero declares war on vice in the ghetto and the white cops who patrol it like colonial overlords.

But Goines wasn't born a ghetto child. From a reasonably well-off family in Detroit, he became hooked on heroin in the army and, returning to Detroit in 1955, robbed, pimped, gambled and stole to support his habit. In jail he began writing cowboy stories to pass the time, until he read a book by the black writer **Iceberg Slim** that inspired him to write the memoir Whoreson, about a ghetto pimp. Another autobiographical tale, Dopefiend, about life as a heroin addict, proved Whoreson was no fluke and made his reputation.

Goines had dreamed he would find some peace as a writer, but the grind of writing and drugs soon returned. He moved his family to Los Angeles in a desperate bid to break the cycle. Two productive years later he returned to Detroit, where he and his wife were killed. Goines, the authors **Andrew Calcutt** and **Richard Shephard** concluded, "wrote fiction the way other people package meat." But his novels are intense, so intense that one reviewer felt he had to shower after reading one. **Chaz Williams**, the producer who organised a soundtrack album to Black Gangster in 1999 – for a film that was later sadly canned – sums up Goines eloquently: "He was in the streets, of the streets and spoke for the streets."

INFLUENCED BY Iceberg Slim; Hemingway; Chester Himes.

INFLUENCE ON Hip Hop (Tupac Shakur, DMX, plus Nas and Royce Da 5'9", who have both cut tracks called Black Girl Lost, after the title of a Goines novel); Walter Mosley, whose **Easy Rawlins** mysteries offer considerable insight into America's social and racial politics.

ESSENTIAL READING **Black Gangster** or **Daddy Cool**, which, among the bodies and bullets, has real breadth.

FURTHER READING The Kenyatta novels are politically ahead of their time, and the first in the series, **Crime Partners**, has real power.

DAVID GOODIS

The dark prince of paperback pulp

David Goodis (1917–1967) made his name – and posthumous reputation – by bringing his personal obsessions to two of the most anonymous genres: pulp fiction and the mass-market paperback. The recurring motif of his late paperback novels – a cycle of failure, recovery and failure – typified his own life.

Born in Philadelphia, Goodis published his first serious novel, Retreat From Oblivion, when he was 21. His debut's failure to sell led Goodis to retreat into more lucrative pulp fiction, which he wrote well enough to earn the time to write Dark Passage, a noir novel about a man wrongly convicted of murdering his wife who escapes to prove his innocence. Warner Bros bought the film rights and Goodis as the screenwriter. For several years he amused himself by running around Tinseltown in creased, stained suits, sleeping on other people's couches and pursuing prostitutes in the worst neighbourhoods until, in 1950, broke and homesick, he fled back to Philadelphia. There he spent the next 17 years in his parents' house writing cheap paperbacks.

Goodis often ignored or circumvented the rules of his new genre. His sex scenes were more often depressing than titillating and his tales weren't that violent. Yet at their best (The Burglar, Nightfall and Down There) his tales of losers condemned to the gutter by their past errors had a terse originality that attracted filmmakers. Typically, when François Truffaut adapted Down There for his second movie (Shoot The Piano Player), Goodis resented his new-found celebrity. By 1966 he had voluntarily entered a psychiatric hospital where he may have had electric-shock treatment. A year later he was dead.

Yet his stories still appeal to French filmmakers, notably **Jean-Jacques Beineix**, possibly because his best, most personal work marries psychological precision with great narrative pace, a rare combination in American mass-market fiction. But then Goodis's martyrs were a reflection of his own life, which may be why, decades after his death, the best still ring true. Dark Passage wasn't just the name of his most famous novel – it summed up his life.

CULT FICTION

ALASDAIR GRAY

"I want to write about folk who aren't specialists in the entertainment industry"

Known as much for his work as an artist as for his writing, **Alasdair Gray** (1934–) was born in Glasgow into a working-class family (his father worked in a factory, his mother in a shop) on a council estate. Educated by the state system, he ended up a student at the Glasgow School of Art from 1952 to 1957, returning there immediately as a teacher from 1958 to 1962.

Lanark, Gray's first novel, drew much inspiration from his evacuation at the beginning of World War II to Glasgow's hinterlands in Lanarkshire and from his student days at the art school, where he started writing. Like his protagonist, Gray painted murals in places of worship, moving on in the early 1960s to become a scene painter for the Glasgow Pavilion and Citizens theatres.

Instinctively socialist and a fierce believer in the benefits of an independent Scotland, Gray found himself at the vanguard of a Scottish literary renaissance that began in the mid-1960s. Though his literary skills were largely self-taught,

THE ULTIMATE TITLE BOUT

Writers of pulp fiction may not have the narrative subtleties of **Nabokov** or philosophy of **Proust**, but, as this list shows, they know how to invent a title. Gorgonzola Won't You Please Come Home? Honk If You've Found Jesus The Man With The Magic Eardrums Men Are So Ardent The Satanic Piano Pigeons From Hell Sugar & Vice by **Hank Johnson**, who may have had 'issues' with the opposite sex, judging from some of his other titles,

like Skirts Bring Me Sorrow, Kill Her For Kicks and Kill Her If You Can, although Roxy By Proxy has a certain assonant charm.

Trailer Tramp by **Orrie Hitt**. The pseudonymous pulp legend inspired some great cover blurbs. On Ellie's Shack the cover groaned: "They Were Always Peeking And Pawing At Her. How Could A Girl Stay Good?"

When The Death Bat Flies by **Norvell Page**, who also gave us The Devil's Death Dwarfs, Hell's Sales Manager and the Benevolent Order Of Death.

he wrote plays, TV and radio scripts throughout the 1960s and 1970s, finding employment as artist-recorder for the **Glasgow People's Palace**, attending **Philip Hobsbaum**'s Glasgow writers' group (where he met fellow writers **James Kelman** and **Tom Leonard**) and revising the early drafts of Lanark.

When, after almost 30 years of gestation, Lanark appeared in 1981, Gray was acclaimed as the great new hope of Scottish literature and almost overnight became a kind of northern focus of resistance to the rampant excesses of Thatcherism. It was followed by Unlikely Stories, Mostly, a collection of short stories in 1983, and by the novel 1982, Janine the following year.

Gray's second novel took him out of the familiar and into a suburban Hades of pornography, obsession and perverted sex. Essentially the internal monologue of one Jock MacLeish, a travelling salesman stretched out on his hotel bed with a bottle of whisky and a filthy imagination, what starts out as an apparently irredeemable exploration of the dirtier corners of a drunken man's mind turns gently, as the night progresses, into a tale of remorse, redemption and even an apology for pornography if it helps a troubled man achieve some kind of rest by helping him forget his own insignificance and misery.

His multiple-prize-winning novel Poor Thing in 1992 made Gray even more famous. Beautifully executed as a series of historical documents (the memoirs of Dr Archibald McCandless) and set mainly in a gothic 19th-century Glasgow full of eerie shadows, it was another fantastic, seemingly allegorical tale that recast Frankenstein's monster as the beautiful, desirable creation of a rogue doctor Godwin Baxter. Bella the beauty has the body of a young and sensual woman but the mind and imagination of a two-year-old child, and she sexually exhausts her first partner to such a degree that he finds himself confined to the lunatic asylum. After the dark night of Jock's soul in his previous book, this curious amalgam of Jekyll And Hyde, Frankenstein and Dracula is strangely light and refreshing.

> "When Chekhov was asked the message of his stories, he said, 'Friends, you should not be living like this.' My message is the same"
>
> Alasdair Gray

Gray's books are richly illustrated, with portraits and allegorical political statements inked painstakingly into the text. Gray takes his politics outside the pages of his books too, notably protesting against nuclear weapons at Faslane, Scotland and against the second Gulf War in 2003.

Since Lanark, Gray – a "self-employed verbal and pictorial artist" – has supported himself mainly by writing and selling his art. After a stint as writer-in-residence, he became professor of creative writing, again alongside Kelman and

Leonard, at the University of Glasgow. His talent can be seen in the heart of Glasgow's West End, where a new mural has appeared in **The Ubiquitous Chip** eaterie, one of his favourite venues (rumour has it he painted the original mural in the 1970s in exchange for £500 in credit). He's recently created a beautiful celestial mural for a new Arts Centre in Partick and still lives in Glasgow.

INFLUENCED BY James Joyce; Orwell.

INFLUENCE ON Will Self; Ian Banks; Rhys Hughes.

ESSENTIAL READING **1982, Janine**; **Poor Things**.

FURTHER READING Novels: **Lanark**; **The Fall Of Kelvin Walker**; **McGrotty And Ludmilla**. Short stories: **Unlikely Stories, Mostly**; **Ten Tales Tall & True**.

Alasdair Gray knows that if all else fails he can always decorate a few cafés

"I've achieved quite a bit and failed a good deal"

Graham Greene (1904–1991) once won a magazine competition to write a successful parody of his own style. But then Greeneland, as created by its enigmatic author, was a domain where the same characters suffered the same wounds. Its inhabitants included: heroes troubled by self-doubt, loss of faith – religious, political, personal or intellectual – and also despised by their superiors; young girls avid for love or sex or both; dashing liars with secret sorrows; innocents who ought to know better and arrogant complacents who somehow evade justice.

You could, as you might expect from an author who was a long-time freelance (as journalist, secret agent and polemicist), tour the world with Greene, as long as you were content to visit the world's troublespots: Vietnam (The Quiet American), Haiti (The Comedians), Paraguay (The Honorary Consul), Cuba (Our Man In Havana), postwar Vienna (The Third Man). In Travels With My Aunt he tours much of the world in one novel. But it was as a religious novelist – in the Catholic tradition of **François Mauriac** – that he made his name.

The evil Pinkie glitters in Brighton Rock, but redemption is more of an issue in The Power And The Glory, The Heart Of The Matter and The End Of The Affair. Although England, in its shabby glory, is brilliantly evoked – especially in Brighton Rock – fiction was a way of escape for Greene and he became something of a literary globetrotter.

He famously divided his output into entertainments and serious novels, yet the labels don't always ring true. The Honorary Consul, while aiming for gravitas, sags as the characters slide into lengthy, predictable, political debate. It's a pity as the opening scenes are among the most beautifully evoked in all of his fiction. He is more convincing in nastier novels like The Comedians and Brighton Rock – the latter the rather unlikely inspiration for a recent musical – in the deeply personal The End Of The Affair and in The Third Man and The Quiet American, where broader themes are blended with personal anguish.

Our Man In Havana is justly admired by many, though **James M. Cain** noted crossly, "His characters lack bone, flesh and blood, and only occasionally seem lifelike. They are dumb when convenience requires, smart when convenience requires, rarely showing initiative on their own." This, though, might be a case of the right criticism, wrong novel. **Robert Stone**, whose own fiction touches on many of Greene's political themes, has made similar criticisms, while admiring Greene's artistry.

Greene felt that by the time he had finished his ninth novel, A Burnt Out Case, he was in danger of becoming, well, a burned-out case (juggling five mistresses as he wrote it couldn't have helped). He felt he should have left

The Human Factor in a drawer; an opinion shared by this reviewer. His anti-Americanism – he declared in 1967 that, given the choice between the USA and the USSR, he'd rather live in the Soviet Union – gets a tad predictable.

He once snapped at someone who congratulated him on inventing

Greeneland, saying "I write what I see." In which case, his gaze was at its most penetrating from 1938 (Brighton Rock) until 1966 (The Comedians), when he looked on the world with the cynical view of a man who, in bouts of depression, had toyed with Russian roulette.

For all the affairs, encounters with prostitutes, refusal to divorce his wife and links to the spy world – Greene's is not, as the monumental biography by **Norman Sherry** shows, one of the most vivid literary lives. His best writing tells us, his readers, as much as we need to know about a professional enigma.

Maybe Greene's obsession with his faith or politics misses the point – and his greatest strengths may very well be his choice of words, his economy of description and his painterly eye. In **Evelyn Waugh**'s Swords Of Dishonour trilogy a character reads The Heart Of The Matter and decides that West Africa "must have been like that."

If Greene never actually took great risks as a novel writer, he was, at least, drawn to the world and not to the bourgeois navel-contemplating that almost killed off the British novel in the 1970s. Among the risks he did take as a public novelist was to weigh in on behalf of **Nabokov**'s Lolita; an advocacy that Nabokov later admitted proved crucial both to the book's publication and its success.

INFLUENCED BY Robert Louis Stevenson; Rider Haggard; Henry James; Joseph Conrad; Ford Madox Ford.

INFLUENCE ON Ian Fleming; John Le Carré; Len Deighton; Patrick Hamilton; Evelyn Waugh; William Boyd; Robert Wilson; Muriel Spark; Paul Theroux.

ESSENTIAL READING Of the great Greene novels – **Brighton Rock**; **The Heart Of The Matter**; and **The End Of the Affair** – John Updike said, "His masterly facility at concocting thriller plots and his rather blithely morbid sensibility had come together, at a high level of intelligence and passion, with the strict terms of an inner religious debate that had not yet wearied him."

FURTHER READING **Travels With My Aunt** is a Greene novel that has consistently delighted many people who don't warm to the usual suspects and grey world of Greeneland.

The man who invented the literary west

Don't judge **Zane Grey** (1872–1939) by his covers. He may have pioneered the western as a genre, but his novels did not simplistically cheer on America's conquest of the wild frontier. In 1918, in The Roaring U.P. Trail, he reminds the reader: "Progress is great but unspoilt nature is greater." In his more intriguing tales his principals are often outlaw heroes trying to protect good and find love, anticipating the complexities of what Hollywood, in the 1950s, would call the psychological western.

Grey was born **Pearl Zane Grey** – Zane after Zanesville, his hometown in Ohio. His first novel was published in 1904 and after that he averaged 100,000 words a month for the rest of his life, which as he may have spent up to 300 days a year fishing was no small feat. His style today may seem antiquated (his formula dismissed as "villains, virgins and varmints") and he is never averse to melodrama, but he took the West seriously, researching his subject and touching upon most of the themes that later defined the western genre on page and on celluloid. He mourned the decline of the native American way of life, touched on inter-racial romance and recorded their rituals with a sympathetic eye.

Ironically, for an author who spent a quarter of a century on the bestseller lists, many of Grey's novels are now fairly hard to find. E-texts are available at

Project Gutenberg and some have been recently reissued – either singularly or in anthologies – as his reputation starts to recover. **Kurt Vonnegut** lists him as a favourite author, and though Grey might have been a better writer if he had modelled his prose on **Mark Twain** rather than **James Fenimore Cooper**, without him the fictional West – as we know it – wouldn't exist at all.

INFLUENCED BY James Fenimore Cooper; Daniel Defoe; Owen Wister.

INFLUENCE ON The western genre; Louis L'Amour; the Japanese-American writer Wakako Yamauchi; and the native American novelist Sherman Alexie.

THE WEIRD WEST

If you like cowboy stories but fancy something a little more unusual, you could start with **Walter van Tilburg Clark**'s Track Of The Cat, an intriguing gothic western that touches on mythology and psychology. For westerns with a hint of **Jim Thompson**-style noir try The Desperado by **Cliff Adams**, in which Tall Cameron can't stop killing, but he's so sweet-natured it isn't his fault. But the weirdest take on the Wild West may be **Joe R. Lansdale**'s Zeppelins West. It stars the disembodied battery-powered head of Buffalo Bill (stored for some reason in a jar of pig urine), Frankenstein's monster, Sitting Bull, Captain Nemo and Annie Oakley. It's stranger than it sounds.

CULT FICTION

ESSENTIAL READING **The Riders Of The Purple Sage** sold the most, although **The Vanishing American** was Grey's personal favourite.

FURTHER READING Grey's successor was Louis L'Amour, whose **Hondo** was described by John Wayne as "the best western novel I have ever read." There is, alas, no evidence that Wayne did read it, but it's still a good book.

BRION GYSIN

"Writing is 50 years behind painting"

The work of artist, writer and socialite **Brion Gysin** (1916–1986) has been almost completely ignored in favour of his collaboration with **William Burroughs**. To many, he is known mainly for his joke recipe in the Alice B. Toklas Cookbook, for his paintings, his interest in experimental techniques – primarily cutting up and reassembling newspapers – and his role in creating the Dreamachine, which uses light flashes to induce overwhelming hallucinations.

Born in England, Gysin grew up in the US and Canada before escaping to Paris, the Sorbonne and the exciting world of expatriate American bohemians. Introduced to some ground-breaking surrealist artists by **Sylvia Beach**, Gysin was invited to show some of his own work in their 1935 exhibition. But before the opening he argued with the group and his drawings were taken down on the orders of **André Breton**. Undeterred, and determined to show his work, Gysin displayed his pictures on the pavement outside.

After the war, during which he was drafted, Gysin wrote a biography of **Josiah Henson** (a prototype for **Harriet Beecher Stowe**'s Uncle Tom) and The History Of Slavery In Canada, which won him a Fulbright fellowship and the chance to return to Europe. In Paris he developed his cut-up technique (discovered when he was slicing mounting for his art work and cut though the newspaper protecting the table below) and worked on the fringes of experimental writing alongside Burroughs, staying at the same run-down rooming house (first discovered by **Allen Ginsberg**), which came to be known as The **Beat** Hotel.

Gysin is widely remembered as a catalyst in the worlds of art and literature and for editing several of Burroughs's novels (even turning the unfilmable Naked Lunch into an equally unproduceable script). But he also produced his own work, notably his Stories, the posthumously published The Last Museum and The Process, an under-rated classic influenced by his Moroccan years.

INFLUENCED BY Dada; Burroughs; Gertrude Stein.
INFLUENCE ON Music concrete; Genesis P. Orridge; Throbbing Gristle.
ESSENTIAL READING **The Process**.
FURTHER READING **Here To Go** (interviews with Terry Wilson).

The godmother of lesbian fiction

In 1928 the novel The Well Of Loneliness by **Radclyffe Hall** (1880–1943) was banned – in the words of judge **Sir Charles Biron,** not for dealing with "unnatural offences between women," but because "not one word suggests that anyone with the horrible tendencies described is in the least degree blameworthy." Even the 'liberal' **New Statesman** huffed: "People who desire toleration for pathological abnormalities certainly should not write about them."

Hall, who her biographer **Diana Souhami** calls "an unpleasant character who had great charm and allure," wasn't too surprised. She had "long wanted to write a novel on sexual inversion, a novel which would be accessible to the general public who did not have access to technical treatises" but expected the abuse.

None of Hall's six other novels caused as much of a stir, although The Unlit Lamp, the most effective, alludes to issues raised in The Well Of Loneliness. In the latter, Sir Philip and Lady Gordon's longing for an heir is so acute that they call their daughter Stephen. Inevitable complications arise as the tale winds to a sad end that led some feminists to question its 'liberating' effect. Others were deterred by its hauteur; this is how Stephen regards a chap in her carriage: "His soft, white hands grew restless making their foolish gestures. She looked at him coldly, wondering how she could tolerate this young man – why indeed, she chose to endure him."

The novel caused an awful fuss for a long time. Hollywood producer **Sam Goldwyn,** hearing the title, told his producer, "They're all talking about a book called The Well Of Loneliness. I'm going to film it." His horrified producer told him it was about lesbians. "Doesn't matter," said the mogul. "Make 'em Austrians."

113

INFLUENCED BY Havelock Ellis (who believed lesbianism was caused by a rogue chromosome); Noel Coward (he may appear, disguised as homosexual playwright Jonathan Brockett, in **The Well Of Loneliness**).

INFLUENCE ON Noel Coward (**Blithe Spirit** alludes to some of her ideas about the supernatural).

ESSENTIAL READING **The Well Of Loneliness**.

FURTHER READING **The Unlit Lamp**.

DASHIELL HAMMETT

The real-life detective who reinvented detective fiction

If **Dashiell Hammett** (1894–1961) was hard-boiled, life made him so. Born in Maryland in 1894, he left school at 13 and joined the **Pinkerton** detective agency at 21. His assignments may have included protecting **Fatty Arbuckle**, the silent comedian accused of rape, and working in **Butte**, Montana in 1917 when union leader **Frank Little** was lynched for organising a strike. His life was shaped by tuberculosis, women and booze and, near the end, blighted by politics. In between all these distractions, he invented hard-boiled detective fiction.

He honed his style in detective stories for **Black Mask** magazine, recreating with terse prose and rapid-fire dialogue the shabby, amoral world he had worked in, where heroes could be as tainted as the criminals. "Hammett," said **Raymond Chandler**, "put these people down on paper as they were and he made them talk and think in the language they used." His finest work, created in a remarkable burst between 1929 and 1934, includes Red Harvest – which inspired Akira Kurosawa's movie Yojimbo and, through that, A Fistful Of Dollars – The Dain Curse, The Maltese Falcon, The Glass Key and The Thin Man.

Red Harvest featured four stories set in Personville, a Depression-era Montana mining town so corrupt its inhabitants rename it Poisonville. In The Maltese Falcon he created his most famous character, Sam Spade (Samuel was Hammett's real first name), the archetypal film-noir detective. Hammett's favourite novel was the The Glass Key – as the book's anti-hero Nick Beaumont is a gambler with a drink problem and tuberculosis, it's not hard to work out why. He finished it after moving to New York, where he became drinking buddies with **Dorothy Parker** (who said his work was "as American as a sawn-off shotgun").

Screenwriting in Hollywood, he met **Lillian Hellman**, a brilliant young playwright who shared his left-wing politics. Her repartee and copious amounts of whiskey fuelled The Thin Man, the story of a crime-fighting duo, former detective Nick Charles and his rich wife Nora, that spawned a series of successful films starring **William Powell** and **Myrna Loy**.

Hammett's subsequent professional life would be defined not by fiction, but by politics, war and political wars. In the anti-Communist hysteria of postwar America, as the trustee of a bail-fund to help people accused of 'un-American activities,' he was jailed for six months and then hauled before **Senator Joe McCarthy**, a corrupt alcoholic opportunist who could have been one of Hammett's villains. Prison broke Hammett's health and the taxman broke him financially. When he died, in 1961, his books were out of print in America.

INFLUENCED BY Dickens; John Carroll Daly, whose stories preceded Hammett's and who invented the hard-boiled detective genre with him.

INFLUENCE ON Hemingway; Chandler; film noir; Tony Hillerman; Charles Willeford; P.D. James; Burroughs.

ESSENTIAL READING **The Maltese Falcon**; **The Thin Man** (although as Paul Theroux notes, the sleuthing is less convincingly depicted than the drinking).

FURTHER READING **Red Harvest**; **Dashiell Hammett: A Memoir** by Hellmann, whose repartee with Dash helped inspire screwball comedies.

The first modernist

The genre-bending experiments of **Knut Hamsun** (1859–1952) place him with modernists like **James Joyce**. Yet he admired **Hitler**, told fellow Norwegians to welcome the Nazi occupation (he gave **Joseph Goebbels** his Nobel Prize medal) and denounced the influence of "African half-apes" in America.

Born Knut Pedersen Hamsund (he shortened his surname after a printer dropped the 'd' by mistake), he published his first novel, The Enigmatic One, when he was 18. Norway's literati weren't interested in this uneducated genius with no great intellectual or political allegiance and, asking writer **Bjornsterne Bjornson** for advice, he was told to become an actor. He left for America, but didn't like it any more than Norway (when he wrote The Intellectual Life Of Modern America, the title was heavily sarcastic). On his return to Oslo, a magazine published extracts of what became Hunger, arguably his best novel.

Published in 1890, Hunger is the story of a proud young writer who decides to starve himself.

> "In old age we are like a batch of letters that someone has sent. We are no longer in the past, we have arrived"
>
> Knut Hamsun in one of his happier musings

Narrated by an increasingly unreliable and erratic anti-hero, it was years ahead of its time. He won the **Nobel Prize** for Growth Of The Soil in 1920, in which two-dimensional Nietzschean superman Isak and his three-dimensional biceps battle to make the farm work. It's also a hymn to the dignity of manual labour and the values of the simple life.

The 1921 black-and-white film of the book looks like a recruitment film for Nazi farmers. And Hamsun, who suffered a kind of breakdown between the wars, began to believe the future lay in a move away from urban chaos, an idea developed in Mysteries and Pan. Perhaps attracted by the Nazi 'blood and soil' philosophy, he started writing articles praising Hitler in the mid-1930s. When the Nazis arrived in Norway in 1940, he told his countrymen: "Throw down your rifles and go home… the Germans are fighting for us all." During the occupation Hamsun allied himself with leading collaborator **Vidkun Quisling**. He met Hitler in 1943, but he was so deaf he couldn't hear a word Hitler said and talked over his idol (upsetting the Führer with complaints about conditions in Norway) in a scene that recalled **Charlie Chaplin**'s The Great Dictator.

A 1996 movie partly blamed his wife **Marie** for this affair, suggesting history's least likely ménage à trois with the catchline: "His wife wanted Hitler – Hitler wanted him." After the war Marie was given three year's hard labour while

Hamsun was confined to a psychiatric hospital, tried in 1947 and fined. He wrote On Overgrown Paths, less of an apology for his beliefs than a justification, and died, broke, in 1952. In his book on America he had criticised **Ralph Waldo Emerson** for having an "overdeveloped moral sense and an underdeveloped psychological sense." As **John Updike**, an admirer of Hamsun's fiction, noted: "Reverse the proportions and you have Hamsun."

Norway hasn't forgiven Hamsun, yet he's hard to dismiss. **Paul Auster** opened his book of essays, The Art Of Hunger, with an eloquent look at Hamsun's book, while the Jewish writer **Isaac Bashevis Singer** wrote: "The whole school of fiction in the 20th century stems from Hamsun."

INFLUENCED BY Nietzsche; Mark Twain.
INFLUENCE ON Kafka; Isaac Bashevis Singer; Henry Miller; Paul Auster.
ESSENTIAL READING **Hunger**; **On Muted Strings**, a rich, sharp novella.
FURTHER READING **The Trial Against Hamsun**, by Danish writer Thorkil Hansen, defended Hamsun and inspired the movie starring Max von Sydow.

JOHN HAWKES

The imagineer who went a bit off at the end

John Hawkes (1925–1998) once said his motto was "Power to the imagination". Hardly controversial for a novelist, yet, for some, too much imagination is where Hawkes went wrong. A mostly admiring **Salon.com** reviewer noted: "What he means by the imagination seems to be some substrate where incest fantasies and pornographic projections are encouraged to articulate themselves in a purple rhetoric that is profusely lyrical and vaguely comic, but mostly fustian horseshit."

Hawkes, born to Irish immigrant parents, grew up in Connecticut and isolated Alaska. His works, novelist **Malcolm Bradbury** noted, were "open-ended, semi-formal and dreamlike, a visionary explanation of the imagination." He produced three fine nightmarish novels, starting with The Cannibal, which blended surrealism and American gothic to create something grotesque, yet significant. By the 1960s, Bradbury says, the novels "became ever more like psychoanalytical texts." Their erotic content grew as Hawkes was influenced by the '**pornosophers**' – a group of writers who combined pornography and philosophy – and his novels increasingly found favour in France, not America.

Hawkes's early admirers often cite the late 1970s tales, Travesty or The Passion Artist, as the last work of the old, lucid, brilliant Hawkes. In interviews Hawkes sounds as if he had read, and believed, his glowing reviews, stating after a notice in **Elle** magazine, "I'm still trying to write fiction the reader wants to eat." Proof, perhaps, that praise can be more fatal for a novelist than abuse.

THE AUTHORS

ROBERT A. HEINLEIN

The dean of science fiction

You can learn a lot from **Robert A. Heinlein** (1907–1988) who is, after **H.G. Wells**, arguably the most influential sci-fi writer of the last century. In Beyond This Horizon we learn that "an armed society is a polite society"; in The Door Into Summer that "love is all you need"; and once in Double Star, then again in The Day After Tomorrow, we're given a lesson in how to cut up a body.

This is how hard it is to categorise a man who wrote 50 novels and collections of short stories, whose titles – Stranger In A Strange Land, Starship Troopers – are known even to those who have never read a sci-fi novel. Even friends found him mysterious. **Isaac Asimov** recalled: "a flaming liberal during the war, Heinlein became a rock-ribbed, far-right conservative afterward, just at the time he changed wives from a liberal woman to a rock-ribbed, far-right conservative woman." His novels are almost as controversial. Stranger In A Strange Land so enraged a **New York Times** reviewer he called it a "disastrous mishmash of science fiction, laborious humor, dreary social satire and cheap eroticism."

Heinlein's fascination with the military, sometimes seen as evidence of fascism, may have had more to do with his regret at being discharged from the US Navy in 1934 for tuberculosis. He drifted for five years before the magazine **Astounding Science Fiction** published one of his stories. A career as a children's sci-fi writer followed until, in the late 1950s, he wrote more ambitious works like Citizen Of The Galaxy – Oliver Twist in space – and Starship Troopers, a vision of a future society in which he reveals a geeky love for high-tech weaponry. Today the novel is often slammed for espousing fascism, but in 1959 his regular publisher Scribners refused to publish it, believing it laid the blueprint for Communism.

His fiction touched on cloning, incest, mysticism, brain transplants, alternate history and time travel, but he made his biggest impact with Stranger In A Strange Land. **Kurt Vonnegut**, reviewing the reissued complete version in 1989, quoted Heinlein as saying: "I was trying to shake the reader loose from his preconceptions. It was an invitation to think, not to believe." The book achieved greater infamy when **Charles Manson** adopted some of its ceremonies and orgies and named one of his follower's sons **Valentine Michael Manson** after the novel's hero.

Heinlein's reputation has survived such notoriety, possibly because, as the man who, fans say, first dreamed up the **water bed**, he's obviously a visionary.

INFLUENCED BY Sci-fi pioneer James Cabell – Heinlein once described his novel **Stranger In A Strange Land** as a "Cabellian satire on sex and religion"; Mark Twain; Edgar Rice Burroughs; H.G. Wells; Jules Verne; and Rudyard Kipling, among many more.

INFLUENCE ON Isaac Asimov; Poul Anderson; Larry Niven; Robert Crais; L. Sprague de Camp; the moon race.

ESSENTIAL READING The obvious choice is **Stranger In A Strange Land**; but **The Moon Is A Harsh Mistress** is often said to be the greater work.

FURTHER READING The best of the rest – though with Heinlein there is wide disagreement even among fans – is probably **The Door Into Summer**.

RICHARD HELL

The punk bass guitarist who knows his sex, drugs, rock'n'roll and fiction

Born **Richard Myers** (1949–), the poet, novelist and performer **Richard Hell** was a high-school dropout from Lexington, Kentucky, who drifted to New York in the 1970s to hook up with his pal **Tom Miller** and make his way as a poet. A shared interest in drugs and poetry led to the creation of Richard Hell and **Tom Verlaine**. Together they were **The Neon Boys** and later **Television**, whose performances ignited the New York new-wave scene.

Between bands Hell wrote the confessional novel The Voidoid, which nods to such French writers as the symbolist **de Lautréamont** while betraying the fact that its creation was fuelled by cheap wine and cough syrup. Hell is also said to

have invented the punk look of spiked hair (inspired by French poet **Rimbaud**), torn clothes and shirts held together with safety pins. Legend has it that after trying to hire Hell, **Malcolm McLaren** adapted this look for the **Sex Pistols**.

New York punk was popular and very influential, but Hell became frustrated with his diminishing role in Television, and the band split. His next band, **The Heartbreakers** (not to be confused with the **Tom Petty** band of the same name), was too top-heavy with heroin users to succeed. Again Hell quit and turned a bunch of proficient New York rockers into the **Voidoids** and released Blank Generation – the depressingly up-to-date response he'd written for Television to **Kerouac**'s Beat Generation – as a single.

Hell and the Voidoids enjoyed some success with their nihilist attitude – Hell famously wore a t-shirt with the legend 'Please Kill Me' – and committed performances of such songs as Love Comes (In Spurts). When the Voidoids died, he returned to writing with the part-autobiographical Go Now. This tale of a heroin-addicted punk is better than the early rhapsodies about the protagonist's genitals might lead you to expect; it gets a decent review on the **Heroin Helper** website ("Richard Hell knows crack") and some see it as a precursor to Trainspotting.

Hell has made occasional returns to the stage, starred as **Madonna**'s boyfriend in Desperately Seeking Susan and reunited with the Voidoids to record a new track, Oh, for a compilation. He gives readings in clubs, universities and bookstores, while his drawings have been exhibited at the Rupert Goldsworthy Gallery in New York; the old punk playing renaissance man in his middle age.

INFLUENCED BY Rimbaud; Jim Carroll; Patti Smith; Hunter S. Thompson.

INFLUENCE ON Art-school punk rockers; Irvine Welsh; Jim Carroll.

ESSENTIAL READING **The Voidoid**.

FURTHER READING **Across The Years** (selected poems cased in a wooden box with a CD of Hell reading the entire book aloud).

ERNEST HEMINGWAY

Tough, wounded, 'Papa' fathered a thousand literary heirs

In **Raymond Chandler**'s Farewell, My Lovely, Philip Marlowe calls **Ernest Hemingway** (1899–1961): "A guy that keeps saying the same thing over and over until you begin to believe it must be good." It was a good shot at a rival. Hemingway's trademark prose style did away with adjectives and adverbs, working with nouns and verbs, building images with repetition and rhythm.

In A Moveable Feast, an under-rated book of sketches describing his literary apprenticeship in 1920s Paris, he recalls: "Since I had started to break down all my writing and get rid of all facility and try to make instead of describe, writing had been wonderful to do." His prose won him the **Nobel Prize** and defined a style of American sports journalism. His subject matter made him spokesman for the **Lost Generation**, a phrase **Gertrude Stein** coined and Hemingway hated.

Hemingway learned the discipline of line and length as a reporter on the **Kansas City Star**, but, excited by war, he spent the final months of World War I in the ambulance corps, getting wounded on the Austro-Italian front. After the war he married and lived in Paris, mixing with the likes of Stein, **Ezra Pound** and **F. Scott Fitzgerald**.

After some early short stories, his breakthrough came with The Sun Also Rises, a description of a group of wealthy expats searching for fulfilling experiences and developing a 'code' by which to live. After that came his superb short-story collection Men Without Women, followed by A Farewell To Arms, based loosely on his experiences of war, injury and falling in love with a nurse. Disillusionment, betrayal and how to live with pain were all regular themes: he married four times but never really trusted women.

Hemingway spent much of the rest of his life in the media spotlight, which he both craved and despised. He spent most of the 1930s in 'masculine' pursuits, hunting, boxing and fishing and all-day drinking, becoming a tourist attraction in bars. His books of this period failed to recapture the raw power of his earlier work, but he came back with For Whom The Bell Tolls. Based on the experiences of an American explosives expert in the Spanish Civil War, the novel had structure, breadth and depth – although there was merit in F. Scott Fitzgerald's lament that "Ernest wrote it for the movies."

JAMES SALTER

In the tradition of heroic, wounded men from **Hemingway**'s stories, **James Salter** is one of the finest practitioners. He regards his early novels The Hunters and The Arm Of Flesh as works of apprenticeship, recommending instead A Sport And A Pastime, a moving tale of the destructive power of passion; Light Years, tracing the havoc lack of passion can cause, and Solo Faces, which ponders why men are driven to climb mountains. Salter is an acquired taste but, once acquired, seldom lost.

120

Hemingway's last book of note was The Old Man And The Sea, ostensibly about a Cuban fisherman but really an allegory about a writer trying to preserve his talent in the face of money and fame. The allegory didn't help: Hemingway took his life with the same shotgun his father had used to kill himself, in 1961.

INFLUENCED BY Mark Twain; Ezra Pound; Sherwood Anderson; Gertrude Stein; Hammett and the hard-boiled crime genre.

INFLUENCE ON Norman Mailer; Raymond Carver; James Salter for starters.

ESSENTIAL READING **The Sun Also Rises**; **A Farewell to Arms**.

FURTHER READING **To Have And Have Not**: not his best work, but for insight into Hemingway's troubled mind, sections of it are unmatched.

CARL HIAASEN

The thinking man's Dave Barry

South Florida's favourite satirist **Carl Hiaasen** (1953–) has earned global fame with his absurdist assaults on faceless corporations, rabid developers and corrupt politicians. "Politicians don't mind if you scream and yell at them…" he says, "but if you're making fun of them that drives them nuts. And that's what I like to do… The more I can humiliate them in print the happier I am."

Hiaasen's satirical career began at high school with a newspaper More Trash. Married at 17, he had a three-year-old son by the time he started as reporter on **Cocoa Today**. In 1976, joining the **Miami Herald** (where he still has a weekly column), he specialised in investigative journalism.

A cocaine assassin, **El Loco**, inspired his first novel Powder Burn, a thriller co-written with fellow-journalist **Bill Montalbano**. They collaborated again on Trap Line and A Death In China before Montalbano became a foreign correspondent.

His first solo novel, Tourist Season, features full-blown Hiaasen craziness, fat with alligators, corruption, a leading character wreaking vengeance on behalf of nature and an undisguised loathing of anyone who fails to respect the Floridian environment. The crazed avenger of nature turns up in various forms in Hiaasen's work: most notably as Skink, a former governor of Florida driven mad by abuses of power and reduced to living in a wood and eating road-kill. Skink makes his first appearance in Double Whammy, but reappears in Skinny Dip, Native Tongue, Stormy Weather and Sick Puppy – by which time he is advising the younger, though no-less odd, Twilly Spree on eco-activism: "Somebody's got to be angry," he tells him, "or nothing gets fixed."

Hiaasen delights in South Florida's perverse life: "[It] is one of the weirdest, most screwed-up places. Nothing that happens in my novels… couldn't happen (or hasn't already happened) in real life." One motif is the perverted trait in an authority figure, such as Reverend Weems, the televangelist in Double Whammy who is drawn to prostitutes. Such characters meet suitably nasty ends: Pedro, the loathsome security guard in Native Tongue, is sodomised to death by a dolphin.

Hiaasen's novels are largely the same: comic crime stories set in South Florida full of ridiculous, if convincingly human, characters, environmental outrage and an abhorrent villain who gets gruesome comeuppance. Even Hoot! – Hiaasen's first children's book, one of the funniest around – follows the pattern.

INFLUENCED BY John D. MacDonald; Joseph Heller; Tom Wolfe.

INFLUENCE ON Christopher Brookmyre; Laura Lippman; Karen Mueller Bryson.

ESSENTIAL READING **Double Whammy**; **Strip Tease** – forget the film.

FURTHER READING Hiaasen's thrillers (co-written with Montalbano) were reprinted in 1998 by Vintage Crime.

121

PATRICIA HIGHSMITH

Mistress of the casual murder, queen of low-key claustrophobia

The recent burst of fame for **Patricia Highsmith** (1921–1995) and her amoral anti-hero Tom Ripley makes it hard to believe that when she died she had no American publisher. Acclaimed in Europe (she won the French Grand Prix de Littérature Policière in 1957), Highsmith never received her due from her countrymen: her last novel, Small g: A Summer Idyll, was rejected in 1994. Only after the Hollywood success of The Talented Mr Ripley and Ripley's Game were her books and short-story collections reissued in the US.

Highsmith was born in Fort Worth, Texas just as her parents divorced. She wasn't really a Highsmith: she took the name of her stepfather and didn't meet her biological father until she was 12. Her childhood was dominated by her cruel mother, who told her daughter she'd swallowed turpentine in a bid to abort her which was why the child liked the smell of it. When Highsmith was a teenager, her mother asked, "Are you a les?… You're beginning to make noises like one."

While her homosexuality was perhaps at odds with her preference for male company, her leading characters are mostly male, except, notably, in her second novel The Price Of Salt. Published under the pseudonym **Clare Morgan**, it's a lesbian romance with a happy ending. The book was inspired by a woman Highsmith saw shopping in the toy department of Bloomingdale's, where she worked. In some ways the poet of stalking, Highsmith was so captivated she followed the woman and watched her.

She wasn't open about her sexuality, but an understated homoeroticism finds its way into her stories. When Ripley murders the wealthy Dickie Greenleaf and assumes his identity, he risks everything for a life he could never afford and exacts revenge on Dickie for rejecting him. To cover his tracks Ripley has to kill again and the reader is persuaded to side with Ripley, to see his point of view.

Similarly, Highsmith's first novel, Strangers On A Train, filmed by **Alfred Hitchcock**, tells the story of two men who agree to kill for each other. The instigator Bruno's carefree amorality establishes the casual ruthlessness that became a central theme and part of Ripley's appeal. In a prescient early diary entry, Highsmith wrote: "The abnormal point of view is always the best for depicting 20th-century life, not only because so many of us are abnormal, but because 20th-century life is established and maintained through abnormality."

Much of the pleasure in a Highsmith novel comes from a frisson-inducing moral and sexual ambiguity, an elusive but present danger that pervades all her stories. She defined herself loosely as a suspense writer. A fan of Crime And Punishment, she wrote: "Most of Dostoevsky's books would be called suspense, were they being published today for the first time. But he would be asked to cut, because of production costs." (An American reviewer slighted her work in the

1960s by calling her a "dime-store Dostoevsky".) Highsmith moved to Europe in 1963 and lived in East Anglia, France and Switzerland, where she died in 1995.

INFLUENCED BY Edgar Allan Poe; Dostoevsky; Kafka; Camus.
INFLUENCE ON Thomas Harris; crime novelist Andrew Taylor; P.D. James.
ESSENTIAL READING All the **Ripley** novels.
FURTHER READING **The Cry Of The Owl; The Tremor Of Forgery.**

CHESTER HIMES

The godfather of black crime fiction

"I thought I was writing realism," **Chester Himes** (1909–1984) once declared. "It never occurred to me I was writing absurdity. Realism and absurdity are so similar in the lives of American blacks that they cannot tell the difference."

Himes was an oddity. A black American master of crime fiction, he discovered his style in 'exile' in France, while his lifestyle, as **James Campbell** notes in his acclaimed book Paris Interzone, anticipated the **Beats**: "Years before **Kerouac**, Himes had long since dropped out; he had been on the road all his life." But Himes was angrier than **Ginsberg** when he was howling and not without reason. The son of a middle-class family from the midwest, his violent temper, anti-social tendencies and skin colour meant he ended up serving a long sentence for armed robbery. In jail he sold a story to **Esquire** and, after wandering to California, wrote his first published novel, If He Hollers Let Him Go, an unblinking account of American racism. Angry, humiliated and isolated, he fled to Europe, following the example of **Richard Wright**.

123

> "Realism and absurdity are so similar in the lives of American blacks that they cannot tell the difference"
>
> Chester Himes on the rationale for his fiction

Broke, Himes accepted the offer and brief of French publisher Gallimard to write a hard-boiled crime novel: "Make pictures. We don't give a damn who's thinking what – only about what they're doing." It was good advice, forcing Himes to restrain his anger, and he invented an outlandish Harlem in which his heroes Coffin Ed and Grave Digger Jones were at home. Funny, satirical, violent, well-told, the novels were a smash in France. His biographer and disciple **James Sallis** says, "Almost every sentence is a two-edged blade – laughter and horror cutting the reader asunder."

The novels gave Himes financial security, although he was not famous in America until 1970, when a film of Cotton Comes To Harlem did brisk business. By then, Himes had dried up. Back in the US, watching the civil-rights struggle, he could not sustain the tone required for detective fiction. Pulp and politics fused in one novel, Blind Man With A Pistol, but the contradictory role of his heroes – black cops working for a white state – meant he could take his fiction no further. In his last, unfinished, apocalyptic novel Plan B, published posthumously, his heroes' careers end in blood, madness and racial civil war.

Himes stopped writing, except a later autobiography, and moved to Spain in 1969. Retired but not content, he insisted: "The only time I was happy was while writing those strange, violent, unreal stories." Writer **Ishmael Reed** says: "Himes taught me the difference between a black detective and Sherlock Holmes."

INFLUENCED BY Richard Wright; James Baldwin; Ralph Ellison; Chandler; Hammett.

INFLUENCE ON James Sallis (he includes Himes as a character in one of his stories); Donald Goines; Ishmael Reed; John A. Williams; Sam Greenlee.

ESSENTIAL READING The Coffin Ed/Grave Digger Jones series starts with **For Love Of Imabelle**, also published and filmed as **A Rage In Harlem**.

FURTHER READING **Pinktoes** was too sexy at first for American publishers, but it can be read as a kind of companion novel to Terry Southern's **Candy**.

RUSSELL HOBAN

The indefinable rightness of being Russell Hoban

To classify **Russell Hoban** (1925–) you have to invent words. He's a children's writer – of more than 60 children's books – and his novels are suffused with child-like wonder. His characters travel beyond conventional awareness, inhabiting a world you might call magical if it weren't so astonishingly real.

Hoban was a literary late starter. Born in Lansdale, Pennsylvania, the son of Jewish immigrants from Ukraine, he was steeped in art and literature as a boy and attended the Philadelphia Museum School of Industrial Art before fighting in the US Infantry in Italy in World War II. After the war, and stints as an artist, teacher, illustrator and television art director, he wrote children's books, finally publishing (in 1967) his first novel, The Mouse And His Child, which recounts the impossible quest of a pair of clockwork mice to become 'self-winding'.

At 44 Hoban moved to London with his wife and four children, but his marriage broke up, precipitating a run of extraordinary novels. In The Lion Of Boaz-Jachin And Jachin-Boaz, a man from the Near East abandons his wife and son and travels to London, where he is forced to confront a lion only he can see. Hoban found his voice in Kleinzeit, in which his wandering protagonist suffers from an acute pain in the hypotenuse and exchanges views with a hospital, a mirror and several sheets of yellow paper. His next novel, Turtle Diary, was a strange, shimmering, yet gentle and accessible story of two lonely people united by a desire to release three green turtles from "their little bedsitter of ocean" in London Zoo. (**Harold Pinter** helped to turn it into a movie – starring **Glenda Jackson** and **Ben Kingsley** – in 1985.)

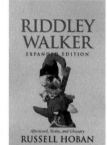

RIDDLEY WALKER
EXPANDED EDITION

Afterword, Notes, and Glossary
RUSSELL HOBAN

Riddley Walker, which took five-and-a-half years and 14 drafts to complete, is unquestionably Hoban's masterpiece. Set in post-apocalyptic Kent, it is written in a futuristic dialect strewn with dislocated references to the late 20th century and centres around a figure called Eusa (suggesting the USA, the USSR and St Eustace). His next work, Pilgermann, opens with an 11th-century German Jew losing his "proper parts" to a sow. Hoban's recent work has focused almost entirely on a mythologised London, tending towards autobiography. The Medusa Frequency and Fremder are as funny and powerful as any of his novels and contain some of his most distinctive images. Since 1998 he has published a book every year, and while Amaryllis Night And Day and The Bat Tattoo were well received, some have struggled to meet Hoban's exceptionally high standards.

INFLUENCED BY Joseph Conrad; Dickens; Gerald Kerch; Charles Williams.

INFLUENCE ON Czech poet Dominika Dery.

ESSENTIAL READING **Riddley Walker**; **Turtle Diary**. For children, **How To Beat Captain Najork And His Hired Sportsmen**.

FURTHER READING **The Moment Under The Moment**, a collection of essays and stories, allowing a rare insight into Hoban's thought processes.

STEWART HOME

Porn, parody and intellectual insurrection

"I checked in and after I'd had a piss, I told a woman cleaning the toilet that she had nice hair. She asked me if I wanted to get it on, and having a thing about women struggling with middle-aged spread, I said 'yes.'" This happens all the time to **Stewart Home**'s protagonists. In a few pages of this novel – whose title rhymes with punt and is the part of the female anatomy that interests his heroes most – the narrator has woken up to find a woman in his bed, had sex with her twice, given her (as a joke) to the miserable bloke downstairs who isn't getting any and had sex with three women at a train station. Home's rationale for all this frenetic activity? "I'm like taking the idea of pulp and deconstructing it."

A Londoner of Afro-Celt descent, Home (1962–) likes deconstructing and pranks (such as handing out **Booker Prize** invitations to the poor). His books tend to read like homages to/parodies of the cash-in Skinhead novels written by **Richard Allen** (see page 17) in the 1970s. One such novel, Blow Job, provoked one reviewer – on a website called **Leftforum** – to respond: "I may have been missing something, but it seems to me that you are no more likely to get oral sex on the Left than anywhere else."

Part of the beauty of such novels is that you don't just get **Henry Miller**, you get **Leon Trotsky** too – kind of. Home has had issues with Leon since he was in a ska band called **The Molotovs** and the singer foisted his dodgy Trotskyite lyrics on the rest of the band. The odd thing about Home, and for the author it is utterly irrelevant, is that he can write. Amid a parodic pulp orgy, his narrator notes: "If I hadn't been drunk, I wouldn't have stayed the night in Lowestoft."

INFLUENCED BY Richard Allen; Jim Thompson; Mickey Spillane; H.P. Lovecraft.

INFLUENCE ON The headline-grabbing art of Damien Hirst; Tracy Emin.

ESSENTIAL READING **69 Things To Do With A Dead Princess**, a cracking tale of a ventriloquist's dummy, stone circles and sex. The **Times Literary Supplement** said it "does for the novel what **Viz** did for the comic strip."

FURTHER READING **Slow Death**, among other things, satirises the way rumours and fabrications become accepted as historical truth.

Houellebecq, looking oddly inoffensive

MICHEL HOUELLEBECQ
A clever man, though not necessarily a clever novelist

Atomised, one of the most controversial recent European novels and a bestselling sensation in France, launched **Michel Houellebecq** (1958–) as one of Europe's great literary cults.

Houellebecq was born in Reunion (a French island off the coast of Africa), but his parents abandoned him to his grandmother when he was just five. Educated in France, he graduated in agricultural engineering and – after unemployment, depression and spells in a psychiatric institution – became a civil servant.

His early poems The Pursuit Of

Happiness, the literary journal **Perpendiculaire** (founded with a group of left-wing intellectuals), a book on **H.P. Lovecraft** and even a first novel, Whatever (a satire on sexually liberal society) – all of these now seem like preludes to the strategic literary missile that was Atomised. Charting the decline in fortunes of two characters, Bruno the hedonist and Michel the rationalist, this eloquent, sexually explicit novel attacked liberalism, free love, free markets, youth culture and individualism, and did so with enough verve to outrage half of France and get Houellebecq expelled from the board of **Perpendiculaire** for misogyny.

"Well, I can see that the plan will work in practice, but will it work in theory?"

Michel Houellebecq sends up French diplomacy

In his next novel Platform he upped the outrage by dwelling on sexual tourism, the art of masturbating over **John Grisham** books and Islamic terrorism. Its anti-Islamic sentiment led him to be sued for inciting racial hatred.

Houellebecq enjoys his enfant terrible image. When a female reviewer from **The Times** visited him, he collapsed face-down in his dinner and told her he'd only answer questions if she slept with him. The author **Julian Barnes** noted "Houellebecq sees through everything in the world except commercial sex, which he describes like one who believes every word and picture of a holiday brochure." Barnes believes Houellebecq could be the most significant French novelist since **Michel Tournier**, but does suggest that he is a cleverer man than novelist.

INFLUENCED BY J.G. Ballard; Camus.

INFLUENCE ON Adam Thirlwell.

ESSENTIAL READING **Atomised**.

FURTHER READING **Platform** asks if sexual tourism can aid the Third World.

DOROTHY B. HUGHES

The first lady of hard-boiled fiction

Dorothy B. Hughes (1904–1993) acquired her terse understated style when her editor demanded she cut 25,000 words from her first suspense novel, The So Blue Marble. Armed with such economy, she wrote a book a year for 12 years until, in 1952, a sick mother and the care of grandchildren forced her to stop.

Hughes (who was born in Kansas City but lived most of her life in New Mexico) knew she wanted to be a writer from the time she was six. Poetry and pulp romance were her first efforts before she perfected suspense stories with paranoid ambiences, haunted heroes and upper-class characters engaged in sinister intrigues. Her best-known novel is In A Lonely Place, adapted – and softened – for the classic noir movie starring **Humphrey Bogart** and **Gloria Grahame**, with a setting borrowed from another of her novels, Dread Journey. (The Fallen Sparrow and Ride The Pink Horse were also made into movies.)

Good as the movie was, the novel was more innovative, narrating the events from the killer's point of view subtly enough to keep the reader in suspense till late in the tale. **Jim Thompson** would use a similar device five years later in The Killer Inside Me. Hughes's books – the best of the others being Ride The Pink Horse – are now slowly being reissued. Had she been born 40 years later, she could have had the profile and hype of a **Sara Paretsky** – only with more talent.

INFLUENCED BY Eric Ambler; Faulkner; Graham Greene.

INFLUENCE ON Sara Paretsky; Marcia Muller; Jim Thompson.

ESSENTIAL READING **In A Lonely Place**; **Ride The Pink Horse**, in which the hero tracks gangsters to a New Mexico town celebrating a fiesta.

FURTHER READING **Sherlock Holmes And The Muffin**, a fine pastiche.

HERBERT HUNCKE

The surname happens to rhyme with junkie

Like **Neal Cassady**, **Herbert Huncke** was an outcast hipster and sporadic writer. He crops up in various **Beat** books including **Allen Ginsberg's** Howl, **William Burroughs's** Junky, **John Clellon Holmes's** Go and **Jack Kerouac's** On The Road and The Town And The City – in which he is known, simply, as "junky".

Huncke (1915–1996) grew up in middle-class Chicago, where his father ("a miserable bastard") owned a machine-parts company. At 12 he escaped into hustling. By 16 he was working for a freakshow hermaphrodite named **Elsie John** who inspired one of his best stories, Elsie John, and introduced him to heroin. For much of the 1930s, Huncke "beat it" across America, pursuing the life of a hobo long before most of his Beatnik contemporaries.

A keen user of amphetamines, heroin and marijuana, Hunke had been to prison many times before he wound up in New York in 1939. Hanging out with pimps, whores, drag queens and drug addicts, he was a perfect muse for Burroughs. The two first met in 1945, when Burroughs was trying to sell a submachine gun. Huncke introduced Burroughs to heroin and the word 'beat' to Burroughs, Kerouac and Ginsberg. "To me it meant being poor," said Kerouac, "like sleeping in doorways like Huncke used to do, and yet being illuminated…"

Huncke was living with Ginsberg when, in 1949, he was jailed for four years for possessing stolen goods. Freed, he worked on Burroughs's cannabis farm and, in the 1960s, more or less gave up the criminal life. His writing, often fragmented and spontaneous, blends the formal and the colloquial, and consists largely of studies of bohemians and outcasts. In his last years he lived at the legendary Chelsea Hotel in New York, financially supported by the **Grateful Dead**.

INFLUENCED BY The Beats.

INFLUENCE ON The Beats.

ESSENTIAL READING **The Herbert Huncke Reader**.

FURTHER READING **Guilty Of Everything**: his autobiography strips the romantic sheen from the Beat legend.

ALDOUS HUXLEY

He imagined a brave new world and opened the doors of perception

Aldous Huxley (1894–1963) was a novelist of ideas. A prolific writer, he spent most of his career wrestling with such major themes as the role of science, culture and religion. While this produced some turgid, intellectually overblown novels, it also led to Brave New World, which ranks alongside 1984 as a classic fictional prophecy. But it was his experiments with LSD that won him lasting cult status as one of the prophets of the first chemical generation.

Huxley came from a well-off Surrey family of writers, poets and scientists – grandfather Thomas had been a friend of **Charles Darwin**. He was fiercely intelligent, but at 16 he lost most of his sight after an eye infection. He gave up

Aldous Huxley realises he's mislaid the key to the doors of perception

hopes of being a scientist and, aided by Braille, read literature at Oxford. Unable to enlist, he spent much of World War I at the ongoing literary house party at Garsington, **Lady Ottoline Morrell**'s country home. Garsington was the inspiration for Huxley's savage satires on English intellectual life, including Crome Yellow, which Clive James has said "teems with bright people making speeches."

Huxley's habit of putting ideas first, character second means his novels are not always an easy read, but Brave New World, as a novel of ideas, still stands out.

Island
Aldous Huxley

Huxley's last novel in which the horrors of Brave New World melt into the vision of an eastern state governed by reason and love

Written at a time when 'progress' meant strong leaders, uniforms and modern architecture, it presents a bitter view of a society that had all three, but was a living hell. Illness and social unrest have been banished by science, stability is maintained by the hallucinogenic drug soma and the vapid populace spends its time having sex. Huxley's future is a **Le Corbusier**-designed concentration camp for the wilfully dumb. He would later suggest he got the future wrong and write the weaker Brave New World Revisited.

After the publication of his acclaimed pacifist novel Eyeless In Gaza, Huxley moved to California in 1937, became interested in Eastern religions and began experimenting with mescaline, believing the hallucinogen offered a gateway to higher mental faculties. The effects are described in The Doors Of Perception and Heaven And Hell. By 1955 he had graduated to LSD, then seen as brain food for the intellectual elite. The ideal society described by Huxley in his final novel, Island, presents his model for how its use could lead to better things.

In 1963, on the day of **JFK**'s assassination, Huxley died of throat cancer, departing in an hallucinogenic blaze after his wife administered a last dose of LSD. As the 1960s wore on, he was resurrected as a guru. The Doors Of Perception gave **Jim Morrison** a name for his band, and when Huxley graced the cover of **The Beatles**'s Sergeant Pepper album, his canonisation as an icon of counterculture was complete. Huxley would have been appalled. He firmly believed LSD was best kept for people who had minds worth expanding – people like him. Yet, after a lifetime of pondering the human condition, he shamefacedly admitted the only firm advice he could give mankind was: "Try to be a little kinder."

INFLUENCED BY William Blake; H.G. Wells; D.H. Lawrence.

INFLUENCE ON Ginsberg; Finnish writer Olavi Paavolainen.

ESSENTIAL READING **Brave New World**; **The Doors Of Perception**; and his best novel **After Many A Summer**.

FURTHER READING **Collected Essays**: Huxley is a fine, very readable critic.

GARY INDIANA ON GANGLAND STYLE

"Seven months after the tragic incidents on Woodrow Wilson Drive, it was assumed that the deaths of Fidel and Peggy Martinez were gangland killings, or, as was sometimes reported, gangland-style killings, since Fidel Martinez, a video distribution company executive, was reputed to have had so-called gangland connections or gangland associates, though it was often noted that a double murder involving fifteen shotgun blasts could not be accurately described as gangland-style killings, even if they had in fact been gangland killings, since the established style of gangland killings is a single bullet fired from a pistol or revolver into the base of the skull, rather than five to ten rounds of birdshot and buckshot fired wildly from a shotgun."

GARY INDIANA

Not to be confused with the town, or the song from The Music Man

You would think there was nothing else to say about the **O.J. Simpson** trial, until you read Resentment by **Gary Indiana** (1950–), aka Gary Hoisington. Some of his novels touch on the most notorious criminal cases in recent American history, but he has also written two collections of short stories and an intriguing study of **Pier Pasolini**'s movie Salo: The 120 Days Of Sodom. Just as you begin to suspect Indiana is a notoriety junkie, he produces a novel like Do Everything In The Dark, in which he dwells affectionately on a group of ageing characters set on outlasting their own extinct promise.

131

Indiana, who lives in New York, published his first novel, Horse Crazy, in 1989. He raised his public profile with a trilogy – Resentment, Three Month Fever and Depraved – that spun off the O.J. case, the parent-killing **Menendez** brothers' trial and the slaying of **Gianni Versace**. Resentment skewers the media hypocrisy over the Menendez trial, sends up the incompetent prosecution of O.J. Simpson and includes an astonishing riff on the media's take on gangland killings (see above).

His notorious novel Rent Boy, about an architecture student who works as a rent boy and gets caught up in organ stealing, shows a tasteless talent for the noir thriller. Indiana can be razor sharp, although there are times you may wish his editor had a sharper razor, but at his best, as novelist **Keith Ridgway** said of Crazy Horse, he is "wonderful, beautiful, funny, breathtaking."

INFLUENCED BY Bret Easton Ellis; Dominick Dunne.

INFLUENCE ON No one yet.

ESSENTIAL READING **Resentment**, a perfect fable of fin-de-siècle madness.

FURTHER READING **Do Everything In The Dark**, not for the squeamish.

CULT FICTION

GUILLERMO CABRERA INFANTE

Havana's finest writer-not-in-residence

Guillermo Cabrera Infante (1929–) was born in the tobacco-growing province of Oriente, Cuba. He was given official posts after **Fidel Castro**'s revolution, but became a dissident. His defence of smoking, Holy Smoke, is as passionate as his dislike of Castro, a man he knew well and whom he calls a monster.

At school Cabrera Infante won English spelling contests and his writing is a fusion of the Anglo style of **Hemingway** and colloquial Cuban – spelling words as they sound and creating witty word games. The title of his most successful novel (though he says he writes books, not novels), Three Trapped Tigers, is in Spanish the first line of a tongue twister: Tres Tristes Tigres.

Movies play a major role in Infante Cabrera's work. In his youth he founded Cuba's **Cinemateca** and wrote reviews for a film magazine he eventually edited. He co-wrote (as **Guillermo Cain**) the screenplay for the cult movie Vanishing Point and has worked with Cuban actor **Andy Garcia** on a film adaptation of his The Lost City. He is so fascinated by the Phantom Of The Opera that he based a short story on the 1970s musical film version, Phantom Of The Paradise.

The constant throughout his work is the city of Havana, particularly after his exile. After a brief stint in Brussels – or Siberia as he called it – he moved to London, where he felt ill at ease in the Swinging Sixties. He says the experience of exile made him a writer, though he was prolific and famous before leaving Cuba. He is outspoken about his bouts of severe depression. His work is based on memories and nostalgia, on the recreation of a world that over time and at a distance has become clearer and more real, like **James Joyce**'s Dublin or **Proust**'s Paris. His most ambitious book, La Habana Para Un Infante Difunto, printed in English as Infante's Inferno, traces every stone, every kiss, every person of his youth.

Only when his wife, Cuban actress **Myriam Gomez**, and daughters joined him did he really make London his home. His famously tropical flat recreates a Havana ambience he has never left behind, though his works are still banned in Cuba.

INFLUENCED BY Cervantes; Hemingway.

INFLUENCE ON Zoe Valdes.

ESSENTIAL READING **Three Trapped Tigers**; **Infante's Inferno**.

FURTHER READING **Holy Smoke**.

TOVE JANSSON

Swedish Finn, best known for The Moomins – kids' books not just for kids

"A genius" was Philip Pullman's assessment of the writer and artist **Tove Jansson** (1914–2001), and who's to argue. Born into Finland's Swedish-speaking

Tove Jansson surveys the watery Moominland

minority, Jansson had the odds for literary fame stacked against her, yet her creation of The Moomins ranks alongside Winnie The Pooh in children's literature: the world she created is as wise, idiosyncratic and as funny as **A.A. Milne**'s. The Moomintrolls – mouthless, hippo-like creatures whom Jansson drew as well as wrote – inhabit a rural, Nordic world of peculiar inventiveness. Their adventures are both small and cosmic: they sail boats, tend to depressed lighthouse-keepers, avoid comets, encounter magic and stand firm against the dark spirits of the north. And in winter, of course, they hibernate.

In the animated TV series, the Moomins are – just about – creations for children. On the page they have a depth, and sometimes haunting melancholy, that ensures they can be read without embarrassment at any age. The characters are quirky, resonant archetypes: the bohemian Snufkin who travels in winter; the philosopher Muskrat who lies in a hammock eating ice cream and reading a book called The Uselessness Of Everything; Little My, the angry punk girl. Jansson began their adventures in 1939 – part comment on the dreadful times, part escapism – and continued the books (and for a time a cartoon strip for London's **Evening Standard**) until she grew tired of them. The last, Moomin Valley In November, written in 1970, dealt with growing old disgracefully.

For those too po-faced to savour great children's literature, Jansson considerately added a coda of adult fiction – half-a-dozen novels and story collections, the best known being The Summer Book. This beautiful, sparse novella is a lightly fictionalised account of life on the tiny one-house island in the Gulf of Finland where she summered with her mother, brother and niece. This is a deceptively simple book, in which almost nothing happens beyond a storm and the arrival of a cat, is big in all the right ways: a tract for life, nature and child-like philosophical questions (are there ants in heaven?).

In the mid-1960s Jansson moved, with her partner, the (woman) artist **Tuulikki Pietila**, to the extreme of the Finnish archipelago, building a house on a treeless islet of rocks and gulls. There Tove and Tuuki (the model for the Moomins' Too-ticky) spent five months of each year until, at 77, Tove became scared of the sea and realised it was time to leave. In those long, light summers and dark Finnish winters in Helsinki, Tove and Tuuki played – writing, drawing, making cine films, creating objects and tableaux. The relationship between the two is depicted in another of Tove's novels, Rent Spel, soon to be published in English as Fair Play.

INFLUENCED BY Nordic myth; A.A. Milne.

INFLUENCE ON A generation of postwar children's authors; Philip Ardagh.

ESSENTIAL READING **Finn Family Moomintroll** is the best of the eight Moomin books. **The Summer Book** is a true cult classic.

FURTHER READING The other seven **Moomin** books; **Fair Play**.

The former pilot who mapped out Biggles's flight path

The Biggles who first appeared in print in 1932 is a figure far removed from the all-England pillar of rectitude he became in the 1960s. The short stories that make up the first Biggles book, The Camels Are Coming, reveal a "slight, fair-haired, good-looking lad, still in his teens" with an "irritating little falsetto laugh" and a serious drinking problem, who's about to embark on a disastrous love affair with an enemy spy. The stories are set in France in 1918, when Captain James Bigglesworth, invariably known by his nickname, is a flight commander of 266 Squadron, flying Sopwith Camel aircraft in close-support actions on the Western Front, when a pilot's life expectancy was reckoned in days and weeks.

Biggles's creator, **William Earle Johns** (1893–1968), knew what he was writing about, having served with Britain's fledgling air service himself during World War I. He left the RAF in 1931 and pitched himself into an incredibly prolific writing career. Over the next 36 years he published 161 books – that's about one every 11 weeks. He wrote about gardening and treasure-hunting and tried his hand at westerns, science fiction and adult thrillers, but the bulk of his output was devoted to Biggles – 96 titles in all, plus two unfinished works published after his death.

The first Biggles tales have a darkness and realism that the later stories lack, though Johns's publishers, mindful of the young audience, took a high-handed approach to bad language and alcohol. In one short story the scotch that Biggles and a fellow officer fight over becomes lemonade. References to Biggles's habits – "he's drinking whiskey – in the morning" – were cut entirely from later editions.

135

Biggles entered the post-World War I world as an adventuring aviator. The miracle of powered flight allowed him to find lost treasures in the South American jungles (Biggles Flies Again), fight descendants of ancient armies in the African deserts (Biggles Flies South), dive for pearls in Polynesia (Biggles In The South Seas) and combat an ancient pirate's curse in the Caribbean (Biggles Flies West). Most of these books are terrific page-turning yarns, glorious products of Johns's interest in history and geography. Increasingly, though, Biggles became the leader of a group, rather than a solitary hero. Though he aged at a slower rate, he was still growing too old for readers to identify with, so Johns introduced a younger sidekick, Ginger. Biggles became more austere, remote and thus less interesting.

The process continued through World War II, where Johns was less sure of his ground on up-to-date combat flying. Many of the plotlines are lifted from the World War I books and they don't quite ring true. After the war Biggles finds a role as an officer with the Special Air Police, a division of the constabulary that Johns dreamed up to create a long series of fairly routine crime thrillers.

Johns wrote better stuff in the 1940s and early 1950s with his Worrals series, about Flight Officer Joan Worralson and her sidekick Betty Lovell (aka Frecks, due to her freckles). A headstrong 18-year-old proto-feminist (Frecks was a year younger) with the Women's Auxiliary Air Force, she raged against not being able to fly in World War II combat, but somehow got involved in all kinds of cloak-and-dagger stuff in occupied France. "Worrals wanted to kick him. Why were men always so stupid?" is not a line you'd expect from the man who created Biggles.

It would be wrong to suggest that Biggles was a great literary figure. His character development stops somewhere in his early twenties, while his language and outlook on life now clunk along in a uncomfortably reactionary way. But the best of the stories, though grouped together haphazardly, are really quite good.

INFLUENCED BY His own experiences and the autobiographies of British fighter pilots, such as **Flying Fury** by James McCudden.

INFLUENCE ON The influence his books had on the young men who made up 'The Few' of the Battle of Britain was considerable.

ESSENTIAL READING **Biggles In The Gobi** – a classic of the later period.

FURTHER READING **Winged Victory** by V.M. Yeates, a much more adult, distinctly more bitter tale of another Sopwith Camel pilot (and one who described **The Camels Are Coming** as "bunk").

B.S. JOHNSON

Not experimental, this English eccentric wrote "like a fiery elephant"

"Where I depart from convention," **Bryan Stanley Johnson** (1933–1973) once said, "it is because the convention has failed." Convention failed almost all the time in Johnson's ten-year reign as leader of Britain's literary avant-garde. Indeed, the formalities of beginnings, middles and ends were complete strangers to him.

> "A page is an area on which I may place any signs I consider to communicate most nearly what I have to convey"
>
> B.S. Johnson gives his readers fair warning

Johnson was born in west London to an adoring mother and an emotionally distant father. His working-class childhood was marked by the trauma of wartime evacuation and failing exams. Thereafter his life was characterised by an intense fear of rejection, death and the impossibly high standards he set himself. (He learned Latin in the evenings and eventually won a place at King's College, London where he read English.)

A combative character, Johnson detested the label 'experimental', feeling it left him firmly outside the established literary order, exacerbating the commercial failure that contributed to his suicide when he was 39. His stunts – from cutting holes in pages to allow the reader to skip through his Albert Angelo, to publishing an entire novel, The Unfortunates, in 27 separate pamphlets to be shuffled at the reader's whim – might seem frivolous, but the sheer quality of his prose excused his indulgences. "His writing sings," wrote poet and author **Adrian Mitchell** in his review of Albert Angelo. "He writes like a fiery elephant."

Such techniques were an attack on readers' laziness. "I want him to see my vision, not something conjured out of his own imagination," he said of his reader. "How is he supposed to grow unless he will admit others' ideas? If he wants to impose his imagination, let him write his own books." Ironically, for contemporaries like **Eva Figes**, it was Johnson's refusal to let his imagination loose on a society that had moved on from the certainties of 1950s Britain that doomed him creatively and, perhaps, personally.

His fifth novel, The Unfortunates, deals with death as seen through the eyes of a football reporter, winning plaudits from **Anthony Burgess** and Johnson's hero **Samuel Beckett**. It was conceived while Johnson was working as a football hack, a career that ended when he called his sports editor at five o'clock one Saturday afternoon to say he would not be filing copy as he'd "just had an idea for a novel".

Christie Malry's Own Double-Entry, published shortly before his death, is Johnson's meisterwork. A malevolent, bleakly comedic tale of a trainee book-keeper who uses the double-entry system of debit and credit to wreak vengeance, it uses Johnson's favourite device – the interruption of the narrative by the author to mull over how the story is progressing: "'Christie,' I warned him, 'it does not seem possible to take this novel much further. I'm sorry.' 'Don't be sorry,' said Christie. 'Who wants long novels anyway?'" **Margaret Drabble** admired its coarseness, while **Alan Sillitoe** praised its easy-to-read virtuosity.

The warmth, the celebration of Englishness and understanding of working-class frustration mark Christie Malry as a vital and original piece of work even 30 years on. After languishing in the wilderness since his death, his work – championed by author **Jonathan Coe** and aided by a movie of Christie Malry – has now mostly been reissued. The temperamental genius would surely have approved of success, at last, on his own terms.

INFLUENCED BY Beckett; James Joyce; Robert Graves – he often reread the poet's **The White Goddess**, celebrating the female muse.

INFLUENCE ON Jonathan Coe; Dave Eggers.

ESSENTIAL READING **Christie Malry's Own Double-Entry**; **The Unfortunates**.

FURTHER READING His **Omnibus**; **Like A Fiery Elephant: The Story Of B.S. Johnson** by Jonathan Coe.

CULT FICTION

THOM JONES

In the acknowledgments in Cold Snap, **Thom Jones** (1945–) thanks friends and the anti-depressant drugs Effexor and Elavil for "expanding the narrow spectrum of happiness available to such gloomy hypochondriacal existentialists as myself."

Jones was born in Aurora, Illinois to a father who had been a professional fighter: "He left when I was a little kid, but he would come back to get me on weekends and take me to the gym, usually with liquor on his breath." Jones became an amateur boxer (over 150 fights), a marine and a janitor, but it was as an advertising copywriter that he learned the writer's trade, at a University of Iowa writers' workshop. To date he has written three collections of short stories.

His first published story, The Pugilist At Rest, named after a famous Roman statue of a boxer, appeared in **The New Yorker** in 1992. The narrator is an ex-marine who believes the statue is **Theogenes**, the greatest gladiator of them all, and recognises his own barely concealed capacity for violence in the pugilist's world-weary posture. As a young soldier he sees his friend killed in action and works out his anger in Vietnam: "I committed unspeakable crimes and got medals for it." Later, in a boxing bout, he acquires a head injury that leaves him with '**Dostoevsky**'s epilepsy'. By the end he's waiting for psychosurgery, wearing a boxer's headguard and gumshield around the house in fear of seizures.

This debut, written in a rush of slang dialogue by a narrator alternatively full of venom and fear, established Jones's major theme – life and survival in a brutal world – and is quasi-autobiographical: Jones has temporal lobe epilepsy and takes anti-depressants after a military brawl brought on epileptic fits.

The story was an instant hit (pun intended): within six months Jones's work had appeared in **Harper's**, **Esquire**, **Mirabella**, **Story**, **Buzz** and twice more in **The New Yorker**. In his first published collection, also entitled The Pugilist At Rest, the prose flashes hot and cold. His characters – boxers, soldiers, amoral lovers, deep-sea divers and cancer sufferers – live in extreme situations, lurching movingly and amusingly between ecstatic pleasure and depression or pain.

Much of his second collection Cold Snap is about a bunch of misfit doctors working under extreme conditions in Africa while fighting mental illness. Why did he choose to write about doctors? "They're insane, they take drugs, some of them are saints and some of them are sinners." It was back to boxing gyms, Vietnam, psychiatric wards and drug use for Sonny Liston Was A Friend Of Mine. Jones says, "I found the gym a sanctuary, a place to hide from the reality of the world… you get familiar with patterns in your life, even if they're bad ones."

He still writes stories for magazines: "Here and there it will all add up to a book. I just try to think of all the most embarrassing stuff I've ever done… for my next collection I want A-grade material cover to cover."

"GOD GAVE ME TWO WEEKS OF SEMI-HAPPINESS"

Exclusively for this book, Thom Jones reviews his life, fiction and drugs

"I don't get into trouble anymore but I have spent more time in jail than any other Guggenheim fellow. I probably took more drugs than **Elvis**, but I've been off alcohol and dope for 20 years. I'm diabetic. I still work out a lot. I am almost 60 years old. I have had a succession of boxer dogs.

If you write a story (in six weeks) and it doesn't get published – rare for me, but it happens – that's not a big expenditure down the drain. Write a novel for three years and have that bomb, as most will – well, put a bullet through your brain. I have written a lot of stories that headed for novel territory, but I would sell them as short stories and that would be the end of it.

Jon Jackson, a pal from the University of Iowa Writers' Workshop, said the exact right stuff that led me to get published: "Editors get paid to reject your stories. You have to write something so good they can't not publish it." It has nothing to do with the writer, it's all about the work.

I used to think there was a conspiracy against me. Early in the overnight sensation deal, I walked by a magazine rack and saw a **New Yorker**, an **Esquire** and a **Harpers**, all containing a story by me. I wish I had remained in hiding like **Thomas Pynchon**. Meanwhile I was swimming nightly in the high-school pool, alone and in the dark, and I was losing two or three pounds a day, which I knew was a lot for a mile or two in the pool. Two weeks after I signed with my publishers I found out I was an insulin-dependent diabetic. But God gave me two weeks of semi-happiness.

Each night I dump my meds – seizure meds, depression meds, anti-psychotic meds and more – in the palm of my hand before bed – and glance down at the pills in my right hand, thrice broken and now an eagle talon from Dupuytren's contracture.

I read medical journals for pleasure, horror and astonishment. I read until daylight. I write from nine in the evening, listening to the **Doors** and **Linda Ronstadt**. Another nifty drug is Provigal, it's meant for narcoleptics but they give it to patients with sleep apnea like me, or people who work nights. You can stay awake three days in a row unimpaired, sleep when desired and wake up without a hangover. But the nightly handful is something to behold.

My grandmother used to say, 'You will show them. Some day you will show them.' The prophecy came true – a kind of minor fame as a cult writer of whom it has been said, 'I like reading Thom Jones, but I surely wouldn't like living next door to him.'"

139

INFLUENCED BY Alan Sillitoe; Somerset Maugham; Hubert Selby Jr.

INFLUENCE ON Chuck Palahniuk; emerging American novelist Stephen Elliott.

ESSENTIAL READING **The Pugilist At Rest** collection, but especially **I Want To Live!**, where a woman dying of cancer reaches an epiphany before she dies.

FURTHER READING His recent story **Cannonball: Love Sinks** describes a pool attendant's first experiences of love and death.

The novelist's novelist who created Dublin and the cult of difficulty

"The only demand I make of my reader," **James Joyce** (1882–1941) once said, "is that he should devote his whole life to reading my works."

James Augustine Aloysius Joyce was always fascinated with language. Born to well-off Irish Catholic parents (before his father lost his job, declined into alcoholism and became a model for some Joyce characters), Joyce was just nine when he wrote his first work, a poem, Et Tu Healy, about the death of **Charles Stewart Parnell**. His father had it printed and sent a copy to the Vatican library.

Joyce loved Dublin, yet hated what he saw as its insular literary community and parochial society. He spent most of his life abroad, in Trieste, Zurich and Paris, but the places, history and people of **Dublin** and Ireland were more intricately real to him, in his self-imposed exile, than if he had lived on the Liffey.

Dubliners, a series of stories examining Dublin society, was his first published work. Joyce described it as his attempt to write a chapter of the moral history of his country, but when he returned home from Trieste he found his publisher had destroyed the first section. Joyce left the country for the last time the next day.

At university he had started writing Stephen Hero. He developed it when he moved to Trieste but abandoned it until **Italo Svevo** – one of the private students he taught English to – encouraged him to return to it. The result was A Portrait Of The Artist As A Young Man. Stephen Hero became Stephen Dedalus, Joyce's alter ego, and in this book Joyce developed his love of interior monologues, rejecting traditional plot narrative for the stream-of-consciousness technique (which, along with **Virginia Woolf** and **Dorothy Richardson**, he pioneered).

With Portrait's arrival, Joyce's genius was declared. **Ezra Pound** compared him to **Flaubert** and in 1918 began serialising Joyce's next novel in his **The Little Review**. Joyce had been working on the idea of a Jewish advertising canvasser called Leopold Bloom since Dubliners, and this now became the mammoth Ulysses: a novel recounting a day in Bloom's life by way of Homer's Odyssey and the history of literature, each chapter written in its own style. Innovative, full of mythological allusion, it is a highly structured, intellectual, creative work that also features sex, masturbation and defecation, reason enough for it to be banned in the US until 1933 and in the UK until 1936, though several bootleg versions appeared. It is also an astonishingly detailed homage to Dublin. Joyce, who had badgered friends with questions about the city, once declared that if Dublin were destroyed it could be rebuilt brick by brick using his work.

Ireland's Committee on Evil Literature branded it the "notorious volume of a well-known degenerate Irishman," but the ban only increased its popularity. Joyce recalled being asked by a fan in Zurich if he could kiss the hand that wrote Ulysses. Joyce declined, telling him, "No, it did a lot of other things as well."

Critics disagree over its merits. Irish writer **Roddy Doyle** says it could have done with a good editor. **Jonathan Franzen** admires the novel, but not its effect on novelists: "It routinely tops lists of the best novels. Which sends this message to the reader: literature is horribly hard to read. And this message to the aspiring writer: extreme difficulty earns respect."

Finnegans Wake is beyond difficult. The book is a dream-like night to Ulysses's day, abandoning plot and character in favour of language. Syntax and words fall apart and snippets of songs, quotations and allusions run through seemingly unconnected thoughts. When the critic **Max Eastman** asked Joyce why it was so hard to read,

Portrait of the artist as an old man

Joyce replied: "to keep the critics busy for three hundred years."

Samuel Beckett, Joyce's protégé and sometime secretary, said it is not about something, it is something itself. Joyce, whose eyesight was fading, dictated large sections of the work to Beckett. During one session someone knocked on the door. "Come in," called Joyce, which Beckett, not hearing the knock, faithfully transcribed. On reading back his work, Joyce said of the error, "Let it stand."

Joyce also wrote poetry and was interested in stage and screen – in 1909 he established Dublin's first, short-lived, cinema and, in 1914, wrote the play Exiles. It is chiefly interesting for its central character who must decide whether to live in Ireland or flee, before deciding: "real adventures, I reflected, do not happen to people who remain at home: they must be sought abroad."

INFLUENCED BY Joyce said he read every line of three writers – Ben Jonson, Flaubert and Ibsen. He also loved Tolstoy and Shelley and ascribed his use of stream of consciousness to Dujardin's **Les Lauriers Sont Coupés**. He also once remarked he loved Dante almost as much as the **Bible**.

INFLUENCE ON After Shakespeare, he is probably the most influential writer of English, influencing, among many others, Beckett; Flann O'Brien, who sent him up in **At Swim-Two-Birds**; Borges; Salman Rushdie; Pynchon; Umberto Eco.

ESSENTIAL READING **Dubliners** (the story **The Dead** is believed by many to be his greatest work); **Portrait Of The Artist**; **Ulysses**.

FURTHER READING: **Finnegans Wake**; **ReJoyce**, an analysis by Anthony Burgess for those "scared off by critics".

CULT FICTION

FRANZ KAFKA

Although his place in the 20th-century literary canon is assured, only a few lesser works by **Franz Kafka** (1883–1924) were published in his lifetime. Indeed, he demanded that all his manuscripts be destroyed on his death. Only by ignoring Kafka did his literary executor **Max Brod** preserve his phantasmagoric The Trial and The Castle, as well as innumerable short stories, parables and fragments.

Born in Prague to a middle-class Jewish family, Kafka's childhood was marked by an intense fear of his father, a businessman overtly hostile to his son's literary hopes. After taking a law degree, Kafka worked at an insurance company and devoted his nights to frenetic bouts of writing that ultimately damaged his health.

In the autumn of 1912 he wrote the tautly oedipal confrontation The Judgement in one nocturnal sitting, the lengthy first chapter of what was to become his novel Amerika (published posthumously in 1927) and The Metamorphosis, in which travelling salesman Gregor Samsa famously awakens to find himself transformed into a giant insect. Told with a matter-of-factness that is initially quite jarring, the story gradually lures the reader into its singular metaphysical world, even as Gregor acquiesces to his own destruction.

This sense of personal powerlessness and impending annihilation permeated Kafka's thought, diaries and letters. "**Balzac** carried a cane," he once noted, "on which was carved the legend: 'I smash every obstacle.' My legend reads: 'Every obstacle smashes me.'" Although he once typed a searing 50-page letter indicting both the elder Kafka and himself for their failures as father and son, he lived at home for much of his adult life. Twice, and with immense anguish, he broke off engagements because he considered the state of marriage beyond him.

Kafka created fictional worlds calibrated by his very neuroses. In The Trial, in which Josef K is suddenly arrested, the notion of guilt comes under kaleidoscopic

Franz Kafka
Das Schloß
Roman

focus. This attempt at escape is inverted in The Castle, where K, the land surveyor, is always seeking admission to the Castle in the face of an inscrutable and irrational bureaucracy. Replete with paradoxes and aphorisms, these novels affirm a unique spirituality that, for all its uncanniness, resounds well beyond Kafka's neurotic hypersensitivity.

After his death Kafka's works were suppressed in Czechoslovakia by the Nazis because he was Jewish and then by the Communists, who found his depictions of authority were ideologically problematic. Only with the **Velvet Revolution** of 1989 was he officially embraced in his native land.

INFLUENCED BY Kabbalah; Goethe; Søren Kierkegaard; Heinrich von Kleist.
INFLUENCE ON Borges; Philip Roth; Bruno Schulz; Beckett; Milan Kundera.
ESSENTIAL READING **The Trial**; **The Castle**; **The Metamorphosis**.
FURTHER READING **The Diaries Of Franz Kafka**.

ANNA KAVAN

"Bizarre studies of tormented women"

Writer, editor, painter, interior designer: there were few things **Anna Kavan** (1901–1968) couldn't do. But kicking her heroin habit was one of them. Whether she first took the drug to numb the pain from a spinal injury or as a way of self-medicating her depression, the addiction overtook both problems while helping to develop her **Kafkaesque** tales of the darker side of the human psyche.

The daughter of wealthy ex-pat British parents, **Helen Emily Woods**, as Kavan was born, enjoyed a cosmopolitan, much-travelled childhood. But her father committed suicide when she was 13, leaving her mother as the driving force in her life (she often appears in Kavan's novels as a remote and selfish figure).

A COMIC GENIUS IN A TRAGIC ERA

143

"He's better than Kafka" was how **Isaac Bashevis Singer** described **Bruno Schulz** (1892–1942). **John Updike** said he was, "One of the great writers... the great transmogrifiers of the world into words."

Schulz was, in the American novelist's fine phrase, "a hidden man, in an obscure Galician town, born to testify to the paradoxical richness, amid poverty of circumstance, of our inner lives." He was born in Drogobych, a small Austrian town in what was then the Austro-Hungarian empire. He died, in 1942, shot by a Gestapo officer while walking out for a loaf of bread. In between he wrote two rarified masterpieces: Street Of Crocodiles, which started out as letters to a female friend, and Sanitorium Under The Hourglass. Both books are packed with verbal brilliance, but the reader dreads some forthcoming, unspecified cruelty.

It is tempting to find such menace in the Holocaust, yet the disaster that infuses Schulz's fiction is more personal – his father's madness. In Street Of Crocodiles he muses on his fictional father's fate: "What remained of him would finally disappear one day, as unremarked as the gray heap of rubbish swept into a corner, waiting to be taken to the rubbish dump."

Schulz wrote in Polish, not Yiddish, suggesting a desire to escape his roots. But after a spell in Warsaw he found he couldn't flourish without his hometown. He returned to Drogobych to write and, though he didn't know it, to die.

In a tragic era, Schulz was a comic genius. In his imagery and freedom, he wrote like Chagall painted. In the leaps of his imagination, he anticipated baroque magic realism. Nobody has ever written quite like Schulz – it's possible no one ever will again.

Anna Kavan, a self-portrait

During her unhappy first marriage (she wed when she was 17) she began to write under the name **Helen Ferguson**. Early novels – A Charmed Circle and The Dark Sisters – were traditional, but her third, Let Me Alone, focuses on a young girl who is brought up by her father until he kills himself when she is 13, and is then adopted by an aunt who eventually rejects her.

The 1930s were a tumultuous decade for Kavan. Her second marriage ended in divorce in 1938, leading to the first of at least three suicide attempts, and her dependence on heroin grew – she often detoxed, only to fall back on what she called her "bazooka". Changing her name to Anna Kavan, after her heroine in Let Me Alone, Kavan's work began exploring the darkest regions of her depressed mind. One reviewer called her short story Asylum Piece "a classic equal to the work of **Kafka**." But, despite her struggles, professionally she was prolific, producing what one critic referred to as "bizarre studies of tormented women", while also working as a painter (she exhibited in the Wertheim Gallery, London) and an interior designer. When she died a full syringe was found next to her body.

INFLUENCED BY Kafka; the nouveau roman; Cocteau.

INFLUENCE ON Too little.

ESSENTIAL READING **Ice**, a fascinating marriage of the Goth novel and sci-fi.

FURTHER READING **Sleep Has His House**, strange, beautiful, drug-fuelled.

WELDON KEES

Missing presumed dead – but keep an eye out for him just in case

If you see **Weldon Kees** (1914–c.1955) be sure to give him a copy of this book. The American poet and short-story writer, described as one of the most bitter of the 20th century by his friend **Donald Justice**, disappeared one July morning in 1955. His car was found abandoned near the Golden Gate Bridge. Before his mysterious departure he was talking to a friend about flying to Mexico. He feared he would never be "up there" with the literary greats, and it is nice to imagine him now, in his 90s, sitting in a bar, staring out at a beach somewhere near Acapulco.

Kees's miserable, bitter, powerful poems didn't suit the movements of his day. His low-key, humdrum stories often set in small communities recall **Hemingway**, but, as in the tale of the shop owner who sells his mute sister's favours to the locals, they have a darker twist. His stories weren't published until 1983, by which time a full-blown cult had emerged. Poems started appearing in his honour, while several young poets name-checked him. In 1995 the British writer **Peter Crowther** wrote a story called Too Short A Death, in which the protagonist searches for Kees and, in the writer's hometown in Nebraska, meets a middle-aged man-cum-vampire called Robinson, a figure from Kees's poems.

The poet **Simon Armitage**, who made the BBC film Looking For Robinson, sums up Kees's work best: "A hot potato but a hard one to get hold of." Kees sold less than 1,000 books in his lifetime. He's back in print now but, while his cult grows, the critics are snippy about him again.

INFLUENCED BY Hemingway; F. Scott Fitzgerald; T.S. Eliot; W.H. Auden.
INFLUENCE ON Hugo Williams; Peter Crowther.
ESSENTIAL READING **The Selected Short Stories Of Weldon Kees**.
FURTHER READING **The Collected Poems Of Weldon Kees**.

JAMES KELMAN

How controversial he is, how controversial

Urban as a back alley littered with syringes, the writing of **James Kelman** (1946–) has done more than most to change the landscape of Scottish literature from what he calls "the tartan-and-heather kind of bollocks" to something far grittier. Kelman's characters aren't heroes: think of them as the odd-job, absent fathers of the cast of Trainspotting: chancers and loners, slipping into middle age, grasping for meaning with an existential unease and a mordant wit.

It's easy to confuse the writer with the writings. Born in Glasgow, Kelman left school at 15 to become an apprentice printer, spending time in America and London before returning home and joining the writing group that led to his first short-story collection, An Old Pub Near The Angel, in 1973. A decade later he published his first full-length novel, The Busconductor Hines. For 11 years he mined the same social seam, before becoming the first Scot to win the **Booker Prize** in 1994 for How Late It Was, How Late – a controversial choice, with one large book chain refusing to buy it because of its profanity and one judge declaring it "crap".

Kelman dealt with the furore in typical style – spotting BBC reporters while making a speech at the Edinburgh Festival he peppered it with profanities. The man who had been labelled a 'literary savage' also made a strong defence of his style. Writing in dialect, he said, was "a way of talking about the validity of your own culture, indigenous culture, as opposed to the dominant culture, whether it's based in London or in Harvard. It's a way of saying 'I have a right to write from my own experiences, from my own community.'"

CULT FICTION

Kelman still rails against the "sentimentalisation and mythology" that accompanies Scottish writers, but has started moving away from Scottish settings. His last two books, Translated Accounts and You Have To Be Careful In The Land Of The Free, were set in an unnamed state and America respectively. The existential problems and dialect continues – the politics have just moved into a global arena.

INFLUENCED BY Beckett; James Joyce; Kafka.
INFLUENCE ON Irvine Welsh; Gordon Legge; Alan Warner.
ESSENTIAL READING **How Late It Was, How Late**.
FURTHER READING **A Disaffection**; some fans rate this above **How Late**.

A.L. KENNEDY

"My books are the best I could do at the time, but no, I don't like them"

Alison Louise Kennedy (1965–) – she uses A.L. in homage to her heroes **J.R.R Tolkien**, **C.S. Lewis** and **E. Nesbit** – loves to write, but she is less than complimentary about the trappings of being a writer. Sharing her views of the pitfalls of publishing, she writes on her website: "Missed newcomers and piss-poor final presentation of texts on the shelves, silly covers, greedy and simple-minded bookshop chains… there is nothing like watching people who care about books being destroyed by publishing to put a blight on your afternoon."

Born in Dundee, Kennedy studied theatre and drama at Warwick University, and, in 1990, released Night Geometry And The Garscadden Trains, a collection of short stories about lonely people pondering sex, death and public transport. Her 1993 debut novel Looking For The Possible Dance continued the theme: Mary Margaret a woman struggling with the relationship with her father, lover and employer, and Kennedy peppered her prose with wry humour and social issues. So I Am Glad was an ambitious project, tackling the subject of child abuse and its consequences on adult life, but with Everything You Need, about a writer living alone on a remote island and struggling to connect with his estranged daughter, Kennedy returned to the same themes of isolation and intimacy.

A.L. KENNEDY

Now that you're back

INFLUENCED BY C.S. Lewis; J.R.R. Tolkien.
INFLUENCE ON Martyn Bedford, whose novels include **The Houdini Girl** and **Black Cat**, cites Kennedy as one of his favourite British writers.

ESSENTIAL READING **Now That You're Back**, Kennedy at her deadpan best.
FURTHER READING **Original Bliss**, her most recent short stories.

JACK KEROUAC

From rebel icon to Ku Klux Klan supporter: one strange trip

The 'king of the Beats' excites mixed feelings. The joy and the verve of his novels and poetry, together with his square-jawed good looks, made him an icon of 1950s youth: a personification of cultural and spiritual liberation. But **Jack Kerouac** (1922–1969) was a man of hopeless contradictions – a bisexual homophobe, a lover of jazz who went on to champion the **Ku Klux Klan** – and many now consider his writing of far greater cultural than literary value.

Kerouac was born to working-class, Catholic, French-Canadian parents in Lowell, Massachusetts. The youngest of three children, he was badly affected by his father's alcoholism and gambling. At high school he was a champion athlete, and he won a football scholarship to New York's Columbia University in 1939, where he began to indulge his interests in women, jazz, drinking and writing.

Kerouac dropped out of Columbia, joined the merchant navy and returned to New York, where he met **Allen Ginsberg** and **William Burroughs**. Together they formed the core of the **Beat Movement**. Emulating the likes of **Rimbaud**, Kerouac experimented with sex and drugs, immersing himself in a world of social outcasts – particularly hobos and "happy, true-minded, ecstatic Negroes". He also started his first published novel, The Town And The City: a semi-autobiographical epic, influenced by **Thomas Wolfe**, which was well-received but a commercial failure.

The arrival of **Neal Cassady** – "the holy con-man with the shining mind" – in New York in 1946 was pivotal for Kerouac. Sports and literature-mad, working class and (mostly) heterosexual, Cassady was a natural companion, and their hitch-hiking adventures provided the material for On The Road. Cassady's wild, uninhibited conversation and letters were used by Kerouac as a basis for his high-speed "spontaneous prose". He wrote On The Road in three Benzedrine-fuelled weeks in 1951, typing uninterrupted on to 12ft rolls of paper. But, while his phrase "Beat Generation" (combining rhythm, beatitude and a 'dead-beat' weariness with conventionality) was widely known, it was 1957 before he found a publisher.

In 1952 he revisited his time with Cassady in Visions Of Cody (finally published in 1960); he also took peyote for the first time and was introduced to The Tibetan Book Of The Dead, igniting a passion for Buddhism. His devotion led to much poetry and prose, notably the ecstatic The Dharma Bums, based on a 1955 mountain-climbing expedition with the Zen poet **Gary Snyder**, although Tristessa is a more honest reflection of his ongoing conflict with Catholicism.

On The Road was finally hailed as "an historic occasion" by the **New York Times**,

> "Offer them what they secretly want and they become panic stricken"
>
> Jack Kerouac's insight into life and literature

but by then Kerouac was weary and disillusioned, not the vibrant Dean Moriarty fans expected. To overcome nerves, shyness and, later, to counter the criticism of The Subterraneans and Doctor Sax, he drank more, and in 1960 suffered a nervous breakdown – "the final horrors" he noted in Big Sur. Living mostly with his mother, he sank into reactionary politics, decrying as Communist the counterculture he had helped create. He died of an alcohol-related illness at the age of 47, but still inspires travellers across the world.

INFLUENCED BY Thomas Wolf; Jack London; Lester Young.

INFLUENCE ON Bob Dylan; Hunter S. Thompson; Jim Morrison.

ESSENTIAL READING **On The Road**; **The Dharma Bums**.

FURTHER READING **Off The Road**, Carolyn Cassady's informed inside view.

GERALD KERSH

A 20th-century Edgar Allan Poe

If the ultimate definition of a truly cult author is to be out of print, **Gerald Kersh** (1911–1968) qualifies. Look him up on Amazon.com and, after a few listings, the words "limited availability" appear with monotonous regularity.

Kersh might not be surprised. He got used to life's tricks early, being declared dead when he was two, selling his novel Night And The City to the movies only for them to throw away every part of his story but the title (he sent the script back suggesting it be nailed to a wall), and, in World War II, getting so fed up with army regulations he deserted – to fly to the front line. His first novel, Jews Without Jehovah, was withdrawn after outraged family members, incensed by what they saw as grotesque derogatory sketches of themselves, threatened to sue.

Born in Teddington, Middlesex, Kersh spent his final years in remote New York state, as far away from creditors as possible. In between, he wrote a bewildering variety of novels and short stories. In the 1940s he was as critically rated in England as **Angus Wilson**, but his versatility, and a certain weirdness, counted against him. His fiction included disguised army reminiscences, noirish underworld tales and short stories in which midgets fight for the love of a beautiful multiple amputee, and a ventriloquist's relationship with his dummy takes a very strange turn.

He began writing novels on toilet paper in Soho bars and his feel for the criminal milieu is obvious in Night And The City, Prelude To A Certain

A percussion of Beats: (from left) Peter Orlosvky, Bill Burroughs, Allen Ginsberg, Alan Ansen, Gregory Corso, Paul Bowles (seated) and Ian Somerville in Tangiers

EXTRA BEATS: JOHN, LARRY AND GARY

John Clellon Holmes (1926–88) was the first member of the **Beats** to publish a novel featuring fictionalised versions of **Kerouac**, **Ginsberg** and **Neal Cassady**. Predating On The Road by five years, Go (1952) describes the Beat scene in 1948-9 New York – "Youth in Search of 'Kicks'" as the cover put it – and offers a fascinating comparison with later accounts. It was in response to a question from Holmes that Kerouac invented the term **'Beat Generation'**. Holmes also wrote The Horn and Get Home Free, as well as collections of essays and poetry.

Lawrence Ferlinghetti (1919–) is a poet, playwright, publisher, bookseller and political activist. Born in New York, he lived the travelling Beat life in the early 1940s before serving in the navy. In 1953, having completed a doctoral degree at the Sorbonne in Paris, Ferlinghetti set up the City Lights Bookstore in San Francisco, where many of the movement's most important early poetry readings were staged. Among the poetry later published by the City Lights Press was Ginsberg's Howl – a book for which Ferlinghetti was tried and acquitted on obscenity charges. His collection A Coney Island Of The Mind is a classic of Beat literature. He continues to write and run City Lights Bookstore.

Gary Snyder (1930–) was the most mystical of the beatniks, motivated by Zen Buddhism, native American culture and ecology, rather than cars and jazz. As the inspiration for Kerouac's The Dharma Bums he introduced the Buddhist craze to the Beat scene, but his own work, with its reverence for nature and emphasis on peace, contemplation and escape from the city, was a key influence on the hippies. He lived on and off in Japan from 1956 to 1968 and was a focal point of the San Francisco **Human Be-In** of 1966.

Midnight and Fowlers End, which **Anthony Burgess** hailed as "one of the best comic novels of the century." The central character, a fast-talking cinema owner called Sam Yudenov, was, Burgess said, almost the equal of Falstaff. But Kersh sometimes had too many ideas and too vast a cast of bizarre characters to handle.

INFLUENCED BY Edgar Allan Poe; Graham Greene; Julian Maclaren-Ross.

INFLUENCE ON Julian Maclaren-Ross; Harlan Ellison; James Sallis.

ESSENTIAL READING **Night And The City**; **Fowlers End**.

FURTHER READING **The Story Of St Paul**, in which the saint is sent to persecute the Nazarenes by a Roman officer, is evidence of his versatility.

KEN KESEY

Sometimes, Ken had too many great notions

Ken Kesey (1935–2001) is often described as the father of 1960s counterculture – the link between beatniks and hippies. He wrote two classics of American literature– One Flew Over The Cuckoo's Nest and Sometimes A Great Notion – and was one of the first exponents of psychedelic culture, combining music, lights and hallucinogenic drugs in his work.

Kesey was born in La Junta, Colorado to Baptist parents. At high school he set state records at wrestling. Studying creative writing at Stanford in California, he wrote two unpublished novels – End Of Autumn and Zoo – and volunteered for a CIA project at a veteran's hospital, in which he had to report on the effect of certain drugs that included mescaline, psilocybin and LSD. Working as an orderly in the hospital psychiatric ward, Kesey found the inspiration for Cuckoo's Nest. The story centres on RP McMurphy, a charismatic figure who organises resistance against the established order in the psychiatric institution. Narrated by a paranoid native American, the book is strange and hallucinatory, reflecting the damaged mind of the narrator and questioning what is real and who, if anyone, is sane.

With the money from Cuckoo's Nest Kesey bought a house in La Honda, California, where he kept experimenting with drugs and began Sometimes A Great Notion, which he deemed his best work. Long, wild and sprawling, it tells the story of a cantankerous family of Oregon loggers and the relationship between two half-brothers, athletic Hank and Leland, an urbanised intellectual, hinting at a conflict between two aspects of Kesey's personality.

In 1964 Kesey and a bunch of friends calling themselves the **Merry Pranksters** set out across America in a painted bus. With **Neal Cassady** at the wheel and a fridge full of LSD, the trip was an instant legend and marked Kesey's abandonment of the novel for 'living theatre'. In 1966, with LSD now illegal, Kesey was arrested on marijuana charges and fled to Mexico. He spent half of 1967 in jail in California, where he wrote Cut The Motherfuckers Loose (renamed The Jail Journal in 2003), before returning to his family farm where he spent the rest of his life.

Kesey's 1973 book Garage Sale was really a ruse to get his friends into print, though it features a fine introduction by **Arthur Miller** and an intriguing dramatised account of Kesey's Mexican exile. Sailor Song left him, and the world, unimpressed, but Last Go Round – about the first world rodeo championship in 1911 – is good. But his unrealised potential as a novelist is much lamented. Late in life, Kesey described "smokin' holes where my memory used to be."

INFLUENCED BY Faulkner; Burroughs; Kerouac.

INFLUENCE ON The Beatles; Robert Stone; Hunter S. Thompson.

ESSENTIAL READING **Sometimes A Great Notion**.

FURTHER READING **Little Tricker The Squirrel Meets Big Double The Bear**, his fine children's book; Tom Wolfe's **The Electric Kool-Aid Acid Test**.

W.P. KINSELLA

No one writes time-travelling baseball ghost stories like W.P. Shoeless Joe, the novel the movie Field Of Dreams sprang from, feels so quintessentially American that it may come as a minor shock to hear it was the first novel of a farm boy from Alberta.

William Patrick Kinsella (1935–) says he works "with the two great subjects: laughter and tears." His emotional speciality may be regret, but he is the undisputed master of a quirky microgenre he has invented in which baseball, time travel and ghosts all collide. In Shoeless Joe, it creates one of the great feelgood novels. In The Iowa Baseball Confederacy the collision creates something odder. The tale of a man determined to prove the Chicago Cubs played a series of exhibition games in Iowa in the summer of 1908 has a simple premise, but the reader is soon immersed in a richly imagined game that lasts for more than 2,000 innings and, in the course of which, several players die. His baseball fiction has its roots in the game's lore (indeed, literal-minded folks have analysed his facts and found him wanting).

INFLUENCED BY Ray Bradbury; Richard Brautigan. The hero of **Shoeless Joe** is called Ray Kinsella after a character in a Salinger story.

INFLUENCE ON Nobody.

ESSENTIAL READING **Shoeless Joe**; **The Iowa Baseball Confederacy**.

FURTHER READING Kinsella's native American fiction deserves to be better known, especially the award-winning **The Fencepost Chronicles**, with their fine central duo Silas Ermineskin and Frank Fencepost.

DANILO KIS

The Serbian magical realist

Danilo Kis (1935–1989) did not believe experience defines a novelist – even though he had witnessed the massacre of friends in the streets of Novi Sad and seen his father deported to Auschwitz. "Technique is at least half of writing," he said, "beginners think to have experience is enough."

His work reveals a fascination with form and style that was unusual at the time in writers working behind the Iron Curtain; both Bruno Schulz ("Schulz is my God") and Borges remained powerful influences on his stories.

Kis's most famous book is A Tomb For Boris Davidovich, a minor classic, which through seven tales captures the political and social destruction of eastern Europe under Communism. Though publication led to personal threats – forcing him to leave Yugoslavia – he later decided that Tomb was too simply political, preferring The Encyclopedia Of The Dead, a more stylistically varied and fantastical collection of stories about death. His masterpiece is Garden, Ashes, a moving and dream-like Holocaust novel in which Kis attempts to retrieve his memories of a father he barely knew.

Kis was not a prolific writer, producing just four novels and a dozen or so short stories, but, as novelist **Aleksandar Hemon**, says: "If writers were paid by unit of meaningfulness rather than per word or per page, he would have been one of the richest."

Hemon sums up Kis's style brilliantly when he says, "His books are not page-turners, whose pages one keeps turning in search of something to read, but page-gazers – one keeps going back to the same page, compelled to go deeper." And in all his stories Kis brought an eye for the telling, immaculately observed minutiae. Garden, Ashes, for instance, begins not with sweeping generalisations, but with a description given in the minutest detail of a tray bearing cod-liver oil, honey and "ringlike layers of grease".

INFLUENCED BY James Joyce's **Ulysses**; Nabokov; Borges; Bruno Schulz.
INFLUENCE ON Alexsandar Hemon.
ESSENTIAL READING **Garden, Ashes**; **A Tomb For Boris Davidovich**.
FURTHER READING **The Encyclopedia Of The Dead**.

The pleasures and perils of taking Kant too seriously

Despite the overriding pessimism of his writings, **Heinrich von Kleist** (1777–1811) was a product of the Enlightenment, albeit one who turned spectacularly against it. Born into a Prussian military family, he abandoned a career in the army in 1799 and enrolled at the University of Frankfurt. Already questioning man's ability to shape his own destiny, his (mis)reading of **Kant**'s Critique Of Pure Reason shook him by suggesting that the limitations of knowledge made truth unattainable. The crisis this provoked unleashed his artistic imagination, but also exacerbated a profoundly unstable personality.

From then on, Kleist's life was a series of restless wanderings: to Paris with his sister **Ulrike**; six months on an island in Switzerland; a stay with veteran author **Christopher Wieland**. In 1803 he tried joining **Napoleon**'s army; the following year saw a spell in the Prussian civil service; while on a trip to Dresden in 1807 he was imprisoned by the French as a spy. At this point Kleist was an established

TALES FROM THE GULAG

Arguably the most troubling literary genre to emerge in the last 100 years – because of what it says about man's inhumanity to man – is the stream of books written by inmates of gulags and concentration camps. Space stops us mentioning all the fine works in this genre, but here are a few of the most significant.

Dostoevsky probably got there first with his novel The House Of The Dead, a fictionalised account of four years hard labour in Siberia, written in the 1860s. **Aleksandr Solzhenitsyn** would, like Dostoevsky, turn his Siberian servitude into fiction with One Day In The Life Of Ivan Denisovich and the much under-rated The First Circle. **Varlam Shalamov**'s Kolyma Tales covers comparable experiences in sparser prose. Solzhenitsyn's work is echoed by **Kang Chol-Wan** in The Aquariums Of

IF THIS IS A MAN
THE TRUCE
PRIMO LEVI

Pyongyang, his account of North Korea's gulags, and **Armando Valladares**'s Against All Hope, a terrible tale of life in Castro's gulags. **Slavomir Rawicz**'s The Long Walk tells how he and six other men escaped from Siberia and walked across Russia to India to escape.

Nazi concentration camps have created a vast amount of literature. **Primo Levi**'s If This Is A Man and The Truce are moving, painfully observed recollections and meditations, made even more agonising by the author's subsequent suicide.

Elie Wiesel's Night, a compressed (the Yiddish original was 900 pages long), lightly fictionalised book of his life in a death camp, is a work of lucid anguish. For painful honesty, it's hard to beat The Cap by **Roman Frister**, which confronts us with the question: what would you do to survive?

153

author, and on his release co-founded a short-lived journal, followed, a few years later, by a newspaper **Berliner Abendblätter**. The failure of these projects, along with his estrangement from **Goethe**, and the success of Napoleon – whom he now despised – deepened his gloom. On a November morning in 1811, he and his friend **Henriette Vogel** (a married woman with a terminal illness) made their way to Lake Wansee, where Kleist first shot her and then himself.

> "The truth of the matter is there was no help for me here on earth. May heaven grant you a death that half-equals mine in joy"
>
> Heinrich von Kleist bids his sister a fond farewell

Kleist wrote while war convulsed Europe, and in all eight of his stories acts of violence – domestic or on a grand scale – play a vital role. Only two have contemporary settings, while the others are derived from historical chronicles as if to impart veracity to the bizarre sequences of events described. This objectivity is reinforced by a detached tone that led **Kafka** to claim Kleist as one of his "blood-relations". And, as with Kafka, the absurd and a sense of alienation are central to Kleist's vision: in The Marquise Of O a highly respectable widow finds herself inexplicably pregnant; in Michael Kohlaas a successful horse dealer is forced to wage war to obtain justice; while in The Earthquake In Chile a young man awaiting execution is liberated when an earthquake destroys the prison where he is held, only to be killed at the hands of an angry mob.

Kleist's characters battle alone with the outrages of fortune: some, usually the females, do so with stoical resolve; others, like the embittered philanthropist in The Foundling, with rage. Even in stories that end happily (The Marquise Of O and The Duel), there is a nagging sense that a nightmare has only temporarily abated.

INFLUENCED BY Immanuel Kant; Jean-Jacques Rousseau.

INFLUENCE ON Kafka; Philip Pullman.

ESSENTIAL READING Kleist's eight short stories are all available in an excellent Penguin Classics translation by David Luke and Nigel Reeves.

FURTHER READING The stories of Kleist's contemporary E.T.A. Hoffmann offer an even weirder assault on rationalism.

TADEUSZ KONWICKI

A dandified Polish Solzhenitsyn with attitude

"A sweltering morning and wonderful news: classes had been cancelled due to the outbreak of war." **Tadeusz Konwicki** (1926–) has always had his own take on life and the tragedies of 20th-century history as they afflicted his homeland,

Konwicki doesn't care if he bores you

Poland. He once called himself a "hideous hybrid formed at the boundary of two worlds" – Poland and Russia. The perverse pride in that phrase explains much of what makes Konwicki so compelling – and downright annoying – as a novelist.

Born in Wilno (then a Polish city, now Vilnius, the capital of Lithuania), Konwicki has offered a distorted mirror to Polish society and its suffering in his 20 novels. He writes in cycles, the novels devoted to the landscape around Vilnius and his childhood there are especially beautiful. He has also published a series of 'lying' journals, featuring witty poisonous diary entries and mini-essays that can be taken as fiction or fact; many of the boasts, notably his admission that he doesn't care if he bores his readers, ring true.

155

In three of this classic books – A Dreambook For Our Time, A Minor Apocalypse and The Polish Complex – he is trapped (in a hospital bed; on a foolish errand of political protest; in a Christmas shopping queue), surrounded by men and women (the women often possess, as he puts it, breasts that would be unfashionable west of Poland), who all demand some response (sexual, emotional, intellectual) from him. His predicament is often the hook for extended flashbacks on the youth of the hero/novelist – in Konwicki, they're usually synonymous.

Read in succession, the bitter cacophony of this chorus of characters can grate, and women may be enraged by the frequency with which beautiful females are depicted as forces of nature, inexorably drawn to his passive, intellectual, Casanova persona. But then Konwicki, no fan of feminism, would claim this is true: that he has been, as a character tells him in his journal, "Lucky with women, unlucky in everything else."

His rambling, sardonic, poetic yet political novels are sharply observed and often surprisingly funny. Read A Minor Apocalypse, which, for Konwicki, has surprising narrative tension, and it is hard not to be haunted by the image of the hero wandering around decrepit Communist Warsaw with a can of petrol debating whether to set fire to it – and himself. The predicament is terribly

Konwickian. This is an author who says, "When I have trouble getting to sleep, I like to think of my funeral."

INFLUENCED BY Kafka; Poland's national poet Adam Mickiewicz; Stalin and Hitler, whose decisions shaped the life his novels dwell on.

INFLUENCE ON Nobody: too famous in Poland – any homage would look like imitation – and too obscure in the West to be influential.

ESSENTIAL READING **A Minor Apocalypse**; **The Polish Complex**.

FURTHER READING **A Dreambook For Our Time**; **Moonrise Moonset**, a refreshingly bitter, and funny, polemical journal.

JERZY KOSINSKI

Charlatan or genius? The mystery endures

Jerzy Kosinski (1933–1991) may have been an astonishing writer or world-class fraud, either way he set the literary world alight. His closest friends were aware of his mischievous love of deception, but it was the rich and powerful who Kosinski liked to deceive and who eventually turned against their 'court jester', even though, as a friend noted, "They were so eager to be entertained and were so confident of their superiority they deserved to be played for fools."

Born into a Jewish family in Lodz, Poland, by the time Kosinski was six he had learned the dangers of admitting who you really are. He survived the Nazi occupation – his parents were wealthy enough to ensure he was given fake Catholic documentation – but had other problems: an accident when he was nine left him mute until he was 14.

After such troubles, Kosinski decided to determine his own fate. An elaborate hoax ensured he was invited to attend Columbia University. His marriage to steel heiress **Mary Hayward Weir** gave him access to America's wealthiest socialites. Then, in 1965, came The Painted Bird, Kosinski's endearing tale of a child learning to survive in Nazi-occupied Poland. The novel marked the pinnacle of a career that also included Being There, in which the enigmatic Chauncey Gardiner becomes a presidential advisor, media icon and tycoon, and The Devil Tree, about an amoral steel tycoon's travels to Africa.

After The Devil Tree was published in 1973, rumours began circulating that Kosinski's novels were merely English translations of works unknown outside Poland. An article in **The Village Voice** cited as evidence the fact that his novels were wildly different from each other and that his English wasn't good enough to be able to write such stories. But one of Kosinski's editors supported the author, saying he only ever edited Kosinski's words, "no more, no less."

The rumours were enough to destroy Kosinski's spirit. He initially responded in 1988 with The Hermit Of 69th Street, inserting footnotes for almost every term used. But the rumours continued and Kosinski threw in the towel on 3 May 1991, his suicide note reading, "I am going to put myself to sleep now for a bit longer than usual."

INFLUENCED BY Hard to say, given the controversy.

INFLUENCE ON **Being There** has influenced the light political fiction of Christopher Buckley.

ESSENTIAL READING Reportedly written in reaction to John Lennon's death, **Pinball** focuses on a fan's search for the world's most popular rock star who no one has seen or heard performing. Also **The Painted Bird**.

FURTHER READING James Park Sloan's entertaining biography.

JAAN KROSS

"My best writing was done under the constraints of censorship"

If you had lived a life like **Jaan Kross** (1920–), ending up as, poet **Fiona Sampson** says, "heir to the great Russo-European 19th-century novelists" was probably inevitable. The Estonian writer was left unscathed by the brief, savage Soviet occupation of his country in 1940, avoided fighting for the Nazis only by swallowing pills and brandy to make his thyroid gland swell up, was sent to the gulags for eight years when the Soviets returned and, after being told his poetry was "insufficiently Bolshevik", began writing historical novels.

His masterpiece The Czar's Madman was derived from the true tale of a 19th-century Baltic aristocrat who was jailed, also for eight years, for sending **Tsar Alexander** his proposals for constitutional reform. Kross wrote the novel under the Soviet regime, the book's parallels between two systems of oppression and the perils of protest too subtle for the censors to spot.

His style can be off-putting. **Doris Lessing** notes, "He's not in the least sensationalist and that makes him a little old fashioned for today's tastes, but he's a great writer in the grand old style." At times, notably in Treading Air, which touches on Estonia's wartime agonies, the rhetoric and the absence of sensationalism can be frustrating.

Kross takes his history so seriously that he got into public dispute over whether one of his characters, a mayor of Tallinn in the 1500s, was an ethnic Estonian. But he is no dyed-in-the-wool

157

"Many of the Russians I met in the gulag, even some of the guards, would have given me their last piece of bread"

Jaan Kross generously recalls his suffering

nationalist. Don't be put off by the fact that, in his homeland, he is almost a national monument. If only all national monuments were this pertinent and generous.

INFLUENCED BY Walter Scott; Thomas Mann; Lewis Carroll.

INFLUENCE ON Estonian prose – in a country whose language seemed threatened by extinction, he has reinvented it.

ESSENTIAL READING **The Czar's Madman**.

FURTHER READING **Four Monologues On St George**, the life of 15th-century Estonian artist Michel Sittow, court painter to Queen Isabella of Spain.

MILAN KUNDERA

Forget the titles, he's not that keen on lightness, laughter or forgetting

To the general public **Milan Kundera** (1929–) may be the bloke who wrote the book for that kinky movie (he hated it) The Unbearable Lightness Of Being. Critics have tended to focus on the politics. Yet if one thing typifies a Kundera novel it's not sex or meditations on political perfidy, it's the tone: sad, playful, rueful, amused, philosophical, cynical, indignant, yet pessimistic.

Although he exploded into Western literary consciousness in the 1980s with The Book Of Laughter And Forgetting and Lightness Of Being, Kundera had been writing novels in his native Czechoslovakia since the 1960s. He joined the Czech Communist party in 1948, wrote some poems glorifying Stalin that were later used against him, was booted out for individualistic tendencies and has since written about the fallacies, deceptions and irrationality of Stalinism with the insight and bitterness of a betrayed lover. Yet many of his themes – memory, deception, our need to simplify everything – had nothing to do with the nature of the regime that both nurtured and persecuted him.

You don't need to agree with Kundera politically to appreciate such tour de forces as Laughter And Forgetting or, for an early novel in a savage, satirical vein, The Joke. He delights in paradoxical tales, unexpected consequences and conflicting perceptions – such as the well-observed account of a threesome in Laughter And Forgetting in which the man feels like a master while the women regard him as an annoying irrelevance. His famous interview with **Philip Roth** starts off in this vein. Asked if he thinks the world will end soon, Kundera observes that such a fear is as old as mankind. "So then we have nothing to worry about," says Roth. "On the contrary," replies Kundera. "If a fear has been present in the human mind for ages, there must be something to it."

Kundera was at his most accomplished from 1965, when The Joke was published, to 1982, when Lightness Of Being was acclaimed. Some Czechs have accused him of air-brushing his past, to minimise his years as a young Stalinist.

The erotic interludes in his novels have begun, one reviewer complained, to feel "banal and tawdry" and his philosophising, so alluring in Lightness Of Being, can overwhelm later novels like Immortality. But Kundera is a master, albeit one whose style has, since, led too many bad novelists astray.

INFLUENCED BY In 1989 Kundera declared: "There are four great novelists: Kafka, [Hermann] Broch, [Robert] Musil, [Witold] Gombrowicz.

INFLUENCE ON Ivan Klima, a more politicised Czech novelist; Hungarian Peter Nadas.

ESSENTIAL READING **The Book Of Laughter And Forgetting**.

FURTHER READING **The Joke**; **The Unbearable Lightness Of Being**.

ANDREY KURKOV

"Everything that is absurd, I take it to the next level of absurdity"

Of all the writers to have recently emerged from the former Soviet Union, few are as dark or as funny as **Andrey Kurkov** (1961–). Death And The Penguin, published in translation in 2001, was an immediate success across Europe –

WHAT JOSEPH STALIN DID FOR FICTION

It might disgust **Joseph Stalin** to know this, but his conquest of eastern Europe has produced some of the 20th-century's finest fiction.

Any list of the great novels 'inspired' by this nightmare would have to include Albanian novelist **Ismail Kadare**'s The Palace Of Dreams, in which an all-embracing dictatorship monitors even its subjects' unconscious lives.

Czech writer **Josef Skvorecky** is more grounded in realism, but his novel The Cowards captures perfectly the moment when eastern Europe was about to swap one tyranny for another, while his Miss Silver's Past is a fine book and bitter reflection of life under the dead hand of Communism.

The problem for Romanian authors was that real life under **Ceaucescu** felt like a collaborative fiction between

Kafka and **Gabriel García Márquez**. But **Augustin Buzura**'s Refuges works both as as protest and as a novel.

In Ukraine, **Volodymyr Dibrova** offers a witty, exhilarating take on Communism's heyday with his story Peltse, available in Writings From An Unbound Europe, using a spaghetti western-style narrative pace to tell his story of the rise, corruption, disgrace and death of its ruling cadre.

The complexities of life during and after Communism as a writer are illustrated by the trials of **Christa Wolf**. She wrote the first great novel to emerge from the German Democratic Republic, The Quest For Christa T. After the fall of Communism, Wolf was accused of informing for the Stasi and defended herself. For all the debate, her novel is well worth reading.

Death and
the Penguin
Andrey Kurkov

introducing Misha the depressive penguin, Viktor the reluctant obituarist whose subjects only die after he's written about them and an army of Ukrainian gangsters and unashamedly corrupt politicians.

Kurkov was born in what is now St Petersburg. Family life centred around his immense cactus collection (he had 1,500 by the time he was seven) and his three hamsters. Two died horribly and his first piece of writing was a poem describing the solitude of the one that remained.

Kurkov trained as a Japanese translator and narrowly avoided a spell of military service in the Russian Far East by working as a warder in an Odessa prison. Later he operated a disinfection machine in a hospital and worked as a film cameraman, writing in his spare time. For 15 years he was on the KGB blacklist, his friends were routinely questioned and his writing was banned. Kurkov describes his work at this time as "more surreal than satirical", but the fact that it was set in the USSR made it subversive. He smuggled his manuscripts to publishers abroad – he received a magnificent 500 rejection letters – and gave readings to underground societies, chess clubs and weddings. His first book was finally published in Kiev two weeks before the end of Communism.

Since 1991 Kurkov has published ten novels in Ukraine and four children's books about the adventures of a baby vacuum cleaner named Gosha. Death And The Penguin – his seventh novel and the first to be translated – is a comic thriller reflecting on the shattered world left behind in the wake of Communism. A lonely would-be writer Viktor Zolotaryov adopts a penguin from Kiev zoo and the two of them live together in a small flat, "two complementary lonelinesses". Viktor begins to write obituaries and the household is joined by Nina and Sonya, six-year-old daughter of a man referred to as Misha-non-penguin. The penguin, Misha, is a fine creation – a superb comic character whose mute yearning echoes Viktor's post-Soviet predicament perfectly.

With Death And The Penguin Kurkov became the only Ukrainian writer in general translation. He has capitalised on his success with a series of novels on a similar theme. The Case Of The General's Thumb is essentially an espionage thriller, but with the same deadpan style and undertow of satire and surrealism as its predecessor.

Penguin Lost is a sequel to Death And The Penguin, although the two books were once a single manuscript. Misha is missing from the outset, so Viktor sets out to find him. The satire is bleak and, despite some fine comic moments, unrelieved by the first book's delicate absurdism. The forthcoming A Matter Of

Death And Life – in which a man commissions his own murder, changes his mind but finds the murderer as committed as ever – is tipped as a return to form.

INFLUENCED BY Andrey Platonov; Daniel Charms; Konstantin Vaginov.

INFLUENCE ON Too little.

ESSENTIAL READING **Death And The Penguin**.

FURTHER READING **The Tower**, the avant-garde classic by Konstantin Vaginov, is available free at websher.net/spub/twr.html.

GAVIN LAMBERT

The dream-factory novelist

Gavin Lambert (1923–) may not have written the best Hollywood novel – a literary title as heavily disputed as any boxing title – but he is the best Hollywood novelist. Yet, sadly, he has largely given up the novel to write compelling biographies of Hollywood personalities, from **Natalie Wood** to **Nazimova**, the bisexual silent-movie legend and godmother to **Nancy Reagan**.

Born in London, Lambert seemed destined for showbiz after producing, with **Lindsay Anderson**, a school musical that the headmaster denounced as disgusting. In photographs he appears low-key, slightly aloof, even conservative, yet he evaded the threat of conscription in World War II by reporting for duty with his eyelids painted gold.

161

After editing the film magazine **Sight And Sound**, Lambert did the inevitable and moved to Hollywood where he became assistant to, and part-time lover of, director **Nicholas Ray** and, in 1954, published a remarkable volume of seven linked stories set on Hollywood's fringes called The Slide Area. The title, from the signs in Hollywood's Pacific Palisades area where the land does slide into the sea, captures the ebb and flow of Hollywood wannabes, in overlapping stories that recall **Christopher Isherwood**'s Berlin books. Isherwood called the tales "the most truthful stories about the film world and its suburbia I ever read."

Inside Daisy Clover
Gavin Lambert

– the happiest, saddest, sexiest Hollywood novel of all!

Lambert's best-known work is Inside Daisy Clover, a sexy, readable diary of an up-and-coming actress, filmed, and scripted by Lambert, with Natalie Wood in the title role. His other novels include The Goodbye People and Running Time. Not easy to find now, they are a fine achievement.

Armistead Maupin noted: "Decades before it was fashionable, Lambert expertly wove characters of every sexual stripe into his lustrous tapestries of Southern Californian life. His elegant stripped-down prose caught the last gasp of Old Hollywood in a way that has yet to be rivalled."

INFLUENCED BY Christopher Isherwood; F. Scott Fitzgerald.

INFLUENCE ON Armistead Maupin.

ESSENTIAL READING **The Slide Area**; **Inside Daisy Clover**.

FURTHER READING **The Goodbye People** is a decent, Generation X tale written when the world was still only on Generation U.

URSULA K. LE GUIN

Magical, versatile, Taoist, graceful and fiendishly hard to pigeonhole

Long before Harry Potter and Hogwarts there was another young wizard and another school where the magic arts were taught. And that's where any resemblance between the works of **J.K. Rowling** and the Earthsea novels of **Ursula K. Le Guin** (1929–) begins and ends.

162 Born Ursula Kroeber in California, Le Guin's work defies pigeonholing. The first Earthsea books, a self-contained trilogy written in the late 1960s, are fantasies for juveniles. Her award-winning Ekumen series is compelling adult sci-fi, though one critic called them "philosophy disguised as science fiction". To which you have to add general fiction, short stories, children's books, poetry and a translation of the Tao Te Ching. Now in her seventies, Le Guin continues to write with what **Margaret Atwood** calls "graceful prose, carefully thought-out premises, psychological insight and intelligent perception".

A Wizard Of Earthsea was first published in 1968, the sequels The Tombs Of Atuan and The Farthest Shore soon followed. They've been compared to **Tolkien**'s The Lord Of The Rings and **C.S. Lewis**'s Chronicles Of Narnia, but the differences are as great as the similarities. In the first book her hero is a teenage goatherd and the great battle he has to fight is with himself.

The science never gets in the way of the fiction, and the fantasy never clashes with reality in Le Guin's books. In The Left Hand Of Darkness she created a planet in perpetual winter with androgynous people. In some ways an old-fashioned romance, it was turned down by one publisher as "so endlessly complicated" and "hopelessly bogged down" as to be "eventually, unreadable". It won the Hugo and Nebulae science-fiction awards in 1969.

Le Guin explored themes of reaching across barriers in her early Ekumen works and brought the anti-war and sexual politics of the late 1960s and early 1970s into her fiction in The Dispossessed: An Ambiguous Utopia, which had as its premise a planet of capitalists with a satellite deliberately populated by an anarchist breakaway movement. Two worlds, one people. Ying and Yang meets **Jung**.

Increasingly, though, it has been to Taoism rather than Jung that Le Guin has turned, and to the feminine voice. Eighteen years after The Farthest Shore, she returned to Earthsea with Tehanu, picking up her characters and looking at them from an older, female perspective. In 2001 she followed that with The Other Wind and a collection of short stories, Tales From Earthsea.

Her Ekumen series had apparently come to an end with 1976's The Word For World Is Forest, but Le Guin brought it back to life with The Telling in 2000. Both books have a political edge; the former influenced by the Vietnam war, the second by Maoist China's crushing of the Taoist religion and traditions. A collection of short stories The Birthday Of The World explored other looks at those Ekumen worlds. We go inside a brothel on the androgynous planet Winter, for example. It's hard to imagine C.S. Lewis or J.R.R. Tolkien taking you there.

INFLUENCED BY Taoism; Carl Jung; J.R.R. Tolkien; feminism; Greek myths.
INFLUENCE ON Too little.
ESSENTIAL READING **The Left Hand Of Darkness**; **The Dispossessed**.
FURTHER READING **The Word For World Is Forest**.

ELMORE LEONARD

A novelist with an eye for the cinematic and an ear for dialogue

"Chili Palmer's a talker," Nick said. "That's what he does, he talks. You should have hit him in the mouth." The fast-talking Chili is the star of Get Shorty and its sequel Be Cool. He's a Mob loan shark-turned-movie producer – just one of a host of fast-talking, low-life characters affectionately drawn by **Elmore Leonard** (1925–) in his crime novels. Leonard is a master of dialogue. His rules of writing advise would-be authors to: "leave out the part that readers tend to skip… the hooptedoodle," adding, "I'll bet you don't skip the dialogue."

His novels, whose plots serve as a vehicle for a galaxy of compelling schemers and big and small-time crooks, cops and lawmen who get along on both sides of the law, read like movies.

Born in New Orleans, Leonard moved to Detroit aged eight, where his father was a car-industry executive. After graduating from a Jesuit high school he was sent to the Pacific, but his eyesight kept him from combat and he served as a store man. After the war Leonard majored in English at the University of Detroit, married and took his first job in an ad agency. But penning commercials for cars

CULT FICTION

> "To me, the good guy is the one who's natural. He's not playing a role. The bad guys play roles, wanting to be somebody else"
>
> Elmore Leonard sorts out virtue and vice in fiction

wasn't fulfilling and his desire to be a published writer – and support his five children – drove him to write for two hours before work every morning.

Trail Of The Apache, his first published story, appeared in **Argosy** magazine in 1951. He continued with the western genre and his early novels include 3:10 To Yuma and Hombre, which were made into films. His first crime novel The Big Bounce was finally published in 1969 after being rejected 84 times, followed by Valdez Is Coming, another western that became a movie. The late 1960s and early 1970s were a lean period for Leonard, who got divorced, realised he had a drink problem and wrote educational scripts to bring in the money.

In the 1980s he developed a loyal cult following with the novels City Primeval, Stick, LaBrava, Glitz and Freaky Deaky. Hollywood snapped up Stick and Fifty-Two Pick-Up, but both films failed. On the advice of his second wife Joan, Leonard wrote stronger female characters. Jackie Burke, the flight attendant in Rum Punch who became Jackie Brown – and black – in the **Quentin Tarantino** film, is a powerful heroine with all the qualities of a classic Leonard character. Struggling to survive, she successfully scams the bad guys and the FBI out of money with the help of an ageing bondsman.

In 1984 Leonard's appeal was acknowledged in the USA when he made the cover of **Newsweek** and was dubbed the 'Dickens of Detroit'. But it wasn't until the 1990s that films capturing Leonard's style brought him global recognition. **Barry Sonnenfeld**'s Get Shorty was followed by Tarantino's Jackie Brown in 1997 and **Steven Soderbergh**'s Out Of Sight in 1998. Some of Leonard's ambitious later novels extend the range of settings to explore historical events and social conscience. Cuba Libre is a kind of western set during the Spanish-American War, while Pagan Babies features a fake American priest in Rwanda during the genocide.

The world Leonard shows us is so convincing it is instantly understandable. The reader is helpless to resist the apparently effortless draw of his people. That's probably because Leonard loves them too: "I'm writing about the kinds of people that interest me the most, savvy people, people who have a hustle going."

INFLUENCED BY Hemingway.

INFLUENCE ON Martin Amis is a great fan; Joseph Wambaugh.

ESSENTIAL READING **Get Shorty**; **Rum Punch**.

FURTHER READING **Maximum Bob**; **Freaky Deaky**.

MARK LEYNER

The titles are so good, the novels can't keep up

I Smell Esther Williams And Other Stories, Tooth Imprints On A Corn Dog, The Tetherballs Of Bougainville… The titles say a lot about what makes **Mark Leyner** (1956–) so prized, yet so specialist. He is probably the funniest experimental novelist writing fiction today, but the comic conceits tumble out of him so fast that even an admiring has reservations, one saying he is, "tremendously entertaining in small doses, but exhausting in the long haul."

The book that made him an undergraduate cult was My Cousin, My Gastroenterologist which, like many of his books, reads like the result of an experiment involving the literary genes of **Kurt Vonnegut** and **Woody Allen**. He is usually a character in his novels and sent up his own success in Et Tu, Babe, telling readers "My life has been one long ultraviolent hyperkinetic nightmare."

Some critics say he hasn't mastered the novel's longer form, that his appetite for gags and one-liners suggest he would be an immensely gifted comic poet. The closest he has come to what Leyner himself calls a "bona-fide novel" is The Tetherballs Of Bougainville, which has an intricate Chinese puzzle quality to it and uses many different tones and voices: a corporate brochure, the **New York Times** Home issue… Told once by an interviewer, "It's like a concept from poststructuralist literary criticism", Leyner replied: "Thank you, don't ever say that to me again."

INFLUENCED BY Jean-Luc Godard; Pynchon; David Foster Wallace.

INFLUENCE ON Nobody yet.

ESSENTIAL READING **The Tetherballs Of Bougainville**.

FURTHER READING **My Cousin, My Gastroenterologist**.

H.P. LOVECRAFT

Altogether ooky

New England's dreamer of dark, forbidden nightmares, **Howard Phillips Lovecraft** (1890–1937) was brought up in Rhode Island by his mother, a brace of aunts and a grandfather after his father was edged into a hospital, where he died of syphilis. Young Howard showed a prodigious interest in literature, writing tales at the age of six, encouraged by his grandfather, who told the boy horror stories of his own.

A sickly child, a nervous breakdown stymied his further education. He grew up a sensitive young man, prone to nightmares (that he incorporated into his work), who conjured up worlds of resonant eerie horror. His decidedly British style, purposely peppered with anachronistic phraseology and adjectives, has a ponderous hypnotic rhythm of unavoidable evil about it. His early works, heavily influenced by fantasy writer **Lord Dunsany**, showed little of the horrors that were to become his trademark, and it wasn't until he fell under the darker spells of **Edgar Allan Poe** and more importantly **Arthur Machen** that Lovecraft's inner fears of ancient evil surfaced in his fiction.

Lovecraft was inspired by Machen to invite his readers into dark new worlds, inventing the Cthulhu Mythos, a crew of ancient alien extra-dimensional deities that ruled the Earth before the coming of man. A key part of this mythos was The Necronomicon (book of dead names) that drove its owners to madness or worse. This new, darker turn was first seen in Dagon and The Tomb published in 1917. These stories attracted such favourable response and thoughtful inquiry from readers that Lovecraft soon found himself embarking on a lifelong sea of correspondence. But he was never able to make a good living as an author.

Depressed by this, and by the suicide of his friend **Robert E. Howard** (author of Conan The Barbarian), he succumbed quickly to the malnutrition and cancer of the intestine with which he was diagnosed, dying in 1937. Virtually ignored in his lifetime, he is now considered one of the giants by devotees of the weird in horror and science fiction.

166 INFLUENCED BY Arthur Machen; Edgar Allen Poe; Lord Dunsany.

INFLUENCE ON Clive Barker; Clark Ashton Smith; August Derleth; Neil Gaiman; Alan Moore; Brian Lumley; Robert Bloch; Algernon Blackwood.

ESSENTIAL READING **The Dunwich Horror**.

FURTHER READING **Others At The Mountains Of Madness**; Frank Belknap Long's **Howard Phillips Lovecraft: Dreamer On The Night Side**.

MALCOLM LOWRY

"The sight of that old bastard makes me happy for days. No bloody fooling"

This friend's tribute offers a useful corrective to the conventional stereotype of **Malcolm Lowry** (1909–1957). Yes, he spent much of his life drunk, depressed, suicidal even, convinced he had failed as a novelist. But his life, when it wasn't harrowing or heartbreaking, could be hilarious. Writing his own epitaph, he noted: "He lived nightly and drunk daily/And died playing the ukulele."

Alcoholism stalked Lowry all his adult life. English respectability stifled him and he escaped to become a deckhand, roaming across Europe and America. But it was Mexico, and the symbolic, magical, inspiring, yet sinister quality of its landscape, that inspired his great novel Under The Volcano, in which a doomed consul drinks to forget the modern world and his own failure.

The setting is crucial because, as **Denis Donoghue** noted in **The New York**

Review Of Books, "Lowry's characters are mere functions of himself"; the less of Lowry that is in them, the less convincing they are. Forget character and Under The Volcano works on many levels – political, religious, even Kabbalistic. The best scenes are extraordinarily rich in their sensations, possibly because the author found it hard to distinguish between one sensation and another.

Nothing else Lowry did came close to that novel's quality. His first book Ultramarine has only found favour with completists, while Dark Is The Grave Wherein My Friend Is Laid was left unfinished. Under The Volcano was supposed to be the heart of a seven-novel sequence, but Lowry's soul gave out before he could finish it. He was dogged by extraordinary bad luck, especially in the form of fires and lightning. He taunted **Paul Fitte**, a friend at Cambridge, into killing himself, an act that haunted him until he died of an overdose of sleeping pills, deliberate or accidental, on Fitte's birthday. The very title of Lowry's unfinished novel seems to hark back to this tragedy.

The author's own fate was no surprise. Studying his idol **Herman Melville** he had noted: "His failure fascinated me and it seems to me from an early age I determined to emulate it."

INFLUENCED BY Dante; Herman Melville; the Norwegian novelist Nordahl Reid; the poet Conrad Aiken; Joseph Conrad; James Joyce.

INFLUENCE ON Graham Greene; Elias Canetti; Borges; Umberto Eco.

ESSENTIAL READING **Under The Volcano**.

FURTHER READING The stories in **Hear Us O Lord From Heaven Thy Dwelling Place** are uneven, but **Through The Panama** is among the triumphs.

ARTHUR MACHEN

The horror, the horror and… the beauty

Arthur Machen (1863–1947) was born **Arthur Llewelyn Jones**, the only child of a Welsh clergyman in Carleon-on-Usk, Wales. He grew up to become the British master of fantasy and horror fiction. Though he moved to London in 1880, while still a young man, he was inspired as a writer by his childhood in Gwent.

He took several semi-literary jobs (book cataloguer, teacher, translator of **Casanova**'s memoirs) until his interest in the occult led him to join the **Order of the Golden Dawn** – a group involved in magic and theosophy – and influenced him to write The Great God Pan, The Inmost Light.

In this beautifully convoluted tale, published in 1894, a woman's mind is torn apart in a disastrous ceremonial that attempts to conjure up the ancient Greek god of nature. Years later London society is unsettled by the arrival of a mysterious woman without a past, who turns the heads and quickens the hearts of the young toffs with whom she becomes acquainted but is gradually revealed as a monster.

The Great God Pan was published with a cover by **Aubrey Beardsley** and, though Machen never considered himself part of the in-crowd, he was immediately associated with the other grand decadents of the 1890s.

He became known as a writer of ghost stories or works of horror, an inaccuracy that persists today. But it gave him the funds and time to write a semi-biographical account of his early life, The Hill Of Dreams, which is his greatest work possibly because his main characters are often barely disguised versions of himself. His characters meet beauty as often as terror, but Machen is rather good at the terror. In his subtle masterpiece The White People, elegantly presented as a girl's diary, the young protagonist begins writing down the innocent tales told to her by her nurse, before becoming trapped in a world of magic.

His legend grew in World War I when, to his annoyance, the plot of his short story The Bowmen inspired the Angel of Mons myth, where angels are reputed to have appeared to soldiers. Confusion over whether the tale pre-dates the legend of the angels continues to this day. He saw the story as little more than a pot-boiler but it was his only financially successful publication.

168

INFLUENCED BY Aleister Crowley.

INFLUENCE ON H.P. Lovecraft; August Derleth; John Betjeman.

ESSENTIAL READING **The Hall Of Dreams**; **The Great God Pan**; **The White People**.

FURTHER READING **The Bowmen**.

COLIN MacINNES

He wasn't an absolute beginner at all, in the literary sense

Colin MacInnes's literary output was far from prolific, yet his London-based trilogy of novels still resonate today. The great-grandson of pre-Raphaelite painter **Sir Edward Burne-Jones** and son of novelist **Angela Thirkell**, London-born MacInnes (1914–1976) seemed destined to shine in the arts. Returning from Australia, where his mother had taken him to live after her second marriage, he worked in business, studied art, served in the British intelligence corps in World War II and briefly wrote scripts for BBC radio. He soon knew he wanted to write but, as a homosexual drawn to the inner-city lights, knew he didn't want to pen genteel stories of English country life like his mother.

The 1950s, although they didn't swing quite as fast as the 1960s, were not a bad time to write about British youth culture, and MacInnes ensured he was in the thick of it, soaking up the bohemian atmosphere of Soho and multi-cultural Notting Hill. His fiction was exciting; it had a beat, but it also had a conscience, MacInnes being drawn to those who, like himself, were outsiders politically, racially or sexually. Not content with sharing his opinions with the denizens of Frith Street pubs, he gave voice to his concerns in magazines such as **Encounter**.

His London trilogy was influenced by his journalism. In City Of Spades, Absolute Beginners and Mr Love And Justice, MacInnes used fiction to show how Britain was changing and how attitudes needed changing. Absolute Beginners, thanks to **Julien Temple**'s film version, is the most famous and probably the best of the three. Combining jazz with the bright lights of the big city and a social commentary on race relations in Britain, the novel impresses not with its plot but with its characters and as a social, almost sociological, chronicle, with the narrator noting, "I don't understand my country anymore."

MacInnes kept writing after his London trilogy. His 1971 novel Three Years To Play marks a distinct change in style, Elizabethan London replacing the capital of the 1950s, but it is still worth a look.

INFLUENCED BY Life; Samuel Selvon.

INFLUENCE ON Barking balladeer Billy Bragg; Paul Weller's Style Council.

ESSENTIAL READING **The London Trilogy**.

FURTHER READING **Out Of The Way**, his collection of essays laying down his thoughts on race, the class system and crime.

JULIAN MACLAREN-ROSS

International man of mystery, Soho chronicler

The fog of scandal and intrigue that surrounded **Julian Maclaren-Ross** (1912–1964)was so great that his long lost son, Alex, asked the author's biographer **Paul Willetts**: "He wasn't a child molester, was he?" (He wasn't.)

If he is remembered at all today it is as the model for X. Trapnel, the famed, doomed writer "theatrically projected" from Maclaren-Ross's persona by **Anthony Powell** for his series A Dance To The Music Of Time. Yet Maclaren-Ross wrote one hilarious novel, Of Love And Hunger, a few fine short stories and a great account of bohemian London in the war years, Memoirs Of The Forties, which he had half-finished when he died of a heart attack: a victim of years in which his daily routine involved 11 hours in a pub, followed by a late meal, followed by writing.

Some of the difficulties Maclaren-Ross presents are summed up admirably in his memoir The Weeping And The Laughter; a book that takes 230 pages to relate the first ten years of the author's life. After declaring "I sometimes wish my early days could have been more exciting," his next sentence is: "My father had been born in Havana, as a baby he had been surrounded by tarantulas and vampire bats; my mother's birthplace was Calcutta: the sight of a rogue elephant trampling one of her brothers to death being a highlight of her childhood and later she lived on an island in the Azores dominated by a smoking volcano."

The definitive example of a writer who failed – through alcohol, debts and womanising – to fulfil his early promise, Maclaren-Ross's great gift to posterity has been his memoirs of London bohemia, in which the likes of **Graham Greene**, **Cyril Connolly** and **Dylan Thomas** make delightful cameo appearances. The encounter with Greene, in which Maclaren-Ross points out that the great author has based an entire film review on the mishearing of a word of American-English, is, in some ways, as fine a glimpse of the enigmatic novelist as the monster authorised biography. Some chapters are as funny in their way as anything in **Hunter S. Thompson**. Which may explain, why when Willett's biography came out, it was called Fear And Loathing In Fitzrovia.

INFLUENCED BY Graham Greene; Chandler; the movies.

INFLUENCE ON Anthony Powell.

ESSENTIAL READING **Memoirs Of The Forties**; **Of Love And Hunger**, front-line dispatches from the vacuum-cleaner sales wars in 1930s Britain.

FURTHER READING **Books Do Furnish A Room** by Anthony Powell, in which a version of Maclaren-Ross appears as the famed, doomed writer X. Trapnel.

NORMAN MAILER

Heavyweight author who wanted to revolutionise our consciousness

"I am imprisoned with a perception which will settle for nothing less than making a revolution in the consciousness of our time," wrote **Norman Mailer** (1923–) in his book Advertisements For Myself. Never a modest man, Mailer planned to write a series of novels that would completely change the landscape of American literature. Now 80, he admits in his book The Spooky Art: Thoughts On Writing: "I certainly failed, didn't I? At the time I thought I had books in me that no one else did."

Born to Jewish immigrants from Lithuania, Mailer grew up in Brooklyn and

studied aeronautical engineering at Harvard. He started writing as a hobby, but it soon became his calling. He was drafted into the army in 1944, where he trained as an artilleryman and was sent to the Philippines. On his tour of duty he was involved in "a couple of firefights and skirmishes" and sent letters home to his young wife that formed the basis of The Naked And The Dead, widely held to be the defining novel of World War II in the Pacific and perhaps Mailer's greatest work of fiction.

It was a hard act to follow. His second novel, Barbary Shore, set in a boarding house, mixed sex and anti-Stalinist Communism. It flopped. His third, The Deer Park, based on his impressions of the movie industry after a short spell as a screenwriter, was often brilliant but at times incoherent (though JFK chose it as his favourite Mailer novel). Its failure shattered Mailer's confidence and he didn't write another novel for ten years, until An American Dream. Instead he channelled his creativity into becoming a public persona, in the Hemingway mould. He stabbed his wife (she didn't press charges), campaigned to become mayor of New York, made dire films and had various literary feuds and several wives.

His saving grace during this time was his journalism. In The Armies Of The Night: History As A Novel/The Novel As History he writes about Norman Mailer in the third person, attending a Vietnam protest march on the Pentagon, filtering the experience through his own warped ego. He followed this with the good, if elephantine, non-fiction The Executioner's Song, about the life, crimes, trial and execution of Gary Gilmore.

Two doorstep-sized novels have since come closest to his grand early ambitions. Ancient Evenings is a story of pharaohs obsessed with sex, politics and dung; Harlot's Ghost covers familiar Mailer ground – the nation's psyche, violence, sexual roles and global politics, told within the structure of a cold-war CIA tale and is still, officially, "to be continued".

The jury is still out on whether Mailer is a great novelist, but he may, as the poet Robert Lowell told him, be "the best journalist in America."

INFLUENCED BY Hemingway; Truman Capote.

INFLUENCE ON Tom Wolfe; Hunter S. Thompson.

ESSENTIAL READING **The Naked And The Dead**; **The Deer Park**.

FURTHER READING **Tough Guys Don't Dance** squeezes Mailer's themes into a slim, overwritten, yet gripping suspense novel; **The Armies Of The Night**.

CULT FICTION

CHARLES McCARRY

Neglected master of the spy novel

Aficionados of **Charles McCarry** (1930–) insist that, in the world of fictional intrigue, he is greater than **John Le Carré**. **George V. Higgins** admires McCarry's craft, while **P.J. O'Rourke** admires his politics. In Le Carré's looking-glass world moral advantage is minimal. McCarry, god bless him, has the confidence to say what's right is right, and in his world what's right is usually right of centre.

McCarry, a CIA veteran, brings a knowing authenticity to his novels, convincingly rendering any part of the world his heroes visit. At times his fiction can read like very clever, entertaining and subtle propaganda for his old employers.

His debut The Miernik Dossier is his best and most technically ambitious novel, consisting of 89 documents about a Pole working for the UN who may be a nerd or

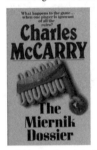

a master spy. The book introduces Paul Christopher, CIA agent and poet, who also stars in The Tears Of Autumn (in which McCarry suggests **JFK** was assassinated in revenge for the death of South Vietnamese leader **Ngo Dinh Diem**); The Secret Lovers; The Last Supper; and, in 2004, Old Boys, a Magnificent Seven-style tale in which Christopher's friends, colleagues and family try to establish whether he really has died in a remote part of China.

McCarry set out to "write naturalistic novels about people who happened to be engaged in espionage," but his audacity is his strength, enabling him to imagine Islamic suicide attacks using airliners blown-up over cities (in The Better Angels, 1979) and stolen presidential elections (in Shelley's Heart, 1995). But, as the Christopher novels progress, he seems to idealise his hero so much you wonder if Christopher is an idealised self-projection or old friend too reverently fictionalised.

INFLUENCED BY John Buchan; Eric Ambler.

INFLUENCE ON 9/11; Bush v Gore, 2000.

ESSENTIAL READING **The Miernik Dossier**.

FURTHER READING His political novels: **Shelley's Heart**; **The Better Angels**.

CARSON McCULLERS

The quality of despair

To **Arthur Miller**, **Carson McCullers** (1917–1967) was a "minor author", but to **Gore Vidal** her work was "one of the few satisfying achievements of our second-rate culture." Posterity has, slightly unfairly, tended to agree with

Miller. Yet McCullers wrote brilliantly, as an outsider, about other outsiders.

The life story of **Lula Carson Smith**, as she was born, is as blighted by tragedy as her characters' lives. She was 15 when she caught the rheumatic fever that triggered a series of strokes which, by the time she was in her thirties, would leave her a virtual invalid and finally, in 1967, kill her. She married her husband, **James Reeves McCullers**, twice, but both had homosexual affairs during the first marriage. The second ended, in 1953, with her husband's suicide. He had tried and failed to persuade her to join him, although she had attempted suicide herself in 1948. Two years later her mother died suddenly, and in 1962 she had a cancerous breast removed and surgery performed on every major joint in her paralysed left hand.

> "I prefer McCullers to Faulkner, she writes more clearly; I prefer her to D. H. Lawrence because she has no message"
>
> Graham Greene
> plays literary favourites

The miracle is that McCullers wrote so much. She was one of the best of several women writers who, in the 1940s, revived Gothic writing in the South. Although homosexuality is a theme in her fiction, McCullers was less concerned with sexual politics than the exploration of loneliness and evil. Her characters are invariably damaged: mute, dwarves or ugly. Even in her most conventional novel, The Member Of The Wedding, the heroine, the groom's younger sister, is as locked out of adult society as her other damaged protagonists.

For black novelist **Richard Wright**, reviewing her breakthrough novel The Heart Is A Lonely Hunter, published when she was 23, "her quality of despair is unique and individual and seems more natural than **Faulkner**'s." The novel revealed her instinctive genius for language but was carefully planned – each character's narrative is cast in a different light by the others' stories. Her debut was matched, in quality, by the novella The Ballad Of The Sad Café and The Member Of The Wedding. Slightly less successful, but worthwhile, are Reflections In A Golden Eye and her final novel Clock Without Hands, attacking racism.

Her fiction has been patronised as a carnival freak show, while some find her morbidly sentimental. But she had an acute eye and ear and her dark visions were disturbingly well-grounded in the reality of society and human behaviour.

INFLUENCED BY Chekhov; Dostoevsky; Tennessee Williams.

INFLUENCE ON Edward Albee; John Hawkes.

ESSENTIAL READING **The Ballad Of The Sad Café**; **The Heart Is A Lonely Hunter**.

FURTHER READING **The Member Of The Wedding**; her autobiography.

CULT FICTION

His imagination is in some bestial hell

It's no coincidence that one of the most famous novels by **Patrick McGrath** (1950–) is called The Grotesque. McGrath's **new Gothic** fiction often errs on the side of the monstrous, usually featuring one or more of his favourite subjects: madness, sexual obsession and evil.

McGrath's father was medical superintendent of Broadmoor mental institute, a fact to which many have attributed the author's rather grim worldview. The flavour of McGrath's debut collection, Blood & Water And Other Stories, is neatly captured by the titles of the stories: The Lost Explorer, Blood Disease and Hand Of A Wanker, the last a terrible cautionary tale.

His first novel The Grotesque was a macabre take on the haunted house, featuring a brain-damaged palaeontologist, murder and sexual depravity. Author **Jeanette Winterson** said: "McGrath's roots are in **Poe** but his imagination inhabits some bestial hell where **Swift** and **Baudelaire** run the butcher's shop." In The Asylum a mental institute is the backdrop for a tale in which a doctor's wife loves a patient who killed his wife in a violent rage.

> McGrath's novel Spider was acclaimed for its insight, though one reviewer found it as 'enchanting as a medical textbook'

174

Doctors and depravation are also present in his novels Dr. Haggard's Disease and Spider. Dr. Haggard's Disease is his finest, with its tale of a doctor, unable to forget a lost love, who becomes obsessive about his lover's son. Spider, which goes inside the schizophrenic mind, shows an innate understanding of human fragility, although one reviewer found it as "enchanting as a medical textbook."

INFLUENCED BY John Hawkes; Edgar Allan Poe; John Fowles.

INFLUENCE ON Nobody yet.

ESSENTIAL READING **Dr Haggard's Disease**.

FURTHER READING **Port Mungo** focuses on a brother and sister's intense relationship in Miami and pre-revolutionary Havana.

Too odd to be mainstream

Rancher, conservationist and quintessential 'writer's writer', **Thomas McGuane** (1939–) has been raved about for decades without ever quite finding mainstream success. He is, as he puts it, "just too weird to have a bestseller."

McGuane was born to an Irish Catholic family in Grosse Ile, Michigan. His parents were both alcoholics and his father was prone to violence, although he inspired McGuane with an early love of nature. At the age of 15 he ran away to his girlfriend's father's ranch and decided to become a cowboy.

After a spell in a boarding school, McGuane attended the University of Michigan and studied play-writing at Yale Drama School. In 1966 he won a fellowship at Stanford, where he became friends with such countercultural icons as **Ken Kesey** and **Robert Stone**. A peripheral hippie himself, he worked hard at writing throughout this period, and the result, The Sporting Club, a satirical tale about a pair of young men who bring down the establishment of a Michigan hunting club, saw him acclaimed as one of America's best young writers in 1969.

McGuane's work broadly falls into two halves: books set in Florida and books set in Montana (although The Sporting Club fits into neither). The Bushwhacked Piano continues the theme of rebellious youth, while exploring the perils of meddling with nature. Having lodged in Key West in the late 1960s, McGuane sold the film rights to The Sporting Club and bought a ranch in Paradise Valley, Montana. Here he embarked on a period of hell-raising and he and his wife divorced. He also wrote film scripts and directed a version of his tragicomic novel Ninety-Two In The Shade, about a man who returns to his native Florida to become a fishing guide, with gruesome consequences.

175

The search for roots in a rootless environment, a recurring theme for McGuane, is reflected masterfully in Panama, the last, most compassionate and best of his Florida novels, in which, using the first person for the first time, he recounts the (semi-autobiographical) crisis of a lovelorn, fading glam-rock star.

After the excesses and failed marriages of the 1970s (he was also married briefly to the actress **Margot Kidder**), McGuane turned to Montana for inspiration in Nobody's Angel. Written as he was coming to terms with his sister's death, it describes the lunatic cattle country for which he is now best known, intricately detailed and awash with crisis-ridden characters. The funny, sexy, mellow Keep The Change covers similar ground. In the past 15 years McGuane has written two novels set in Montana: the picaresque Nothing But Blue Skies and The Cadence Of Grass, about the fallout from the death of a patriarch. On the evidence of these two, his prose is as exquisitely observed as ever.

INFLUENCED BY Hemingway; Faulkner; John Steinbeck.

INFLUENCE ON Kent Nelson; T. Jefferson Parker; Tom Bissell.

ESSENTIAL READING **Panama**; **Keep The Change**.

FURTHER READING **The Longest Silence: A Life In Fishing** is a beautiful account of one of McGuane's chief preoccupations.

CULT FICTION

MARTIN MILLAR

Buffy the Vampire Slayer, **Aristophanes** and grunge rock aren't usually on your average cult author's list of influences, but that's **Martin Millar** (1959–) for you. This is a writer who has been dubbed both "Brixton's answer to **Kurt Vonnegut**" and "the **Armistead Maupin** of South London."

As Millar he celebrates London's thriving counterculture, while as **Martin Scott** he writes of the weird world of Thraxas, in which a fantasy version of Sam Spade faces indescribably weird and wonderful criminals. Yet Millar admits: "I don't know anything about modern literature, or art really. My favourite cultural experiences of the moment are my gigantic new history of Rome and my huge collection of Buffy videos."

Born in Glasgow, Millar headed to London aged 20, taking various menial jobs until his writing found a publisher. With no formal literary training, Millar's writing often has an autobiographical edge, with Glasgow and Brixton, his home for the last 20 years, favoured backdrops. In his debut, Milk, Sulphate And Alby Starvation, Alby spends his days collecting comics, selling speed and listening to **The Fall**, but his days of bumming around are threatened when a series of degenerate characters try to kill him. Written in just five weeks (it took two years to publish), the novel has a fantastic cast of dealers, druggies, Chinese warlords and drug-crazed lesbian punks.

He capped this with another study of human idiosyncrasy, Lux The Poet, in which the 17-year-old title character, believing himself to be the prettiest man – and greatest poet – on Earth, can't understand why TV cameras would rather show riots in Brixton than footage of him reciting his own odes. More frenetic than his previous work, Lux is full of Millar's usual wit and irony.

Frequently calling himself a "medium-ranking author" (he has had to change publishers to get some of his work accepted), Millar has sold screen options for most of his books; written – for the money – a script for the forgettable movie Tank Girl; and co-authored a modern adaptation of **Jane Austen**'s Emma with comedian **Doon MacKichan**. Millar remains, on the evidence of his latest semi-autobiographical novel Suzy, Led Zeppelin And Me, as pertinent, brilliant and self-indulgent as ever.

INFLUENCED BY Buffy; Jane Austen.

INFLUENCE ON Nobody yet.

ESSENTIAL READING **Suzy, Led Zeppelin And Me**, a fabulously funny semi-autobiographical novel set at a Led Zeppelin gig in Glasgow.

FURTHER READING If you like to read about weird private detectives surrounded by orcs, elves and dragons, **Thraxas** will be just up your street.

Chronicles of a death foretold

Yukio Mishima (1925–1970) changed his name from **Kimitake Haroaka** to spare his father, a government official, the 'disgrace' of having a writer for a son. In his first major work, Confessions Of A Mask, published in his early twenties, he discussed his homosexuality but suggested he would have to wear a mask of normality. He did go as far as marrying **Yoko Sugiyama**, daughter of one of Japan's most famous traditional painters (though he insisted that she should never interfere with his writing or his bodybuilding). Yet either he forgot his own advice or he had a very unusual definition of normality, as he often posed for photographs as a drowned sailor, **St Sebastian** shot to death with arrows or as a samurai committing ritual suicide.

His lyrical fiction has been described as chronicles of a death foretold. His obsession with death may not be unconnected to the death he saw around him as a young man who, to his shame, was excused from the Japanese army to work in a factory. In November 1970, after launching a failed attempt to persuade soldiers to save Japan from the Americans, he ritually disembowelled himself – the act is called **seppuku** – and his head was severed by one of his co-conspirators at the fourth attempt. An odd end for a man who, in life, had been obsessed by the body beautiful – but perhaps that was the point. Others have suggested his suicide was driven by fear of physical decay or chagrin at not winning the **Nobel Prize**, which went to fellow Japanese novelist **Yasunari Kawabata**.

His death has overshadowed his reputation and his fiction. But for some, notably **Gore Vidal**, that is not altogether a bad thing as: "Whatever Mishima's virtues in his native language and relative importance among the writers of his own country, he is a third-rate novelist in English." Harsh, but Vidal has a point. Mishima's fame rests as much on his life and death as his art – witness the acclaimed **Paul Schrader** movie Mishima.

177

Mishima said that, as a homosexual, he would wear a mask of normality. But he then posed for pictures as drowned sailors and St Sebastian

Although his first story was published when he was 16, his fiction doesn't suggest he was as fascinated by writing as a craft as he was, say, by bodybuilding. His heroes meet their grim fates with repetitive monotony, but his canvas is broader than his obsessions suggest. In After The Banquet he thoughtfully depicts the marriage of an ageing widow and an old-school conservative aristocrat. His best works – The Sailor Who Fell From Grace With The Sea, which kicks off his famous The Sea Of Fertility tetraology, and The Temple Of

178

Yukio Mishima was obsessed – in life, fiction and in his suicide – with samurai

The Golden Pavilion – make something universal out of his obsessions; perfect reading for adolescent romantics like Mishima.

INFLUENCED BY Oscar Wilde; Raymond Radiguet; Rainer Maria Rilke; T.S. Eliot.
INFLUENCE ON Japanese underground fiction.
ESSENTIAL READING **The Sea Of Fertility**.
FURTHER READING **The Temple Of The Golden Pavilion**.

MOHAMMED MRABET

Moroccan storyteller taped and edited by his friend Paul Bowles.

During **Paul Bowles**'s long postwar residence in Tangier, Morocco, he began taping, then translating, stories told to him by people he came to know in the city.

ES'KIA MPHAHLELE AND DRUM MAGAZINE

Just as South Africans like **Miriam Makeba** provided some of the best non-American jazz music of the 1950s and 1960s, the writers of Johannesburg's **Drum** magazine provided some of the best jazz writing.

Nurtured in the segregated township of Sophiatown, **Drum**'s writers – **Can Themba, Nat Nakasa, Es'kia Mphahlele, Bloke Modisane** and others – confronted apartheid and poverty through their vibrant, defiant tales of gangsters (tsotsis), jazz and illegal drinking dens (shebeens).

Edited by **Anthony Sampson**, **Drum** began as a means of expression for black culture but, by 1953, was selling 500,000 a month across the continent. The line between fiction and journalism was often ill-defined, and the stories were as autobiographical as the fearless investigative reporting of Mr Drum (**Henry Nxumalo**).

In 1955 Sophiatown was bulldozed to make way for a white suburb, but in the early 1950s this huge, noisy, crime-ridden ghetto bred a live-for-today attitude which permeates the best **Drum** short stories, countering the desperation of black life with satire, thoughtfulness and honesty, as well as the fleeting highs of drink, violence and "nice-time" girls.

Tragically, but inevitably, many of **Drum**'s contributors died young, and the magazine lost momentum after the murder of Nxumalo in 1957. Can Themba, whose best-known work is The Suit, died of alcoholism in 1968, and Nat Nakasa committed suicide in New York in 1965. But Es'kia Mphahlele and Bloke Modisane wrote acclaimed autobiographies Down Second Avenue and Blame Me On History.

Mphahlele spent many years as a writer and academic in exile, fleeing to other African states and then to America, before, in 1977, returning to South Africa, where he became professor of African literature at the University of Witwatersrand.
ESSENTIAL READING
The Drum Decade; Good Looking Corpse; both anthologise some of the best **Drum** material. Mphaphlele's roman á clef novel The Wanderer.

179

"They issued," as he put it, "from the repertoire of Moroccan folk humor," and the translator's challenge was to "find the elements to reconstitute the voice." In his work with **Mohammed Mrabet** (1940–), Bowles found the voice that came most easily: that of a virtuoso story-teller – as you still find on any big city public square in Morocco, telling tales of trickery and magic, innocence and violence. Bowles arranged publication of Mrabet's first 'novel', Love With A Few Hairs, in 1967, and over the next thirty years he and Mrabet produced a shelf-full of story collections and novellas, published by small presses in America and the UK, often with covers of Mrabet's hallucinogenic-looking drawings.

Mrabet's stories, too, were clearly inspired by kif, or hashish. He was born in Morocco's cannabis-growing region, the Rif, and as a child set out for Tangier, where he lived on the streets, making money from tourists, from fishing and, so he claims, as a boxer. He tells a story of his life, and his meeting Paul and **Jane Bowles**, in an autobiography, Look And Move On, which is hard to tell apart from his fiction, with its matter-of-fact narrative of strange and often violent episodes, propelled largely through dialogue.

Mrabet and Bowles had a long and close relationship. Mrabet would show up most afternoons at Bowles's apartment, smoke pipes of kif, tell stories, intimidate Bowles's Western visitors and cook dinner. Then the two might work together, with Bowles recording or reading back his renderings to Mrabet in Spanish (which he understood better than English). The quality of Bowles's prose translations, and his choice as de facto editor of Mrabet's stories, gave Mrabet's writing a consistent quality. There is no progression to it: the stories are street tales or fables. Some are very funny, others tragic: but the narrator remains detached and fatalistic, accepting that this is how the world is.

Bowles used to tell a story (with Mrabet adding violent exclamations) of how a noted Paris-based Moroccan novelist had dismissed Mrabet's work as being by Bowles, even going so far as to suggest that Mrabet didn't exist. This was trash, of course. If anything the current could have been said to have travelled as much the other way. Bowles's short fiction, from the 1950s on, became increasingly Moroccan in character, revolving on the fable-like twists that came naturally to Mrabet's tales.

INFLUENCED BY Traditional Moroccan storytelling.

INFLUENCE ON Paul Bowles.

ESSENTIAL READING **M'Hashish** (continuously in print from City Lights since 1969), a classic story collection of 'behashished' characters; **Love With A Few Hairs**, a powerful take of Tangier and a relationship ruined by magic.

FURTHER READING Mrabet's autobiography, **Look And Move On**.

Japanese-Western novelist who writes his own soundtracks.

The stories of **Haruki Murakami** (1949–) – not to be confused with the fiction of his near contemporary **Ryu Murakami** – have been described by an admirer as like watching a soap opera written by **David Lynch**. The description doesn't flatter Murakami, but does point to a central fact about his 'weird stories'. Unlike most Japanese novelists, his work is usually discussed entirely in reference to Western authors like **Vonnegut**, **Salinger** and **Chandler**. Murakami's strangeness is not the step-by-step guide to ritual suicide weirdness of **Yukio Mishima**'s fiction. Murakami's fiction feels neither Japanese nor Western. He has created a fictional kingdom, Murakamiland, where his characters live, love and drift.

Like many Japanese of his generation, Murakami fell in love with the artefacts of Western – especially American – pop culture as a child. In the late 1960s, with anti-Western radicalism almost compulsory on Japanese campuses, he turned his back on Japanese literature to read authors like Vonnegut and **Richard Brautigan**. After university he ran a jazz bar in Tokyo, observing at first hand the city's bored, but hyper, youth culture – vital experience for his early coming-of-age novels, notably Norwegian Wood, a cult book if ever there was one, published in two volumes (red and green).

Norwegian Wood was such a huge success in Japan – albeit one unpopular with local critics, who condemned what they saw as his fiction's emptiness – that Murakami felt obliged to escape into voluntary exile to Europe and the US. His

BANANA MANIA AND OTHER JAPANESE CRAZES

Yasunari Kawabati
Won the Nobel Prize but don't be put off. His semi-fictional The Master Of Go, about a master's attempt to retain his title in the complex Oriental board game Go, is a classic work.

Shusaku Endo
A Japanese Catholic, Endo writes about the struggles of faith. Silence is his greatest work.

Ryotaro Shiba
Too little known in the West, his Samurai stories Drunk As A Lord are a good introduction to his fiction.

Koji Suzuki
Suzuki wrote the novel, Ring, on which the recent horror movie The Ring was based.

Juniro Tanizaki
His masterpiece is The Makioka Sisters, but The Secret History Of The Lord Of Musashi, a brisk tale of human mutilation, is one of the most vicious novels ever written.

Banana Yoshimoto
Her first novella, Kitchen, sold six million copies in two years, prompting "Banana-mania" headlines.

reputation there grew – he is now Japan's best-known novelist abroad – nurtured by a succession of novels and stories that mixed quests for memory and love with a particular sense of identities adrift or un-forged. South of the Border, East of the Sun was a particular triumph, while the surreal The Wind-Up Bird Chronicle, which tackled broader political and historical themes. He returned to his obsession with love in the acclaimed Sputnik Sweetheart. Yet his most remarkable recent work may be his eloquent, dispassionate Underground, based on interviews with the victims – and planners – of the **Aum** cult's Tokyo subway attack.

Murakami's novels – which often feature post-noir outsiders who drift through life, meet enigmatic women, odd circumstances and confront some existentialist conundrum – can sound clichéd in summary, but Murikamiland is distinguished by the references, the detail (which often resonates with the music his characters listen to), the surreal imagery and their quirky first-person narratives.

INFLUENCED BY Jazz; Chandler; Ross Macdonald; Camus; Raymond Carver.

INFLUENCE ON Banana Yoshimoto; David Mitchell.

ESSENTIAL READING Start with **South of the Border, West of the Sun**; then try **Norwegian Wood**.

FURTHER READING **Underground**.

VLADIMIR NABOKOV

"Yes, sometimes I feel the blood of Peter the Great in me"

After reviewing a slew of books by and about **Vladimir Nabokov** (1899–1977) for the **New York Review Of Books**, the poet and critic **D.J. Enright** concluded that much of the celebrated writer's ouevre was "like farting a tune through a keyhole: it may be clever but is it worth the trouble?"

Novelists and critics have decided that, on the whole, Nabokov is very much worth the trouble. His style, conceits and techniques have influenced thousands of writers, for good and ill. The trouble is that you have to be as smart as Nabokov to carry off something like Pale Fire – a novel consisting of a 999-line poem by an exiled east-European king and a commentary by a man who, we slowly realise, is a deluded, paranoid fool. Intellectually, this is humour – and literature – of a very high order, but he makes it beautifully easy to read.

With the exception of **Kafka**, **Proust** and **James Joyce** no other European novelist has had as much impact on the 20th-century novel. But then few novelists have been as affected by 20th-century history. He lost estates he inherited to the Russian revolution, his father was murdered by a monarchist and his brother, a homosexual (a fact Nabokov did not like to acknowledge), died in a Nazi concentration camp.

Nabokov's fiction is prized for its style – the riddles, the puns, the wit, the asides and the intensely visualised descriptions – but even in a work as personal as his memoir Speak Memory, there is a cold detachment; the real Nabokov is as elusive as his heroes. (The exception to this criticism is the tender tale of an academic in exile, Pnin.)

If classics like Pale Fire and The Real Life Of Sebastian Knight are often concerned with identity, there is, as Enright pointed out, a rather disturbing strain in his fiction, an "obsession with the superman hero, arrogant and (except where he himself is concerned) callous, lording it over his 'natural' inferiors." True, the superman hero is often revealed to be mad or undone by fate, but it's clear where Nabokov's sympathies lie. In a very Nabokovian paradox, he was a cultured Russian aristocrat who liked to encourage rumours that his family had, albeit illegitimately, the blood of the Tsars running through their veins, yet he is best known as the author of one of the 20th century's most notorious novels, Lolita.

He is, as **Malcolm Bradbury** has noted, "one of the great tragic ironists of modern fiction." Like **William Burroughs** he deconstructed the novel but, unlike Burroughs, rebuilt it for his own ends. Beneath his oh-so-stylish surface lie enough obsessions – with madness, identity and with obsessives (be they chess champions, as in The Defence, or pursuers of nymphets) – to make his novels intriguingly, endurably odd and challenging.

183

INFLUENCED BY Gogol; Alexander Pushkin; Proust; Kafka; Edgar Allan Poe.
INFLUENCE ON Mary McCarthy; Martin Amis; Paul Auster; W.G. Sebald.
ESSENTIAL READING **Pale Fire**; **The Defence**; **Pnin**.
FURTHER READING **Lolita**; **The Real Life Of Sebastian Knight**.

JEFF NOON

He thinks English fiction lacks whimsy

Manchester-born **Jeff Noon** (1957–) has ambitiously declared he'd like to put the 'whimsy' back into English fiction. While his novels do have a distinctly fantastical side, his cyberpunk tales of gangs addicted to a mysterious drug have done far more than add a little whimsical seasoning to the English novel.

Noon's start in writing is rather romantic. He was working in Waterstones when his boss decided to start a publishing company and suggested Noon write a novel. He started that night, his first line "Mandy came out of the all-night Vurt-U-Want, clutching a bag of goodies" leading to his debut novel, Vurt.

Often likened to **Michael Moorcock**, Noon has a differing emphasis, exploring technology in a world of fantasy and even magic; a good example being his novel Automated Alice, in which Alice becomes a gun-toting robot, and finds herself in Manchester and the prime suspect in the 'jigsaw murders'.

Inspired, as he is, by certain writers (notably **Borges**) and comic-book heroes, music is his key influence. His acute ear for music gives his dialogue an almost lyrical quality. His most recent novel, Falling Out Of Cars, shows Noon expanding his repertoire, writing an unusual road novel about a woman travelling around England in search of herself.

INFLUENCED BY William Gibson; Bruce Sterling; Borges; Lewis Carroll.

INFLUENCE ON Nobody in particular, but give him time.

ESSENTIAL READING Noon's jarringly original debut, **Vurt**.

FURTHER READING **Alice In Wonderland** is a great accompaniment to Noon's **Automated Alice**.

PATRICK O'BRIAN

A triumph of naval gazing

It took **Patrick O'Brian** (1914–2000) sixty years to become an overnight sensation. He was 15 when his first book, Caesar, a **Kiplingesque** novella about the offspring of a giant panda and a snow leopard, was published in 1930. His 1952 novel Testimonies was rated above the contemporary works of **Ernest Hemingway**, **John Steinbeck** and **Evelyn Waugh** by a leading US critic. But, as recently as 1990, if his name rang any bookstore bells at all it was as the translator of **Henri Charrieré**'s Papillon or, possibly, as **Picasso**'s biographer.

Bubbling under the surface, though, was a growing crew of fans for his series of **Nelsonian** seafaring novels. The first, Master And Commander, was published in 1969, but although his fans included such people as **Mary Renault** and **A.S. Byatt**, O'Brian's work sold poorly. Despite this, US publishers W.W. Norton took the brave decision to reissue the whole series – 13 books by the early 1990s – and they were hailed in the **New York Times Book Review** as "the best historical novels ever written."

O'Brian was a secretive, reclusive and scholarly man. Born **Richard Patrick Russ** in England, just before World War II he walked out on his wife and their two children. He worked in black arts propaganda during the war and, afterwards, reinvented and renamed himself as an Irish-born writer, living in remote spots first in Wales and then in the south of France.

An American publisher asked O'Brian if he could create a character to replace **C.S. Forester**'s Horatio Hornblower in the cutlass-and-cannon genre. O'Brian

O'Brien was born **Brian O'Nolan** in Strabane, Co. Tyrone, the son of a customs officer. Until the age of six he spoke only Gaelic, and he was educated at home until 1923, when his family moved to Dublin. In 1929 he entered University College, where he studied English, German and Irish, acquired an early reputation as a wit and intellectual and began to write fiction, despite his devotion to billiards and drink. Scenes From A Novel (Probably Posthumous) By Brother Barnabas was serialised in the college magazine and, with its conceit that the author has been murdered by one of his characters, foreshadows At Swim-Two-Birds. Having completed an MA on nature in Irish poetry, O'Brien joined the civil service and began to write in earnest in his spare time.

At Swim-Two-Birds is widely considered O'Brien's finest novel; a book of many layers, concerning an idle, hard-drinking Dublin student who lives with his uncle and is writing about a long-suffering writer named Dermot Trellis, who, in turn, is writing about a cast of characters, many of whom have been appropriated from other novels or from Irish folklore, and whom conspire to overthrow him with a story of their own. Written in numerous styles, including Middle Irish lays and the clichés of popular westerns, it creates a brilliant collage of Irish culture, high and low. Even **James Joyce** thought it a "really funny book".

> "This is just the book to give your sister if she's a loud, dirty, boozy girl"
>
> Dylan Thomas spots the present-giving potential of At Swim-Two-Birds

186

But the novel was a commercial failure and, with the death of his father in 1937, O'Brien had to support his mother and ten siblings. Working relentlessly, by 1940 he had completed The Third Policeman. This was, very loosely, a murder mystery set in a bleak, surreal Irish village, and dominated by bicycles – indeed, due to "the interchanging of the atoms" between seats and backsides, many of the characters are partially bicycles themselves. Largely nonsense, it is also a study of identity and quite possibly the funniest book you'll ever read.

The Third Policeman was rejected, and, claiming to have lost the manuscript, O'Brien failed to write another book in English for 21 years. By this time (as **Myles na Gopaleen**) he was writing a regular satirical column for the **Irish Times**. In 1941 he published An Beal Bocht (The Poor Mouth), a satirical novel in Gaelic about a miserably poor community in western Ireland at the turn of the century, which finds itself idealised by the wealthy Dubliners of the Gaelic Revival.

In 1953 O'Brien lost his job at the civil service, due to his columns and his alcoholism. With the enormous success of the reissue of At Swim-Two-Birds in 1960, he wrote two more novels in English: The Hard Life and The Dalkey Archive, which plunders many of The Third Policeman's ideas, although **De**

Selby's conversation with **St Augustine**, whose "Dublin accent was unmistakable", makes the book worth reading. O'Brien died on April Fool's Day, 1966. The Third Policeman was published in 1967 to universal acclaim.

INFLUENCED BY James Joyce; Lewis Carroll; Giambattista Vico.
INFLUENCE ON Anthony Burgess; Gilbert Sorrentino; William H. Gass.
ESSENTIAL READING **At Swim-Two-Birds**; **The Third Policeman**.
FURTHER READING **The Best Of Myles**, a blinding collection of his columns.

FLANNERY O'CONNOR

A ruthless misfit and mistress of Southern Gothic

Flannery O'Connor (1925–1964) once said of her own work: "I can write about Protestant believers better than Catholic believers – because they express their belief in diverse kinds of dramatic action which is obvious enough for me to catch. I can't write about anything subtle."

From the Southern Gothic school of writing, there certainly wasn't anything restrained about O'Connor's description of a man beating his grand-daughter's head against a rock in A View Of The Woods. O'Connor's fascination with the damned stemmed from her childhood. The only daughter of a Catholic family living in the **Bible**-belt Protestant region of Savannah, Georgia, her life's work focused on those suffering from issues of faith, with tragicomic results.

Her first short story, The Geranium, was published in 1946 while she was still studying at the University of Iowa. The following year she spent seven months at Yaddo in Saratoga Springs, the estate left by the **Trask** family for aspiring writers, painters and musicians, and produced what would become Wise Blood, her most acclaimed work. In the completed novel, not published until 1952, a religious enthusiast establishes his own church, but a church without **Christ**. A savage satire, **John Huston** directed the cult screen version in 1979.

Shortly after Wise Blood's success, O'Connor discovered that she had lupus, the same disease which had killed her father. At this point, as her friend and editor **Sally Fitzgerald** said, "She took stock characteristically, and began to plan her life in the light of reality." O'Connor was reasonably content as long as she could "write every day for at least two hours, and spend the rest of my time largely in the society of ducks" – and peacocks, which were a lifelong obsession.

O'Connor finished her second novel, The Violent Bear It Away, in 1960, in which an orphan struggles with his faith and his possible destiny as a prophet. But her collection A Good Man Is Hard To Find is generally considered her best work, "nine stories of original sin" as she called them. Her disease finally overcame her in

187

August 1964, when she was just 39, but another collection of stories, Everything That Rises Must Converge, rewarded her with further posthumous acclaim.

INFLUENCED BY Faulkner; the **Bible**.
INFLUENCE ON Alice Walker; Harry Crews; Nick Cave.
ESSENTIAL READING **Wise Blood; A Good Man Is Hard To Find**.
FURTHER READING **The Habit Of Being**: O'Connor's letters.

GEORGE ORWELL

"Big Brother is watching you"

Though he regarded himself as a socialist, **George Orwell** (1903-1950) was one of the most powerful and effective critics of Communism (in his brilliant allegory Animal Farm) and of totalitarianism (in his futuristic novel 1984). He created such convincing visions of overwhelming state control that his name has given rise to an adjective: Orwellian.

The cult status of Orwell – real name **Eric Blair** – rests on these two novels, and also on his memoir of the Spanish civil war, Homage To Catalonia – a painfully honest and vivid account of one of the most romanticized of 20th-century conflicts. An Old Etonian and the son of a colonial civil servant, Orwell worked for the Indian Police in Burma before breaking out of the world he was born into; first by investigating poverty in two European capitals (written up as Down And Out In Paris And London), then by fighting on the Republican side in Spain, while at the same time analysing the deadly, factionalism which plagued the various left-wing groups involved. Orwell was also a brilliant essayist, covering a wide range of subjects, from an account of a public execution to the saucy postcards of Donald McGill.

Both Animal Farm and 1984 were banned in the Communist bloc, while an American left-wing journal dubbed 1984 **'Maggot Of The Month'**. But as the Polish writer **Czeslaw Milosz** noted, the book was known to

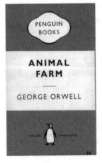

"members of the inner party, Orwell fascinates them through his insight into details they know well... they are amazed a writer who never lived in Russia should have so keen a perception into its life." But as well as extrapolating from existing regimes, Orwell was also predicting the future – often with startling accuracy. Several critics have pointed out the strong parallels between the book's permanently maintained state of war and the way in which Islamic terrorism has replaced Communism as the perceived threat to western civilisation.

Orwell borrowed many ideas from **Zamyatin**'s novel We, but 1984 had the greater impact. Several of its key concepts – doublethink, the idea of 24-hour surveillance, the degradation and manipulation of language, the re-writng of history – are now routinely employed by states throughout the world. The tragedy is that Orwell's book did not inspire us to resist them.

INFLUENCED BY Cervantes; Dicken; James Joyce; Yevgeny Zamyatin.
INFLUENCE ON Anthony Burgess; Octavio Paz; Camus.
ESSENTIAL READING **1984; Animal Farm; Homage To Catalonia**.
FURTHER READING **Collected Essays** – arguably his finest work.

CHUCK PALAHNIUK

He writes fiction in which the monsters and monstrous are all too visible

It is ironic that American author **Chuck Palahniuk** (1961–) is best known for Fight Club, his first novel to be published. Successfully adapted for the big screen, the novel was Palahniuk's angry response to the rejection of an earlier draft of his novel Invisible Monsters, which was viewed as being too risky.

Instead of toning his book down he made it more disturbing. This would become a familiar pattern. Each of his novels tries to be more offensive than its predecessor. Invisible Monsters tells of a supermodel who receives horrific facial injuries in a car accident, Survivor is a story of plane hijacking and death cults, Choke is about a sex addict who attends Sexaholics Anonymous meetings to find partners, and Lullaby follows a journalist with a Zulu death spell stuck in his head that makes him a mass murderer.

He was destined for cult status. Violence, dark humour and rants on contemporary America recur in his novels, which centre on lonely people looking to connect with others – what he calls "the invention of self... the central, most American, literary theme."

Don't ask Chuck to read a bedtime story

189

Palahniuk didn't start writing until he was 31. He grew up in Burbank, Washington, where he graduated from high school before studying journalism at the University of Oregon. His family history reads like the plot of one of his novels. When his father was a young child, Chuck's grandfather killed his grandmother with a gun before turning it on himself. His father and his father's girlfriend were shot dead in 1999 by the woman's jealous ex-husband.

Palahniuk has turned to non-fiction with Fugitives And Refugees and Stranger Than Fiction: True Stories (Nonfiction in the UK), but this seems a temporary shift. There are few subjects he views as too disturbing to use in his fiction. As he told **The Guardian**: "I want to have the story that makes people weep uncontrollably…"

INFLUENCED BY Thom Jones; Amy Hemple; Joan Didion; Bret Easton Ellis.

INFLUENCE ON Nobody yet.

ESSENTIAL READING **Fight Club**.

FURTHER READING **Choke**, a philosophical, pornographic tour de force.

WRITTEN ON OPIUM

Traditionally, the opium of the literary class has always been, well, opium, which wasn't illegal the 19th century. While we're not advocating that all frustrated authors use opium, without it we wouldn't have the last chapter of The Picture Of Dorian Gray, **Samuel Taylor Coleridge**'s Kubla Khan and most of the works of **Paul Bowles**.

Thomas De Quincey famously proclaimed: "Thou has the keys of Paradise, oh just, subtle and mighty opium." But then De Quincey dedicated a book to his favourite drug (see page 346). Other notorious opium-taking literary types include the eccentric Estonian-English aristocrat **Eric Stenbock** (see page 300); **Graham Greene**, who gave his journalist in The Quiet American an opium habit; **Coleridge**, who first tried opium to relieve his toothache (that old excuse) but became addicted; **Wilkie Collins** (who called it "my only friend"); and

Elizabeth Barrett Browning, who began taking it after a stomach illness, once proclaiming her pain: "Opium, opium – night after night! And some evenings even opium won't do."

Some took opium more seriously than others. In Artificial Paradises **Charles Baudelaire** detailed his addiction to the drug that would eventually kill him. But then French authors had always had a certain regard for opium. As far back as the 1790s, even before De Quincey admitted eating the stuff, French novelist **Charles Nodier** decided opium gave him insights that he never had sober. Sadly, these insights only seemed profound to other opium takers.

Ironically, there is evidence that **Edgar Allan Poe**, whose name has become synonymous with opium after a tell-all and invent some more posthumous biography, was not actually that keen on the stuff.

191

There are those who say that Paul Bowles smoked his way to greatness

MERVYN PEAKE

He caught the "blindingly exquisite fish of the imagination" for a while

"Titus Groan never reached the widest public; it was destined to be something of a coterie obsession…" wrote **Anthony Burgess** in his introduction to the 1968 reissue of the novel, after the death of its author. "There is no really close relative to it in all our prose literature. It is uniquely brilliant…" **Mervyn Peake** (1911–1968) was an artistic jack of all trades, with a strong reputation as a quirky illustrator before he took to fiction, but Titus Groan, Gormenghast and Titus Alone make up the epic Gormenghast trilogy for which he'll be remembered.

Born to missionary parents in China, Peake returned to England in 1923. He trained as an artist and joined an artists' community on the Channel Island of Sark, where he was finally accepted by the locals after punching someone who said his clothes were effeminate. He returned to England to take up teaching at the Westminster School of Art, but was later drafted. In the army he wrote Titus Groan. He showed the finished manuscript to his friend **Graham Greene**, who suggested changes, and it was published in 1946.

Gormenghast is a castle in a self-contained fantasy world that is reminiscent of 19th-century England. The ancient family of Groan has occupied it for millennia, but is bound by the strict and suffocating rituals of its traditions.

Peake writes like a painter, building up scenes and detailing characters like brush strokes applying oils to a canvas. The characters have descriptive names – Rotcodd, Sourdust, Flay and Swelter – but they're not remotely comical, and the atmosphere is stifling. Over the first two books the plot is linked to the rise and fall of the Machiavellian Steerpike, who charms, tricks and murders members of the family. Only Titus, the young Earl, stands in his way.

Peake's wonderful manipulation of language conjures up startling images and there are some unforgettable set-pieces, such as the fight to the death between the creaking, monosyllabic Flay and the hideously fat Swelter in the cob-webbed Hall

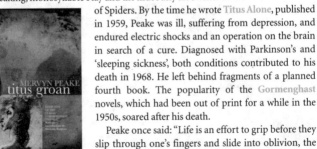

of Spiders. By the time he wrote Titus Alone, published in 1959, Peake was ill, suffering from depression, and endured electric shocks and an operation on the brain in search of a cure. Diagnosed with Parkinson's and 'sleeping sickness', both conditions contributed to his death in 1968. He left behind fragments of a planned fourth book. The popularity of the Gormenghast novels, which had been out of print for a while in the 1950s, soared after his death.

Peake once said: "Life is an effort to grip before they slip through one's fingers and slide into oblivion, the startling, the ghastly or the blindingly exquisite fish of the imagination, before they whip away on the endless current and are lost for ever…" He landed his fish – before the current swept it away again.

INFLUENCED BY Lewis Carroll; Dickens; Robert Louis Stevenson.

INFLUENCE ON Joanne Harris; Michael Moorcock.

ESSENTIAL READING The **Gormenghast** trilogy.

FURTHER READING **Mr Pye**, a quirky, comic morality story.

VICTOR PELEVIN

The pre-eminent spinner of post-Communist fiction

Buddhism, psychedelic drugs, 'New Russian' gangsters, space flight and the ravages of capitalism, **Victor Pelevin** (1962–) is the foremost Russian writer of the post-Communist generation, and the most controversial. Denying him the Russian Little Booker Prize in 1997, the chair of the judges described his work as a type of virus, intended to "destroy the cultural memory".

Pelevin grew up on a Moscow army base – "a big playground full of soldiers" – where his father was an officer. He studied at the Moscow Institute of Power Engineering, working on MiG jets before turning to journalism, copywriting and, in his mid-twenties, to the stories that would later comprise The Blue Lantern. 193

The Blue Lantern, like much of his work, is concerned with the nature of reality. In Hermit And Six-Toes a pair of misfit philosophers prove to be battery chickens. The prostitutes of Mid-Game were once (male) activists in the Young Communist League. These stories capture a mutability of identity whose roots lie both in Russian absurdism and in the sudden collapse of the Soviet Union.

Pelevin completed his first novel, Omon Ra, just days before the coup that brought down the USSR. Set in the long stagnation of the Brezhnev years, it is a metaphor for the lie of the Soviet era: a model youth becomes a cosmonaut, only to find that his mission is suicidal and his lunar lander a poorly-disguised bicycle. Unlike some of his peers, Pelevin has focused as much on the Soviet Union's chaotic aftermath. In The Life Of Insects, for example, the residents of a decaying Black Sea holiday camp change periodically from humans to insects.

Buddhism is a theme Pelevin returns to, particularly in The Clay Machine-Gun (Buddha's Little Finger in the US). It is, he says, "the only religion that didn't resemble the projection of the Soviet power onto the domain of spirit", and reflects an easterly urge which balances the Westernisation of Russia in Pelevin's books. The Clay Machine-Gun contains many loosely connected stories, but is essentially about a poet named Pyotr Voyd, an inmate in a 1990s mental hospital who considers himself an aide to **Chapaev** – a Bolshevik hero of the Russian civil war, who, in Pelevin's tale, ponders the illusory nature of reality.

Babylon (**Homo Zapiens** in the US) is a satire of the burgeoning Russian advertising industry which opens itself to charges of unsubtlety and self-indulgence. In Russia there are those who consider Pelevin to be far too cool for his own good: he is, for instance, never seen in public without a pair of dark glasses. But with book sales somewhere round the million mark and a reputation as "the saviour of Russian literature", it does seem a bit churlish to complain.

INFLUENCED BY Mikhail Bulgakov; Kafka; Chekhov; Andrey Platonov.

INFLUENCED ON Nobody yet.

ESSENTIAL READING **The Clay Machine-Gun**; **Omon Ra**.

FURTHER READING Try Andrey Platonov's **The Portable Platonov**. (Stalin described him as "scum", a recommendation of sorts.)

GEORGES PEREC

Sadly, Georges died before the letter E became a cult character

Parisian writer, literary innovator and master of language, **Georges Perec** (1936–1982) structured much of his work with literary puzzles, word play and complex logic. But Perec likened the structures he used to scaffolding, something to be discarded once the work was complete, so his work, unlike that of many experimental writers, also has great substance.

194

Born to Polish immigrants living in a largely Jewish Parisian suburb, Perec was left orphaned at six – his father having been killed in the war, his mother having disappeared in Paris, presumed to have been taken to Auschwitz. Raised by an aunt and uncle, he studied before serving in the army.

Perec loved wordgames and was fascinated by palindromes (he created what is considered the longest-ever written, at over 5,000 letters). From his first book, 1965's The Things, he began experimenting with language – the story, about a couple obsessed with consumerism, explores **Flaubert**'s method of using syntax for stylistic purposes (the first chapter is written in the conditional tense, the final in future tense). In writing about the perils of a consumer society he was labelled a sociologist – a label he tried to correct with his next book, Which Little Bicycle With Chrome Handlebars At The Back Of The Courtyard?.

In 1967 he joined **Oulipo**, a Parisian group of writers including **Italo Calvino**, **Raymond Queneau** and **François LeLionnais**. Oulipo's aim was to create literature which borrowed formal patterns from maths, logic and chess. Perec felt at home in this group – perhaps because, as he felt he didn't have a personal history to draw on for his writing, such structure helped focus and direct his mind.

Under Oulipo's influence Perec wrote A Void, a detective novel written without the letter E, which explores a parallel universe where one William Shakspar wrote a famous soliloquy which begins: "Living or not living, that is what I ask." Later Perec redressed the balance with The Return Of E, containing no vowels except E.

Perec was intensely private, although in 1973 he published La Boutique Obscure, where he recounted 124 of his dreams. He followed this in 1975 with W, Or The Remembrance Of Childhood. In it he describes a simple childhood domestic scene in astonishing detail, only to say: "That's what happened in the books I read at school", yet it shows how often he must have thought of such scenes of domestic bliss, longing for them to be true memories.

While writing, Perec worked as a research librarian for a neurophysiological research lab and earned money scripting a radio serial The Adventures Of Mr Eveready, sponsored by the battery company of the same name. Only with the success of his 1978 **Prix Medicis**-winning novel Life: A User's Manuel could Perec afford to become a full-time writer. Hailed as on a par with Ulysses (although far easier to read), the novel describes people living in a Paris apartment block, with over 100 stories interwoven through a complex chessboard/jigsaw structure full of the minute detail and observations of the eccentric people Perec loved.

INFLUENCED BY Oulipo writers, especially Queneau and Harry Mathews.
INFLUENCE ON David Mitchell.
ESSENTIAL READING **Life: A User's Manual**.
FURTHER READING **W, Or The Remembrance Of Childhood**.

MARGE PIERCY

A woman on the edge of fiction and feminism

Marge Piercy's political commitment runs through all her writing. Her work explores questions of gender, class and power in a way that may no longer be fashionable but has won her a devoted following. **Thomas Pynchon** described Piercy (1936–) in the 1970s as "somebody with the guts to go into the deepest core of herself, her time, her history, and risk more than anybody else has so far."

Born in Detroit, Piercy grew up in the Depression. Her father was often unemployed. Her mother was a housewife with a tenth-grade education and a profound influence on Piercy's chosen craft. As she says, "We would try to guess the stories of people we saw on the bus and would argue to prove or disprove each other's theories." Piercy was close to her maternal grandmother, who told her endless stories of her Jewish family history, and her maternal grandfather was murdered for organising a union. The first person in her family to attend college, Piercy won a scholarship to the University of Michigan and left home, later gaining an MA from Northwestern University.

Throughout university she baulked against the strictures imposed on women in the 1950s. Moving to France with her first husband, she protested against the Algerian war. The marriage ended with Piercy restless and desperate to see her writing taken seriously. She moved to Chicago, taking low-paid part-time jobs while writing novels and poetry (none of which were published). In 1962 she married again. Realising her feminism was stopping her getting published, she wrote a novel from a male point of view: Going Down Fast was her first published work. Her third novel, Small Changes, won her fame in the US as a timely fiction of women's liberation.

The novel that brought Piercy renown in the UK was Woman On The Edge Of Time, published by the (then new) feminist publisher The Women's Press in 1979. This angry, powerful classic of feminist literature uses sci-fi to tell the story of Connie Ramos, a poor, Hispanic woman confined in a brutal mental hospital who discovers she is a 'receptor' and can travel to a utopian future where gender inequalities are a thing of the past. Piercy's subsequent novels vary in setting, although she often uses futuristic science fiction to comment on the present. Her fiction can sometimes be overdrawn, the meaning too explicit, and she can overwrite – in one novel the rain doesn't fall, it "insinuates" down. But her fiction continues to address public and private themes, adding ecology and religious heritage to her continuing concern with feminism and civil rights.

INFLUENCED BY Adrienne Rich; Audre Lorde; Henry David Thoreau and Walt Whitman; Simone de Beauvoir.

INFLUENCE ON Grace Paley.

ESSENTIAL READING **Women On The Edge Of Time**.

FURTHER READING **Gone To Soldiers** is an epic, feminist, story of war.

SYLVIA PLATH

A lifetime struggling with the bell jar

Few writers embody female angst quite as powerfully as **Sylvia Plath** (1932–1963) Even now, 40 years after her death, undergraduates who wish to be taken seriously will wander through quads clutching a copy of her only novel The Bell Jar or frown over her poems.

Plath's life and work have been obscured by the controversy surrounding her relationship with **Ted Hughes** and by her tragic suicide. The Plath-Hughes affair is more interesting to non-biographers as an example of the turbulence which marked Plath's life. She met Hughes at a party in Cambridge in 1956 and four months later married him. They went to Spain on honeymoon and, according to the letters Sylvia wrote back to her mother, had an idyllic time. Yet in her journals she noted: "The world has grown crooked and sour as a lemon overnight."

Presenting a smiling, all-American happiness to the world, Plath fought depression all her life. This has often been traced to the death of her father, a biology professor, when she was eight. In her bitter poem Daddy she closes, "Daddy, daddy, you bastard, I'm through." Her finest, personal, dark poetry exemplifies the confessional style perfected after studying with **Robert Lowell** in 1959. She was recognised as a great poet, albeit posthumously, with the publication of Ariel, a collection full of humour, strong imagery and emotion.

At 20, after getting rejected from a creative-writing course, Plath spent six months in a mental hospital after an unsuccessful suicide bid. This experience is the root of the semi-autobiographical The Bell Jar, about Esther Greenwood, a young woman who suffers a breakdown and is cured with electric-shock treatment. The bell jar is the claustrophobia that makes her feel trapped. This lifts as she is cured, but, towards the end of the book she notes: "How did I know that someday the bell jar, with its stifling distortions, wouldn't descend again?"

197

In 1963 – just a month after the publication of The Bell Jar, initially under the pseudonym **Victoria Lucas** – Plath killed herself. Hughes had left her for another woman, and despite battling with the 'dark days' and writing much poetry, she put her head in a gas oven on 11 February 1963, after sealing the kitchen door with tape so no fumes would harm her children who were sleeping upstairs.

INFLUENCED BY: Robert Lowell; W.H. Auden; Anne Sexton; and, in a very direct way, Ted Hughes.

INFLUENCE ON: Anne Sexton; Matthew Sweeney; Erica Jong.

ESSENTIAL READING: **The Bell Jar**; **Ariel**.

FURTHER READING: **The Journals Of Sylvia Plath**.

EDGAR ALLAN POE

The definitive misunderstood genius of American fiction

Sadomasochist, dypsomaniac, drug addict, pervert, egomaniac, manic depressive… **Edgar Allan Poe** (1809–1849) has been called all these things, often by his admirers. He was, the critic **James Russell Lowell** once noted, "three-fifths genius". And it is these three-fifths which are in need of reclamation from those aficionados obsessed by the baroque fiction which surrounds his biography.

Even without his troubled life, with its perfect death-in-the-gutter dénouement, Poe's work would be savoured. He created, in some stories, a fictional world which, in its sense of meaningless suffering, anticipates **Kafka**. He virtually invented, in the Dupin stories (notably The Murders In The Rue Morgue), the modern police procedure. With The Fall Of The House Of Usher he wrote a classic horror story which has inspired such different souls as Czech animator **Jan Svankmajer** and **Stephen King**. In his only novel, The Narrative Of Arthur Gordon Pym Of Nantucket, he created a deliberately experimental structure in which the chapters oscillated between optimism and despair. And in other work he seemed to anticipate – some say create – science fiction.

All of which isn't bad for a writer who died when he was 40, after being found delirious in the streets of Baltimore; a death variously ascribed to drink, syphilis and even rabies. Most critics rewind from his horrendous end, projecting such misery back to his childhood. True, the young Poe hardly knew his parents, being taken into the house of a Scottish tobacco merchant after his mother died. But his letters – and testimony from schoolmates and teachers – hardly suggest that he was a youthful soul in torment.

As a man he was plagued by poverty, illness (suffering from an irregular heartbeat which made him abnormally receptive to stimulants) and by the grief of watching his wife, **Virginia Clem**, the cousin Poe married when she was 13, driven to invalidity and premature death by tuberculosis. The image of Poe as a drug-crazed fiend, so popular with French admirers like **Baudelaire**, was perpetuated by his self-appointed executor **Rufus Griswold**, a writer and critic who had feuded with Poe in life and wrote a biography of him which now seems as impartial as **Albert Goldman**'s hatchet jobs on **Elvis** and **John Lennon**.

This isn't to demystify or belittle Poe, merely to correct the stereotype. Because the fact he was, for the most part, "a gentle comrade, a conscientious editor and a solicitous husband" makes his fiction – variously labelled Gothic, baroque, existentialist, morbid and deranged – all the more remarkable.

GOTHIC CHIC

Castles, suspense, prophecies, omens, visions, supernatural or inexplicable events, overwrought emotions, women in distress (possibly threatened by a tyrannical male), the baying of unseen hounds… you will find all or most of these in the Gothic novel as invented by **Horace Walpole**, author of The Castle Of Otranto. Published in 1764, the novel sold well but was no great read. The works of **Ann Radcliffe** (notably The Italian, with its malevolent monk Schedoni) and **Matthew Lewis**'s spicier The Monk were a marked advance, but the classic Gothic novel would finally be perfected by **Mary Shelley** with Frankenstein and **Charles Maturin**'s Melmoth The Wanderer. This was the legacy that **Poe** reinvented.

THE AUTHORS

INFLUENCED BY Coleridge; Keats; Percy Bysshe Shelley; the Gothic novels.

INFLUENCE ON Conan Doyle; H.P. Lovecraft; Baudelaire; Nabokov; Borges; Robert Louis Stevenson; Stephen King.

ESSENTIAL READING **Tales Of Mystery And Imagination**.

FURTHER READING **The Narrative Of Arthur Gordon Pym Of Nantucket**.

RICHARD PRICE

He wanders around a bit and then writes what he sees

"I'm a great believer in osmosis. I just put myself with people that I want to write about and see what happens," says **Richard Price** (1950–). His career as a novelist splits into two halves, with a screenwriting dalliance in between. His early books drew on his own experiences. When he had exhausted those he looked to other people, immersing himself in their routines and absorbing details, gestures and language to help build his fictional characters. "A plot to me always feels like something obligatory. I'm much more interested in character."

Price grew up in a housing project in the Bronx and, though he studied at some of the nation's top colleges, it was his experiences as a teenager that he returned to for his first book, The Wanderers, now often billed as the "anti-Grease" novel of teenage angst. His dark, disturbing, hilarious story of gang war and racial feuding, set in the 1960s Bronx, shows the kind of urban realism he has specialised in ever since. The members of a gang called The Wanderers face their own rites of passage, while the prospect of the Vietnam war looms on the horizon.

The Wanderers was such a startling success that Price struggled to cope. He developed a serious cocaine habit and critical praise cooled for his follow-ups, although they still have their own cult following. Bloodbrothers occupies the same working-class teenage territory as his debut, Ladies Man is a tale of urban loneliness and The Breaks is again about coming of age. At a dead end, Price used his gift for snappy dialogue to write film scripts. "By the time I went off to write screenplays, I'd written about myself so much even I was bored," he said.

The novel Clockers, a story of drug dealing, murder and morality in New York, marked Price's return to fiction in 1992, but in the heavyweight style of **Charles Dickens** or 19th-century Russian novelists, with massive casts and painstaking social detail.

Freedomland followed, based loosely on the story of **Susan Smith**, a South Carolina woman convicted of murdering her two young children then blaming a black car-jacker for their disappearance. In Samaritan he puts strong characters from different ethnic backgrounds into the framework of a police investigation. Oddly, Price has often claimed that he doesn't like writing very much, but "the only thing worse than writing is not writing…"

INFLUENCED BY Hubert Selby – his **Last Exit To Brooklyn** made Price "so crazy I felt I had to get out there and write"; Tom Wolfe.

INFLUENCE ON Nick McDonnell.

ESSENTIAL READING **The Wanderers**.

FURTHER READING **Freedomland**, a gripping portrait of a city set to riot.

MARCEL PROUST

The most celebrated cake-dunker in literature

In the first volume of **Marcel Proust**'s (1871–1922) seven-volume novel *Remembrance Of Things Past* (more accurately translated as *In Search Of Lost Time*), the narrator describes dipping some cake (a 'petite madeleine') into a cup of tea given him by his mother: "No sooner had the warm liquid mixed with the crumbs touched my palate than a shudder ran through me and I stopped, intent upon the extraordinary thing that was happening to me." This apparently innocuous action – the original Proustian moment – triggers a series of memories and reflections which form the basis of the novel. The moment is also symptomatic of the work as a whole: both in the way it focuses on memory as a key element of personality and the way it takes a seemingly ordinary moment and unravels it in the minutest detail.

The vast array of characters that parade through *In Search Of Lost Time* are very much a reflection of Proust's own social milieu, in which aristocrats and the well-to-do rub shoulders with aesthetes and courtesans. The son of a professor of medicine, Proust spent his twenties frequenting the most fashionable salons of Belle Époque Paris. But his chronic asthma and the death of his beloved mother turned him into a recluse, and after 1900 he rarely left his cork-lined bedroom on the Boulevard Haussmann. It was here, looked after by various servants (including his chauffeur and lover Alfred Agostinelli), that he embarked on his great rambling masterpiece – publishing the first volume, *Swann's Way*, at his own expense.

PROUST BY NUMBERS

12 The number of times Proust rewrote the first page of his novel.

38 The age at which Proust started his novel.

200 The percentage tip Proust usually gave waiters.

950 The number of words in what is thought to be Proust's longest sentence (in the English translation).

2,360 The number of times, it is estimated, Albertine's name is mentioned in this novel.

7,000 The number of pages in the new Pléiade edition, edited by **Jean-Yves Tadie**.

12,000 The sales of **Stephane Heuet**'s graphic novel based on Proust's work in France in its first three months on sale.

200

Oddly enough, one of Proust's most important influences was the English art critic **John Ruskin**, whose acute sensitivity to the visual world inspired in Proust a similar obsession with detail. In Proust, however, it is focused on the mental mechanisms by which the characters make sense of experience – in particular the inner life of the narrator-hero (a virtual self-portrait). It's this emphasis on revealing the complex web of motivations that lie behind human actions that led the critic **Alexander Woollcott** to say that "reading Proust is like bathing in someone else's dirty water." But while there are moments when you seem to have been give just too much information, it's also true that much of the book reads like a gossipy, up-market soap opera. The dilettante Swann's infatuation with Odette, the predatory behaviour of Baron Charlus, the sorrow of the composer Vinteuil over his failed relationship with his daughter, the narrator's pursuit of the elusive Albertine – all are scrutinized (and sometimes satirized) with remarkable insight. Through all these characters Proust explores his main themes – the vicissitudes of love and desire (nearly all shades of gay and straight), and how these can be rarified through the process of memory and the transformative power of art.

201

Proust's achievement as a writer was to wrest the novel out of the straitjacket of a purely linear narrative and create a new subjective mode of fiction, one that more accurately conveyed the fluidity and atemporality of consciousness. As such he altered the course of nearly all modern literature, and inspired art-house cinema luminaries **Volker Schlöndorff**, **Chantal Akerman** and **Raúl Ruiz** to attempt the impossible, that is, to capture the subtle magic of Proust's prose on the big screen (Hollywood need not even think about trying).

INFLUENCED BY Balzac; George Sand; John Ruskin; Tolstoy; Henri Bergson.

INFLUENCE ON Virginia Woolf; Anthony Powell; Jonathan Franzen.

ESSENTIAL READING If you don't read French, the Scott Moncrieff/Kilmartin/ Enright translation is the version to go for.

FURTHER READING Alain de Botton's **How Proust Can Change Your Life**.

PHILIP PULLMAN

"There's a sort of embarrassment about telling stories"

Philip Pullman (1946–) is the inventor of one of the most completely realised fictional worlds since Middle Earth, an author read by millions of children whose work explores fairly hefty philosophical and religious ideas, and a mild-mannered bloke who wrote his novels in the garden shed and who has been told, by the Catholic Herald, that his books are "worthy of the bonfire".

Pullman had an averagely dysfunctional childhood (father died when he was nine; mother remarried an eccentric) and, by his own account, spent much of his time at Oxford (studying English), drinking and reading cheap thrillers. As a teacher he discovered a talent for telling stories and a conviction that storytelling was a neglected art: "Since modernism, we suspect stories… The value of writing books for children is that they couldn't care less if you're **Jeffrey Archer** or **Dostoevsky**. All they want to know is what happens next."

The His Dark Materials trilogy centres on the characters of Will and Lyra and the struggle between good and evil in a fantastically imagined universe which owes more than a little to Oxford. The books pose significant spiritual and philosophical questions for adult readers, yet enthral children of 12 and over. Indeed the first book, The Northern Lights, has been enjoyed by eight-year-olds.

Pullman is no fan of God, or of organised religion, and the way his narrative retells the **Biblical** tradition of the Fall has led to it being derided as Satanic by the religious right. Yet his trilogy, while taking on Christian theology, stresses such Christian values as love, humility, loyalty and compassion. Ultimately, though, for an admirer like novelist **Michael Chabon**, what matters isn't the theology or the philosophy, but "the sheer unstoppable storytelling drive" which, in his opinion, sags somewhat in the final instalment, The Amber Spyglass, as the author tidies up his themes and schemes.

His Dark Materials has, rather as The Lord Of The Rings did for **Tolkien**, overshadowed everything else Pullman has written. His Sally Lockhart novels are more conventional children's literature, but still good page-turners, while The Scarecrow And The Servant is a witty, intriguing, picaresque classic.

INFLUENCED BY Jonathan Swift; William Blake; Milton.

INFLUENCE ON Nobody yet – but give him time.

ESSENTIAL READING **His Dark Materials**.

FURTHER READING **Sophie's World**, the intriguing philosophical children's novel by Jostein Gaardner.

THOMAS PYNCHON

He makes J.D. Salinger look like a media tart

When **Thomas Pynchon**'s first novel V was published to rave reviews in 1963, **Time** magazine sent a photographer to his house to catch the new literary genius. Pynchon (1947–) supposedly leapt out of his window and has avoided the public eye ever since. His fierce privacy – he is said to feel his buck teeth make him look like Bugs Bunny – mean that nobody really knows what he looks like. Weird rumours still follow him – in the 1990s some people said he was the **Unabomber**. In 1997 a CNN crew spent days staking him out in New York, finally capturing him on film. They broadcast three minutes of footage of street scenes without identifying the one-second clip that actually features Pynchon.

Taught by **Nabokov** at Cornell University, Pynchon is remembered there as being "the type to read books on mathematics for fun… one who started the day at 1pm with spaghetti and a soft drink and read and worked until three the next morning." You sense this in the books – hugely erudite works, massive in breadth and depth, peopled by crazy characters and caricatures, full of paranoia, espionage and government control, countercultures and luminous prose.

V is the story of two characters pursuing what may or may not be the elusive female principle. One drifts along in artsy New York City, the other travels the world in his search. Many critics say it's the best debut novel of the 20th century.

Its slim successor, Crying Of Lot 49, is Pynchon's most digestible work. After the death of her ex-lover, Oedipa sets out on a trail of weirdness that takes her across America. But Gravity's Rainbow, published in 1973, is his meisterwork. Tyrone Slothrop tracks a ballistic missile throughout the novel, which makes massive demands on the reader's knowledge of science, military history and literature. Pynchon reportedly told a friend: "I was so fucked up while I was writing it… I go back over some sequences and can't figure out what I could have meant."

Seventeen more years passed before Vineland – the Norse term for America – again full of paranoia and secret police; and a further seven before Mason And Dixon, a kind of historical tale of the two English surveyors **Charles Mason** and **Jeremiah Dixon** charged with marking the boundary between Pennsylvania and Maryland. Thumbnail sketches don't do the novels – or their literary and intellectual pyrotechnics – justice. Pynchon's fiction is like entering a maze in the company of an eccentric, voluble, polymath.

INFLUENCED BY James Joyce; John Barth; physics

INFLUENCE ON Don DeLillo; David Foster Wallace; 20th century fiction.

ESSENTIAL READING **Gravity's Rainbow**, chosen for the Pulitzer Prize, but rejected as "unreadable" and "obscene" by the advisory board. **V**.

FURTHER READING **The Crying Of Lot 49** can be read at a sitting. If you like it, you'll love Pynchon, if not, you've wasted hardly any time.

RAYMOND QUENEAU

Playful experimenter, Groucho Marxist, cabaret songwriter

Albert Camus said – of the Nazis – "Where you have no character, you have to have a method." And too many contemporary novelists have used method as a convenient alibi to cover up a lack of personality. **Raymond Queneau** (1903–1976) comes encumbered with theory. He flirted with **surrealism** (and married **André Breton**'s sister), founded the **Oulipo** literary school (with its suggestion that by applying formal constraints to their work, writers could achieve a new kind of freedom) and wrote a book, Exercises In Style, in which the same story is told 99 different times. Yet Queneau used his wealth of learning with a light touch in his fiction. One of his most famous novels, Zazie In The Metro, even made some readers laugh out loud. Another, We Always Treat Women Too Well, intelligently parodied **Mickey Spillane** thrillers so adroitly it was regarded by his admirers as an appalling lapse in taste.

Born in Le Havre, Queneau was an unhappy child and a brilliant student who, in 1920, moved to Paris to study philosophy at the Sorbonne. In his spare time he also studied English, the cinema, mathematics and billiards. On holiday in Greece, he became intrigued by the differences between classical and colloquial Greek and became determined to create a third French language, a written language that corresponded to the French people spoke. He put this into practice in his first novel The Bark Tree. All his novels are elegantly plotted, full of unusual yet believable characters, erudite but not elitist (it's often the 'normal' characters who have his most intriguing monologues) and cheerfully coarse. His linguistic innovations, such as the creation of compound words to emulate speech, are usually amusing rather than irritating. This idiosyncratic blend, coupled with a storyline that seems to nod toward **Jean-Luc Godard** and **French New Wave** cinema, made Zazie In The Metro an unlikely bestseller – and inspired **Louis Malle** to film it.

His autobiographical novels – The Last Days, Odile and A Harsh Winter – are his most accessible. But he indulged his passion for history in The Blue Flowers, which travels from 1264 to 1964 via 1789; sends up and celebrates fairytale and folklore in Saint Glinglin; and goes for broke in his last novel, The Flight Of Icarus, in which half the cast are various novelists and the other half are the characters they are writing about.

What unites all his work is Queneau's intellectual and artistic independence and his humour. He was slave to no school or movement and, unlike many of his peers, more **Marx Brothers** than **Karl Marx**.

INFLUENCED BY James Joyce; **The Odyssey** and **The Iliad** (he said all novels sprang from Homer); Dostoevsky ('the Idiot' was his favourite character).

INFLUENCE ON **The Oulipo school; Camus; Italo Calvino; Monty Python.**

ESSENTIAL READING **Exercises In Style**: one story told 99 different times – but don't be put off, it's wittily done; **Zazie In The Metro.**

FURTHER READING **We Always Treat Women Too Well.**

ANN QUIN

"I want to write 1,000 words an hour – but half will be cut out"

Ann Quin (1936–1973) is the most under-rated of a generation of British writers led in part by **B.S. Johnson** who, in the 1960s, reacted against the working class novel of **John Braine**, **Stan Barstow** and **Alan Sillitoe** to experiment unfashionably with the novel as art form. These novelists were rewarded, largely, with indifference, and Johnson and Quin both committed suicide in the same year.

Quin was born in Brighton, where she lived alone with her mother, and the opening line of her first published novel, Berg – "A man called Berg, who changed his name to Greb, came to a seaside town intending to kill his father…" – recalls the opening line of **Greene**'s Brighton Rock. This is, though, a slightly unrepresentative sample of her fiction. She found her voice with her second published novel, Three, in which the story of a couple who take in a girl who later commits suicide is fragmented with diaries and tape recordings representing the girl's view and the differing recollections – and imaginings – of her by the couple. For an experimental novel, with no speech marks and passages that are almost **Joycean**, Three is remarkably easy to read. Passages isn't quite as satisfying, but Tripticks, in which a man may or may not be on the run across America from his "No. 1 X-wife" and her schoolboy gigolo lover, breaks down into letters, asides, cartoons and the occasional over-explanatory paragraph.

205

Quin long struggled with depression and mental illness and, after Tripticks was published in 1972, suffered such a severe breakdown she was unable to speak for a month. She then began writing her fifth novel and was admitted to study at the University of East Anglia, but drowned herself in the summer of 1973.

INFLUENCED BY **Jane Bowles; B.S. Johnson; R.D. Laing; Eva Figes.**

INFLUENCE ON **Stewart Home; Kathy Acker.**

ESSENTIAL READING **Tripticks**: at times it reads like a pop-art novel – and that's meant as a compliment.

FURTHER READING **Berg** and **Three.**

CULT FICTION

RAYMOND RADIGUET

"In three days I am going to be shot by the soldiers of God"

This prophecy, by **Raymond Radiguet** (1903–1923) to his friend **Jean Cocteau**, didn't come true. The precocious French novelist, author of the succès de scandale The Devil In The Flesh, did die when he was 20, but from typhoid fever.

Radiguet was born in a meteorological station eight miles from Paris. By the time he was 16 he had met Cocteau and dabbled with Dadaism, cubism and surrealism, although isms weren't really his thing. He wrote poems that Cocteau read out to friends, one of whom fell asleep, and, in 1920, The Devil In The Flesh. It's a remarkable tale from Radiguet's life, of a schoolboy who has an affair with a married woman whose husband is away at war, and its boldness shocked critics. Watching the women throw flowers to the soldiers passing on trains, the narrator notes: "The whole thing reminded me of a firework display. Never was there so much wasted wine, so many dead flowers." His second novel, Count d'Orgel's Ball, is a fascinating relic of an age when a taxi ride was cause for excitement.

Alcohol and opium abuse took its toll on Radiguet and he caught a fatal typhoid fever, establishing him as what he despised: a suffering, romantic artist. His fiction, for all the intellectual megastars he knew, is distinguished by a simple unilinear style, and drew heavily on his own life.

206

INFLUENCED BY Pierre Chaderlos Laclos; Madame de Lafayette.

INFLUENCE ON Cocteau; Erik Satie; F. Scott Fitzgerald.

ESSENTIAL READING **The Devil In The Flesh** – brilliant, energetic, callous.

FURTHER READING **Count d'Orgel's Ball**, a careful, virtuoso piece.

DEREK RAYMOND

The godfather of gore

The fiction of **Derek Raymond** (1931–1994) is so full of grisly crime, depicted in such detail, it has puzzled readers and critics. Was Raymond confronting us with the evil that men can do or just out to shock? It's easy to be repelled by his work – even Raymond said he didn't think he could finish writing I Was Dora Suarez.

Born **Robert Cook**, Raymond quit Eton and worked as pornographer, money-launderer and pig-slaughterer. In his 1962 debut (as **Robin Cook**) The Crust On Its Uppers, a prisoner recounts an unsuccessful counterfeiting venture. The novel was praised by the **New Statesman** as "one of the great London novels, peopled by queens, spades, morries, slags, shysters, grifters and grafters…"

While jobbing around French vineyards he wrote his most famous books, the Factory novels. Written as Raymond – in homage to **Raymond Chandler** – they feature an unnamed police officer immersing himself in the minds of London's most monstrous criminals. Savage yet absorbing, the Factory tales were a hit in France, though largely unknown across the Channel.

Like a bad hairstyle, Raymond enjoyed a British revival in the 1980s, leading him to pen his autobiography The Hidden Files and a fifth Factory novel, Dead Man Upright. His book I Was Dora Suarez made one publisher physically sick with its doses of coprophagy (feeding on excrement) and necrophilia.

He died in 1994, drink taking its toll, but he left a body of macabre crime novels that made even the author feel as if he had been, "on a terrible journey through my own guilt."

INFLUENCED BY Chandler; the French crime novelist Jean Patrick-Manchette.

INFLUENCE ON Peter Lovesey; Maxim Jakubowski.

ESSENTIAL READING **He Died With His Eyes Open**, a classic noir piece.

FURTHER READING **The Hidden Files**, a good insight into his influences.

> Derek Raymond's novel I was Dora Suarez caused one publisher to be physically sick with its coprophagy and necrophilia

207

ISHMAEL REED

Too funny for his own good sometimes

Ishmael Reed (1938–) is a trickster. If detailed delineation of character intrigues you, go elsewhere. But if you fancy reading a novel that offers the laughter, energy and exhausting mania of a **Lenny Bruce** concert then Reed is for you.

The Bruce comparison isn't entirely flattering because, just as the comedian could exhaust his audience's patience, you might find Reed works best in short bursts. Because he's so funny, he's under-rated; his innovations often overlooked (he mixed up historical and fictional figures in his 1972 novel Mumbo Jumbo, three years before **E.L. Doctorow** struck gold with the device in Ragtime).

Reed almost didn't get to write, quitting his English degree for lack of funds. But work as a radio-show host and journalist helped him find the time to write The Free-Lance Pallbearers, a scathing satire on radical black politics that puzzled many with its use of black slang and advertising slogans. He has sent up sexual politics in Reckless Eyeballing, parodied the detective novel in Mumbo Jumbo and with Flight To Canada offered his most sustained work, blending fact and fiction into a traditional slave narrative.

Hip-Hop writer **Lee Hubbard** praised Reed as an "unorthodox writer who has taken on the media, the writing establishment, feminists, politicians, blacks, whites and the American institution of higher learning." Not that Reed needs defenders. He has a knack for insults – referring to **Tom Wolfe**, for example, as a neo-Confederate – but sadly, he may be more admired than read.

INFLUENCED BY John A. Williams; Chester Himes; W.E. Dubois.
INFLUENCE ON Steve Cannon.
ESSENTIAL READING **Mumbo Jumbo**; **Flight To Canada**.
FURTHER READING **The Free-Lance Pall Bearers**.

LUKE RHINEHART

The enigmatic Dice Man

The works of **Luke Rhinehart** (c.1932–) are 'cult' in two senses of the word. For while The Dice Man and its offshoots have been cherished by readers, others have used these fictions as a way of life. Heck, your neighbour could be a dice man.

Rhinehart is the nom de plume of **George Cockcroft**, a former English lecturer from New York (according to a scant biography that admits it may contain outright lies). The Dice Man, published in 1971, was his first, most extraordinary book. In it, Rhinehart the character, a bored psychiatrist, gives his life over to chance, rolling dice to choose from a set of options reflecting mundane and extreme parts of his personality. By expressing our less socially acceptable desires we will, the theory goes, be happier, more complete people. In the novel, this means the dice man raping his neighbour and leaving his wife and children – for starters.

Cockcroft switches moods, styles and tenses with ease and intersperses a breakneck plot with psychology and philosophy. It's laugh-out-loud funny in places (Rhinehart's televised dénouement), chillingly bleak in others. Banned in several countries and heavily censored in the US, The Dice Man has inspired thousands to try 'dice living'. There is anecdotal evidence of attempts to start dice centres in the US and Europe, including one involving Cockcroft himself.

Cockcroft also published two philosophical novels, Adventures Of Wim and Matari, as Rhinehart. Many readers are as intrigued by the pseudonymous author as by dice life. His last known address was in Canaan, New York and

the dice man
Novelist of the century.
Loaded.
LUKE RHINEHART

208

there are rumours that he and **H.F. Keating**, author of Memoirs Of An Invisible Man, are the same person.

INFLUENCED BY G.I. Gurdjieff (Russian philosopher and author).

INFLUENCE ON Beer commercials; wannabe cult leaders; David Bowie.

ESSENTIAL READING **The Dice Man; The Search For The Dice Man**.

FURTHER READING **The Book Of The Die** is a 'self-help' book explaining many of the principles surrounding dice living.

JEAN RHYS

Self-confessed "doormat in a world of boots"

The cult status of one of the key writers of the 20th century owes much to the fact that **Jean Rhys** (c.1890–1979) didn't achieve global recognition until she was in her sixties, when Wide Sargasso Sea – the story of the first Mrs Rochester, the mad wife in the attic in **Charlotte Brontë**'s Jane Eyre – was published in 1966.

After this late success Rhys's earlier books, written in the 1920s and 1930s, were republished. The first, The Left Bank And Other Stories, covers the lives of the Parisian demi-monde of writers, artists and ex-pats, a world Rhys knew. Encouraged to write by **Ford Madox Ford** (a writer she met in Paris, who became her lover), she wrote four linked novels: Quartet, After Leaving Mr Mackenzie, Voyage In The Dark and Good Morning, Midnight. The female protagonist of each novel is a composite character, marked by loneliness, poverty and alienation. For writer **A.L. Kennedy**, Rhys's prose conveys "something of the insidious, banal horror of a simply unhappy life," leavened by her grim humour.

Born in Dominica, West Indies, around 1890 (she never liked to give her date of birth), Rhys's early years were spent in colonial respectability in the family's slightly crumbling estate. In 1906 she left for England, where, after the death of her Welsh father, she struggled to make it as a chorus girl, touring the provinces and finding comfort in alcohol while longing for the warmth of her native Dominica.

After moving to Holland she met her first husband **Jean Lenglet** and they lived in Vienna, Paris and England. She wrote the Quartet series as her life lurched from crisis to crisis. Rhys was left broke after Lenglet was imprisoned for currency misdemeanours; their first baby died and she was unable to keep her daughter because of her unsettled life. Her precarious existence continued through her second marriage to agent **Leslie Tilden Smith**. When he died in 1945 she married his cousin **Max Hamer**. Depressed and drinking constantly, they were already desperately poor when Max was jailed for three years for fraud.

Rhys's sense of not belonging originated in post-slavery Dominica: despised

209

there by blacks, she was snubbed by whites in England. In her unfinished autobiography Smile Please she wrote, "I knew in myself I would never really belong anywhere, and I knew it, and all my life would be the same, trying to belong and failing." Wide Sargasso Sea is a product of Rhys's rage at the English attitude to their colonial subjects. In the 19th century, rich West Indian heiresses were often married for money, then abandoned – this was part of what drove her to see Rochester from the mad woman's point of view.

Her reputation faded completely during the war. She was thought to be dead, and when the BBC planned to broadcast a play of Good Morning, Midnight an ad was placed for information on the "late Jean Rhys". When she answered in person, she was sought out by London's literary set. Editor **Diana Athill** nursed Wide Sargasso Sea to publication and, with a group that included **Sonia Orwell** (George's widow), she cared for Jean in her last years.

INFLUENCED BY Modernism; Ford Madox Ford; Charlotte Brontë.

INFLUENCE ON Too little – A.L. Kennedy perhaps; Anita Brookner.

ESSENTIAL READING **Wide Sargasso Sea; Quartet**.

FURTHER READING **Smile Please – An Unfinished Autobiography**.

210

ANNE RICE

Queen of the Damned chronicles

Forget garlic, crosses and stakes through the heart, the group of vampires whose story is told in the Vampire Chronicles are the kind of undead the post-Buffy generation understands – gorgeous creatures of the night who span human history from the time of Ancient Egypt to contemporary San Francisco.

This compulsively readable series has made **Anne Rice** (1941–) a bestselling cult author. The first volume, Interview With The Vampire, introduces her key character, Lestat. The story is told by Louis – a sensitive 'all-too-human' young vampire – created by Lestat at the time of the French revolution. Lestat and Louis love each other and turn six-year-old Claudia into a child vampire. Claudia's mind matures while her body doesn't, leading her to loathe her creators.

Rice says, "The vampires are a natural metaphor for people because of their affluence, powers and greed." Her preoccupation with mortality may also reflect her life. Her mother died when Rice was 14 (causing the family to leave New Orleans) and in 1972 her young daughter, with poet husband **Stan Rice**, died from leukaemia. As therapy, Rice began to write Interview With The Vampire. The second and third volumes, The Vampire Lestat and Queen Of The Damned, were so successful that the Rice family moved back to New Orleans to live in a grand mansion that often features in the stories.

Anne Rice, dressed in her inimitable casual style, at a book signing

The novels offer a completely realised other world that is almost **Tolkienesque**. The vampires' physical beauty, access to wealth, sexual freedom and homoeroticism infuse the gothic ambience with blockbuster glamour. The central theme of the chronicles is immortality, yet at times Rice can be portentous and overblown. The vampires discuss their angst as if at an academic symposium: 'Immortal versus Mortal: binary oppositions in the iconography of the undead' or 'Media Vampires: whither the modern bloodsucker?' – discuss.

INFLUENCED BY J. Sheridan LeFanu; M.R. James; Emily Brontë.

INFLUENCE ON Chelsea Quinn Yarbro; Poppy Z. Brite.

ESSENTIAL READING **Interview With The Vampire**; **The Vampire Lestat**; **Queen Of The Damned**.

FURTHER READING Rice's interest in erotic writing is given full expression in the **Beauty** novels written under her pen name A.N. Roquelaure.

ARTHUR RIMBAUD

The boy-genius of French symbolism

"The poet of revolt, and the greatest," said **Albert Camus** of **Arthur Rimbaud** (1854–1891) – whose extraordinary, hallucinatory work resonated throughout the 20th century and into the 21st. He has been called the precursor of surrealism, gay liberation, the **Beat** movement and even 'the godfather of punk'.

Rimbaud's father, an army captain, left his wife and four children in 1860. The stern, pious 'Widow Rimbaud' (as she termed herself) brought up the family in poverty in north-east France. Rimbaud was described by one teacher as a "perfect little monster", yet by the age of 14 he won competitions for poetry and at 16 his first lines (in Latin) were published. Two years later, Rimbaud set out on a course of poetic destruction – placing "an ulcer on the anus" of the goddess of beauty in Venus Anadyomene and making distinctly homosexual allusions.

With the Franco-Prussian war raging, the teenage Rimbaud embraced anarchism, alcohol and violence, celebrated in such poems as The Parisian Orgy. In his quest "to reach the unknown by the derangement of all the senses" he sent poems to **Paul Verlaine** (to his mind, the only living "seer" in French poetry), who invited him to Paris. Rimbaud arrived in the capital with one of his most inspired poems, The Drunken Boat: a dizzying vision that describes a boat after the loss of its crew – interpreted as an allegory of human life, a drinking binge, the Paris Commune and the poet's detachment from morality. Dirty, beautiful and foul-mouthed, Rimbaud lived briefly with Verlaine and his wife (who threw him out), then gave several brilliant, incest-ridden poems to the album of the **Zutistes** – a group of poets who wrote verse in a notebook – while drinking absinthe, smoking hashish and having a debauched affair with Verlaine.

In 1872 Rimbaud persuaded Verlaine to go with him to London, where Rimbaud began Illuminations: a collection of poems described as the origin of free verse. After Verlaine shot Rimbaud in the wrist and was jailed for two years, Rimbaud returned to live with his mother, locked himself in the attic and finished A Season In Hell, a series of prose poems considered to be his greatest and most original work.

At the age of 19 he stopped writing and set out on foot across Europe, pursuing the life of a vagabond. He taught in Germany, unloaded cargo in Marseilles, joined then deserted the Dutch army, lost his clothes and money in Austria, toured with a circus in Denmark and laboured in a quarry in Cyprus, before moving to Aden (in present-day Yemen) in 1880, where he was based until his death. As a trader and gun-runner, Rimbaud became an expert on East Africa, travelling through some of its most remote and inhospitable regions, and was the first European to see Ogaden in Abyssinia.

> "Every form of love, of suffering, of madness; he consumes all the poisons, and keeps only their quintessences"
>
> Arthur Rimbaud's how-to tips for aspiring poets

213

INFLUENCED BY Charles Baudelaire; Paul Verlaine; the **Bible**.

INFLUENCE ON Cocteau; Ginsberg; Bob Dylan; Patti Smith.

ESSENTIAL READING **A Season In Hell; Illuminations**.

FURTHER READING **Rimbaud** by Graham Robb.

ALAIN ROBBE-GRILLET

The experimental genius

The leading exponent of the **nouveau roman** (new fiction) and still one of the world's leading experimental writers, **Alain Robbe-Grillet**'s work is based on the belief that there is no objective truth, only subjective impression. His novels centre on precise physical descriptions, subverting conventional elements like plot and character. His compelling writing mixes various popular genres (particularly detective and spy fiction) and owes much to surrealism and even **Alfred Hitchcock**.

Robbe-Grillet (1922–)was born to a family of scientists and engineers in Brest, north-west France. He followed the family tradition, but his professional life varied: he laboured in a German tank factory during the war and supervised banana plantations in the West Indies. Falling ill in 1951, he wrote what became his first published novel, The Erasers. But it was The Voyeur, published in 1955

"Balzac knows
society but
Mersault
doesn't know
if his mother
died today.
The world is too
incoherent for
authors to look
at it like God"

Alain Robbe-Grillet on
the novel's evolution

with several critical essays, that made nouveau roman part of the critical lexicon. It was followed by Jealousy, which **Nabokov** called one of the century's greatest novels. In The Labyrinth – a **Kafkaesque** tale of a soldier's attempt to deliver a parcel before the enemy arrive, although he can't remember the name of the street – completed a quartet that still stands as his best work. As his star rose he wrote the screenplay for **Alain Resnais**'s Last Year At Marienbad.

Robbe-Grillet's subsequent novels are more cinematic, focused on setting, incorporating more violence and eroticism. Much of his work centres on mysteries: a murder, an abduction, an affair. As the novel folds in on itself the reader is left doubting who was the murderer and whether anyone was actually murdered. Time and space are often confused, events repeat themselves with slight variations. The effect can be hypnotic. For too long little of his work was translated into English, but a revival of interest has seen the publication of the first of a three-volume autobiography, Ghosts In The Mirror, and the European bestseller Repetition.

214

INFLUENCED BY Beckett; Borges; Kafka; Virginia Woolf.
INFLUENCE ON Roland Barthes; Christine Brooke-Rose; Umberto Eco.
ESSENTIAL READING **In The Labyrinth**.
FURTHER READING R.C. Smith's **Understanding Robbe-Grillet**.

TOM ROBBINS

The rewarding results of taking acid

Unusually for an American countercultural writer, **Tom Robbins** (1936–) only began to publish in the 1970s – finding spectacular success with Even Cowgirls Get The Blues in 1976. In his eight wildly imaginative novels he develops a philosophy – combining Buddhism, Christianity, mysticism and shamanism – that may have roots in the "embryonic golden age" of the 1960s, but which is consistently inventive and funny enough to avoid being a throwback.

Born in Blowing Rock, in North Carolina's Appalachian Mountains, Robbins wrote his first book of stories at the age of five. After three years in the air force in Korea – where he taught meteorology and sold black-market goods – he hitched across America, working periodically on newspapers, got married and divorced and, on 16 July 1963 – "the most rewarding day of my life" – took **LSD**. The drug has affected Robbins's outlook to this day: the spoon, sock, can, shell and stick travelling to Jerusalem in Skinny Legs And All, for example, stemming from his realisation that inanimate objects have "a secret life" of their own.

Robbins says he found his voice as a novelist in 1967, reviewing a **Doors** concert in which he called their music "early cunnilingual, late patricidal lunchtime in the Everglades." Moving to Washington State, marrying (and divorcing) for a second time, he started Another Roadside Attraction: a typically odd story about a group of American dropouts, who steal the mummified body of **Jesus Christ** from the Vatican and exhibit it at their roadside zoo. The book became a cult favourite and, with its female narrator and irrepressible wordplay, was something of a blueprint for his later work.

In Even Cowgirls Get The Blues, beautiful young Sissy Hankshaw turns hitch-hiking into an art form with the help of her enormous thumbs and winds up in the company of lesbian cowgirls and a cave-dwelling escapee of the World War II Japanese internment camps. One mark of the book's immense success is that the reclusive Robbins was by now widely assumed to be a woman.

He has been remarkably consistent, publishing several good books in the last three decades. Still Life With Woodpecker and Jitterbug Perfume are highly regarded, though many critics find him self-indulgent. His most recent novel, Villa Incognito – in which a group of ageing Americans are unwittingly involved with a semi-mythical, badger-like creature – is, some say, his best yet.

215

INFLUENCED BY Joyce Cary; Mark Twain; Gabriel García Márquez.

INFLUENCE ON Terry Pratchett; Tony Vigorito.

ESSENTIAL READING **Even Cowgirls Get The Blues**; **Jitterbug Perfume**.

FURTHER READING **Another Roadside Attraction**.

JOSEPH ROTH

"The roads I have travelled are the years of my past"

Joseph Roth (1894–1939) was a teller of autobiographical fiction, full of people who had, in the words of one of his characters, been "found unfit for death". Living in central Europe as the Austro-Hungarian empire collapsed and **Hitler** emerged, Roth tells the story of central Europe from the latter half of the 19th century to World War II, on the eve of which he died, in exile, in Paris.

If that makes him sound dull, Roth was anything but. Born an Austrian Jew in Galicia in 1894, he invented stories about the father he never knew: Polish nobleman, Austrian officer – it didn't matter to Roth, who said he only ever felt

at home in his own self although, in retrospect, he regarded the Hapsburg empire with some fondness. In exile in Paris he used to bribe tailors to make him the unfashionable trousers he had worn as a soldier of the empire on the Russian front in World War I.

His fiction is both historically specific and shaped by his life's sadnesses. After the loss of his father, there were other losses – his homeland, with the rise of Nazism his adopted homeland Germany, followed by flight to Paris. His novels – his golden decade stretching from 1928 to 1938 – were often written in cafés and hotels. His wife **Friedl** suffered from schizophrenia, a disease that triggered his alcoholism as if, says author **Michael Hoffman**, he felt he owed her that self-destruction.

Unlike **Malcolm Lowry**, another alcoholic teller of autobiographical fiction, Roth was no literary narcissist. His best novels, The Radetzky March and The Emperor's Tomb, use families to tell a broader tale of decay. Caught between two brutalities – one monarchical, the other revolutionary – he was drawn to neither, but observed both. As early as 1923 his novel Der Spinnennetz highlights the rise of right-wing nationalism and mentions Hitler by name.

Inevitably he is compared to **Robert Musil**, but as **Nadime Gordimer** put it, "Musil's evocation of that time is a marvellous discourse; Roth's involves [the] creation of a vivid population of conflicting characters expressing that time." His characters live for us, even though ultimately they express the author's belief in "the old and eternal truth that the individual is always defeated in the end."

INFLUENCED BY His journalism; Emperor Franz Josef II.

INFLUENCE ON Thomas Mann; Christopher Isherwood; Alan Furst.

ESSENTIAL READING **The Radetzky March; The Emperor's Tomb**.

FURTHER READING **Job** prefigures Singer's work; Tunda, the protagonist in **Flight Without End**, closely resembles Roth as the author imagined himself.

JUAN RULFO

Capturing the flavour of Mexico in words and images

He only published two books in his lifetime, but **Juan Rulfo** (1918–1986) is one of the most influential Latin American writers; **Jorge Luis Borges** called Rulfo's only novel Pedro Páramo one of the most important of the century.

Born **Neponucemo Rulfo** in Mexico, he lived through the Mexican Revolution and was raised in an orphanage after his father was killed and his mother died. The search for the missing father and death are crucial subjects in Pedro Páramo – and a constant concern in Rulfo's stories. The novel blends fantasy and reality, presents new narrative structures and its characters are dark and joyless, but he captures the life and language of rural Mexico in all its intimacy. **The Guardian** compared it to: "Wuthering Heights located in Mexico and written by **Kafka**." In his book of short stories El Llano en Llamas he develops the slow pace, inner dialogue and introspection that also characterise his work.

Rulfo wrote all his life, but often destroyed his stories once finished. He kept detailed notebooks, published posthumously, revealing the graft behind the craft. He had a passion for photography: all that is praised in his writing – his ability to evoke images, non-judgemental observation – is even more evident in his collection of portraits, landscapes and buildings.

INFLUENCED BY Emily Brontë; Faulkner; Mariano Azuela; Martin Luis Guzmán.
INFLUENCE ON Gabriel García Márquez.
ESSENTIAL READING **Pedro Páramo**.
FURTHER READING **El Llano En Llamas** (only in Spanish).

DAMON RUNYON

Gamblers, gangsters, guys and dolls

Best known for his short stories – centred on a fictitious golden age in and around Times Square in Prohibition-era New York – **Damon Runyon** (1884 –1946) brought a journalist's eye for detail and ear for conversation to his stories.

Born in the wrong Manhattan (the one in Kansas), young **Alfred Damon Runyan** joined the family trade, newspaper journalism, on being expelled from school. In 1898 he fought in the Spanish-American war, writing for local papers in the Philippines. He then wrote for newspapers in the Rocky Mountain region, one of whom renamed him 'Runyon', and moved to New York City in 1910, spending ten years covering professional boxing for the **New York American**. He was a notorious gambler, believing, in the words of Ecclesiastes: "The race is not always to the swift nor the battle to the strong, but that's the way to bet."

Runyon fictionalised the gamblers and bookies, gangsters and petty hangers-on he met in the New York sports world, for a straight audience appalled by and enthralled by his lurid tales. Nathan Detroit, Big Jule, Harry the Horse, Good Time Charlie, Sky Masterson and the rest appeared in Runyon's recognisable, vivid style, using a mixture of formal speech and unbelievably appealing slang.

By the end of the 1930s he had become a national celebrity, holding court in Mindy's, smoking heavily while he argued the toss each night. Since his death his reputation has grown, helped by the splendid 1955 Hollywood production of the Broadway musical Guys And Dolls (based on his celebrated and convoluted short work, The Idyll Of Miss Sarah Brown). He lives on in the **Oxford English Dictionary**, which uses the word 'Runyonese' to describe "slang or underworld jargon characteristic or suggestive of that used in the short stories of Runyon."

INFLUENCED BY Chekhov; Mark Twain.

INFLUENCE ON Nelson Bond; P.G. Wodehouse; Brian Jacques.

ESSENTIAL READING **Guys And Dolls: The Stories Of Damon Runyon**.

FURTHER READING **Broadway Boogie Woogie: Damon Runyon And The Making Of New York City Culture** by Daniel R. Schwarz.

MARQUIS DE SADE

The original lust for life

As a writer, poet, playwright and lover, the **Marquis de Sade** (1740–1814) was committed to breaking down all moral and sexual boundaries, and so explored the very depths of human perversion.

Born in Paris, the son of one of the queen's ladies-in-waiting, at the age of four Sade attacked a playmate and was sent to live with his uncle in a castle whose dungeons would profoundly influence his work. Demobilised from the army in 1763, Sade was forced by his father to marry the rich but socially inferior **Renée-Pelagie de Montreuil**. Undeterred, he retained a Paris apartment for prostitutes, one of whom reported his sacrilegious perversions to the police – leading to his arrest and imprisonment. In 1768, having whipped a prostitute, he was jailed again. The following year he was convicted of poisoning and sodomy when several Marseilles prostitutes became ill after one of his elaborate, aphrodisiac-fuelled orgies, and he fled to Italy with his wife's sister, **Anne-Prospère**. Arrested in Savoy, he was imprisoned again, but staged a dramatic escape.

In 1777 the father of one of Sade's servant girls tried to shoot him. But Sade was soon back inside, where he mostly remained until his transfer to the Bastille in 1784. It was at this time that he wrote most of his most famous work, 120 Days Of Sodom, which was rescued by a guard during the revolution and rediscovered only in 1904. Horrific, though often very funny, it is the story of a group of "sexual adventurers" who repair to a secluded castle to indulge in incest, rape, paedophilia and other perversions (some of them, surely, physically impossible) until the meagre plot degenerates into a simple list of atrocities.

Before the 1789 revolution Sade also wrote The Misfortunes Of Virtue – later adapted into Justine – in which God is a force of evil, but his other manuscripts were lost in the storming of the Bastille. Released under the 1790 amnesty, he was published under a nom de plume – books such as *The Philosophy Of The Bedroom* and *Juliette*, a sequel to *Justine* – and twice avoided the guillotine. But in 1801 he was arrested and spent the last 11 years of his life in a prison/asylum without charge. Sade wrote several books during his time here, including an unfinished ten-volume erotic novel, *The Days Of Florbelle*, which was confiscated and later burned. He was having an affair with a 17-year-old member of staff when he died, aged 74.

> "Either kill me or take me as I am, because I am damned if I will ever change"
>
> The Marquis de Sade writing home to his wife

INFLUENCED BY Ann Radcliffe; Henry Fielding; Matthew Lewis.
INFLUENCE ON Charles Baudelaire; Georges Bataille; Angela Carter.
ESSENTIAL READING **120 Days Of Sodom; Justine.**
FURTHER READING Neil Schaeffer's **The Marquis de Sade: A Life**.

ANTOINE DE SAINT-ÉXUPERY

Author of the third most popular book of all-time

Aviator, adventurer and author of *The Little Prince*, **Antoine de Saint-Éxupery** (1900–1944) wrote several no less magical books for adults. "All grown-ups were first children, but few of them remember it," he says in the dedicatory of *The Little Prince*.

Saint-Éxupery was born **Antoine-Marie-Roger de Saint-Éxupery** to an aristocratic family in Lyon, France. In 1912 he had his first flight in an aeroplane, an ecstatic experience that inspired a poem and encouraged him to train for a pilot's licence. In 1926 he published his first story, *The Pilot*. For three years he flew mail across North Africa, suffering several near-fatal accidents and run-ins with hostile tribes, and became director of an airfield in the heart of the Spanish Sahara, where he wrote his first book *Southern Mail*: an unashamedly romantic account of the pioneering mail pilots and beauty and danger of the desert. He celebrated the dizzying challenges involved in flying across the Andes in similar spirit with *Night Flight*, with an introduction by **André Gide**.

He returned to Africa with his wife Consuelo in 1931 and four years later, in an incident that proved key to *The Little Prince*, he crashed in the Sahara, walking for five days before being rescued by a Bedouin caravan. In 1937 he crashed in Guatemala, smashing his shoulder and fracturing his skull. While in hospital he recalled his years as a pilot in *Wind, Sand And Stars*. In World War II he was permitted to fly reconnaissance missions, which inspired *Flight To Arras*.

The Little Prince is ostensibly a children's book, but it is as much directed at adults who might have forgotten the need for love and friendship. Narrated by an aviator who has crashed in the desert, it tells of his encounter with a boy-prince who comes from an asteroid that he shares with three small volcanoes and a temperamental rose, who is travelling through space in search of a friend.

Simple, poignant and beautifully illustrated by Saint-Éxupery, it was the last book he published in his lifetime. In July 1944 his Lightning P-38 was lost over southern France, presumed shot down. Its wreckage was discovered in 2000.

INFLUENCED BY Voltaire; Gide.

INFLUENCE ON Hugo Pratt; Jean Renoir; Wulf Zendik; Paolo Coelho.

ESSENTIAL READING **Wind, Sand And Stars**; **The Little Prince**.

FURTHER READING **The Tale Of The Rose: The Love Story Behind The Little Prince** by Consuelo de Saint-Éxupery.

J.D. SALINGER

Iconic recluse who's most definitely not a phony

In recent years it has been claimed that **Jerome David Salinger** (1919–) has written film scripts under aliases; is the acclaimed author **Thomas Pynchon**; has travelled halfway across the world secretly to meet female readers; and has stockpiled enough material to release hundreds of books on his death.

The iconic author won't be answering any of the above charges any time soon. He has lived as a recluse in New Hampshire since 1953 and not published a sentence since 1963. He ventures from his house only to buy groceries and apparently does not own a telephone. It's hard not to link this withdrawal to the publication, in 1951, of The Catcher In The Rye.

Salinger never liked publicity, eschewing what his hero Holden Caulfield dismissed as "that David Copperfield kind of crap" by refusing to issue dust-jacket photos or biographies. Born to a successful, emotionally distant middle-class New York family, he was educated, like Caulfield, at boarding school and was disturbed by his experiences in the infantry in World War II. He acquired a cult following with whimsical short stories in literary magazines before publishing his only full-length book, which relates Caulfield's weekend of discovery in New York after being kicked out of school for under-achievement.

Salinger combined the ear for colloquial speech and warm characterisation of his hero **Ring Lardner** with the romanticism of **F. Scott Fitzgerald**. Simplicity itself to read, Catcher is subtly anti-establishment in tone: Caulfield opts out of mainstream education, shuns the sexual machismo of his peers and dreams of retiring to a ranch. Such ideas have proved oddly controversial; many

US states banned the book for decades, denouncing it as "communist", "anti-white" and "obscene". Meanwhile, obsessive Salinger fans deluged him with sackloads of mail. All this and the book's implication in the murder of **John Lennon** (see box) may explain Salinger's recalcitrance.

Salinger published a collection of prose, Nine Stories, and two books containing novellas based around the fictional Glass family before disappearing. Yet, in 2001, he mysteriously listed an old short story, Hapworth 16, 1924, for publication as a new book. After six months it was withdrawn, fuelling the suspicion that Salinger might secretly be laughing at the furore he has provoked.

INFLUENCED BY Mark Twain; Ring Lardner; F. Scott Fitzgerald.

INFLUENCE ON Bret Easton Ellis; Kurt Vonnegut; Harold Brodkey; W.P. Kinsella.

ESSENTIAL READING **The Catcher In The Rye**; **Nine Stories**, which is sometimes published as **For Esme: With Love And Squalor**; **Franny And Zooey**, two Glass family novellas collected in one book.

FURTHER READING **In Search Of J.D. Salinger** by Ian Hamilton.

THE CATCHER IN THE RYE CONSPIRACIES

"Then that morning I went to the bookstore and bought The Catcher In The Rye. I'm sure the large part of me is Holden Caulfield, who is the main person in the book. The small part of me must be the Devil."

So reads an excerpt from the statement **Mark David Chapman** gave to the Parole Board in 2000 while appealing for parole from his sentence for the murder of **John Lennon** 20 years earlier. The part Salinger's novel played in Lennon's shooting is unclear, but Chapman was certainly obsessed with the book and with Caulfield in the months leading up to the crime.

As his mental state deteriorated and he made plans to confront Lennon, Chapman began to sign his name as Holden Caulfield and told his wife he was planning to change his name by deed poll. He bought a copy of the book on the morning of 8 December,

inscribed it with the words "This is my statement – Holden Caulfield" and, after shooting Lennon, read it as he waited for the police. Chapman may have seen Lennon as one of the "phonies" Caulfield despised due to the apparent contradiction of his anti-capitalist message and his vast wealth. He later said the killing had been carried out to "promote" the book.

According to **Fenton Bresler**, author of Who Killed John Lennon?, the FBI used key words from the book as "triggers" to induce a psychotic state in Chapman and encourage him to murder Lennon, a leading anti-war campaigner. Three months later **John Hinckley** shot and wounded **President Reagan**. On his bedside table in his hotel room police found a copy of The Catcher In The Rye, in which he had methodically detailed his plan. Hinckley submitted the book as his sole defence.

CULT FICTION
JEAN-PAUL SARTRE

PENGUIN BOOKS

The Age of Reason

Jean-Paul Sartre

"I have done what I had to do"

"Hell is other people" is perhaps the quote most often attributed to **Jean-Paul Sartre** (1905–1980), but France's most famous novelist and philosopher wasn't quite the old curmudgeon most people think.

Born and educated in Paris, Sartre was a novelist and philosopher, political activist, playwright, biographer and critic. He published several psychological studies, but it was his first novel *Nausea* and his stories *Intimacy*, both published in 1938, that brought him success. In the 1940s young writers hung out in Paris, hoping to glimpse him with the feminist thinker **Simone de Beauvoir**. After she first met him, **Iris Murdoch** said, "His presence… was like that of a pop star."

The novels promoted Sartre's existentialism. He assumed there is no God and that man is condemned to freedom, which he has to face if he is to make his life meaningful – committing himself to a role – because there's no such thing as fate. All his characters are concerned with the struggle to remain free. In *Nausea* the narrator is soul-sick with himself: "My thought is me: that's why I can't stop. I exist because I think… and I can't stop myself from thinking. At this very moment – it's frightful – if I exist, it is because I am horrified at existing." Gloomy, but strangely liberating stuff.

His big existential philosophical treaty was *Being And Nothingness*, a book destined to be more talked about than read. But this existential humanism was the theme for his series of novels, *The Roads To Freedom*, from 1945 to 1949. Feminists have accused him of misogyny. **Angela Carter** once said, "Why is a nice girl like Simone de Beauvoir sucking up to a boring old fart like Jean-Paul Sartre?"

When he'd lost his eyesight and could no longer read or write, aged 70, he said "In one sense, it robs me of all reason for existing; I was, and I am no longer, if you wish." He declined the **Nobel Prize** for Literature in 1964 as he didn't want to be turned into "an institution". Like it or not, he had already become one.

INFLUENCED BY Martin Heidegger; Nietzsche; Simone De Beauvoir.

INFLUENCE ON Camus; Michel Foucault.

ESSENTIAL READING **Age Of Reason**; **Nausea**: "From a purely literary point of view, it is the best thing I have done," Sartre once said.

FURTHER READING **Words**.

222

Move other Agatha, Ngaio and Margery

Of all the queens of detective fiction's Golden Age (**Agatha Christie**, **Ngaio Marsh** and **Margery Allingham**), **Dorothy Sayers** (1893–1957) raised the genre above the drawing-room whodunnit. Her stories don't subjugate everything to the puzzle. Crime novelist **P.D. James** says: "She used this well-worn genre to say something true about men and women and the society in which they lived."

Sayers spent her childhood in the Fens, where her father was parish priest, guided, she said, by duty, self-control and obedience. She was one of the first women to graduate from Oxford and her first book, Whose Body, was the first of 14 novels and short stories to feature her upper-class sleuth Lord Peter Wimsey.

The 'olde-worlde charm' of Lord Peter still appeals, despite the quaint "damn it", "how beastly" and "it was rotten of me" remarks. His slight physique and fey manner disguise a sharp intellect and strength. The four novels that pair him with novelist Harriet Vane: Strong Poison, Have His Carcase, Gaudy Night and Busman's Honeymoon are judged her best work.

It's hard not to see Vane as a barely disguised self-portrait. Like her character, Sayers's relationships with men were unhappy. On the rebound from her great love, novelist **John Cournos**, she had an affair that ended in pregnancy and to avoid disgrace had her son in secret, paying her cousin to bring up the child.

In the first Harriet Vane novel, Strong Poison, Vane is on trial for poisoning her lover. Lord Peter falls in love with her instantly and Sayers's own struggle between the romantic and the intellectual life is played out in their troubled courtship. Gaudy Night shows Sayers's skill with a large cast of characters, while The Nine Tailors perfectly depicts village life in the Fens between the wars. She prided herself on her research, but it would be nigh impossible to commit murder by many of the methods she devises. In Unnatural Death an elderly woman is killed by an injection of air. **P.D. James** says the syringe would have been too heavy to carry and the mere sight of it would have scared off the victim.

Sayers also published plays, works of theology and a translation of **Dante**'s Divine Comedy. Her work rate is reflected in her letters – anyone writing to her, especially with obscure theological questions, received a response of many pages.

223

INFLUENCED BY Wilkie Collins; Conan Doyle; Sheridan LeFanu.

INFLUENCE ON Francis Fyfield; Jill Paton Walsh; and, most of all, P.D. James, chair of the Dorothy L. Sayers Society.

ESSENTIAL READING **Gaudy Night**, and the other Vane novels if you're keen.

FURTHER READING For diehards, Jill Paton Walsh's completion of Sayers's unfinished novel **Thrones, Dominations**.

Delmore Schwartz's life, death and work haunted Saul Bellow and Lou Reed

"Into the Destructive element… that is the way"

The life and death of **Delmore Schwartz** (1913–1966) are even more magnificent, terrible, funny, perplexing and moving than his own short stories and verse. In the kind of bitter irony that plagued Schwartz, he is now better known as the model for Humboldt, the self-destructive writer in **Saul Bellow**'s novel Humboldt's Gift, than for his own work.

At the age of nine, he was woken by his Romanian-Jewish parents, who demanded that he choose between them. The failure of their marriage was the first of many failures, loading down a scale that Schwartz could never balance.

He published his first acclaimed short story, In Dreams Begin Responsibilities, when he was 22. Three years later that story gave its title to an anthology praised by the likes of **Nabokov** and **T.S. Eliot**.

His star soared in public while in private the cracks widened. He was, Bellow says, "the **Mozart** of conversation," but unwritten masterpieces pained him. His first marriage, after a wedding at which the bride's parents wept openly and bitterly and the groom passed out drunk, somehow lasted six years. Of his second marriage he said, "I got married a second time in the way that, when a murder is committed, crackpots turn up at the police station and confess to the crime."

Fuelled by drink and pills, Schwartz's eruptions became more prolonged and strange, inventing adulteries for his wife and, after attacking an art critic, being committed. His unravelling is one of the threads in **Donald Margulies**'s play Collected Stories, in which a protagonist recalls her love for Schwartz. Bizarrely, one of Humboldt/Schwartz's complaints in Bellow's novel is that his life has been turned into a Broadway play. His final years were punctuated by intoxication, incarceration, accusation and sightings on a park bench, where he seemed like a man waiting for death. Yet he also managed to teach at Syracuse University. He died of a heart attack in 1966, in the corridor of a New York hotel. He was, some say, working on a meisterwork. A note in his room read: "Into the Destructive element… that is the way." His body lay unclaimed in the morgue for days.

THE WIT OF DELMORE SCHWARTZ

When drunk, or high on pills, some of Delmore Schwartz's monologues could sound like early exercises in the postmodern miniaturism of **Donald Barthelmes**. His riff on **T.S. Eliot**, **Queen Elizabeth II** and fellatio being a case in point. In writing, his parodies could be deadly sharp. He was obsessed by Eliot and in one letter he perfectly caught the dafter nuances of Eliot's intellectual posturing: "Anyway, at present, I am entirely, for the remainder of January, a royalist in literature, a classicist in politics (eg the Athenian republic) and an Anglo-Catholic in all questions of lyric poetry."

Schwartz's short stories are too rarely read, but he exerts influence. He is probably the writer who first said "Even paranoids have enemies." At Syracuse, one student, **Lou Reed**, called Schwartz his "spiritual godfather" and dedicated a track to him on the first **Velvet Underground** album. His friend **John Berryman** recalls Schwartz in one poem: "We never learned why he came or what he wanted. His mission was obscure. His mission was real but obscure."

INFLUENCED BY T.S. Eliot; Ezra Pound (though he wrote to Pound: "I want to resign as one of your most studious admirers"); James Joyce; the **Bible**; Kafka.

INFLUENCE ON Robert Lowell; Saul Bellow; Philip Roth; Bernard Malamud.

ESSENTIAL READING **In Dreams Begin Responsibilities**, depressing, funny, moving, painful: the short stories have Joycean qualities.

FURTHER READING Bellow's novel **Humboldt's Gift**.

LEONARDO SCIASCIA

Introducing Pirandello into the detective novel

Leonardo Sciascia (1921–1989) stood the mystery story on its head. This Sicilian genius created remarkable novels, notably Equal Danger, in which the detective, not the suspect, is the character who behaves suspiciously and is left fatally isolated. They investigate crimes without a culprit, committed not by an individual but by a system or organisation (the Mafia) which, in a touch from **Luigi Pirandello**, is constantly said not to exist. As **Gore Vidal** notes, the fate of these loners is "not only to be defeated, but worse, never to be understood."

Sciascia (it's pronounced 'Sha-sha') acquired his suspicions early, growing up on an island where he had to evade the compulsory ludicrousness of **Mussolini**'s Fascism and the tangible menace of the Mafia. He grew up reading **Denis Diderot** and Pirandello and, after working as a teacher and clerk in a state granary, was given a lifetime pension in 1969 that enabled him to become a full-time writer, though he briefly ventured into politics out of anger and despair.

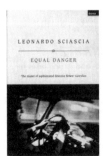

Sciascia's fiction is haunted by the politics, history and criminology of his island and his country. His first mystery novel, The Day Of The Owl, concerns the mysterious death of a building contractor in Sicily. Never a laugh-a-minute man, he brings a strange blend of cynical, insightful humour and quiet indignation to his best stories. His fiction often anticipated reality. In One Way Or Another, a tale of power brokers at a spiritual retreat, a murder victim has paid fixers with secret cheques; such payments later figured in a real scandal, discussed in the article The President's Cheque that disappeared before publication, written by a journalist who was shot. One of the real people recognisable in the film of this novel is **Aldo Moro**, the prime minister kidnapped and executed by the Red Brigades, an episode that provoked Sciascia to write The Moro Affair, a chilling examination of Italian realpolitik.

The stain on Sciascia's reputation – and it is a large one – is that just before his death he wrote an article criticising two anti-Mafia judges who had, ironically, been inspired by Sciascia. The Mafia practice, as Sciascia knew, is to isolate and discredit victims before they are killed. His article did that and the two judges were both soon dead; a dénouement that prompted one Mafia historian to decide he could read no more Sciascia.

INFLUENCED BY Pirandello; Diderot; Faulkner; Orwell.
INFLUENCE ON Crime writer Andrea Camilleri; Pier Paolo Pasolini; Paul Auster.
ESSENTIAL READING **Equal Danger**; the short stories **The Wine Dark Sea**.
FURTHER READING **The Moro Affair**.

HUBERT SELBY JR   227
Turning profanities into rhythmic urban literature

Born in Brooklyn, New York, **Hubert Selby Jr** (1928–2004) wrote fiction as gritty and dangerous as the streets of his hometown. A high-school dropout, at 18 he caught tuberculosis and was told he had only months to live. Surgery and treatment with a newly synthesised drug, streptomycin, saved his life, although left him short of a lung and 11 ribs. He was virtually confined to bed for the next ten years, with a morphine habit and pulmonary problems that would endure until they finally killed him.

Selby began to write, weaving life stories for the characters he observed from his bed. While holding down jobs as a secretary, insurance analyst and copywriter in the 1950s, he gradually assembled the cast and plot for a loosely linked series of short stories called The Queen Is Dead. Several of these stories were published in literary journals across the US, including **The Provincetown Review**. In a foretaste of trials to come, **The Provincetown Review**'s editor found himself accused of selling pornographic literature to a minor for publishing the story Tralala.

When Last Exit To Brooklyn appeared in 1964, Tralala was in its pages, together with a crew of unredeemed Hogarthian grotesques, drag queens, hoodlums, closeted homosexuals, prostitutes and junkies. Selby didn't care for reform or social protest: he just reported what happened to the urban poor and recorded the language of the streets. But his novel caused a worldwide riot of controversy. When, after three years of prosecution, the book was finally back on the shelves, it had sold half a million in paperback alone.

Money, fame, success and increasingly pointed inquiries from his publishers regarding a second novel pushed Selby into alcoholism and a serious heroin addiction. He kept writing, always when he was sober. He would shut himself away for five or more hours a day, always leaving a line at the end so he would have an easy place to start again the next morning.

INFLUENCED BY Henry Miller; Norman Mailer; Hemingway.
INFLUENCE ON Darren Aronovsky; David Lynch; The Smiths.
ESSENTIAL READING **Requiem For A Dream**; **Last Exit To Brooklyn**.
FURTHER READING **Song Of The Silent Snow**.

WILL SELF

The rock star of the literati

Will Self (1961–) famously made headlines in 1997 when he was sacked by **The Observer** for taking heroin on **John Major**'s election campaign plane, just the surreal sort of thing that could afflict one of his fictional characters.

Will doesn't want you to identify with him

Self was born in London to an English professor and a Jewish-American mother who encouraged his rebellious streak, even his early experimentation with soft drugs. But by 17 he was taking heroin, a habit he kicked only in 1999. At 19, at Oxford University, he was diagnosed as borderline schizophrenic, and was on bail when he sat his finals. He quit drugs for the first time in 1986 and wrote The Quantity Theory Of Insanity, a short-story collection full of the themes that have preoccupied him since: drugs, sex, violence, mental health and the trials of urban living. The wit and wordiness was reminiscent of **Martin Amis** – there were rumours he was writing under the alias of Self (John Self is the hero of Amis's Money). By the time it reached the bookshops in 1991, Self was writing prolifically and back on drugs.

Self admits he struggles with plot and character. Elaborate imagery, clever ideas and a nihilistic world view are his strengths. He styles himself a "destructive intellectual force" and he targets all the absurdities of modern life. The novellas Cock And Bull describe a woman who grows a penis and rapes her husband and a man who grows a vagina behind his knee and is seduced by his male doctor. His best book to date, How The Dead Live, expands on a story from Quantity Theory in which the dead just move to live in another part of London. At worst, his fiction is unstructured, overblown and is designed to be read with a thesaurus. At his best, he's a clever satirist. "I don't write fiction for people to identify with… I write to astonish people," he has said.

INFLUENCED BY Lewis Carroll; J.G. Ballard; Jonathan Swift; Martin Amis.

INFLUENCE ON D.B.C. Pierre.

ESSENTIAL READING **The Quantity Theory Of Insanity**; **How The Dead Live**.

FURTHER READING **Junk Mail**, an amusing collection of Self's journalism.

IAIN SINCLAIR

A visionary or crackpot or both

Iain Sinclair's work was once described as belonging "to a branch of literature that might be described as visionary. Crackpot might be another word." The clue here being that Sinclair, like his novels, isn't always easy to understand.

Born in Cardiff, Sinclair (1943–) came to writing late, having struggled for 15 years to break into the movie industry – an experience he likened to "Russian roulette with thousands of blanks and a single golden bullet," but which at least gave him fuel for Lights Out For The Territory. He self-published books of poetry to some acclaim, but he is best known for his prose, often focusing on the people, topography and culture of London. White Chappell, Scarlet Tracings is a tale of two halves; one side the **Jack the Ripper** murders, the other the obsession of a group of booksellers (Sinclair among them) to find a copy of a rare book.

In Downriver Sinclair further complicated his narrative by blending together hundreds of narratives of people as diverse as **Stephen Hawking** and **Lewis Carroll**. The Thames in the late 1980s was the backdrop for each, and the 12 linked journeys take the reader on a surreal, obscurely referenced tour of the city. The key figure is The Widow, a literary take on **Margaret Thatcher**, of whom Sinclair said "I can't understand her except as demonically possessed."

Of late Sinclair has branched out to focus on his native Wales in Landor's Tower, although the novel retains his passion for blending past and present: it is about a London-based journalist commissioned to investigate and write about a 19th-century writer and his attempts to revive a medieval abbey.

INFLUENCED BY Arthur Machen; surrealism; Derek Raymond.

INFLUENCE ON Peter Ackroyd; Alan Moore.

ESSENTIAL READING **Downriver**, praised by Angela Carter.

FURTHER READING **London Orbital**, a book about the M25: it's a bit like being trapped as a passenger with a very intelligent, anoraky cab driver.

ICEBERG SLIM

The poet of pimping

Iceberg Slim (1918–1992) was the pen name of **Robert Beck**; born **Robert Lee Maupin** in Chicago, Illinois to brutalising poverty, who became the poet of pimping, the writer who brought beauty, elegance and a degree of honour to a profession despised by the right-thinking folks of mainstream society.

He drifted into pimping, starting with his first girl at 18, and moved through the penal system until he found himself in solitary confinement, during his third stretch in jail. At the age of 42 he decided to "square up" and turn his life into some of the most fascinating accounts of underground life ever written.

Having spent most of his professional career sweet-talking naïve young women into a life of vice and degradation, Slim had a built-in advantage over most first-time authors. He knew how to use words (in the 1970s he released a

ALAN SHARP GOES TO THE MOVIES

At the age of 14, **Alan Sharp** (1934–) left school in Greenock, Scotland, to become an assistant to a private detective. To a compulsive storyteller like Sharp the job seemed romantic, intriguing and glamorous – until he realised the mystery consignment he was collecting from a railway station was a gas cooker.

That didn't stop Sharp from spinning stories. His first novel, A Green Tree In Gedde, was hailed – and banned from public libraries in Edinburgh, as two of

the main characters had an incestuous relationship. The author remembers it mainly as "baton-twirling prose" but it's worth reading. The novel was supposed to start a trilogy but after a follow up – The Wind Shifts – Hollywood called. **Peter Fonda** chose to film Sharp's western story (subsequently published as a novel) The Hired Hand. Sharp has been tied to the movies ever since, his biggest literary impact being to encourage his one-time partner **Beryl Bainbridge** to write again.

spoken-word album showing his silver-tongued skill) and with his first novel, Pimp, injected black fiction with the language of the streets – pure, undistorted and, compared to the Uncle Tom texts that had come before, savagely honest.

Pimp was typecast as part of the black revolutionary literary boom sparked by the aftermath of the civil-rights movement. Yet it reads like a blaxploitation movie adaptation of a **Shakespearean** tragedy; major characters die horrible deaths and trust is repaid with treachery. Although Slim saw his success as a pimp taking money off a mainly white clientele as a blow for black freedom, the **Black Panthers** saw him as a leech. Despite the tensions, Slim's books were on shelves next to the revolutionary tracts and, easier to read, were quick to sell.

Universal Pictures bought the rights to Pimp, though they never pursued the project. A film of his second novel, Trick Baby, was made in 1973. 'Trick Baby' was Chicago street slang for mixed-race children, the assumption in the ghetto being these kids were the offspring of black prostitutes and their white clients.

There's precious little true love in Slim's world. But we grow to care for his characters as, finding themselves warm, drunk, stoned and rich for the night at least, they temporarily appear to care for one another. He died reformed and respected, surely the only one-time pimp to sell more than six million books.

INFLUENCED BY School of Hard Knocks.　　　　　　　　　　　　　231

INFLUENCE ON Donald Goines; 'Gangsta' rappers Ice-T, Ice Cube; Irvine Welsh.

ESSENTIAL READING **Pimp**.

FURTHER READING **Airtight Willie & Me**, six tales from the underground.

GERTRUDE STEIN

Brilliant, unreadable: a writer's writer, a "great pyramidal Buddha"

As **Gertrude Stein** (1874–1946) said, "America is my country, Paris is my hometown." Born into a rich family of German immigrants, she left America for Paris in 1903, where she was a mentor to young artists like **Picasso** and, 20 years later, to expat American novelists **F. Scott Fitzgerald** and **Hemingway**. Even **Edmund Wilson**, no intellectual midget, was in awe, rambling about her **Buddah**-like aura. In his memoir A Moveable Feast, Hemingway recalls her advising him to buy paintings from young artists and not waste his money on clothes and drink.

But more than just a patron of the arts and a brilliant conversationalist, Stein was a serious writer, committed to the modernist style. Her first novel QED was only published after her death, largely because it was a semi-autobiographical book that described a lesbian love triangle. Her first published prose work Three Lives was three novellas drawing on **Henry James**, studies in psychology and experiments with automatic writing. But, in writing style, Stein was breaking

THE ORIGINAL STEVIE WONDER

Sylvia Plath was, she admitted in a letter to her idol, "a Smith addict, a desperate Smith addict." English poet **Stevie Smith** (1902–1971) is best known for her oft-anthologised poem Not Waving But Drowning. Yet when, in 1934, she showed her poems to a publisher she was told to write a novel. She did, lightly adapting her life as a publisher's secretary into Novel On Yellow Paper, the title referring to the paper she had typed it on at her office.

Born in Hull, as Florence Margaret Smith, she suffered from tuberculosis as a child, her father ran away to sea and, when Stevie was 16, her mother died of a heart attack. So her obsession with death is perhaps understandable.

She spent much of her life being mothered by, and later mothering, her aunt Madge. Her romantic life was troubled – she was engaged but never married and may have had a lesbian affair. Her poetry often had a little-girl-lost air and she fell out of favour in the 1950s. But a decade later she was adopted by **Beats** touring Britain – and their audience – who warmed to her directness and charm. She once wrote: "My life is vile/I hate it so/I'll wait a while/And then I'll go." But she relished her unlikely renaissance. Her two later novels – Over The Frontier and The Holiday, both thinly disguised memoirs – didn't make the same splash as her first. **George Orwell** was the model for two of the characters in The Holiday.

She brought her gifts as a poet to her novels, but the charming whimsy of her verse can grate in novel form. They are not for readers who insist on narrative. But Notes On Yellow Paper, which prefigures **Muriel Spark**'s A Far Cry From Kensington, and The Holiday (her favourite) are worth a read.

new ground by using simplistic language, repetition and rhythm. Until, that is, her work became eccentric, or at least that's what her critics complained – with Tender Buttons for example, with its "Chicken: alas a dirty word, alas a dirty third alas a dirty third, alas a dirty bird." She was deadly serious, however, trying to rid words of the associations readers normally attached to them.

One of her most renowned works was The Making Of Americans, written before World War I but published in 1925. Stylistically, she tried to emulate the cubist movement – to present experience from every angle possible. Frustrated when her masterpiece didn't sell, Stein started her own company to publish her works, including The Autobiography Of Alice B. Toklas, the book that is actually Stein's autobiography – she used Toklas's voice to write about herself.

INFLUENCED BY Henry James, Picasso.

INFLUENCE ON Hemingway; Sherwood Anderson; William Saroyan.

ESSENTIAL READING **The Autobiography Of Alice B. Toklas**, full of humour and vignettes of some of the most famous artistic figures of the 20th century.

FURTHER READING The heavy-going **The Making Of Americans**.

More than a missing link between Kleist and Kafka

The short stories of **Adalbert Stifter** (1805–1868) have been described as the literary link between **Kleist** and **Kafka**. Such a description fails to do justice to their unique combination of strangeness, psychological depth and extraordinary compassion. In Stifter's world – no less than in Kleist's – people are frequently at the mercy of fate, but rather than be victimised by their experiences they are transformed by them – usually into richer, more complex human beings.

Stifter's own life was often touched by tragedy. The son of linen weavers, he was born in the heart of the Bohemian Forest in what is now the Czech Republic. When he was 12 his father was crushed to death by a wagon. Stifter studied law in Vienna (he failed to graduate), where he met the great passion of his life, **Fanni Greipl**, but – perhaps for reasons of class – her parents disapproved of him and in 1837 Stifter married a milliner instead.

His first story appeared in 1840, and throughout the 1850s his reputation as a writer grew. He also worked as a landscape painter, his small but powerful canvasses reflecting the feeling for the detailed texture of the natural world so evident in his writings. Following the failed revolution of 1848 he retreated to the provincial town of Linz and for 15 years worked as an inspector of primary schools in the region. Stifter was fascinated by the way children's minds develop (it's a recurring theme in his stories), but he and his wife were childless and their efforts to adopt various nieces ended in disaster. Increasingly depressed, in constant pain from cirrhosis of the liver, Stifter slit his throat with a razor.

Although he completed two novels, Der Nachsommer and Wikito, he is celebrated as a writer of short stories. After his death he largely fell from favour. Only in the early 20th century did writers like **Thomas Mann** recognise the intense emotional currents ebbing beneath the placid surface of Stifter's prose. For Mann, it was Stifter's "tendency towards the excessive, the elemental and the catastrophic, the pathological" that made him so compelling.

One of Stifter's best stories, Brigitta, parallels the life of a woman damaged by childhood neglect with that of her neighbour, a dashing major with an adventurous past. The mysterious way their lives intertwine, and the fractured, wounded existences that are slowly revealed, is both moving and disturbing.

INFLUENCED BY Jean Paul Richter; E.T.A. Hoffmann.

INFLUENCE ON Thomas Mann; Peter Handke; W.G. Sebald.

ESSENTIAL READING The stories **Brigitta**, **Abdias**, **Limestone** and **The Forest Path**; **Rock Crystal**.

FURTHER READING **Der Nachsommer**, almost plotless but hypnotic.

CULT FICTION
D.M. THOMAS

"This book is light reading, excessively dependent on private jokes, **Nabokovian** allusiveness and what might be termed interlewds. Anyone who takes it seriously is either an academic or a chump." **D.J. Enright**'s review of Swallow, by **David Michael Thomas** (1935–), captures the critical consensus of the British novelist's career after the success of his audacious, dazzling, controversial novel The White Hotel in 1981. Such is the critical neglect into which Thomas, the novelist, has fallen that even that novel now seems an inspired fluke.

Thomas is partly to blame. Few English-language novelists have explored the grey zone between visionary and daft as relentlessly as he. He takes unusual risks that don't always come off, but when they do – The White Hotel and Flying In To Love – he creates a fictional world unlike any other writer. He was an academic, a translator and a poet before he became a novelist and, at his best, he writes, noted **John Updike**, "with a poet's care, an academic's knowledgeability and the originality of a thorough unprofessional." His first two novels, Birthstone and, most of all, The Flute Player, read now like rehearsals for The White Hotel. The Flute Player, which shares with its successor a forgiving female protagonist, an erotic charge and a sense for the ebbs and flows of history, doesn't really meld these ingredients; Thomas seems to want to jam too much history into his narrative and the novel stalls two-thirds of the way through.

For The White Hotel he found a structure to suit his story: an inspired, daring structure, but one that gave the novel what Updike called "propulsive telescopic action, where the epistolary prologue yields to the heroine's erotic poem, the poem to its prose retelling, the retelling to **Freud**'s psychoanalysis, this analysis to her history, her history to the historical horror of Babi Yar, and Babi Yar to a miraculous Palestine." Controversy followed the acclaim when Thomas was accused of plagiarising another book for his account of the Nazi massacre at Babi Yar, but it remains a stunning achievement: ambitious, warm and epic.

After its success, the big question for Thomas was: where next? At first, in novels like Ararat, he wrote as if he were stumbling around in the same fictional world – holocausts, sex, Freud – hoping to repeat the magic. At times he has looked to dazzle with virtuosity, language and humourous conceits, but focused in Flying In To Love he gave a convincing fictional sketch of **JFK**, exploring our reaction to Kennedy's political and erotic power. The reviews, however, focused on scenes of nuns masturbating.

Thomas now seems to have retreated into non-fiction, awaiting inspiration or re-evaluation. A pity because, for all his flaws, he can bring inventive humour, artistic audacity and a gift for the sudden, shockingly appropriate image that is all too rare in contemporary fiction.

INFLUENCED BY Boris Pasternak; Anna Akhmatova; Alexander Pushkin; Freud.
INFLUENCE ON Nothing much.
ESSENTIAL READING **The White Hotel**.
FURTHER READING **Flying In To Love**; **The Flute Player**.

HUNTER S. THOMPSON

"The author has become larger than the writing… and it sucks"

Honing his writing in the late 1960s, **Hunter Stockton Thompson** (1937–)
typed out The Great Gatsby and A Farewell To Arms in their entirety, trying to
work out what had made **F. Scott Fitzgerald** and **Hemingway** such powerful
authors. He then set about unlearning everything he had discovered.

Thompson is many things: journalist and stylist, observer and participator and
relentless self-promoter. But he is also one of the greatest countercultural icons of
the last 50 years, whose persona has come to rival, even overshadow, his output.
Born in Kentucky, he began his journalistic career with a brief spell as a sports
reporter on a USA Air Force newspaper. There followed a few years of travelling
before he moved to South America, where he developed a reputation for
enigmatic, insightful prose for **National Observer** magazine. Returning home,
he was commissioned to write on Hell's Angels; the articles (the result of a year
on the road with the gang) so popular they became a book in 1966.

Hell's Angels is arguably his most important work. While more linear than
anything since, the sense of detachment lacking in his later work allowed him to
debunk many myths about the bikers, and take a perceptive dig at the state's
failure to engage with the margins of society. This superb example of an
observing journalist at work ends with Thompson receiving a savage beating:
"There was no vocal aftermath, then or later. I didn't expect one – no more than
I'd expect a pack of sharks to explain a feeding frenzy."

Five years later Fear And Loathing In Las Vegas propelled Thompson to
stardom. Sent to cover a motorcycle race, he instead took vast quantities of drugs,
gatecrashed a district attorney convention and left a trail of unpaid bills as the
police chased him across Vegas. The result was sheer madness, surreal, hilarious
and sobering; a piece of drug-crazed travel writing quite unlike anything before.
With his alter ego Raoul Duke at the centre of the book and the 'plot' merely a
starting point from which to jump around wildly, Thompson cemented a style of
'**gonzo**' journalism that won him acclaim and cult status. His championing of
hedonism still seems bold: "I hate to advocate drugs, alcohol, violence or insanity
to anyone," he said, "but they've always worked for me."

He carried the momentum on into Fear And Loathing On The Campaign
Trail '72, in which he joined the press corps covering **Richard Nixon**'s election

battle with **George McGovern**. Thompson's eerily prescient comments on political manipulation make it a minor classic, full of honesty and intelligence.

His insistence on being the centre of his work (and his admission that only three-quarters of his reportage was based on fact) overshadowed much of his later writing: a series of gonzo papers about various aspects of modern America (with Better Than Sex the pick of the bunch), a crazed travelogue called Curse Of Lono, two collections of letters and a novel, The Rum Diary, based on his time in Puerto Rico. Generation Of Swine showed that his caustic wit and distaste for the ruling elite was as sharp as ever.

In the 1970s he set up the short-lived political party **Freak Power** and came tantalisingly close to being voted sheriff of Aspen, Colorado. He has also carefully cultivated his shaman-like persona, Doctor Gonzo, through a series of anarchic brushes with the law (the Duke character in **Garry Trudeau**'s Doonesbury comic strip is based on Gonzo).

236

INFLUENCED BY Hemingway; F. Scott Fitzgerald; George Plimpton; Thomas Wolfe; Kerouac.

INFLUENCE ON Timothy Edward Jones; P.J. O'Rourke.

ESSENTIAL READING **Hell's Angels**; **Fear And Loathing In Las Vegas**.

FURTHER READING **The Great White Shark Hunt**, a great anthology.

JIM THOMPSON

"The world was a shit pot with a barbed wire handle"

A prolific output amounting to little success would push most writers into utter despair. However, Oklahoma-born **Jim Thompson** (1906–1977) was more resilient than most. Conscious he didn't have long to live, Thompson told his wife to take care of his manuscripts and protect his copyrights, saying, "Just you wait, I'll become famous after I'm dead about ten years."

As it turned out Thompson couldn't have been more right, his tales of the criminally insane, pimps, gangsters and losers are popular fodder for today's filmmakers, Thompson's The Getaway, The Grifters, The Killer Inside Me and After Dark, My Sweet having all been turned into movies.

Born in a jailhouse, his father 'Big Jim', the sheriff of Anadarko, Thompson was introduced to the seedier aspects of life from an early age. His father pilfered

$31,000 from the sheriff's office, gambling it away and fleeing to Mexico. He later, Thompson said, died in an asylum, having eaten his mattress stuffing.

Working as a bell-hop by night and studying by day while smoking and drinking heavily, Thompson had his first nervous breakdown aged 19. Luckily he had already begun writing for a selection of 'true-crime' magazines. His wife and sister would comb the newspapers in search of murders Thompson could adapt. His first novel, Now And On Earth, published in 1942, featured a fictionalised take on Thompson's own interview with the **FBI** about his communist activities (Thompson was a Communist Party member from 1935 to 1938, noting the attraction lay in the "good conversation").

His breakthrough came when his fifth novel, The Killer Inside Me (written in two weeks), attracted maverick filmmaker **Stanley Kubrick**. Kubrick called the book, about a small-town sheriff pretending to be dimwitted, the most chilling account of a criminally warped mind he had ever encountered. The pair subsequently collaborated on scripts for The Killing and Paths Of Glory, before Thompson continued his Hollywood career scripting for the TV series Dr. Kildare.

Despite an escalating drink problem, documented in The Alcoholics, Thompson's most prolific period was the 1950s, with 20 novels almost completed, although not all highly polished. His work was barely acknowledged in his lifetime and by the time he died he was struggling with the bottle and bills. He may well have made more money playing the Judge in the **Robert Mitchum** retread of Farewell My Lovely in 1975 than he did as a writer.

237

INFLUENCED BY Chandler; Hammett; James M. Cain; crime novelist Lionel White.

INFLUENCE ON Stephen King; Harlan Ellison; Quentin Tarantino.

ESSENTIAL READING **The Killer Inside Me**.

FURTHER READING **Savage Night** if only for the end, where the protagonist literally falls to pieces.

J.R.R. TOLKIEN

He invented a genre, a kingdom, a franchise

"In a hole in the ground there lived a hobbit" are the unobtrusive opening lines to a saga that would engulf the life of **John Ronald Reuel Tolkien** (1892–1973) and his reputation. The Hobbit, Tolkien's tales of a funny, little, hairy-footed creature called Bilbo, started out as stories to amuse his children, but marked the creation of a literary adventure-fantasy genre.

Born in South Africa, but raised in England after his father's death, Tolkien spent his childhood roaming the countryside outside Birmingham. These were his formative years, old haunts such as Bag End and Moseley Bog later cropping up in Middle Earth. He was 12 when his mother died and under the care of a priest, almost as therapy, Tolkien studied hard, indulging his passion for the

classical world and teaching himself Old Norse before starting to invent languages of his own.

Encouraged by his circle of friends – including **C.S Lewis** – at Oxford University, Tolkien took his writing from a hobby to a profession. Released in September 1937, The Hobbit was a sell-out by Christmas. What made Tolkien's Middle Earth so appealing was his attention to detail. Each place has a history, each character a language and every cause an effect. After this success, Tolkien was ready to move on, writing to his publisher, "What more can hobbits do?" But he reluctantly gave in to demand and the The Lord Of The Rings trilogy was published by 1955, almost a decade after Tolkien had begun working on it.

Despite his sales success (100 million copies and counting), Tolkien has been criticised for his popularity, accessibility, failure to engage with females in fiction and, most of all, for his songs. Many have tried to find a deeper meaning within the tales of Frodo and Sam Gamgee, convinced they represent an allegory of World War II, religious truth or repressed homosexuality. But Tolkien insisted they were to be taken at face value: stories of friendship, self-sacrifice and loss.

INFLUENCED BY C.S. Lewis; Beowulf, **Sir Gawain And The Green Knight**.

INFLUENCE ON Philip Pullman; Terry Pratchett; Stephen Donaldson.

ESSENTIAL READING **The Hobbit**; **The Lord Of The Rings**.

FURTHER READING **The Silmarillion** is for diehards only.

B. TRAVEN

"The biography of a creative man is completely unimportant"

That quote is **B. Traven**'s little joke. As an author, he is probably better known for the riddle over his identity than the fact his most famous novel, The Treasure Of The Sierra Madre, became one of **Humphrey Bogart**'s best movies.

The argument about his identity may never be conclusively settled, but the consensus is that he was born **Hermann Albert Otto Max Fiege** (c.1882–1969) in what was then Prussia. In 1904 he left his parents, after upsetting them by spouting socialist rhetoric, and was never seen again, under that name or by his original family. He later became Bavarian activist **Ret Marat**, wrote a novella and took part in the doomed 1919 Communist rebellion in Munich. By Traven's own subsequent account, he escaped execution and arrived, after various misadventures, in Mexico in 1924, noting in his journal: "The Bavarian of Munich is dead."

This is the condensed version of an impassioned debate, and some, notably **Michael L. Baumann**, still insist Traven was American or one of Fiege's cousins. Whoever Traven was, his first novel The Death Ship, in which a hero with identity papers is kicked from one country to another, was a smash in Germany, **Albert Einstein** choosing it as the book he would take with him to a desert island. Encouraged, Traven soon followed up with a slew of novels (notably The Treasure Of The Sierra Madre and The White Rose) that married a tough, suspenseful prose style with a passionate concern for social justice. In Mexico he had found his landscape and his subject, spending most of the 1930s writing a cycle of novels about the Mexican revolution.

By the time The Treasure Of The Sierra Madre was filmed in 1948, Traven had another identity (**Hal Croves**), a new lover (**Esperanza Lopez Mateos**, who committed suicide in 1951) and film had replaced literature as his most ardent interest. After the Bogart/**John Huston** movie and with the aid of his wife, **Rosa Elena Lujan**, Traven was rich, but his secret life still plagued him: a novel, Aslan Norval, about an American millionaire, was published in Germany in 1960 but is now regarded as fake. That was, with superb irony, the last Traven novel published in his lifetime. He died nine years later, allowing his widow to reveal he had been Ret Marut – but not who Marut was.

239

INFLUENCED BY Marx; Mikhail Bakunin; Hemingway; the Chiapas tribes in the Mexican jungle;

INFLUENCE ON Paul Theroux, who has studied his life and works.

ESSENTIAL READING **The Treasure Of The Sierra Madre**.

FURTHER READING The whole of the jungle series, especially the climactic novel **The General In The Jungle**.

ALEXANDER TROCCHI

Drugs, pornography, prostitution and existentialism

Scotland's – if not Britain's – only **Beat** writer, **Alexander Trocchi** (1925–1984) lived a life so colourful and depraved it has often eclipsed his writing. Much heralded in the 1950s and 1960s by the likes of **William Burroughs**, by the time of his death he was remembered, if at all, for his pornography. Yet with the rise of **Irvine Welsh**, Trocchi's influence has finally been recognised.

Born in Glasgow, Trocchi was the youngest son of a well-off family – one relative was a cardinal – whose parents were forced to run a boarding house during the Depression. On graduating from Glasgow University he won a scholarship, which he used to explore the Mediterranean and settle in Paris. Immersing himself in the literary scene, he set up **Merlin** – a literary magazine funded by his American lover **Jane Lengee**, which published the likes of **Jean Genet** and **Henry Miller**.

This was the most productive period of Trocchi's life. While indulging in some truly graphic depravity, he wrote at least six pornographic novels for the notorious **Olympia Press**, including Thongs, an ambiguous, sado-masochistic tale that opens with the discovery of a naked, flagellated, crucified woman in the Spanish countryside. He also finished Young Adam, a surprisingly straightforward story about a barge hand who pulls the body of a woman from the river (made as a film in 2003, starring **Ewan McGregor**). It becomes clear that he and the woman had been having an affair, but – recalling **Camus**'s The Outsider – Young Adam is really shocking for its amorality and condemnation of conventional society. Colourless, rain-drenched and packed with emotionless sex, the story becomes a metaphor for passing through life without participating.

240

Britain's only Beat genius, fortunately

By the mid-1950s Trocchi was replacing literary experiments for sex and drugs. He left for the US, where his pregnant, drug-addicted wife prostituted herself at Trocchi's instigation to support their habits. In New York he found work on a scow on the Hudson River and it was here that he wrote the erotic, disconnected Cain's Book.

Arrested on the capital charge of supplying heroin to a minor, Trocchi fled to Canada, then to London. In the 1960s he was a countercultural icon, organising the 'tribal gathering' of poets in the Royal Albert Hall in 1965 – pivotal in the development of 'Swinging London' – and spearheading the **Sigma Project**: a movement that drew attention to the avant-garde. He wrote some fine translations (including **De Mandiargues**'s The

Girl On A Motorcycle), but wrote no more fiction and in the last years of his life became an antiquarian bookseller, remaining an addict till the end.

INFLUENCED BY Kafka; Antonin Artaud; Cocteau.
INFLUENCE ON Irvine Welsh; Kathy Acker; Leonard Cohen.
ESSENTIAL READING **Young Adam**; **Cain's Book**.
FURTHER READING **A Life In Pieces: Reflections On Alexander Trocchi** (1997), ed. Allan Campbell.

KONSTANTIN TSIOLKOVSKY

"First, inevitably, the idea, the fantasy, the fairy tale. Then scientific calculation"

Konstantin Eduardovich Tsiolkovsky (1857–1935) is one of the great prophets of science fiction. He was also a great scientist – the father of the Russian space programme – and his frequently bizarre novels and stories contain the world's first sightings of spacesuits, spacewalks, space stations and even space rockets.

Born in Izhevskoye, a village southwest of Moscow where his Polish father was a forester and amateur philosopher, Tsiolkovsky lost his hearing as a result of scarlet fever aged ten. Unable to attend the village school, he began to teach himself physics and mathematics. In 1873 he travelled to Moscow to continue his self-education in the Chertkovskaya Library, where the chief cataloguer was **Nikolai Fedorov** – the 'cosmic' philosopher who believed it was mankind's duty to resurrect its ancestors, via technology, and colonise other planets to provide them with accommodation. As Tsiolkovsky discovered From The Earth To The Moon by **Jules Verne**, he also began to study with Fedorov.

Tsiolkovsky began writing in the early 1880s. Free Space, cast as a diary, is easily the earliest description of a rocket engine as a means of propulsion in outer space. But he was by then an impoverished school teacher in Borovsk, a village 70 miles south of Moscow, so it was years before he found recognition. Even in Borovsk he was deemed at best eccentric – sailing down the river in winter on an armchair fitted with skates, or attaching a centrifuge to the village watermill to test the effect of increased gravity on chickens. In 1893 his first story, On The Moon, was published in a Moscow magazine. The fantastical tale describes a dream in which the narrator finds himself exploring the lunar surface. All his life Tsiolkovsky had a loathing for the 'shackles' of gravity.

He worked in virtual isolation until 1920 when Beyond The Planet Earth, which he began in 1896, was published. His best work of fiction, it contains many of his most prophetic ideas: an orbiting space station with an international crew, docking ports and artificial gravity; a multi-stage, liquid-fuel rocket; and tethered spacewalks to name a few. Publication coincided with a reassessment of

241

his neglected, pioneering earlier papers on rocket dynamics, and, in the revolutionary climate of the early 1920s, the deaf, ageing schoolmaster was declared a proletarian hero, granted a pension and a new house in Kaluga.

Since the fall of communism, Tsiolkovsky's suppressed 'cosmic' works such as Essays On The Universe have been published – summarising his ideas on the future in space and human perfectibility – and a recent revival of interest in Russian mysticism has earned him a sizeable cult following.

INFLUENCED BY Jules Verne; Fedorov; Ivan Turgenev – particularly the austere, materialistic Bazarov in **Fathers And Sons**.

INFLUENCE ON Alexandr Beliayev ('The Soviet Jules Verne'); Sergei Korolyev (the designer of Sputnik); Arthur C. Clarke (space elevators, solar sails, geostationary satellites… Many of his best-known ideas, in fact.)

ESSENTIAL READING **Beyond The Planet Earth; The Science Fiction Of Konstantin Tsiolkovsky**, ed. Adam Starchild.

FURTHER READING Fedorov's **What Was Man Created For?**

JULES VERNE

The father of science fiction

Jules Gabriel Verne (1828–1905) has been translated into more languages than any other novelist: 148. In such classic adventures as Twenty Thousand Leagues Under The Sea, in 1870, he imagined everything from the car to the submarine – influencing the world of science almost as much as he influenced literature.

> "The sea is everything, its breath is pure, it is an immense desert on which man is never lonely"
>
> Jules Verne's ode to the sea in 20,000 Leagues

Verne was born in Nantes, the son of a wealthy lawyer. As a teenager he wrote short stories but, pressured by his father, studied law in Paris. Here, he became friends with **Victor Hugo** and **Alexandre Dumas, Jr**. Verne passed his degree, but never became a lawyer. Instead he worked as a secretary at the Théâtre Lyrique, co-wrote an operetta and published several more plays and short stories, heavily influenced by **Baudelaire**'s 1854 translations of **Edgar Allan Poe**. Success still eluded him and he reluctantly joined a stockbrokers.

In 1862 Verne met **Pierre Jules Hetzel**, who was to remain his publisher until Hetzel's death in 1886. Although Hetzel rejected Verne's first novel, Paris In The Twentieth Century, he did accept Five Weeks In A Balloon – about a group of explorers crossing Africa in a hot-air balloon. Producing one or two novels a year, Verne abandoned stockbroking and began to write full-time – researching his work meticulously in a bid to remain within the bounds of scientific possibility. From The Earth To The Moon, for example, involves a manned capsule fired to the moon by means of an enormous gun located in Florida, close to Cape Canaveral. It was extraordinarily prescient in its description of space flight, even if the gun would have killed all of the passengers instantly.

This emphasis on scientific accuracy is perhaps the key distinction between Verne and other fantastical writers such as **Lewis Carroll**. Journey To The Centre Of The Earth – in which a professor leads adventurers through an Icelandic volcano and into the world's cavernous interior – is, admittedly, an exception; but such books as Twenty Thousand Leagues Under The Sea demonstrate Verne's desire to educate his readership and the astonishing power of his imagination: Captain Nemo's Nautilus predated the first powered submarine by almost 25 years.

Around The World In Eighty Days is perhaps Verne's most famous novel, recounting the funny and fast-moving adventures of Phileas Fogg and his butler as they try to circumnavigate the world. By 1875, however, the sense of optimism that permeates his earlier work was beginning to fade and his later darker novels often end in the death or madness of the protagonist. Robur The Conqueror is classically Vernian in its prediction of heavier-than-air flying machines, but Robur himself is insane and in the sequel has evolved into a megalomaniac.

After 1882 Verne lived sedately with his family but in 1886 his mad nephew Gaston tried to kill him, shooting him in the shin and leaving him lame for the rest of his life.

243

INFLUENCED BY Edgar Allan Poe; Victor Hugo; Walter Scott.

INFLUENCE ON Conan Doyle; Mark Twain; Arthur C. Clarke; Sartre.

ESSENTIAL READING **Around The World In Eighty Days**.

FURTHER READING **Twenty Thousand Leagues Under The Sea**.

KURT VONNEGUT

Bombed into writing novels

It is hard to imagine **Kurt Vonnegut** (1922–) without the horrific events of World War II. His experiences of the Dresden fire-bombing provided the basis of his one unquestionable masterpiece, Slaughterhouse-Five, but an awareness of mankind's capacity for destruction underlies all of his work, transforming his fantastical sci-fi into devastating satire.

Vonnegut was born in Indianapolis, Indiana, the son of a wealthy architect who lost most of his money in the Great Depression. To please his father, he studied biochemistry, but enlisted in the US Army partly to avoid being expelled. His time as managing editor of the **Cornell Sun** was more successful, and it was during this period he developed an interest in science fiction.

In 1944 Vonnegut's mother committed suicide (on Mother's Day) while he was at home on leave. Soon after, he was posted to Germany, where he was captured and imprisoned in a disused slaughterhouse in Dresden. There, in February 1945, he witnessed the infamous Allied bombing raid in which 135,000 people died and he survived by sheltering in an underground meat locker.

On his return to America, Vonnegut worked for the **Chicago City News Bureau** and studied for a Master's degree in anthropology. Although his thesis 'Fluctuations Between Good And Evil In Simple Tales' was rejected, this scientific training was crucial to his writing. He began to see science fiction as the only way

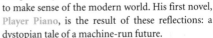

to make sense of the modern world. His first novel, Player Piano, is the result of these reflections: a dystopian tale of a machine-run future.

The Sirens Of Titan is the novel in which he really found his voice. A wildly imaginative trip through the cosmos, it explores the nature of time and reality and introduces the Tralfamadorians (of the planet Tralfamadore) who would recur throughout his work. The book earned Vonnegut a cult following, but it was not until Cat's Cradle that he began to experience mainstream success, with **Graham Greene** declaring him "one of the most able living writers."

Slaughterhouse-Five was published in the midst of America's involvement in Vietnam, and its surreal, cyclical account of the Dresden bombing is one of the most memorable indictments of warfare in modern history. As absurd as it is terrifying, it is also – improbably – very funny, and the contrast between Billy Pilgrim's time spent sheltering in a meat locker beneath the burning city and his time as an exhibit in a Tralfamadorian zoo is irresistible.

Not long after publication Vonnegut became seriously depressed. His next book, Breakfast Of Champions, received poor reviews but is one of his best, featuring the prolific but dire science-fiction writer Kilgore Trout, who first appeared in God Bless You, Mr. Rosewater and bears a marked resemblance to Vonnegut himself between 1950 and 1970. Vonnegut attempted suicide in 1985 just before the publication of Galapagos: a powerful satire in which human brains have become too big for their own good. He wrote two more strong novels in the 1980s, Bluebeard and Hocus Pocus, but after the lacklustre Timequake swore never to write again. His novella God Bless You, Dr. Kevorkian was a real return to form.

INFLUENCED BY H.G. Wells; Aldous Huxley; Orwell.
INFLUENCE ON Douglas Adams; John Irving; Haruki Murakami.
ESSENTIAL READING **Slaughterhouse-Five**.
FURTHER READING Mark Vonnegut's **The Eden Express: A Memoir Of Schizophrenia** is an intriguing insight into life with his father.

DAVID FOSTER WALLACE

Convoluted syntax, plainspeaking language, fun with dictionaries

Depending on who you ask, wunderkind American author **David Foster Wallace** (1962–) is either the greatest living writer or a particularly exasperating example of what's wrong with contemporary American fiction.

His big break came in 1996, with the publication of his 1,079-page (including nearly 100 pages of endnotes) magnum opus Infinite Jest. With three previous titles to his name – the uneven Broom Of The System, the irresistibly strange short-story collection Girl With Curious Hair and the essays A Supposedly Fun Thing I'll Never Do Again – Wallace pulled his talents together in true fireworks fashion for Infinite Jest. It's a sad but touching portrait of a near-future America in which a deadly "entertainment" has begun to circulate, killing (by eliminating their desire to do anything but watch the entertainment) all who view it.

245

Yet the conceit is not really the point. The characters and their feelings are what's important, despite the oversized servings of life in a halfway house for recovering drug addicts (addiction is a primary, serious theme of Infinite Jest) or a nuclear Armageddon-themed tennis game played by prodigies at an academy. These two institutions are where the book's two main characters – a dictionary-memorising, dope-smoking tennis star and a big-hearted, former drug-addict and criminal bruiser – hail from. Infinite Jest spirals its way towards a harrowing, heartbreaking conclusion that happens more between the lines than on the page itself.

Since his masterpiece, Wallace has published two short-story collections, Brief Interviews With Hideous Men and Oblivion: an e-book about 2000 presidential aspirant **John McCain**; a book about 18th-century mathematician **Georg Cantor**, who developed a working theory of infinity; and essays and articles for various magazines (who could imagine that a 20,000-word dictionary review could be inspiring and – no, really – knee-slappingly funny). But, as in his fiction, Wallace writes with panache and generosity to boot, alternating easily between convoluted syntax and plainspoken earthiness.

INFLUENCED BY Pynchon; Don DeLillo.

INFLUENCE ON Nobody, so far.

ESSENTIAL READING **Infinite Jest**.

FURTHER READING **Girl With Curious Hair**; **Oblivion**.

IRVINE WELSH

"I hope the author will soon be dead"

The 1996 movie of **Irvine Welsh**'s (c.1961–) first novel Trainspotting shot the Scot to fame as the spokesman for a new youth culture – an E'd-up poet laureate of the chemical generation, if you will. Yet would he rather have been a rock star?

Welsh's early life, including his date of birth, are a mystery perpetuated by the writer. He was born in Leith in the late 1950s/early 1960s and grew up in a jobless, gloomy, drug-ridden Edinburgh housing estate. Backpacking in America, Welsh wrote seriously, penning short stories for the influential Edinburgh magazine **Rebel Inc.** A mix of drug-fuelled fantasy and harsh realism, many of these stories ended up in The Acid House, published in 1993 to critical acclaim.

Later that year he published his first novel, Trainspotting – the horrific but hilarious adventures of heroin addict Mark Renton, his likeable but idiotic mates

Irvine Welsh, moustache about town

Spud and Sick Boy and the psychotic Begbie. His needles-and-all portrayal of a disenfranchised, drug-dependent culture was a triumph, which had much to do with the universal characters, the random narration and swear-happy, phonetic use of the Scots dialect; readers had to interpret words like "gadge".

His second novel, Marabou Stork Nightmares about the ruminations of a comatose football hooligan, and Ecstasy: Three Tales Of Chemical Romance received lukewarm receptions. Two years later Filth – the story of an abhorrent, morally corrupt copper – made him look like a one-hit wonder. But then came Glue in 2001. Underscored with black humour, the story follows the lives of four childhood friends and was praised for its maturity and ambition. The release of Porno a year later was a return to top form, with his best-loved characters Renton and the gang a decade on from Trainspotting, preoccupied with home-made pornography rather than pills.

Welsh often says he isn't enamoured with writing – "I've no fucking respect for the writer's craft. It's a lot of fucking nonsense. It's all application. It's nothing to fucking do with skill" – and has hailed the internet as the death of the novel.

INFLUENCED BY Burroughs; Kerouac; Bukowski; Gary Indiana; Cormac McCarthy; Alexander Trocchi; Alasdair Gray; James Kelman; Iggy Pop.

INFLUENCE ON Scottish heroin fiction.

ESSENTIAL READING **Trainspotting**.

FURTHER READING **The Acid House**; **Glue**; **Porno**.

NATHANAEL WEST

An apocalyptic dreamer, out of place, out of time

If the French can be perennially ridiculed for the intellectual reverence with which they regard **Jerry Lewis**, they should take the credit for the rediscovery of **Nathanael West** (1903–1940), a neglected American writer whose works seem to anticipate the grotesque, apocalyptic evil of holocausts and gulags.

247

Born **Nathanel von Wallenstein Weinstein** to Lithuanian Jewish immigrants, West was an obsessive collector of grotesque stories from real life – of strange tortures, exotic diseases, occult happenings – and his fiction, as **Edmund Wilson** noted, has an east European sense of suffering and humour reminiscent of **Gogol**. One of the few established writers to recognise his genius was his friend **F. Scott Fitzgerald**. He died a day after his mentor, just as his life – with a new marriage and increasingly lucrative commissions from Hollywood – seemed set to take a turn for the better; a bitter irony straight out of a West novel.

With his second novel Miss Lonelyhearts, in which the journalist-author of an agony column assumes **Christ**-like responsibility for America's personal griefs, West found his voice, based, as **Malcolm Bradbury** perceptively put it, "on a perception of the pain and anguish underlying the myths of American society."

The black humour would infuse his next two novels: the satire A Cool Million and the

> "Good reviews: fifteen per cent. Bad reviews: twenty-five per cent. Brutal personal attacks: sixty per cent"
>
> Nathanael West reviews reviews for his novel

apocalyptic The Day Of The Locust, for many the definitive Californian novel, with its depiction of crazed fantasists drawn to the Golden State by their dreams. The freakish characters, comic-surrealism and apocalyptic imagery are remarkable for an American novel written in the 1930s. Too remarkable for West's own good. Writing to Fitzgerald, he noted: "So far the score stands – good reviews: fifteen per cent. Bad reviews: twenty-five per cent. Brutal personal attacks: sixty per cent." But by the 1960s West's savage, gloomy humour seemed utterly contemporary. The title of his final masterpiece is famous globally, as is the name of one of the main characters, a man with a murderous body, like a "poorly made automaton", called Homer Simpson.

INFLUENCED BY Humorist S.J. Perelman (the two were friends; West started out drawing cartoons with Perelman); F. Scott Fitzgerald; Gogol.

INFLUENCE ON Joseph Heller; John Kennedy Toole; Flannery O' Connor.
ESSENTIAL READING **Miss Lonelyhearts**; **The Day Of The Locust**.
FURTHER READING The Library of America edition of his works and letters.

OSCAR WILDE

248 Poor Oscar. Brilliant, flamboyant, outrageous, moving and disastrous

The life of **Oscar Wilde** (1854–1900) was a work of art, a Victorian fin-de-siècle tragedy that almost outshines his work. Wilde subverted the mores of his age and became literature's reigning wit. As **Dorothy Parker** wrote: "If, with the literate, I am/Impelled to make an epigram/I never seek to take the credit/We all assume that Oscar said it."

Born in Dublin, Wilde came from a rich family – his father was a knighted eye surgeon. At Oxford, he stood out as 'odd', wearing outrageously coloured clothes, the aesthetic's long hair and a notorious frock coat shaped liked a cello. Despite this, it's often forgotten that Wilde married in 1884 and had two children. He seems to have ignored or suppressed his homosexuality until later in life.

Wilde's great and only novel, The Picture Of Dorian Gray, is a masterly twist on the Faust story. The eponymous hero sells his soul for aesthetic and physical pleasures and for the privilege of remaining young: youth, in the novel, being the greatest prize of all. The novel is a window into Wilde's soul, but Wilde is as much Sir Henry Wootton, the Mephistophelian elder 'tempter' of Dorian, as Dorian. It is the witty, urbane Sir Henry who fuels Dorian's obsession with youth and beauty, at the expense of everything, yet Sir Henry rejects this doctrine in his life. In Dorian we may see Wilde's longing for a life of passion and unrestrained free expression that he desired and feared – and for which he paid the ultimate price. But it is for his plays that Wilde is best known. Vacuous, witty, polished, The Importance Of Being Earnest contains, apart from Lady Bracknell's handbag, Wilde's finest aphorisms ("All women turn into their mothers. That is their tragedy. Men never do. That is theirs").

That such genius shone so brightly makes it all the more tragic that it was snuffed out so cruelly. After his rash libel action against the **Marquess of Queensberry**, Wilde was famously imprisoned for homosexual offences and spent two years in Reading Gaol. Wilde's motivation for bringing the suit is unclear. Many ascribe it to love for **Sir Alfred Douglas**, who loathed his father the Marquess and urged action against Wilde's better judgment. We cannot know, but Wilde's lifelong presentiments of tragedy, and its awful inevitability in so many of his works, suggest he acted in ghastly awareness of what would follow.

Stock can go down as well as up, but Wilde's has soared stratospherically since he died, exiled and broken, in Paris in 1900. Arguably more popular than ever, his works still entertain all over the world, and often in surprising places – in Russia, for instance, he is the most quoted author after **Pushkin**.

INFLUENCED BY Wilde spoke fluent French and must have been influenced by Theophile Gautier's romantic aesthetic, but he is a genuine one-off.

INFLUENCE ON Every English writer since, especially Ronald Firbank.

ESSENTIAL READING **The Picture Of Dorian Gray; The Ballad Of Reading Gaol; De Profundis**, his moving essay on spirituality and suffering.

FURTHER READING Wilde's sublime fairytales, particularly **The Happy Prince** and **The Nightingale And The Rose**. Read them and weep.

249

CHARLES WILLEFORD

A crime-writer's crime writer

Psychotic, amoral, obsessive and cruel best describe the characters penned by **Charles Willeford** (1919–1988). The author of 16 novels, a number of collections of poetry and two pieces of non-fiction, Willeford's work is a disturbingly accurate portrayal of criminal life; his people, whether murdering fathers or cock-fighting obsessives, always written with an innate sense of empathy for what motivates them. An orphan by the time he was eight and homeless by the time he was 15, Willeford's experience of life, as **Donald Westlake** noted, "led him to a certain attitude towards the world and his place in it, and his attitude, ironic without meanness, comic but deeply caring, informed every book he ever wrote."

Before writing for a living, Willeford spent 20 highly decorated years in the forces. His day-to-day duties not hindering his literary output, rather providing inspiration: "A good half of the men you deal with in the army are psychopaths. There's a hefty overlap between the military population and the prison population, so I knew plenty of guys like Junior in Miami Blues and Troy in Sideswipe."

In 1949 he penned his first novel, High Priest In California – "one continuous orgy of prolonged foreplay" according to one reviewer – featuring a womanising car salesman. Set in San Francisco, it displays Willeford's sardonic wit and tough prose. Although it was four years before the book was published, Willeford kept writing. The black comedy that infused his earlier work became more prominent, as did the level of depravity in his tales. In his 1960 novel The Woman Chaser he again used a womanising car salesman as his lead. He also wrote a pulp novel, with **W. Franklin Sanders**, called Whip Hand, published without Willeford's approval.

With Cockfighter he found a more original story and his tale of an obsessive cock-fighter desperate to win a medal was filmed, starring **Warren Oates** and **Harry Dean Stanton**. Yet, to his annoyance, success still eluded him. Novelist **James Hall**, who asked Willeford to lead creative-writing classes, noted: "He developed an extremely cantankerous persona… winding up students like a radio talk-show host." Fame came finally in 1984 with detective Hoke Moseley in Miami Blues. His publishers chose the title, hoping to cash in on the TV series Miami Vice, and the book was praised by **Elmore Leonard** among others. The author's response to requests for a sequel was to write Grimhaven, in which Moseley kills his two daughters.

250

INFLUENCED BY Hemingway; Chandler.

INFLUENCE ON James Lee Burke.

ESSENTIAL READING **Miami Blues**.

FURTHER READING **The Collected Memoirs Of Charles Willeford**.

WHY COLIN WILSON IS STILL THE OUTSIDER

Colin Wilson (1931–) made his name with a study of alienated geniuses, The Outsider, published in 1956. He then became an outsider: his next book, Religion And The Rebel, was slammed for elitism, he left his wife and was threatened with horsewhipping by the father of his new girlfriend, who had read his pornographic diaries.

He retired to Cornwall and has, in between investigating UFOs, editing anthologies of strange but true stories and writing Edward Scissorhands-style profiles of serial killers, written several novels from the autobiographical (Adrift In Soho) to sexy, doomy, psychological thrillers (Ritual In The Dark; Janus Murder Case). His novels can be formulaic and often humourless but **Edith Sitwell**, reviewing the Ripper-inspired Ritual In The Dark, noted: "so good is Mr Wilson's prose you can see and smell it all". A better summary of the effect of Wilson's fiction comes from a reviewer of The Mind Parasites, a philosophical sci-fi romp, who said: "I was fascinated and disappointed by turns but I couldn't put it down."

"Shall I tell you my favourite conspiracy theory?"

Just to key the name **Robert Anton Wilson** (1932–) into Google is to feel that you are stepping into a strange, parallel, slightly sinister universe. It's not every novelist of whom such questions are asked in cyberspace as: "Is Robert Anton Wilson the great beast of the Apocalypse?"

Wilson has written tons of fantasy novels, the most famous of which – Schrodinger's Cat trilogy and the Illuminatus trilogy he co-wrote with fellow **Playboy** journalist **Robert Shea** – trip into a strange hinterland where paranoia, conspiracy theories, drugs and some of the more arcane legacies of **Beat** writers like **William Burroughs**, meet and mingle. Both trilogies draw on real events and paranoid theorising (often taken from readers' letters written to **Playboy** when Wilson and Shea were on the staff). These are Wilson's best-known works, but he may have had more impact as a disseminator of esoteric philosophies and an advocate of **Timothy Leary**'s theories about neurosomatic/linguistic engineering.

Wilson is fated to be regarded as the world's foremost conspiracy-theory novelist – not, in an age full of such theories, that that's such a bad thing. The Illuminatus cult (see page 252), Wilson's suggested secret ruling elite, has been taken seriously by many and both trilogies are, perhaps intentionally, full of the rambling, suggestive, overlapping plots later deployed in The X Files. The Illuminatus books also present lashings of drugs, sex and self-mockery and were so popular that Wilson wrote sequels and spin-offs, following up the original trilogy with another entitled The Historical Illuminati Chronicles.

Not all of the many ideas suggested in these trilogies are unique to Wilson and his writing partner. Schrodinger's Cat takes Dr Strangelove as one of its departure points, while the idea of a 'fnord', a code word that has hypnotic power over people who come into contact with it, is an obvious spin on techniques that control the brainwashed assassin in The Manchurian Candidate. The word 'fnord' comes from the Principia Discordia, the 'sacred' cut-up text of a group called the Discordians, a sect that has been described as the world's first post-modern religion; a religion disguised as a joke and a joke disguised as a religion.

The question is: are the novels worth reading? Yes, if you go with the flow. But his first published work, remember, was Playboy's Book Of Forbidden Words.

INFLUENCED BY Leary; Aleister Crowley; Pynchon; philosopher Eric Voegelin.

INFLUENCE ON **The X Files**; **The Nose** magazine; cyberspace.

ESSENTIAL READING The original **Illuminatus** trilogy (**The Eye In The Pyramid**; **The Golden Apple**; **Leviathan**) and **Schrodinger's Cat**.

FURTHER READING **Cosmic Trigger**, a tour of the mind and a tour de force.

23 AND THE ILLUMINATUS CONSPIRACY

Number 23, to many, is synonymous with the shirts of **Michael Jordan** and **David Beckham**. But to readers of **Robert Anton Wilson**'s Illuminatus novels – and a growing band of professional 23 watchers influenced by **William Burroughs** – it has a much deeper and sinister significance.

When Burroughs was in Tangiers, he began keeping a scrapbook of 23s after a conversation with a **Captain Clark**. The ferry captain told Burroughs he had been doing the route to Spain for 23 years without an accident. That day, the boat sank. That evening, on the radio, Burroughs heard that Flight 23 from New York to Miami, piloted by a Captain Clark, had crashed.

The figure is said to be the sacred number of **Eris**, the Greek goddess of discord. One random literary reference: when Sydney Carlton is guillotined in A Tale Of Two Cities, he is the 23rd victim that day. Some say this is where the phrase '23 skidoo' ('23 and move on') comes from.

Karl Koch, a German hacker, became so obsessed by the figure's significance, he allegedly committed suicide on the 23rd day when he was 23 years old. His life – and death – were the subject of a German movie, 23, released in 1998. Koch was obsessed by the Illuminati, for whom 23 is a secret significant number. Wilson named his sect in homage to the

Illuminati (it means 'enlightened ones' in Latin), which had been the name for various sects in 15th- and 16th-century Europe. The Illuminati most conspiracy theorists look to are the **Bavarian Illuminati**, a group of 18th-century freethinkers (whose adherents may have included **Goethe**) and masons who wanted to establish republican government across Europe.

This group was defunct by 1785, but various writers have claimed that through their masonic influence they have had a decisive effect on Western history. As Wilson himself says, "A theory I like claims the United States has been run by Freemasons ever since the beginning, but the Freemasons are really a gay secret society, and **George Washington** was gay right?" Others have suggested that the **Skull & Bones**, the Yale fraternity to which **George W. Bush** and **John Kerry** belonged, is an offshoot of the Illuminati/masons.

All of this should be taken in the same spirit Wilson regards The Holy Blood And The Holy Grail and The Da Vinci Code (see page 284). "The Priory of Sion [the secret order which, the books suggest, protects Jesus's bloodline] has all the appearances of a real conspiracy but, look at it another way and it looks like a very complicated practical joke by a bunch of French intellectual aristocrats."

CORNELL WOOLRICH

First you dream, then you die

This title of **Francis Nevin**'s biography of **Cornell Woolrich** (1903–1968), taken from an unfinished story found in his hotel room when he died, captures the life – and work – of one of America's darkest pulp writers. In his memoirs, Woolrich recalls a performance of Madame Butterfly he watched as an eight-year-old. The romance and tragedy left him with the realisation that he too would die, like the heroine: "I had that trapped feeling, like some… insect… inside a downturned glass, and it tries to climb up the sides, and it can't."

In his first novel, Cover Charge, written after an infected heel had left him bedridden, the protagonist is left contemplating suicide after the two older women he has loved are both dead. "I hate the world," declares Woolrich's hero, "Everything comes into it so clean and goes out so dirty."

If Woolrich's prose trembled on the brink of parody, his plots could be slick. **Raymond Chandler** called him "the best ideas man in the business." Hollywood, appreciating the ideas, hired him to adapt his second glitzy serious novel, Children Of The Ritz. He married, but it was annulled after his wife found she had married a shy, gay, mother-dominated man who kept a sailor's uniform in a locked briefcase so he could patrol the waterfront in search of sex.

He lived with his mother in a New York hotel from 1932 to 1957, from where he wrote most of his fiction, some of which, in its depiction of uncertain, alienated, fearful lives, had a rare quality. The French adopted Woolrich for his série noire novels. He had a certain knack for titles, The Corpse Next Door and Death Sits In The Dentist's Chair being just two of his more lurid.

Alfred Hitchcock was a fan, making Rear Window from It Had To Be Murder, as was his acolyte **François Truffaut**, whose The Bride Wore Black and La Sirène Du Mississippi, adapted from Woolrich's work, are fine movies. After 1957, when his mother died, Woolrich's unhappy life unravelled. His writing became less prolific; the booze bit deep and he died of a stroke, aged 65, leaving two unfinished novels and scores of titles in his room.

INFLUENCED BY F. Scott Fitzgerald; pulp pioneer MacKinlay Kantor; G.T. Fleming-Roberts, master of 'weird menace' pulp fiction.

INFLUENCE ON Jim Thompson; Fredric Brown; Gary Indiana.

ESSENTIAL READING The best single anthology is **Nightwebs**.

FURTHER READING The hard-to-find fiction of Charlotte Armstrong, who wrote Woolrich-influenced noir, but with a harder political edge.

RICHARD WRIGHT

An outsider from birth to death

Of the Afro-American writers of the 20th century, few have written so powerfully or earned such respect as **Richard Wright** (1908–1960). His ideas had a profound effect on the black liberation movement of the 1950s and 1960s and, crucially, he rid American literature of the cowed, subservient Negro once and for all.

Wright was born on a Mississippi plantation. His father walked out when he was six and he and his brother later lived with his maternal grandmother – a Seventh Day Adventist who frowned on Wright's literary aspirations as she deemed all books the work of the devil. Yet in 1924, a year before he dropped out of high school, Wright published his first story, The Voodoo Of Hell's Half Acre, in the **Southern Register**, a local black newspaper. He had developed a passion for **H.L. Mencken**, borrowing his books secretly from the whites-only library.

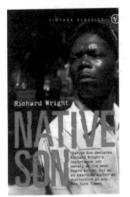

Moving to Chicago three years later, he wrote most of a novel, Cesspool (published posthumously as Lawd Today in 1963), and in 1938 won an award for his story Fire And Cloud that led to a Guggenheim Fellowship.

Native Son followed, the story of the provocatively named Bigger Thomas: a young, uneducated black man trapped by poverty and racism who is offered work as a chauffeur for a wealthy white family but, in a moment of panic, accidentally murders their daughter. Wright's protagonist is no pitiable Uncle Tom, but rather the brutal, damaged consequence of his society.

254

In 1941 Wright married a second time, to a white member of the **Communist Party**, and, in 1946, they moved to Paris with their daughter, partly because his skin colour meant he couldn't buy an apartment in New York. He had left the Communist Party, but stayed involved in left-wing politics, and – with **Sartre** and **Camus** among his friends – began to study existentialism.

Wright's The Outsider was published in 1953. Called the first existentialist American novel, it concerns a black Communist – the ultimate marginalised figure of 1950s American society. Aside from the slim, critically panned Savage Holiday, it was his last work of fiction for years. Five years later he published The Long Dream, a surreal take on the racist South, which was to be part of a trilogy, but the second instalment, Island Of Hallucinations, has never been published and the third never begun. In 1959 Wright became fascinated by haiku and wrote over 4,000 in a year. He died, officially, of a heart attack, although rumours persist that he was murdered.

INFLUENCED BY H.L. Mencken; R.H. Blyth; Camus.
INFLUENCE ON Ralph Ellison; Chester Himes; James Baldwin.
ESSENTIAL READING **Native Son**.
FURTHER READING James Baldwin's **Go Tell It On The Mountain**.

RUDOLPH WURLITZER

The slow fade of a promising author

Little is known about the life of Texan novelist **Rudolph Wurlitzer** (1938–), although he has added to the intrigue with tales of his family, claiming his father spent the fortune created by the Wurlitzer music empire before he could enjoy it.

Wurlitzer made a quiet, cultish, debut with Nog in 1969, hailed by **Thomas Pynchon**, who noted: "Rudolph Wurlitzer is really, really good," and boosted by others as the best stoned novel of all-time. But, as **Toby Litt** has suggested, there's a craft to the novel that's rare in chemically-driven fiction – this is writing, not typing. Flats followed in 1970, then Quake, an apocalyptic tale of a major earthquake rocking Hollywood, which has some fine passages in it, but is more convincing if you also happen to be on whatever Wurlitzer was when he wrote it.

Wurlitzer is probably best known today for Two-Lane Blacktop, his play filmed by **Monte Hellman** in 1971. He then wrote the screenplay for **Sam Peckinpah**'s Pat Garrett And Billy the Kid, starring **Kris Kristofferson** and **Bob Dylan**, and published a brilliant Hollywood novel, Slow Fade, about a declining western director. Four years later, in 1984, he directed Candy Mountain, a movie about a struggling musician with a bizarre cast – **Tom Waits**, **Jim Jarmusch**, **Joe Strummer**. Since then, there's been Hard Road To Sacred Places, an account of a spiritual journey through Asia after the death of Wurlitzer's 21-year-old son, but the title Slow Fade is probably an apt, sad summary of his career as a novelist.

INFLUENCED BY Beckett; Buddhism; Burroughs.

INFLUENCE ON Don DeLillo.

ESSENTIAL READING **Nog**; **Slow Fade**.

FURTHER READING **Quake**; **Hard Road To Sacred Places**.

RICHARD YATES

"All the people who knew how to live had kept the secret to themselves"

In 1961 two great novels failed to win America's National Book Award. One, Catch-22 by **Joseph Heller**, became a critically acclaimed global bestseller. The other, Revolutionary Road by **Richard Yates** (1926–1992), fell into such neglect that, by the time Yates died, his books were out of print. As writer **Stewart O'Nan** noted: "To write so well and then to be forgotten is a terrifying legacy."

The titles of Yates's short-story collections – Liars In Love and Eleven Kinds Of Loneliness – identify his fictional terrain: the masterful depiction of the banal failures of ambition and affection. In Revolutionary Road his trapped protagonist Frank Wheeler observes that the people who know how to live well weren't sharing that vital information.

Yates didn't know how to live well. Neither did his parents, who were probably alcoholics and separated when he was a boy. He lived with his mother who brought home many boyfriends, climbed into bed with her son when drunk and once vomited on his pillow. Yates developed a stutter, was bullied at school and, after a stint in the army, developed tuberculosis. He missed out on university, writing press releases and short fiction instead. His two wives left, he had a succession of poorly paid teaching jobs and his own alcoholism achieved legendary proportions. Martini breakfasts didn't help his manic depression nor the fact that, by the mid-1960s, his unexperimental fiction, in the great tradition of **F. Scott Fitzgerald** and **John Updike**, was deemed old hat. In the 1970s his fine novel The Easter Parade was almost ignored.

Death, a few influential literary fans (**Julian Barnes**, **Michael Chabon**) and the 40th anniversary of Revolutionary Road have forced a reappraisal. His fiction has no massive emotional range but he brought authority and compassion of failure to his subject. For Chabon, "He is a master of finding the revealing episode or culminating incident in the history of a human relationship and dramatising it through sharp dialogue and a terse, vivid, style."

INFLUENCED BY F. Scott Fitzgerald; Hemingway.

INFLUENCE ON Richard Ford; Chabon; Robert Stone; Tobias Wolff.

ESSENTIAL READING **Revolutionary Road**; **The Collected Stories**.

FURTHER READING **The Easter Parade**, flawed but moving and, unusually for Yates, holding out the possibility of redemption.

RICHARD ZIMLER

Richard Zimler (1956–) found his inspiration in Portugal. Born in a New York suburb, he worked as a journalist in San Francisco before moving to the University of Porto in 1990, where he still teaches journalism.

Although he has written many short stories, Zimler's breakthrough novel was The Last Kabbalist Of Lisbon which, in 1998, became the most surprising cult bestseller since The Name Of The Rose. An engrossing tale, tracing a murder mystery against the slaughter of Jews in Portugal in the 16th century, it was garnished with just enough ancient wisdom from the currently fashionable Kabbalah sect to be a feel-good philosophical thriller.

He has returned to the subject of the lives of Portuguese Jews in Hunting Midnight, an impressive book that doesn't hold together as well. When the tale leads into American slavery, Zimler invites comparisons to the works of such writers as **Toni Morrison**, a parallel that does him no favours. But Zimler remains one of the most intriguing American novelists in exile.

GRAPHIC NOVELS

FOR A GENRE THAT HAS BEEN AROUND SINCE 1827,
GRAPHIC NOVELS STILL DON'T GET THE RESPECT
THEY DESERVE. ALLOW US TO INTRODUCE YOU TO OVER
30 OF THE FINEST EXPONENTS OF THE ART

"We do what we must, Lucien.
Sometimes we can choose the path we follow.
Sometimes our choices are made for us.
And sometimes we have no choice at all"

Dream In Sandman: Seasons Of Mists,
Episode 1 by Neil Gaiman

 Waldo D.R. Dobbs has an IQ of 280 and likes to blow things up; don't we all?

GRAPHIC NOVELS

So what are graphic novels exactly? In this case 'graphic' doesn't mean 'explicit' or 'pornographic' (though there are those for adults only), but simply 'told in pictures'. Nor does 'novel' necessarily mean 'an extended fictional work'. True, there are some 'novelistic' graphic novels thousands of pages long across multiple volumes, but many are much shorter – graphic novellas really – or even short-story collections, and a good number are definitely not fiction. In the end, 'novel' just refers to being in a book format, hardcover or soft, with a spine.

It was American fan and critic **Richard Kyle** who first coined the term 'graphic novel' in November 1964, in an attempt to escape the humorous and childish connotations of the word 'comics' and to imply an aspiration to greater sophistication and respectability. However, comics in book form have existed for nearly two centuries – at least since 1827, when Swiss pioneer **Rodolphe Töpffer** drafted his earliest satirical album. But it was **Will Eisner** – already a veteran of the comics medium – who crystallised the format and ambition of the modern graphic novel with A Contract With God in 1978 – four short stories interconnected by their setting: the Bronx slums of the 1930s.

Since then, a body of substantial works has emerged in the form of original stories created specifically for the format, compilations of serialised comic books and translations from Europe, Japan and beyond. Contrary to some people's misconceptions, their subjects are not just confined to superheroes or fantasy either.

Graphic novels have scaled the bestseller lists, won prestigious awards, been praised by the media and intelligentsia and adapted into hit films. Over the past four years they have become by far the fastest-growing category of books sold in the USA. You'll find the widest range in specialist comics stores, but more general bookshops and libraries now carry a selection. Here are over 30 American, British, Canadian and Maltese graphic novelists to start you exploring…

BRIAN AZZARELLO

This Chicago writer scripts 100 Bullets (Vertigo/Titan), probably today's smartest, seamiest mainstream crime comic book. Why is rebel hitman Agent Graves baiting his former employers by giving their victims an untraceable loaded gun and the chance to avenge themselves? Immerse yourself in the taut pacing, vivid characterisation and moody noir graphics by Argentina's **Eduardo Risso**, as all gradually becomes clear by the 100th issue.

PETER BAGGE

Meet New Jersey's wonderfully dysfunctional Bradley family and their number-one son – alienated, pessimistic twentysomething Buddy, desperate to escape to Seattle's grunge scene, only to get caught up there in sex, drugs and managing a talentless punk band. **Bagge**'s big-nosed, big-hearted Buddy Bradley comedies (Fantagraphics) stand as a bitingly satirical chronicle of 1990s slackerdom.

> "Damn! I forgot this all started because I was crying over a pair of lousy boots"
>
> Maggie in Locas Tambien in Jaime and Gilbert Hernandez's Love & Rockets

BRIAN MICHAEL BENDIS

Bendis is a writer and sometime artist grounded in crime fiction, films and TV. His work ranges from his female bounty hunter Jinx and serial-killer case Torso (Image) drawn by **Marc Andreyko**, to his gritty reworking of blind lawyer-superhero Daredevil (Marvel). At his best he shows real wit, as in the quickfire repartee and exposure of celebrity in Powers (Image/Icon) with artist **Michael Avon Oeming**, about streetwise detectives in a superpowered world, and in his fraught diatribe about Hollywood development hell, Fortune And Glory (Oni).

RAYMOND BRIGGS

Best known for his children's classics The Snowman and Father Christmas, **Briggs** caused uproar in parliament with When The Wind Blows (Cape), in which he criticised government preparations for a nuclear attack by showing a trusting elderly couple's slow, sad death from radiation sickness. Another English couple, Briggs's parents, unfold the story of their everyday lives amid the rush of technology and social change in Ethel And Ernest (Cape), a tender remembrance.

CHESTER BROWN

Canada's most versatile underground cartoonist, **Brown** recalls his teenage anxieties over porn, swearing, his budding sexuality and his mother's mental health with haunting candour in The Playboy and I Never Liked You. His range also encompasses bizarre humour in The Little Man (Drawn & Quarterly), a biography of radical **Louis Riel** and a critical retelling of the Gospels.

CHARLES BURNS

This modern horror master (born in Seattle – where he went to high school with **Matt Groening** – but now based in Philadelphia) dissects the American nightmare and draws his freakshow characters – transplant victim Dog Boy, Mexican wrestler-detective El Borbah and troubled kid Big Baby – with an almost inhuman precision. Even more disturbing undercurrents seethe through Black Hole (Fantagraphics), a story of 1970s high-school students deformed by a sexually transmitted plague and ostracised.

HOWARD CHAYKIN

Chaykin's ribald satire on American politics and media, American Flagg (First/Image) pits maverick marshal and womaniser Flagg against a corrupt, corporate-run government and a racist, survivalist opposition. It remains his sharpest comic, though his unapologetically raunchy Black Kiss (Vortex/ Fantagraphics) offers some guilty pleasures.

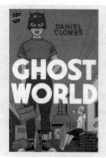

DANIEL CLOWES

261

If you liked the Ghost World movie (**Clowes** co-wrote the screenplay), his original graphic novel takes you much deeper, focussing on the self-destructive relationship between suburban outsiders Enid Coleslaw (an anagram of Clowes's name) and Rebecca Doppelmeyer. His other books are as good, if not better, especially his **David Lynch**-like chiller Like A Velvet Glove Cast In Iron, the alienated romance David Boring, and new issues and compilations of his solo anthology Eightball (Fantagraphics).

ROBERT CRUMB

The most influential cartoonist from the 1960s American underground 'comix' generation, **Crumb** enjoyed wide popularity for his oversexed Fritz The Cat, but was so furious about **Ralph Bakshi**'s animated travesty that he drew a strip in which Fritz was killed off by an ice-pick to the head. To **Crumb**, who lives in France these days, comics are an outlet for his erotic fantasies, unflattering confessionals and inner demons. His entire output is gathered in The Complete Crumb series (Fantagraphics), or sample some of his best in the R. Crumb Coffee Table Book (Little Brown/Bloomsbury).

CULT FICTION

WILL EISNER

An acclaimed comics veteran, **Eisner** was nearing 60 when he underwent a renaissance creating his first graphic novel, A Contract With God (DC), more accurately four vignettes set in a Depression-era Bronx tenement. Memories and research of the Jewish immigrant experience fill his books, whether exploring the racial tensions of his own childhood in To The Heart Of The Storm (DC) or reappraising the origins and fate of **Charles Dickens**'s Fagin (Doubleday). Incredibly, Eisner (who was born in 1917) is still working at his peak.

WARREN ELLIS

In The Authority's take-charge battalion and Planetary's conspiracy paranoia, British writer **Ellis** pumped up his widescreen superheroics beyond even Hollywood's biggest budgets. With more than 35 graphic novels to his name, he's equally adept at hard-science speculation in Orbiter and at vitriolic commentary via his bitter futuristic hack Spider Jerusalem in Transmetropolitan (DC).

GARTH ENNIS

With a penchant for pithy dialogue, outrageous violence, blasphemy and pitch-black humour, Irish writer **Ennis** made his mark with cynical magician Constantine in Hellblazer (with artist **Steve Dillon**), before embarking on their nine-volume contemporary horror-western Preacher (DC), in which a possessed priest searches for God to take Him to task for the world's injustices.

NEIL GAIMAN

Sandman (DC) is British author Gaiman's most admired graphic novel: ten referential, century-spanning books that construct a mythology around the Endless, a family of seven symbolic beings that includes Morpheus, king of dreams, and Death herself, personified as a perky, pale Goth. **Gaiman**'s partnership with artist **Dave McKean** resulted in fractured family stories Violent Cases (Escape/Titan) and Mr Punch (DC), their experiment Signal To Noise and a pair of thoughtful children's books (Bloomsbury). For Marvel, he transposed their cast to 17th-century England in the clever game of 1602.

JAIME AND GILBERT HERNANDEZ

The women featured by these Hispanic American brothers in their comic Love & Rockets (Fantagraphics) are strong, sensual and fully realised. Jaime's Locas

EUROPE: A CONTINENT OF COMICS

Beyond the perennial favourites Tintin and Asterix lies a vast continent of outstanding European comics. These range from Franco-Belgian hardback colour albums to the black-and-white pulps of Italy, and many are now available in English translations.

Comics in mainland Europe have enjoyed far greater acceptance for decades and some – such as **Jean Giraud**'s wild-west hero Blueberry – are bestsellers.

Crumbling dystopias are the settings for exiled Yugoslav **Enki Bilal**'s richly painted science fictions, while **Jacques Tardi** has adapted novelist **Léo Malet**'s Parisian P.I. Nestor Burma for comic-book form. Tardi has also created a Belle Epoque detective, Adèle Blanc-Sec.

Among France's latest generation are **David B**, with his frank account of his elder brother's illness in Epileptic, and Iranian-born **Marjane Satrapi**, who vividly conveys the impact of the Islamic revolution on her family in Persepolis.

The seafaring Corto Maltese by Italy's **Hugo Pratt** is another man-of-action bestseller. Italy's other maestros include erotic specialists **Guido Crepax** and **Milo Manara**; **Tiziano Sclavi** (creator of horror investigator Dylan Dog); and **Lorenzo Mattotti**, **Igort** and **Francesca Ghermandi**, products of the Valvoline art-comics movement.

For European humour try **Claire Brétecher**, Germany's gay satirist **Ralf König** and the prolific French phenomenon **Lewis Trondheim**.

263

As Time Out put it, Love & Rockets is about "real women in a surreal world"

charts the lives of Maggie Chascarillo and Hopey, her on-off lover, in the 1980s punk scene of southern California, while Gilbert's magic-realist Palomar is the smalltown location for his indomitable heroine Luba.

DAVE McKEAN

As well as his collaborations with **Neil Gaiman**, **Iain Sinclair** and others, Berkshire-born **McKean** writes stories of his own. His ambitious Cages (NBM/Titan) revolves around the occupants of an apartment block and their issues of creativity and identity, while his short-story collection Pictures That Tick (Hourglass) demonstrates his stylistic repertoire.

FRANK MILLER

At heart, **Miller** always hoped to resurrect America's toughest crime comics, but as superheroes dominated the market, he injected a noir grittiness into Daredevil (Marvel) and Batman in The Dark Knight Returns (DC/Titan), influencing the

THE MAGIC OF MANGA

Comics are, ahem, big in Japan, filling multi-million-selling weeklies as fat as phone directories and accounting for 40 per cent of all publications sold. Translated into English, manga paperbacks around 200 pages long have invaded the West.

Japan's 'god of manga' is **Osamu Tezuka**, best known for his robot Pinocchio Astro Boy, who established the techniques and traditions. His masterpieces include the alternative Hitler history Adolf, the life story of **Buddha** and the allegorical firebird **Phoenix**. Among the generations of artists that Tezuka has influenced is **Keiji Nakazawa**, whose anti-war autobiography Barefoot Gen records his harrowing childhood surviving Hiroshima's atomic bomb.

People often discover manga via the animated versions such as **Katsuhiro Otomo**'s Neo-Tokyo nightmare Akira and **Masamune Shirow**'s techno-future Ghost In The Shell. Film director and animator **Hayao Miyazaki** has also crafted manga, notably the eco-fable Nausicaä Of The Valley Of Wind.

Brutal and touching, the 28 volumes of Lone Wolf and Cub by **Kazuo Koike** and **Goseki Kojima** chronicle a rogue samurai assassin on the run with his infant son. But for sheer horror, as well as manga adaptations to The Ring and Battle Royale, it's hard to top **Junji Ito**'s Uzumaki, **Hideshi Hino**'s many titles and the decadent 'erotic-grotesque' Ultra-Gash Inferno by **Suehiro Maruo**. In contrast, urban Japanese have lost none of their sensitivity to nature, exquisitely captured in **Jiro Taniguchi**'s The Walking Man.

From Passion (a gay romance in the 'beautiful boy' genre), to Apocalypse Meow (the Vietnam war fought between cute rabbits and cats), there is something for every taste in Japanese comics.

Tim Burton films. His sequel The Dark Knight Strikes Again disappointed many Bat-fans, but wickedly subverts the genre's clichés. Miller has written for other artists, notably **Bill Sienkiewicz** on Elektra Assassin (Marvel), **Geoff Darrow** on Hard-Boiled and **Dave Gibbons** on Martha Washington, leading to him letting rip on a solo crime series, his brutal, compelling Sin City (Dark Horse/Titan).

PETER MILLIGAN

Milligan seeks out strange ideas and surprising angles in his writing, from examining superheroes' homosexual subtexts in Enigma (DC/Titan) and their celebrity stature in X-Force/X-Statix (Marvel), to blending **James Joyce** with The Godfather in Skreemer (DC). Particularly striking are his books with designer **Brendan McCarthy**: their Indian mind-trip Rogan Gosh and the banned Skin (Tundra), about a thalidomide skinhead's violent vengeance.

ALAN MOORE

Northampton-born **Moore** brings daring intelligence, political passion and human understanding to every genre and theme he touches. V For Vendetta (DC/Titan) is a high point, insisting on individual freedom in an Orwellian future Britain. In Marvelman/Miracleman and Watchmen (DC/Titan), Moore

reinvigorates superheroes by addressing how they would affect our real world for better or worse. More recently, he masterminded his own universe of heroes, the America's Best Comics line, and in one heroine, Promethea, personified the magic of creation. In Lost Girls (Top Shelf) with artist **Melinda Gebbie**, he celebrates explicit erotica, unveiling the sexualities of three ages of 'fairytale women' in the forms of Dorothy, Wendy and Alice. Forget the films; his Swamp Thing, League Of Extraordinary Gentlemen and From Hell originals are infinitely richer reads. Moore is the medium's greatest living writer.

265

GRANT MORRISON

Whether revamping established characters like the JLA and X-Men or devising his own, **Morrison** (who still lives in Glasgow) is a restlessly innovative writer, always intriguing if not always accessible. He transformed such worn-out concepts as Animal Man and Doom Patrol into fascinating vehicles for his imagination and produced the memorable Batman psychodrama Arkham Asylum with painter **Dave McKean**. Prompted by a 'contact experience' with aliens, Morrison let his most outré ideas overflow in the apocalyptic conspiracy epic The Invisibles, a key inspiration for The Matrix, and the paranormal chiller The Filth. Some feel his shorter, more restrained pieces, such as St. Swithin's Day, New Adventures Of Hitler, Sebastian O and We 3, are among his best.

HARVEY PEKAR

In the words of Cleveland everyman **Pekar**, "Ordinary life is pretty complex stuff!" For nearly 30 years the hospital administrator has been finding magic in the mundane and transcribing his everyday experiences (and those of others) into his annual comic American Splendor, illustrated by **R. Crumb** and many more. He also narrates and appears in the big-screen version released in 2003. As well as the assorted compilations, Pekar and his wife **Joyce Brabner** wrote an arresting full-length graphic novel, Our Cancer Year, illustrated by **Frank Stack**.

CHRIS REYNOLDS

What lies behind the enigmatic Monitor's clandestine operations, and how will life in semi-rural Wales change now that it is occupied by eerily benign alien invaders? Drawn with almost woodcut boldness, a unique vision of the near future fills **Reynolds**'s subtly nuanced graphic novels Mauretania (Penguin) and The Dial (Kingly Books).

JOE SACCO

A Maltese citizen who studied journalism in the US, where he now lives, **Sacco** has virtually invented his own genre, 'Comics New Journalism': part documentary, part autobiography. Influenced by his mother's wartime experiences in Malta and based on thorough research and extensive interviews on his visits to modern frontlines, he has captured the harsh effects of war on ordinary people in Palestine and Safe Area Gorazde (Fantagraphics), while in The Fixer (Drawn & Quarterly) he returns to **Bosnia** a decade later, only to discover how little life has improved.

SETH

Nicknamed 'the nostalgia guy', Canada's **Seth** (born **Gregory Gallant**) harks back to the better, or less ugly, days of the past in his quiet stories and his elegant cartooning. His work is often full of melancholy and lonely characters searching for meaning in life: It's A Good Life If You Don't Weaken (Drawn & Quarterly) fictionalises his quest for an obscure gag cartoonist, while Clyde Fans is the memoir of a failed fan salesman who collects postcards.

> "Satisfactory!!!
> Are you
> shitting me!!?
> Maimed,
> one-legged
> for life,
> and you
> find that
> satisfactory!!?"
>
> Nikopol in Bilal's
> Gods In Chaos

DAVE SIM

What began in 1977 as Cerebus The Aardvark, a funny pastiche of Conan The Barbarian using animals, concluded in 2004 as an unprecedented 300-issue graphic novel of over 6,000 pages, created and self-published by Canadian **Sim**, assisted by **Gerhard** on backgrounds. Along the way, Sim narrates the travels and travails of the mercenary Cerebus, parodies the famous, from **Mrs Thatcher** and **Ernest Hemingway** to **the Marx Brothers** and **Woody Allen**, and engages in a freewheeling questioning of ideologies and philosophies.

POSY SIMMONDS

She's the 'First Lady' of English comics, not that her **Guardian** newspaper strips are ever prim. Her Weber Family sitcom and Literary Life essays show how observant and sometimes scathing she can be. **Posy**'s masterpiece is Gemma Bovery (Cape), a romantic thriller that mixes typeset prose with graphic novel and updates **Flaubert**'s Madame Bovary as a listless London wife enamoured with French provincial living.

267

JEFF SMITH

Twelve years in the making, **Tolkien** meets **Pogo** in **Smith**'s 1,300-page Bone (Cartoon Books), a beautifully illustrated saga of intricate fantasy leavened with pathos and humour to enchant all ages.

ART SPIEGELMAN

The **Pulitzer Prize-winning** Maus (Pantheon/Penguin) is the unflinching family history of **Spiegelman**'s father Vladek, a Polish Jew and survivor of Auschwitz, combined with the present-day life of the author in New York as, approaching 40, he tries to rebuild his relationship with his father and understand himself. By portraying Jews as mice and

Cat and mouse: the horrors of the Holocaust

Nazis as cats, Spiegelman draws on both the cat-and-mouse antics in early animation and comics and the racist propaganda that uses such imagery. Maus not only gives a firsthand account of the Holocaust, but is also a brave attempt to address the pain of the survivors' children today. With his wife **Françoise Mouly**, he edited the comics magazine RAW, providing a platform for a raft of talent, and he has created a fantastic series of large-format Little Lit comic anthologies for kids, putting fresh twists on fairytales and other subjects (memorably, It Was A Dark And Silly Night). His most recent work is the extraordinary In The Shadow Of No Towers, a series of strips, originally for **The New Yorker**, exploring September 11 and its aftermath.

CAROL SWAIN

Like **Chris Reynolds**, **Swain** is a distinctly English voice championed in **Escape** magazine. Drawn with spare dialogue and atmospheric charcoal shades, her alienated youths stumble along the wavering line between society and the primal Welsh landscape in Invasion Of The Mind Sappers and Foodboy (Fantagraphics).

BRYAN TALBOT

Inspired by **Nick Roeg** and **Michael Moorcock**, Lancashire-born **Talbot** is the link between the British underground comics of the early 1970s and 2000AD, for whom he began work in 1983. His complex, multi-layered Adventures Of Luther Arkwright (Dark Horse) was Britain's first epic graphic novel, involving a parallel timeline where **Cromwell**'s Civil War never actually ended, and led to

an alternative Victorian age in the colour sequel Heart Of Empire. In the multi-award-winning The Tale Of One Bad Rat, Talbot sensitively relates how a sexually abused runaway girl finally returns to confront her father, and even manages to include a fitting homage to **Beatrix Potter**.

ADRIAN TOMINE

This American artist writes and draws stories about people and their struggle to connect with each other. He published his early work in his mini-comic Optic Nerve (later collected as 32 Stories), but it is his 2002 collection Summer Blonde (Drawn &

Tomine's yearning masterpiece

Quarterly) that is a must-read and indicator as to why Tomine fans count **Dave Eggers** and **Nick Hornby** among their number. With his ear for the dialogue of everyday narratives, he pretty much lives up to his publisher's billing as the "Raymond Carver of comix".

CHRIS WARE

Deeply affecting, bleakly funny and at least partly autobiographical, Jimmy Corrigan: The Smartest Kid On Earth (Pantheon/Cape) is a study of the family secrets and emotional void between fathers and sons across three generations. Born in Nebraska and now living in Chicago, **Ware** composed all 380 colour pages – each one a precise mechanism of motion and emotion – by hand. He is the smartest cartoonist in the world.

HERGÉ'S ADVENTURES OF TINTIN

George Rémi, or **Hergé** as he's known to the world (it's a phonetic rendition of his initials reversed), died more than 20 years ago. But his creation – the plucky young hero of indeterminate age (some fans say he's 21, others 14) with the cowlick hair – shows no sign of fading, despite charges that some of the stories are racist and that Hergé was a Nazi collaborator. His admirers have included **Andy Warhol** (who admitted: "Hergé has influenced my work in the same way as Walt Disney"), **Charles de Gaulle** (who insisted: "Deep down, my only international rival is Tintin") and a surprising number of pop stars.

Evidence as to whether Hergé was a Nazi collaborator – as suggested by film director **Jan Bucquoy** in his comic book The Secret Life Of Hergé – is inconclusive. Detractors seize on one villain with a Jewish-American name and on racist depictions of Africans in Tintin In The Congo – though these were typical attitudes for the time.

Against that, he lampooned **Hitler** in another non-Tintin book and, in the Tintin story King Ottakar's Sceptre (published in 1938), depicted a warlike nation called Syldavia, whose soldiers wore SS-style uniforms and whose air force flew **Heinkel-style** planes.

After fleeing to Paris on the Nazi invasion, Hergé returned to occupied Belgium – a patriotic, if daft, response to **King Leopold**'s appeal to his subjects to return home – and worked for **Le Soir**, a newspaper approved by the Nazis. He was certainly unpopular in Belgium after the war.

The Tintin titles have sold over 200 million copies yet their appeal is mysterious. The mechanics are visible enough: the long-running cartoon series was on TV all over the world and the films helped (although if **Steven Spielberg** ever joins the gang, Tintin could be as big as Harry Potter).

Hergé's canniest decision was to create a hero young enough – and of

CULT FICTION

... THE CONTINUED ADVENTURES OF TINTIN

THE ADVENTURES OF
TINTIN
REPORTER FOR "LE PETIT VINGTIÈME."
IN THE LAND OF
THE SOVIETS

vague enough age – for boys to think they were him. In his heyday most boys couldn't tour the world and Tintin visited all its exotic corners, in travels obviously influenced by **National Geographic** magazine, getting into all kinds of scrapes on their behalf.

Chipper, brave but not rash, innocent but not stupid, with a sense of humour, Tintin is almost a blank canvas readers can project on to. Maybe that's why he has never had to be remade, though

some of the attitudes in the books have changed – and he was briefly, disastrously, given bell bottoms and a peace pin in an attempt to look trendy.

Tintin has exerted a surprising pull on the pop world. British bands of the 1980s, notably the **Thompson Twins** and **Stephen 'Tin Tin' Duffy** (the original lead singer of **Duran Duran**, who went solo as Tin Tin), were obsessed. And on **The Shadows**'s album, **Live At The Liverpool Empire**, there's a seven-minute tour de force by drummer **Brian Bennett** entitled Captain Haddock Is Missing. But first came the obscure Australian pop-rock band **Tin Tin**, formed in 1968 and led by **Steve Kipper**, whose quirky US hit Toast And Marmalade For Tea was produced by the **Bee Gees**'s **Maurice Gibb**. Fast forward 20 years and **Emma Bunton** collaborated with **Tin Tin Out** – DJs **Darren Stokes** and **Lindsay Edwards** – on her single I Am What I Am.

Albert Camus said that a great man shows his greatness not by being at one extreme, but by touching two at once. On that definition, Tintin – who can touch **Charles de Gaulle** and **Baby Spice** – must be very great indeed.

ISOLATION WARD

SIXTY-SEVEN NOVELS THAT HAVE WON ENOUGH
ACCLAIM, ABUSE OR AFFECTION TO EARN THEM – BUT
NOT NECESSARILY THEIR AUTHORS – CULT STATUS

"Some American writers who have
known each other for years have never met
in the daytime or when both were sober"

James Thurber

Dino and Jerry: more inspirational than Ben & Jerry; for proof see p.285

THE ISOLATION WARD

The isolation ward is dedicated to authors who have produced one classic cult novel, but didn't take enough drugs (or took the wrong kind), challenge a fellow writer to a race on all fours across a square in Paris (as a drunken **Arthur Koestler** once did with **Albert Camus**), become secluded mystics or were inconveniently alive for too long and so cannot be considered truly cult themselves, even though they may have written other good novels. Some of the novels are not that well-written, but they have all prompted a reaction more intense than 'So what?' And at least one of these books spins off **Dean Martin** and **Jerry Lewis**. At the end of each review we suggest a work similar in context, subject or spirit that you might enjoy. The key word here, of course, is 'might'.

———

253 Geoff Ryman 1998

One of the earliest, most successful literary experiments on the internet. 253 takes as its basis the fact that a tube train has 253 seats. From this **Ryman** creates 253 mini-stories – each 253 words long – about every traveller on one particular train during the seven-and-a-half minutes before it crashes. Initially this can seem constrained, but the more you read, the more you start to see connections between the stories. The print 'remix' footnotes shed extra light on references in the text, and indices help build connections between the characters, based on their places of work, tastes, mutual friends and so on.

IF YOU LIKE THIS, TRY... **David Thomson**'s Suspects, in which the lives of great film noir characters gradually and tellingly intersect.

———

A REBOURS (AGAINST NATURE)
J.K. Huysmans 1884

The 'poisonous' yellow book that corrupted **Oscar Wilde**'s Dorian Gray. A Rebours is a decadent classic: the story of Des Esseintes, a highly strung,

hyper-aesthetic aristocrat who forsakes the world and its "waves of human mediocrity" to live in sumptuous seclusion. Here he embarks on a doomed experiment to detach himself from nature – surrounding himself with art and waking only at night. To "point out the way to new possibilities," he undertakes various bizarre projects, such as encrusting his tortoise with so many gemstones it can't stand and blending liqueurs in his "mouth organ" to generate a music of flavours.

IF YOU LIKE THIS, TRY... **Fyodor Dostoevsky**'s The Eternal Husband: perfect, grim – and horrid – short fiction from the master.

———

THE AERODROME: A LOVE STORY Rex Warner 1941

This is often described as the best novel ever written about fascism, a verdict that doesn't quite do it justice. The **Kafka**-influenced tale of an adopted boy who is attracted to the gleaming efficient world of the aerodrome near his village – and by the air vice-marshal who runs it – is more than a simple narrative of how a thuggish air force takes over the village. It points out, as the writer **John Gray** noted, "the thwarted religious need" that underpins events and suggests how inadequate the response of liberal democracy is. **Warner** makes his point subtly – and more effectively – because we can see the seductive appeal of a world without inefficiency, irresolution and indolence. Reading this makes the author's later suggestion – "I've bollocksed up my life" – even sadder.

IF YOU LIKE THIS, TRY... **Richard Hughes**'s Fox In The Attic. The first in an historical trilogy, in which the hero's love for a girl blinds him to Nazism.

———

ALL THE KING'S MEN Robert Penn Warren 1946

A roman à clef about the career of **Huey Long**, who governed Louisiana as his personal fiefdom between 1928 and 1932. As such All The King's Men is the most gripping and vivid novel written about US politics (which seems, perhaps by dint of being so personality-driven, to generate much better fiction than British politics). But this sensuously written novel is much more than a book about politics. Its core is the decay of promise. Even the ruthless governor, here named Willie Stark, had promise: he entered politics because he wanted to put things right for the common man. It is through the narrator Jack Burden, once a bright young newspaperman, that we see the corrosive effects of power. Burden left his paper to work as an aide to the governor, but years of corruption, minor and major, are revealed to have rotted his soul. Maybe **John Dean** should have read this before he joined the Nixon White House. Too late, Burden realises he has surrendered everything that might once have made his life worthwhile. IF YOU LIKE THIS, TRY... **Gore Vidal**'s **Lincoln**, a bestseller with brains and a refreshingly candid reappraisal of a national icon.

AUNT JULIA AND THE SCRIPTWRITER
Mario Vargas Llosa 1977

Mario is a 19-year-old law student working at a radio station in 1950s Lima when two chaotic forces crash into his life. The first is his recently divorced, vibrant Aunt Julia: the pair begin a playful affair that turns into love. He brings the fun back into her life; she encourages his desire to be a writer in Paris. The second force is a famous radio soap-opera writer Pedro Camacho, who, after enlivening the airwaves with his hot and steamy novellas, loses the plot quite literally: his characters pop up in the wrong stories, some returning from the dead. In this semi-autobiographical tale, **Vargas Llosa** alternates between Mario and Julia's tragicomic love story, the pair battling with their family, and Camacho's tragic destiny, as his plots unravel and intertwine, one soap opera leading seamlessly into another. All soap writers will read this and shudder.

275

IF YOU LIKE THIS, TRY... **Julia Urquidi Illanes**'s What Mario Didn't Say. Vargas Llosa married his aunt, Julia Urquidi Illanes, and dedicated Aunt Julia And The Scriptwriter, his fictionalised account of their relationship, to her after their divorce. Alas, the sentiment backfired, with Urquidi Illanes writing the vengeful What Mario Didn't Say in reply. It may not be great literature, but there are few occasions when you're able to read two sides of the same story.

BLACK LIST, SECTION H Francis Stuart 1972

Many may not want to read this semi-autobiographical novel because its Irish author voluntarily moved to teach in Berlin in World War II where, according to the journalist **Robert Fisk**, he broadcast on behalf of the Nazi regime to Ireland. Controversy still rages over whether **Stuart** genuinely repented, though he did tell one interviewer that he came to realise that **Hitler** was possessed by evil. Black List, Section H is, as novelist **Colin Toibin** (who prefaced the book for Penguin) put it, "something special, strange and haunting". H is a drifter, a gambler, a damaged unsettling soul who can't connect with the world, suffers internment and goes to Nazi Germany. Often praised for its brutal honesty, the book, in presenting its anti-hero, offers no excuses or explanations though he does gloss over H's reasons for his trip to Germany. For all that, it is a powerful work and there is a passionate, intriguing review of it by Stuart's cousin on Amazon.

IF YOU LIKE THIS, TRY… Collected Stories by **John McGahern**. Elegiac tales of the Irish psyche set in a decaying rural way of life, popular with both intellectuals and the public, from the man often called **the Irish Chekhov**.

THE BLIND OWL Sadegh Hedayat 1937

One of the most important works in the Persian language, this hallucinatory, labyrinthine, yet effectively written narrative was criminally overlooked for decades until Rebel Inc. republished it a few years ago. The nameless narrator is a pen-case decorator who retells an event that has "shattered" his existence. The story is dominated by imagery of a cypress tree, an old man and a woman in black. The resulting book effectively conveys an oppressive heat, the haze of opium and a fear of death. The story is increasingly eerie, with an ending that unsettles and is made all the more macabre when you find out **Hedayat** eventually committed suicide (in 1951).

IF YOU LIKE THIS, TRY… **Juan Rulfo**'s Pedro Paramo has a similar eeriness and recurring imagery, but both books are unlike almost any other novel.

CARTER BEATS THE DEVIL Glen Gold 2001

The book opens with Carter, a magician in Prohibition America, performing a grisly trick with audience volunteer, president Warren Harding, who is later found dead in his hotel room. Bumbling sleuth Jack Griffin sets out to uncover

the trick he believes has been played. Like its subject, **Gold**'s colourful debut is a work of illusion – a hypnotising blend of historical detail and fiction melded with seamless sleight of hand. Enjoy the blend of vaudeville, villains, political scandal and escapades in this fictional portrait of Carter, but don't try to separate fact from fiction. It took Gold five years to research this and like any good magician he won't be giving away his secrets lightly. This, **The Guardian** noted, is from the "school of **Doctorow** with flourishes of **John Irving**". But it should, as the same review concluded, "blow you away".

IF YOU LIKE THIS, TRY… **Michael Chabon**'s The Amazing Adventures Of Kavalier And Clay, an intriguing tale of magic, love, betrayal and superheroes.

CATCH-22 Joseph Heller *1961*

Heller should have thanked **Leon Uris** for writing a novel, Mila-18, that forced him to change the title of his fabulous debut from Catch-18, which doesn't have the same snap. The book is one of the finest anti-war novels (it's set in Allied-occupied Italy during World War II) but that tag doesn't quite do this fierce, funny, bitter masterpiece justice. It is, as **Will Self** says, "a veritable manual of satire", but its greatness lies, in part as Self says, in its blend of "deep cynicism and deep humanism". The mad messiness of war is superbly sent up, but the satire would work if Heller's characters were working for a US multinational. War makes the absurdities – the colonel impressing his bosses by constantly raising the number of missions his pilots have to fly – that much more extreme and tragic. With savage genius Heller turns the laughter into darkness. The book's obsessive entrepreneur Milo Minderbinder, who seemed outlandish at the time, would now be working for a Halliburton-style conglomerate in Iraq, while Yossarian is a cynical everyman, a perfect anti-hero for the latter half of the 20th century.

IF YOU LIKE THIS, TRY... All **Heller**'s books – except Picture This – have their admirers. Good As Gold comes closest to his debut, with its riffs on the 'fake Jew' **Henry Kissinger** and puns and verbal games.

———

CHATEAU D'ARGOL Julien Gracq *1938*

The first Surrealist novel, said **André Breton**, who ought to have known. **Gracq** (real name **Louis Poirier**) might not have agreed, since he kept his distance from the Surrealist movement with much the same reticence as he turned down the Prix Goncourt in 1951. But this is, as Breton rightly recognised, a remarkable novel. A disturbing love story, set in a lonely gothic castle, told with an unusual mix of linear narrative and poetry, in which two men are seriously disturbed by the amorality of a beautiful woman.

IF YOU LIKE THIS, TRY... **Gracq**'s other acclaimed masterpiece, The Opposing Shore. A novel that seems both to refer to France's postwar predicament and yet has nothing in it to tie it to a certain country or epoch.

———

CHRIST STOPPED AT EBOLI Carlo Levi *1947*

"Many years have gone by… years of war and what men call history." So begins this remarkable documentary novel, narrated by a Turin doctor exiled to the remote southern province of Luciana for his opposition to Fascism, that made social realism fashionable in Italian literature. Sixty years after its publication, **Levi**'s delicate prose appeals as much for its humanity, the painterly eye with which landscape is depicted and for the light it sheds on life in a neglected region of Italy where outsiders have often been enemies, conquerors or bigoted temporary visitors. Christ, insist the locals, didn't make it to their part of the world, a saying that points to the continual neglect they have suffered from priests and politicians. Levi never wrote anything this popular again. His fine, bitter novel The Watch, about Italy's moral post-war decline, was too fierce to appeal as broadly, but it's not as good as this book, a work of rare durability that you'll want to reread whenever a few years of what men call history go by.

IF YOU LIKE THIS, TRY... **Mario Rigoni Stern**'s novella, The Story Of Tonle – a classic, concise account of peasant life in northern Italy.

A CLOCKWORK ORANGE Anthony Burgess 1962

Burgess's disturbing, dystopian and sometimes humorous vision of the future shows an amoral youth obsessed with law-breaking "ultraviolence" and **Beethoven**. Part of Burgess's inspiration for the book was an assault on his pregnant wife by four army deserters, but the real genius is in the Nadsat language spoken by Alex, our "humble narrator" and anti-hero: think Russian meets cockney rhyming slang via baby-talk and you get words like 'droogs', 'moloko' and 'vidying real horrorshows'. The book is, as **David Lodge** points out, something of a rarity – a successful novel of ideas by an English author. The work became truly notorious when director **Stanley Kubrick** withdrew his cinematic creation after it apparently inspired real-life violence. The American edition of the book carries a final chapter with an older Alex appearing to fully repudiate his actions.

IF YOU LIKE THIS, TRY... Earthly Powers, also by **Burgess**, if only for the opening line and the immense gusto with which the author tells his tale. Many believe it to be superior to A Clockwork Orange.

A CONFEDERACY OF DUNCES John Kennedy Toole 1980

No **Pulitzer Prize**-winning novel has endured such a tragic history, yet even the remarkable tale of its publication does not overshadow this timeless comic masterpiece. **Toole**, a troubled English lecturer from New Orleans, completed the book in 1965, but was rejected by publishers who claimed it "wasn't really about anything". Despondent, Toole committed suicide in 1969 aged 31. Only his mother's dogged determination saw the book reach the hands of celebrated writer **Walker Percy**, who found it "a gargantuan, tumultuous human tragicomedy" and ensured it finally reached print. Toole's hero, the obese, sociopathic Ignatius J. Reilly, is obsessed with what he sees as the moral depravity of modern life, yet is forced to fit in by taking on various menial jobs, with increasingly ridiculous results. Toole's humour is, as you might expect from his fate,

An ultra-violent horror show, a novel of ideas and a dystopian classic

simultaneously funny and sad. But the numerous subplots and flawlessly authentic New Orleans characters are deftly and amusingly handled. Reilly is one of 20th-century fiction's great originals, described by historian **Simon Schama** as "the only serious medieval historian to ponder the legacy of Aquinas while selling hotdogs in New Orleans" and by Percy as "a mad **Oliver Hardy**, fat Don Quixote and perverse **Thomas Aquinas** rolled into one."

IF YOU LIKE THIS, TRY… **Dorothy Baker**'s Cassandra At The Wedding, a fine tragicomic novel. Toole's other novel, The Neon Bible, is for completists only.

CONFESSIONS OF ZENO Italo Svevo 1923

Obsessive, whiny, self-deluding, comically excruciating, depressing, **James Joyce**'s favourite Seinfeld episode – these are a few of the verdicts applied to this account of a backsliding, bumbling businessman trying not to give up nicotine. Written under a pen name (**Svevo** was really an Italian-German called **Ettore Schmitz**), the title can mean Conscience Of Zeno or Consciousness in Italian, but there are no **St Augustine**-style soul-baring confessions in these unreliable memoirs, published, say the foreword notes, by the hero's doctor as an act of revenge. With verbal and stylistic echoes of Joyce's Dubliners (the two authors were friends), influenced by **Freud**'s psycho-analytical theories, this reads, at times, like a distant precursor of Catch-22, while the narcissistic, hypochondriac hero can feel like George Costanza's alter ego.

IF YOU LIKE THIS, TRY… As A Man Grows Older, his most rounded work.

CORNER BOY Herbert Simmons 1957

A lyrical, violent bildungsroman, set in the back streets of St Louis, in which a young black drug-pusher for the Mob sees his dreams – and life – threatened when he is caught by cops with a white woman in his new Cadillac. **Simmons**'s debut, published when he was just 26, is the best of an often overlooked genre now dubbed 'black pulp fiction'. This – and his second novel Man Walking On Eggshells (about a militant jazz musician) – more than deserve the comparisons to **James M. Cain** that reviewers made on their re-issue. Gritty, glittering and relevant – the novels make you wish Simmons hadn't given up the form.

IF YOU LIKE THIS, TRY… **Charles Perry**'s Portrait Of A Young Man Drowning, a powerful account of a thug's rise and fall and how psychosis flowers.

THE CURIOUS INCIDENT OF THE DOG IN THE NIGHT-TIME Mark Haddon 2003

When **Haddon's** novel – about a boy suffering from Asperger's Syndrome (a form of autism) who finds a murdered poodle on his neighbour's lawn and sets out to unravel what happened – won a top literary prize, the **Times Literary Supplement** sniffed that this was a step towards "the juvenilisation of everything". Haddon wanted to emulate what he saw as **Jane Austen's** great gift – writing about humdrum lives with such empathy that they seem fascinating – and he succeeds brilliantly. As this has sold squillions, you might ask how it can be cult, but, possibly because of the tone set by its boy narrator, it's one of those novels that still prompts thousands to turn to friends, significant others, commuters and insist, "You must read this." So ignore the **TLS**.

IF YOU LIKE THIS, TRY... I Capture The Castle by **Dodie Smith**, an intense, evocative recollection of a childhood spent in poverty in a ruined castle.

THE DEATH OF NAPOLEON Simon Leys 2002

This delightful novella imagines what would have happened had **Napoleon** escaped exile in St Helena and returned incognito to Europe. **Leys** handles this scenario with such rare deftness and boldness that it feels entirely logical when, after plans go awry, the undercover emperor returns to the scene of Waterloo as a tourist and ends up selling melons in Paris. You finish the book feeling that somehow, through all the bizarre misadventures, you know the real Napoleon better. Leys's parting gift is to stop the conceit just before it runs out of steam. This is, as the ubiquitous **Susan Sontag** noted, "a marvellous book".

IF YOU LIKE THIS, TRY... Eva's Cousin by **Sibylle Knauss**, a chilling imagining of **Eva Braun**'s life from her cousin's point of view.

281

DELANO John Orozco 1998

An American campus novel with some of the biting wit **Heller** brought to war in Catch-22 applied to academia. Perennially underachieving, **Delano's** odyssey starts with him shooting off his big toe to avoid further entanglement in the Vietnam war, but shifts to a California campus, populated by nutty professors, rabid women's libbers, deluded leaders of the revolution – and the dark lady of his dreams. You know those reviews on Amazon that begin, "I haven't laughed so much since…" Well, the title they're often talking about is this one by Orozco.

IF YOU LIKE THIS, TRY... Holiday On Ice, a collection of stories by **David Sedaris**, one of the wittiest American writers and commentators today.

282

Foer's debut novel proves that you can, sometimes, judge a book by its cover

DISTANT STAR Roberto Bolaño *1996*

The author's nationality and subject, Chilean politics and history, automatically invoke misleading comparisons with **Isabelle Allende**. But **Bolaño**, who died (aged 50) in 2003 of liver failure, is too fierce, too satirical and too dark for the comparison to stand. In Distant Star, his hero exploits the 1973 Chilean revolution to launch a multimedia enterprise that encompasses sky-writing, torture, poetry and photography. As **Richard Eder** noted in the **New York Times**, this "dark, glittering" novel is like nothing else written about the **Pinochet** years.

IF YOU LIKE THIS, TRY... **Bolaño's** By Night In Chile – the hallucinatory recollections of a dying priest who imagines teaching Pinochet about Marxism.

ELVIS AND THE APOCALYPSE Steve Werner *2001*

An affectionate satire on celebrity and fan worship in its most extreme form – the worldwide adoration of **Elvis**. The narrator, stopping at a café, is besieged by a waitress who tells him how Elvis's coming was predicted in the Bible and how her ex-husband Bubba was voted Most Likely To Lose His Teeth In An Altercation at school. This lovingly done spoof makes it clear that **Werner** has spent an inordinate amount of time pondering the intricacies of the King's more pointless films of the 1960s. Compelling – even if you're not an Elvis fan.

283

IF YOU LIKE THIS, TRY... Cheese Chronicles: The True Story Of A Rock And Roll Band You've Never Heard Of. **Tommy Womack's** hilarious account of life on the road is autobiographical but, with tales of motel dog-breath and crashing out next to a litter tray, it reads like a novel.

EVERYTHING IS ILLUMINATED
Jonathan Safran Foer *2002*

Heartbreaking, hilarious, serious... **Foer's** novel is all of these. A young Jewish American returns to Ukraine to find the woman who saved his family from the Nazis. This familiar idea becomes strange and puzzling as the author's quest, aided by an incompetent translator called Alex, Alex's grandfather and a flatulent mongrel called Sammy Davis Jr, is interspersed with episodes from a magic-realist novel about life in the Jewish shtetl and letters from Alex in horrendous, yet hilarious, Russian-English. Foer does have some irritating quirks, chiefly his habit of capitalising large swathes of text, but, as the **Financial Times** reviewer put it so eloquently, this "pulses with life and is haunted by vile madness."

IF YOU LIKE THIS, TRY... Dreams Of My Russian Summers: civilisation and barbarism in Siberia by **Andrei Makine**, in the style of **Proust** and **Pasternak**.

JESUS, BRITNEY AND THE DA VINCI CULT

In that genre of fiction defined by the fact that authors have their names embossed on the cover, The Da Vinci Code is a cult masterpiece, proof that success can be generated by word of mouth around the water cooler without being that well-written. It is probably the biggest word-of-mouth cult in publishing since, well, Harry Potter.

Dan Brown's meisterwork (the biggest selling hardback novel ever) is designed to be scanned, not read. It is, as **Richard Eyre** noted in **The Guardian**, "as badly written as the most badly written bad book you've ever thrown across a room in disgust". As for the dialogue, well, if the characters aren't engaged in breathless exposition of the back story, they are saying lines like "the capitane is waiting", which would have been cut from a poor 1940s B-movie as old hat.

Eyre says the best way to see The Da Vinci Code is as a computer game – in which the only goal is to move to the next level, though the ultimate level, Brown's finale, is a letdown. Aficionados have found hints of brazen postmodernism – Brown doesn't describe his hero, just says he looks like **Harrison Ford** – if **Nabokov** were alive today, he could have just told us Lolita looked like a pigtailed **Britney Spears** in the Baby One More Time video.

The intrigue lies in Brown's secret history of Christianity – secret, that is, to everyone but the 20 million or so who read The Holy Blood And The Holy Grail – presciently praised by **Anthony Burgess** in 1983 as "marvellous material for a novel" – or any of the similar titles (The Gospel Code, The Passover Plot, The Bloodline Of The Holy Grail etc) which, together, could fill the library of a small monastery.

The best way to regard The Da Vinci Code is as a cursor pointing intrigued readers to such classics as Jesus Lived In India, by **Holger Kersten**, who co-wrote The Jesus Conspiracy (with **Elmar R. Gruber**). The latter suggests the Holy Grail isn't a cup or Jesus's genes but the Turin Shroud, which, the authors say, is real.

> The existence of Jesus's big brother James, whose letter is in the New Testament, makes the virgin birth even more of a leap of faith

Among the even more scholarly tomes, there is **Robert H. Eisenman**'s (middle initials, in this field, being de rigueur) weighty James The Brother Of Jesus. James's letter in the New Testament isn't by any old James, it's from Jesus's big brother – a historical figure whose existence, Eisenman notes, makes the virgin birth even more of a leap of faith.

Eisenman lacks Brown's verve. His digging for the secret history of Jesus's family in the New Testament isn't just painstaking, it's painful. But his book is well-argued and provocative, unlike **Michael Drosnin**'s The Bible Code, which is provocative only in finding a hidden code in the good book that can pinpoint the world's end but not, strangely, help you win the lottery.

A FAN'S NOTES Frederick Exley 1968

Memoirists are meant to be honest, but we know they rarely are. If **Exley** had been any more honest, you wonder who would make it to the end of this book. Although Exley says it should be taken as a work of fantasy, A Fan's Notes is unmistakably an account of some variant of real life. It is dominated by four themes: Exley's drinking (life-threateningly excessive), his mental health (sufficiently precarious that he is frequently institutionalised), his team (the **New York Giants**) and his ability to fail. Failing is what Exley succeeds at most. This is not comfortable reading. But the mark of Exley's writing is that we can never quite hate him: we want him to live, though we fear that this is the best we can hope for him. A strangely powerful book, this didn't sell well at first, ironically convincing its author that it was a failure.

IF YOU LIKE THIS, TRY... Father And Son by **Edmund Gosse**, an early male confessional memoir. **Paul Theroux** is among the book's fans.

FAST ONE Paul Cain 1932

Somehow Gerry Kells had become "mixed up" in "five shootings in the last 32 hours." But then this hard-boiled slice of Depression-era noir reads at times as if the author (real name **George Carrol Sims**) had taken **Raymond Chandler**'s dictum – "when in doubt have a man come through the door with a gun" – literally. Chandler, perhaps recognising the debt, regarded this as "the high point in the ultra hard-boiled manner". Bleak, bloody, taut – **Cain**'s only novel reads like **James Ellroy** with no political/sociological pretensions. Kells wants to muscle in on the west-coast Mob; cue what one critic called "a welter of bloodshed".

IF YOU LIKE THIS, TRY... **Norbert Davi**'s Mouse In The Mountain: shrewd, badass pulp, served up with the comic genius of **Preston Sturges**.

285

FUNNYMEN Ted Heller 2002

Factional life of a hyperactive Jewish funnyman and a laid-back, but hard-living Italian-American crooner... Now whose story might have inspired **Heller** (son of Joseph) to write this? That said, this 'oral history' transcends its source as friends (past and present – well, mostly past) and family retell the inspiring, brutal, sentimental and bizarre odyssey of two stars condemned to shine together – and detest each other. The best take on the **Dean Martin** story since **Nick Tosches**'s richly imagined, often overwritten, yet compelling biography, Dino, with its fine sub-title Living High In The Dirty Business Of Dreams. Even if you never liked Dino or laughed at **Jerry Lewis**, Heller's novel still works.

IF YOU LIKE THIS, TRY... Slabrat, **Heller**'s debut: mostly a laugh-out-loud send-up of the glossy, facile, poisonous world of US magazine journalism.

GEEK LOVE Katherine Dunn 2002

It's hard to summarise the strange variety of this astonishing novel. Suffice to say the reader is invited into a circus by a bald, humpbacked, albino dwarf, the freakish result of a drug-controlled breeding programme by her sinister parents, who own the circus. After that, to use an old gag, things get really weird. Not easy to get into – "it is not heartening to see a novelist pushed around by her own book" huffed the **New York Times** – this is unlike almost any other modern novel. It will repel you or entrance you, but it won't bore you.

IF YOU LIKE THIS, TRY... Niagara Falls All Over Again, **Elizabeth McCracken**'s funny, sad, vaudeville novel. Like **Carson McCullers**, only funnier.

---

286 ## THE GOLEM Gustav Meyrink 1915

Jorge Luis Borges and **Herman Hesse** are two of the more famous admirers of this novel, possibly the finest modern work of supernatural fiction. **Meyrink** was an Austrian author, banker and Buddhist who wrote several surreal, esoteric novels. In retelling the legend of the golem, a creature supposed to protect Jews in 16th-century Prague, Meyrink depicts the city in the 1890s as surely as **Charles Dickens** captured Victorian London. The narrator, Pernath, who can only remember life since he moved to Prague's Jewish ghetto, drifts through the first three chapters half-asleep, half-awake. This is a strange brew in which the influence of Dickens, **Dostoevsky**, **Mary Shelley** and Jewish legend can all be detected yet is unlike anything else. Aficionados argue over the right translation – the choice seems, essentially, to come down to eloquence (**Madge Pemberton**'s 1928 version) or faithfulness (**Michael Mitchell**'s recent reinterpretation).

IF YOU LIKE THIS, TRY... **Robert Aickman**'s The Wine Dark Sea, the best collection of stories from the spookiest novelist of the 20th century.

A GOOD SCENT FROM A STRANGE MOUNTAIN
Robert Olen Butler 1992

Butler had written six neglected novels before this collection of short stories won him the **Pulitzer Prize**. Most of his earlier novels probably deserved that neglect, yet here he found his subject – and the right strangeness of style – as his narrators, Vietnamese exiles in Louisiana, tell their stories. In one, a housewife on the quiz show Let's Make A Deal appears dressed as a duck, bearing a sign that reads "Don't duck a deal." The most haunting tale, from which the collection takes its name, begins marvellously: "Ho Chi Minh came to me again last night, his hands covered in confectioners' sugar." Even the weaker stories have scenes that pop up at random in your memory, like toast in a toaster.

IF YOU LIKE THIS, TRY… Close Range: Wyoming Stories: spare, telling short tales of life in an unforgiving land by **Annie E. Proulx**.

HADRIAN VII Baron Corvo 1904

A self-styled baron, failed schoolmaster, apprentice gondolier and pornographic photographer, the literary genius of **Frederick Rolfe** (aka **Baron Corvo**) was exceeded only by his paranoia, which finally proved fatal – he died destitute and unknown in Venice in 1913. One of Rolfe's strongest recurring fantasies was that he be elected Pope – a fantasy he lives out in this, his most famous novel. It is, as **Graham Greene** recognised, "a novel of genius" by, to use **W.H. Auden**'s phrase, "a master of vituperation". Corvo's diatribes and sculpted style make for an oddly intriguing read: the novel has never been out of print.

287

IF YOU LIKE THIS, TRY… The Quest For Corvo, often described as the first postmodern biography, by **A.J.A. Symons**.

HANGOVER SQUARE Patrick Hamilton 1941

Hamilton once wrote that there is only one great theme for novels: "That this is a bloody awful life, that we are none of us responsible for our own lives and actions" and that "Hangover Square is the embodiment of that ethic." Set in a world of dingy pubs in London's Earl's Court, in the last brooding months before World War II, it describes George Harvey Bone's hopeless pursuit of the cruel Netta. As his sexual humiliation by Netta continues, he plots her death during recurring, dark mood swings, and the grim inevitability of the ending creates a sense of mounting terror that wouldn't be out of place in **Hitchcock**.

IF YOU LIKE THIS, TRY… Murder Book, **Richard Rayner**'s noir tale in which the cop hero breaks almost every rule to close the book on a murder.

HEART OF DARKNESS Joseph Conrad 1902

After more than a century, this story still won't go away, though **Conrad** might have been stunned to hear that, in 2004, a company offered "The horror! The horror!" themed holidays in Indochina, exploiting the film Apocalypse Now, drawn from his tale. Conrad's journey into the dark heart of nature and man has inspired everyone from **T.S. Eliot** to **Jean-Paul Sartre**. The story, in which the unreliable narrator Marlow recounts his encounter with the hollow, demented maverick Kurtz, anticipates modern history's worst horrors – from the Holocaust to Vietnam and beyond. Yet you can't please everyone. An Amazon reviewer noted: "The paragraphs are all really long and the author tries to throw a lot of ideas at the reader all at once. The main character seems to ramble on and on about things that could have been kept out of the book. There are a lot of symbols for the 'darkness' in the story."

IF YOU LIKE THIS, TRY... **Mario Vargas Llosa**'s The War At The End Of The World, inspired by another deluded genius, **Antonio Vicente Mendes Maciel,** a 19th-century Brazilian revolutionary: an epic, intelligent tale of fanaticism.

HEARTLAND Wilson Harris 1964

Anthony Burgess picked this as one of the best 99 novels written in English since 1939. Although **Harris** emigrated to Britain from Guyana in 1959, this, like most of his work, is set in the landscape of his childhood and youth. A government agent is travelling alone in the jungle undergrowth; his self-realisation ends with him disappearing – from the jungle and the novel itself. Prose ultimately breaks down, a few browned poems are left behind. Harris, as Burgess notes, excels in the fictional territory where logic meets magic.

IF YOU LIKE THIS, TRY... **Harris**'s first collection The Guyana Quartet.

A HERO OF OUR TIME Mikhail Lermontov 1840

A **Byronic** hero who died in his twenties in a duel, **Lermontov** influenced the two great Russian writers who were the best of enemies, **Tolstoy** and **Dostoevsky**. His only novel – five linked stories about a doomed, bored, immoral, cynical anti-hero called Pechorin – seems strangely modern today. Lermontov said it was a portrait of a generation: at one point Pechorin admits, "I'm still in love with her, I'd give my life for her... yet I'm bored with her" – a perfect paradox that positions him as a prototype rebel without a cause.

IF YOU LIKE THIS, TRY... **R.C. Hutchinson**'s Testament: a neglected gem by an English author, set in the Russian revolution.

THE HISTORY MAN Malcolm Bradbury 1975

The novelist makes a **Hitchcockian** cameo as himself here, as "a lecturer in the English department who, ten years earlier, had produced two tolerably well-known and acceptably reviewed novels." This self-deprecation almost came true as, when he died in 2000, the obituaries invariably read: "**Malcolm Bradbury**, author of The History Man…" English literature is so awash with campus novels that it's easy to forget how good The History Man is. Its 'hero', academic Howard Kirk, cuts a swathe through academia like a Marxist Iago. Bradbury's satire is at its fiercest when a colleague tells Kirk: "If you wanted someone through a window, you wouldn't push him yourself. You'd get someone else to do it or persuade the man he should do it himself, in his own best interests." With its delightfully neutral moral stance on the 'hero', this really is, as his fellow campus novelist **David Lodge** noted, Bradbury's masterpiece.

IF YOU LIKE THIS, TRY… **Saul Bellow**'s The Dean's December, a fine novel, set partly on a campus, which also evokes **Ceaucescu**'s Romania superbly.

THE HISTORY OF LUMINOUS MOTION
Scott Bradfield 1989

So many superlatives have been hurled at this over the years – and so many of them seem almost contradictory – that it's tempting to disbelieve the hype. Don't make that mistake. This tale of a mother and her psychotic eight-year-old son drifting round California, stealing and murdering, with a prepubescent existentialist as its anti-hero, really does expose the hollowness of the American dream. And, on top of that, it is darn near impossible to put down. This deserves to be considerably better known.

IF YOU LIKE THIS, TRY… **Elizabeth Vaughn**'s Many Things Have Happened Since He Died – a fictional, stream-of-consciousness memoir by a battered wife in the Deep South who hopes her story will lead to her becoming a celebrity.

289

HOMEBOY Seth Morgan 1990

Morgan was the drug-dealer boyfriend of **Janis Joplin** at the time of her death: a pimp, heroin addict, sometime armed robber and jailbird. His only novel – he died in a motorcycle accident just months after it was published – is a guided tour of the vice-ridden underbelly of American society, from the drug-lined streets of its cities to the violence-strewn corridors of its prison system. The plot, set in seedy San Francisco and later a Californian jail, hangs on the whereabouts of a priceless diamond, but the book's brilliance lies in its many characters and their voices. On every page you meet an array of "hookers,

hustlers, thieves and thugs; pennyweight ponces and flyweight flimflammers; diddyboppers, deadbeats and dopefiends." Morgan's language zings off the page as if it were rap – "A homeboy is someone you trust more than money," says Joe Speaker (the strip-joint barker and junkie hero) – and each gritty episode carries, as he hoped once, "the conviction of someone who really been there."
IF YOU LIKE THIS, TRY... The Fuck Up by **Arthur Nersesian**, in which the main man starts with nothing and it gets worse from there.

I AM STILL THE GREATEST SAYS JOHNNY ANGELO
Nik Cohn 1967

Cohn is one of the great writers on rock and roll. Here he creates a pop star who, in his narcissistic, self-destructive, mock-heroic way, is more interesting than most of today's pop stars – and, for that matter, more interesting than **P.J. Proby**, the trouser-splitting 1960s pop icon whose interviews with Cohn inspired this work. The final scene, where the idol is ripped apart by fans, is derived from Orpheus and was later borrowed by **David Bowie** for Ziggy Stardust.
IF YOU LIKE THIS, TRY... **Michael Felwell**'s The Harder They Come: the story of a Jamaican country boy who travels to the city to make a hit record but turns to drugs and violence in the ghetto. Made into a movie starring **Jimmy Cliff**.

IN THE HEART OF THE HEART OF THE COUNTRY
William H. Gass 1969

If you have read one book by **Gass**, it is likely to be his first novel, Omensetter's Luck. Yet this short-story collection is arguably the finer work – the form suits his self-confessed weaknesses (lack of dramatic imagination, inability to narrate) better than the novel. In most of these tales of Midwest austerity, the central image is winter, with all that implies: Gass's prose is, as **Gore Vidal** put it, "blazing with energy at actual zero". The novella The Pederson Kid, in which a boy travels to tell a family he's found their half-frozen son, is the stand-out.
IF YOU LIKE THIS, TRY... The Stories (So Far) Of Deborah Eisenberg. Compared (at her best) to **Flannery O'Connor**, **Eisenberg** writes brave, provoca-tive stories that plumb the depths of the heart to capture feelings and states of mind.

THE INVENTION OF MOREL Adolfo Bioy Casares 1940

Argentinian author **Casares** was a master of the fantastic genre and his close friendship and professional collaboration with **Jorge Luis Borges** changed the course of western literature. His masterpiece, The Invention Of Morel, anticipates virtual reality by almost half a century. A fugitive arrives on an island inhabited by strange people, one of whom is Faustine, with whom he falls in love. Slowly he realises these people are no more than images projected on to a screen. This novel poses two apparently contradictory ideas: the possibility of reaching immortality through a machine and the suspicion that love and even life itself are a continuous fiction. The plot, which Borges praised as "perfect", is widely considered one of the finest in contemporary literature and inspired many films such as L'Année Dernière A Marienbad by Alain Resnais.

IF YOU LIKE THIS, TRY... The **H.G. Wells** novel The Island Of Dr Moreau, was the inspiration for this – and many other novels and films.

THE LAND OF GREEN PLUMS
Herta Müller 1996

The author, like the narrator, grew up in a German minority in Communist Romania. The title refers to the plums wolfed down by the country's arrogant cops. **Müller**'s flights of poetic fancy can be hard to follow – perhaps the events described here are too intensely recalled – yet ultimately this is a menacing, evocative portrayal of a group of friends who try to survive totalitarianism. The details clinch this – such as the hair she puts in her letters so her friends know if they've been read, hairs that the spies collect and replace with similar strands.

IF YOU LIKE THIS, TRY... **Ismail Kadare**'s The General Of The Dead Army, in which an Italian and a German general try to retrieve the bodies of their World War II dead from Albania. As grim and unsettling as being stranded in downtown Tirana on a Saturday night.

291

THE LEOPARD Giuseppe Tomasi de Lampedusa 1958

This tale of a proud, sensual Sicilian aristocrat, facing the painful realities of life in a soon-to-be unified Italy in the 1860s, is easily misunderstood. The Italian writer **Leonardo Sciascia** (whose works dwell on power and corruption) confused the Sicilian prince who wrote the novel with the prince in the novel and complained that **Stendhal** could have written it a century earlier. The left dubbed Lampedusa a reactionary, yet the **Catholic church** slammed the work as anti-clerical, while others called it the Sicilian Gone With The Wind. On one level it's a love story, yet Lampedusa said: "Every word is weighted. Every scene has a hidden sense." He challenges the rationale for the unification of Italy and draws implicit parallels with the rebirth of postwar Italy – the mayor in the novel has the same first name (and shabby appearance) as the Sicilian capo who welcomed American soldiers – and American mobsters – to Sicily in 1944. All this he does in elegant, haunting prose. The final tragedy is that the author died of cancer a year before it was published, having had it deemed unpublishable (while incomplete) by Italy's biggest publisher. Italian novelist **Giorgio Bassani** assembled a version from his manuscripts, a novel ironically greater than Bassani's own.

IF YOU LIKE THIS, TRY... **Bassani's** The Garden Of The Finzi-Continis, a haunting, elegiac novel of young love in Fascist Italy.

———

LITTLE BIG MAN Thomas Berger 1964

The deft, enjoyable reminiscences of Jack Crabb, the sole white survivor of the battle of Little Big Horn and (at the time he's telling his tall tales) a mere 111 years old. No other novel gives you as good a sense of how characters in the Wild West talked, looked or smelled. That **Arthur Penn**'s film (starring **Dustin Hoffman**) is better known than the book is an injustice that may partly be explained by the author's frightening versatility. If **Berger** had stuck to one genre – or theme – he might be more acclaimed. Instead, he has touched on the West, Arthurian legend, dystopia, noir and even strayed into tender semi-autobiographical reminiscences of his childhood in his smalltown novels. This novel, though, is a bona fide masterpiece.

IF YOU LIKE THIS, TRY... **Berger's** Killing Time, madly derided at first, but since hailed, by **Salon**, as "**Jim Thompson** noir done by an American **Flaubert**".

———

LOST HORIZON James Hilton 1933

Hilton had a knack for creating novels – Good-Bye Mr Chips, Rage In Heaven – filmmakers wanted to buy, perhaps because his tales have no great authorial voice or fine prose style to be missed on screen. For pure thrills, this doesn't offer the tension of, for example, **Anthony Hope**'s The Prisoner Of Zenda. Yet, more than 70 years since its publication, Lost Horizon still wins converts with its tale of a world-weary hero who stumbles into a magical kingdom, Shangri-la, and bumbles out of it again. Two years ago, Chinese officials said they had found Shangri-la, even though Hilton imagined it from a desk in London. On one hand, this is a sentimental, conservative novel in which the magical kingdom is an oasis of civilisation. On the other, it anticipated the **Zen**, mystical strain in Western culture that saw many – notably **The Beatles** – turn east in the 1960s seeking answers to life's conundrums. Hilton would not, you suspect, have been impressed by The Beatles, yet 30 years before their heyday, penned a thoughtful, upper-middlebrow novel that anticipated their quest.

IF YOU LIKE THIS, TRY... **Hilton**'s Random Harvest – a novel of war and romance that prefigures The English Patient.

THE MAGIC CHRISTIAN Terry Southern 1959

Southern, best-known for Candy and Blue Movie, swapped sexual politics for a wild and original flight of fancy in this novel. Bored billionaire Guy Grand decides to use his wealth to test the limits of human greed and poke fun at all corners of society. A ridiculous but riveting set of pranks and challenges ensue, including dropping a million dollars in a vat of offal and excrement to see who will try to retrieve it; paying soap-opera actors to deliver mysteriously oblique lines; and taking money-eyed passengers on a terror cruise aboard The Magic Christian, a luxury liner where disaster is around the corner. **Peter Sellers** was so taken with this astonishing – and astonishingly slim – book he handed out copies to new acquaintants. (He even appeared alongside **Ringo Starr** in an ill-conceived film version.) This exceptionally funny, delightfully ambiguous novel is a work of unexpected class and craft.

293

IF YOU LIKE THIS, TRY... **Ken Kesey**'s Merry Pranksters, which may have been inspired by this book. **Southern**'s other novels are also worth exploring.

THE MAN WHO WAS THURSDAY G.K. Chesterton 1908

A comic fantasy, a mystery novel with surreal twists, a Christian allegory with points to make about free will and the existence of massive, irrational evil – The Man Who Was Thursday is all this and more. Gabriel Syme is the spying policeman who is so successful in his disguise as an anarchist poet that he is elected to the anarchists' council of seven, taking the code name Thursday (each member assumes the name of a day in the week). Even **Kingsley Amis**, a fan, struggled to sum up Chesterton's masterpiece: "not quite a political bad dream, nor a metaphysical thriller, nor a cosmic joke in the form of a spy novel, but something of all three... [and] a boy's adventure story."

IF YOU LIKE THIS, TRY... **Geoffrey Household**'s Rogue Male. It's more limited in scope but it's still a stunning, vivid tale of a man who, for unspecified reasons, goes to shoot a foreign leader, is caught, tortured and then flees for his life.

THE MAN WITHOUT QUALITIES Robert Musil *1930*

For a seemingly interminable (and unfinished) novel in several parts, described by one reviewer as the work of "a sort of jet-powered literary no-good", The Man Without Qualities has proved surprisingly durable. The 1996 translation by **Sophie Wilkins** has enabled this masterpiece of the intellectual imagination to be savoured anew. **Musil** was a complex German-Austrian who left a military academy and then a promising university career to write. The titular hero drifts through the crumbling Austro-Hungarian empire just before World War I, having a vague role in staging a ludicrous Hapsburg anniversary celebration, while being drawn to a murderer and eventually an incestuous relationship with his sister. It's a slow-motion, mentally realised world that reads like a longer, stranger alternative to **Proust**'s Remembrances. You might take this in fits and starts but plunge in at first – otherwise you'll never finish. It's worth the effort, even at 1,774 pages, though it is marred by anti-Semitism and, as the author himself admitted, "overburdened with essayistic material."

IF YOU LIKE THIS, TRY... **Elias Canetti**'s Auto Da Fe: a **Kafka**-like study of a bibliophile's inability to deal with everyday life, set in inter-war Germany.

THE MANUSCRIPT FOUND IN SARAGOSSA
Jan Potocki *1815*

Over the course of 66 days, a young Walloon officer recounts his adventures with secret societies, cabbalists and corpses. The aristocratic Polish author began this narrative to entertain his first wife. When he finished his master-piece, he finished his life – with a silver bullet, in 1815. Any work that uses the Hanged Man tarot card motif, embraces real occult figures like **Simon Magus** (a first-century Biblical sorcerer) and includes tales within tales where reader – and hero – are unsure what is real and what is the product of too much hashish, is open to reinterpretation. The esoteric magazine Fortean Times convincingly argues that the novel is the work of a man who belonged to a sect called the Bavarian Illuminati, that schemed for a free, egalitarian, republican Europe. The book is demanding and compelling – pretty much the kind of novel you'd expect from a man who, later in life, suspected he had become a werewolf.

IF YOU LIKE THIS, TRY... **Umberto Eco**'s bulky Foucault's Pendulum, a demanding, erudite, cunningly crafted fable drawing on the Templar mystique.

MOSCOW STATIONS Venedikt Yerofeev *1997*

All of us, as **Oscar Wilde** noted, may be in the gutter, but some are looking at the stars. But **Yerofeev**, a Russian who died in 1990, is more than happy to stare at the gutter a while longer, as he contemplates the correct treatment for drunken hiccups, runs through a variety of cocktails that would appal 007 (the one based on sock deodoriser being, perhaps, the nadir) and rips away every pretension and hypocrisy of the Brehznev era. Written in 1970, this tale of an alcoholic's erratic progress around the Moscow subway system was available only as a typescript for many years but has found deserved, overdue recognition in this translation by **Stephen Mulrine**, who also adapted it for the stage. It's not often a book can be compared, simultaneously, to the farce Jeffery Bernard Is Alive And Unwell and **Gogol**'s Dead Souls. The best summary comes from Yerofeev himself: "Ninety pages of funny stuff and ten pages of sad stuff."

IF YOU LIKE THIS, TRY... Twelve Chairs by **Il'ia Ilf and Evgenii Petrov**, a fantastic, accurate satire of Russian culture under the Soviet system.

PAVANE Keith Roberts 1968

"I don't know about you but I can never smell more than four odours at a time," sniffed one cyberspace reviewer about **Roberts**'s penchant for ornate descriptions. But such quibbles should not deter you from exploring one of the finest alternative history novels, written before the trend became horrendously fashionable. In this collection of linked stories, Roberts imagines that England, after the assassination of **Queen Elizabeth I** in 1588, has been ruled by the Church of Rome with strange consequences. In his England, there is no electricity, though there is an Inquisition; steam trains are running, but radios have to be smuggled in. The Papal attitude is justified in a strange coda that you may find superfluous. The novel's real strength, as **Anthony Burgess** noted, is that it is "a striking work of the imagination". And, in case you were wondering, in one ornate passage, Roberts asks the reader to imagine 17 smells at once.

IF YOU LIKE THIS, TRY... SS-GB by **Len Deighton**. Deighton is no great prose stylist but his strength – his documentary technique – suits this imaginary tale of what might have been were a defeated Britain run by Nazis. Predates, and betters, the **Robert Harris** novel on the same subject, Fatherland.

THE PILOT'S WIFE Anita Shreve 1998

When "the man from the union" knocks on Kathryn Lyon's door to tell her her pilot husband has died in a plane crash off Ireland, her world as she knows it unravels. Time barely seems to pass at all as each instant is played out in meticulous detail. The love she cherished is cast into doubt as the realisation that, however well you think you know the person you love, you never really do, hits home. But the book's real strength is the way it details the minutiae of grief – the way she longs for the numbness of a coma – while telling a gripping whodunit.

IF YOU LIKE THIS, TRY... The Curse Of The Appropriate Man: **Lynne Freed**'s spare, unflinching meditation on what women really want – astonishingly it isn't a **Mel Gibson** romantic comedy.

THE PRIVATE MEMOIRS AND CONFESSIONS OF A JUSTIFIED SINNER James Hogg 1824

Written in Scotland in 1824, and set there some hundred years earlier, this tells of the dire consequences of religious fanaticism pushed to its logical conclusion. Estranged from his father, the laird of Dalcastle, Robert has been brought up by his mother and her spiritual adviser Mr Wringhim. They are extreme Calvinists who believe the just are predestined and everyone else, however godly, is eternally damned. The very day Robert discovers he is one of the elect, he meets a young man who encourages him to commit terrible crimes – including the murder of his own brother – by convincing him his status frees him from guilt. Who is this strange young man who can assume the form of others? The Tsar of Russia, as Robert believes? A manifestation of Robert's diseased psyche? Or something more sinister? Part of the book's brilliance is that we are never given a definite answer. Robert's fevered confession, which forms the novel's central section, is framed by an editor's narrative. Such apparent objectivity only increases the moral ambiguity of this very original, disturbing book.

IF YOU LIKE THIS, TRY... **R.L. Stevenson**'s Dr Jekyll And Mr Hyde. It was powerfully influenced by Hogg's novel, which also inspired **Emma Tennant** to write The Bad Sister, a profoundly spooky, modern version of Justified Sinner.

Q Luther Blissett 1999

"Along the walls of the university curiosity grows like ivy." You didn't know Watford strikers could be so eloquent, did you? Actually, **Blissett** – who had a fairly wretched spell at AC Milan in the 1980s – had his name adopted as a pseudonym by a group of sympathetic Italian artists, among them four authors from Bologna who describe themselves as – no postmodern irony intended – leftists. Together they have written an apocalyptic, conspiratorial, thrilling epic, set in the Europe of the Reformation and the abortive Peasants' Revolt. Q, the titular 'hero', is an undercover papal spy. As novelist **Sarah Dunant** noted fairly "at 650 pages it simply can't hold the narrative tension," but this is still a marvel, its

early sections transcending the thriller genre to become utterly compelling.
IF YOU LIKE THIS, TRY... Money To Burn by **Richard Piglia**, an intriguing blend
of documentary, myth and fictional tension, based on a real heist in Argentina.

———

THE RIDDLE OF THE SANDS Erskine Childers 1903

Written by a House of Commons clerk executed in 1922 for his devotion to Irish
Republicanism, The Riddle Of The Sands was not the first literary fruit of the spy
fever that gripped Britain before World War I, but it is the most enduring. At first,
it's like reading a spin on **Jerome K. Jerome's** Three Men In A Boat, but Childers
throws in a dash of romance, large lumps of political and military theory and
seasons it all with rip-roaring adventure as Carruthers, the crashing snob hero,
and his pal expose a German plot to invade Britain. Many devices – the phoney

WRITER'S BLOCK... AND BLOCKED WRITERS

There's a lot to be said for writer's block
– most of **Harold Robbins's** novels and
the complete works of **Jeffrey Archer**
for starters. Nobody dislikes **Harper
Lee** for the simple reason that, after the
worldwide smash that was To Kill A
Mockingbird, she sat down to write
the sequel and realised that she could
only write a page or two a day. Now,
45 years after her debut, and as she
nears her eighties, it seems likely that
she will not besmirch the reputation of
that unfussy masterpiece by producing
To Kill A Mockingbird Again.

In France and Germany, the term
writer's block doesn't even exist. In
England and America, the blocked
writer is almost a cult object. **Joseph
Heller**, inhibited by the 20 million or so
copies Catch-22 had sold worldwide,
initially struggled to match Harper Lee's
productivity. **Dashiell Hammett**,
realising he had mysteriously acquired
a style, published his last, fifth and most
famous novel, The Thin Man, when he
was 34. After that, 27 years of literary
inactivity followed and then death. Still,
Hammett looks prolific when compared

to **Henry Roth**, whose Call It Sleep,
published in 1934, was followed, 60
years later, by the first instalment of
what proved to be a four-volume novel
called Mercy Of A Rude Stream. Roth
had an excuse: he had spent many
years in between in complete obscurity.
Howard Brodkey declared his
intention to write the novel A Party
For Animals in full view of New York's
literary glitterati in 1957. He didn't
actually publish a novel until 1991
and even then it wasn't the work he
had so triumphantly announced.

For some, the issue isn't blockage,
it's focus. After his 1952 debut
Invisible Man, **Ralph Ellison** spent
42 years working on a symphonic
novel that was left unfinished, with
2,000 pages of manuscript and notes,
when he died in 1994. Out of this, his
executors created an unacclaimed
single-volume novel Juneteenth.

If there's anything worse than writer's
block, it's being a blocked writer.
Aldous Huxley, **James Joyce** and,
inevitably, **Marcel Proust** all suffered
the ultimate indignity: constipation.

297

introduction to convince the reader the story is real – became staples of the genre.
IF YOU LIKE THIS, TRY... **Kingsley Amis**, under the pseudonym **Robert Markham**, wrote one 007 novel, Colonel Sun, which is the equal of the later Fleming opuses and in a different class from later Bond fiction. **Sol Weinstein**'s Matzhohball, a spy spoof starring **Oy Oy Seven**, is, alas, hard to find.

ROCK SALT AND GLISSANDOS Steve Fisher 1991

Certain books seem to inspire critics to invoke pairings – "like **Jane Austen** meets **William Burroughs**" – you know the drill. This collection of prison stories has had readers – as well as critics – invoking Burroughs, **Jim Morrison**, **Jean Genet**, **Charles Bukowski** and **Jim Thompson**. The names are, in a sense, irrelevant, because this book is good enough to need no comparisons: a raw, powerful, moving account of one man's personal hell, of drugs and prison cells, by someone who has been there, done that and, in 1993 at the age of 37, killed himself with a fatal injection of heroin and cocaine.
IF YOU LIKE THIS, TRY... **Michael Tournier**'s The Ogre: a different kind of hell (a French innocent becomes a POW in World War II) but almost as compelling.

298

SOME HOPE: THE PATRICK MELROSE TRILOGY
Edward St Aubyn 1998

In this trio of early-1990s UK novellas (Never Mind, Bad News and Some Hope) the upper-class hero is raped at five by his sadistic father, turns to drugs in his twenties and then tries to find some reason and way to live amid his anger and despair (and ends up at a country-house party in honour of Princess Margaret). For all that, this knowing satire of the idle and rich is surprisingly funny in a gruesome way. **Will Self** enthused about its "savage wit and scalpel-sharp prose", while **Edmund White** felt compelled to compare St Aubyn to both **Graham Greene** and **Evelyn Waugh**.
IF YOU LIKE THIS, TRY... The Confessions Of Max Tivoli by **Andrew Sean Greer** – not as coruscating or as funny, but the life of a man born looking like a 70-year-old whose body grows younger as his mind matures. In the words of **The New Yorker**, it pinpoints "the tiny, hidden madnesses in ordinary people".

SPOON RIVER ANTHOLOGY Edgar Lee Masters 1915

Masters was a successful Midwest lawyer who seemed to take everything – literary endeavour, the direction of American society, success – personally. His natural literary genre was epitaphs on gravestones. The epitaphs in this book, which form a poetic novel about the fictional small town of Spoon River, tell a powerful tale of the unlucky, the eccentric and the scorned, stripping away all romance from American smalltown life to reveal citizens who died in brothels and brawls. It became the bestselling book of American poetry ever and, to Masters, probably felt as heavy as a gravestone as he struggled to repeat the success of what, today, reads like an antidote to Lake Wobegon Days.

IF YOU LIKE THIS, TRY... **Upton Sinclair**'s The Jungle: morbid, sad, un-put-downable – an angry account of working conditions in the Chicago meat-packing industry in the early 1900s, as experienced by a young immigrant.

THE TIN DRUM Günter Grass 1959

Grass's debut is the fictional autobiography of Oskar Matzerath, a child who decides to stop growing and in recompense acquires a glass-shattering scream. Though Oskar observes the rise of Nazism in Germany, Grass's symbolic dark fable has a certain underestimated wit. The writing is rich and often fantastical, and Grass's message, that a better understood past (the author was, as a boy, a member of Hitler Youth) is key to the future, doesn't just apply to Germany. This is the first – and best – of a trilogy of novels about Danzig – the stronger of the last two being Cat And Mouse.

IF YOU LIKE THIS, TRY... **Salman Rushdie**'s Midnight's Children also has supernaturally talented children, a political undertone and a great deal of wit.

299

TOO LOUD A SOLITUDE Bohumil Hrabal 1976

According to **Milan Kundera**, **Hrabal** is the most important voice in Czech literature. If not his most significant novel, this is one of his most beguiling. At the centre of this strange tale, akin to being trapped in a cellar with a slightly drunk man who insists on telling you his obscure life story, is a man paid to compact waste paper, who finds himself compelled to rescue books rejected by the regime from the jaws of his hydraulic press. Hrabal was a dissident in the darkest days of **Czech Communism**, the 1950s and 1960s, and it is tempting to look for political significance here. Yet ultimately the hero's struggles with paper and words seem like an allegory for the writer's lot. As he admits: "I've got those books weighing down on me like a two-ton nightmare."

IF YOU LIKE THIS, TRY... Closely Observed Trains, a comical story of an apprentice signalman in Nazi-occupied Czechoslovakia, made **Hrabal**'s name.

THE TRIBES OF PALOS VERDES Joy Nicholson 1997

There are almost as many American coming-of-age novels as there are Americans coming of age. But this, despite some late flaws when **Nicholson** reaches too far for metaphor and message, is a fresh mood piece about a girl whose adolescence seems not so much angry or insecure as pointless. Surfing is Medina Mason's escape from the classroom's petty degradations. The disintegration of the heroine's twin brother Jim doesn't always ring true, or perhaps it just pales beside the immediacy and accuracy with which Medina is drawn.

IF YOU LIKE THIS, TRY... **Hugo Claus**'s The Sorrow Of Belgium. The translation doesn't quite do it justice, but this boy's coming-of-age tale, set in Nazi-occupied Belgium and the period after World War II, is a powerful read.

THE TRUE STORY OF A VAMPIRE
Eric Stenbock 1894

Stenbock was a Swedish-Estonian aristocrat who spent most of his life in England. A homosexual alcoholic and opium addict, he died (at 36) on the first day of **Oscar Wilde**'s trial after trying, in a furious drunken state, to hit his stepfather with a poker and falling into the grate. Even by Stenbock's standards (this was a man who liked to wear live snakes round his neck), the last five years of his life were odd – he took to travelling with a dog, a monkey and a life-sized doll he addressed as 'le petit comte'. Now known as 'the first Goth', he was obsessed by death – Studies In Death, his best collection of stories, which includes The True Story Of A Vampire, earned **H.P. Lovecraft**'s seal of approval.

IF YOU LIKE THIS, TRY... **Sheridan Le Fanu**'s In A Glass Darkly, recommended by none other than **Henry James**.

300

UNCLE PETROS AND GOLDBACH'S CONJECTURE
Apostolos Doxiadis 1992

Pure maths and fiction are not the snuggest of companions, but this Greek novel – praised by everybody from the inevitable George Steiner to the official organ of the British Communist Party – may help change that. An anonymous narrator investigates the story of his shunned, elderly uncle, broken by his quest to prove the 200-year-old Goldbach Conjecture (every even number greater than two is the sum of two prime numbers), and he too must decide whether he will take up mathematics as a career. This is still a tour de force.

IF YOU LIKE THIS, TRY... Dork Of Cork by **Chet Raymo**, probably the greatest novel ever written about a 43in-tall, 43-year-old Irish astronomer.

VALLEY OF THE DOLLS Jacqueline Susann 1966

The dolls are 'downers', not the wannabe Hollywood actresses who star in **Susann**'s memoir disguised as trashy fiction. Susann's acting career peaked with a role as Lola the cigarette girl in The Morey Amsterdam Show in 1948. But her struggle wasn't wasted. This novel alerted America to prescription-drug addiction and anticipated **Jackie Collins**'s 'sex-and-shopping' novels. After developing cancer, Susann asked God for ten years to write a bestselling novel. He gave her 12. Her last words, spoken like one of her heroines, were: "Let's get the hell out of here."

IF YOU LIKE THIS, TRY... **Geoff Nicholson**'s The Hollywood Dodo, a hilarious tale of extinct birds, starlets and murder in Tinseltown.

VERNON GOD LITTLE D.B.C. Pierre 2003

A 15-year-old misfit wrongly fingered as an accessory to a high-school massacre committed by his now-dead best friend might not sound like a laugh-out-loud read. But this tale, told by the naïve but wiser-than-his-years Vernon, could, as one reviewer noted, be an episode from South Park. Vernon lives with his self-obsessed mum in Martirio, Texas, a junk-food-filled, consumer-driven, tabloid town whose folk are seeking vengeance, media exposure and the perfect diet. A violently satirical look at modern-day American culture, this black comedy follows Vernon as the evidence builds against him and he goes on the run to Mexico – only to be bungeed right back home and into the ultimate reality TV show.

IF YOU LIKE THIS, TRY... **Botho Strauss**'s The Young Man, a quirky tale in which the older hero meets a seductress who traps lovers in her memory, and a man who has half of **Baudelaire**'s face and half of **Hitler**'s – just everyday kind of people.

301

THE VULTURE Gil Scott-Heron 1969

The godfather of rap, radical poet who coined the line 'The revolution will not be televised', sometime convict and latterly voice of **Tango** (it is him saying "You've been Tangoed" in those ads) wrote two fierce, stunning novels. The Vulture (published when he was just 19) is a work of impressive, even scary, technical maturity. A fine twist on the thriller genre, it captures the life of a murder victim as retold by four men who knew him as a boy. The milieu – New York's black community in the late 1960s – is finely drawn. The Nigger Factory (published when he was a venerable 22) reworks the -

traditional campus novel, as black students try to bring radical reform to a college in conservative Virginia. Both are fresh, hip and streetwise, but The Vulture shades it as the finer work. Both are now available in an omnibus edition from Canongate.

IF YOU LIKE THIS, TRY... Drinking Coffee Elsewhere, a sharp collection of short stories by **Z.Z. Packer**, recommended by **Zadie Smith** and **John Updike**.

WE Yevgeny Zamyatin 1920

The One State is a glass city of the future built on strictly mathematical lines and presided over by The Benefactor. Citizens ('unifs') have numbers rather than names and their lives follow a prescribed order laid out in the Tables of Hourly Commandments. Sexual partners are booked by filling out a pink coupon and behaviour is monitored by the Bureau of Guardians. D-503, chief engineer of a rocketship built to colonise other planets, believes fervently in all this and his journal entries make up the novel. But there's a world beyond the city, a world of the past, of nature and disorder, where nobody reasonable would wish to go. Unfortunately, certain unifs are committed to this world, including the seductive E-330. How D-503 wavers between loyalty to the state and his newly discovered feelings is what makes We such a compelling read. Written in Russia by a former Bolshevik, it is both a brilliant dystopian fantasy and a scathing satire on Soviet totalitarianism. Banned in the USSR, it was translated into English in 1924 and influenced both **Huxley's** Brave New World and **Orwell's** 1984.

IF YOU LIKE THIS, TRY... Other nightmare vision of authoritarian futures: **Ray Bradbury's** Fahrenheit 451 and **Thomas M. Disch's** Camp Concentration.

302

THE WIND IN THE WILLOWS Kenneth Grahame 1908

For **A.A. Milne**, **Grahame's** classic was a test of character. If you didn't like it, you could be cut out of a will or dumped by your other half. It's that kind of book – dismissed by many, fervently championed by a few (Milne, **Theodore Roosevelt**, **Alan Bennett** and **Terry Jones** among them). Different interpretations abound. Is Toad a representative of the upper classes while the Wild Wooders are the unruly proletariat? Is it a protest against technological change? Is Grahame a pantheist? Or is it a deeply personal book about a tragic love between a father and the son for whom he invented these bedtime stories? The son, who shared some character traits with Toad, later broke his father's heart by committing suicide when he was 19. Certainly, the laughter is tempered by a melancholy strain, which may be why it continues to touch so many adults and inspire so many spin-offs. This pervasive sense of regret may also explain why no adaptation has quite captured the complex charm of the original.

IF YOU LIKE THIS, TRY... **Jerome Fletcher**'s Escape From The Temple Of Laughter, a book, a game and a feast of fun (and puns) from an author who is, his publisher says, "a professional real tennis player and elver [young eel] catcher".

WONDER BOYS Michael Chabon 1996

Chabon's darkly comic novel is a work of rare subtlety that uses a tuba, a dead dog, a **Marilyn Monroe** ermine jacket and a squashed boa constrictor to telling, hilarious effect. The 'hero' is Grady Tripp, a fading wunderkind novelist-cum-creative-writing teacher whose life unravels over a weekend. The details of the unravelling sound far-fetched in summary, but as the ante is upped, the reader is intrigued, appalled and delighted. Chabon has written other good novels (notably The Amazing Adventures Of Kavalier And Clay) but this is his best, a quirky suburban nightmare that has you rooting for some very odd heroes.

303

IF YOU LIKE THIS, TRY... **Chabon**'s debut The Mysteries Of Pittsburgh. Set in his home town, it's a flawed, yet haunting portrayal of adolescent angst, which some prefer to The Catcher In The Rye.

WONDERFUL, WONDERFUL TIMES
Elfriede Jelinek 1980

The Austrian Nobel Prize winner has a rare gift for creating horrible people with pointless existences – in this case four self-pitying, self-indulgent and often self-delusional students trying to work out how to live their lives – who you somehow can't stop reading about. **Jelinek** brings what, in lesser hands, could be juggernaut-heavy ideas – the responsibility of intellectuals for the ideas they create – into her stories without the reader's stomach getting that sagging sensation when a bit of literary preaching is imminent. It's a pity **Tolstoy** isn't alive – if he'd read Jelinek's stuff the second part of War And Peace (all that theory of history malarkey) might have been a lot livelier. There's a nice wit in the way one wannabe existentialist spends much of the novel reading (and misinterpreting)

Camus's The Stranger and then announces, just before the final tragedy, that he and the woman he loves (but who doesn't love him) will next read the much more constructive, and hopeful, The Plague.

IF YOU LIKE THIS, TRY... The Piano Teacher, a bitter, metaphorical novel about a mother and daughter which is **Jelinek**'s most famous work.

WATERGATE: THE ONE-OFF FICTION

If you remember **Howard E. Hunt** at all, it's probably from his role in the Watergate conspiracy. The most controversial burglary ever may have earned the former CIA agent a prison sentence but it did wonders for sales of his pulp spy novels. For a while.

Hunt's spy novels aren't up there with **Ian Fleming**'s or indeed **Charles McCarry**'s. But there are a lot of them – over 30 – and they're not devoid of all interest. Read just one – The Judas Hour, a mad caper in which the miserable alcoholic hero is wooed by a female Communist agent whose deadly weapon, in Hunt's elegant phrase, is a "small waist that widened into full, firm buttocks". Trying to woo our hero, she exhorts him: "It's getting in on the ground floor of an irresistible power that's destined to sweep the world."

You don't have to read Hunt's Bimini Run, just remember that its hero is supposed to be based on the author's pal and fellow conspirator **Frank Sturgis**. Hunt isn't the only person connected to Watergate to turn his hand to fiction. **John Ehrlichman**, one of **Richard Nixon**'s closest advisers, wrote two novels, only one of which,

The China Card, is worth reading. The other, The Company, inspired a decent TV mini-series, Washington Behind Closed Doors, but as a novel it makes Hunt look like **Le Carré**.

G. Gordon Liddy, another conspirator who spent four-and-a-half years in prison, wrote two novels – The Monkey Handler and Out Of Control – but neither is a patch on Gordon Liddy Is My Muse, a breezy spy novel by **John Calvin Batchelor** in which he has his own theory for the identity of **Deep Throat**, the source who tipped off the Washington Post.

Batchelor's novel is entertaining enough, although possibly the greatest fiction spun off Watergate is Liddy's suggestion that the burglary was a giant decoy, designed to distract attention from a call-girl scandal involving leading Democrats.

You could take this up personally with Liddy but be warned: he is a bit scary. Remember that character Major — De Coverley in Catch-22, so called because nobody had the nerve to ask him what his first name was? Liddy's just like that – nobody's dared ask what the **G.** stands for.

304

CULT CHARACTERS

ALLOW US TO INTRODUCE YOU TO 35 FICTIONAL
CREATIONS – MALES, FEMALES, FALLEN ANGELS AND
WHALES – WHO STARTED OUT ON THE PRINTED PAGE, BUT
BECAME, BY OSMOSIS, PART OF THE FABRIC OF OUR TIMES

THE CHARACTERS

Some fictional characters jump off the page, into our hearts and minds and into popular culture. Heroes like Jay Gatsby and Walter Mitty become reference points for a lazy media – every upwardly mobile chancer is compared to **Fitzgerald**'s doomed hero, just as the phrase 'Lolita complex' is understood by those who haven't read **Nabokov**. Here are 26 fictional men, five fictional women, a vampire, a monster, a fallen angel and a whale who have struck a chord.

———

RABBIT ANGSTROM

APPEARS IN **John Updike**'s Rabbit series (Rabbit Run, Rabbit Redux, Rabbit Is Rich and Rabbit At Rest).

PERSONA Middle-class American Harry Rabbit (a nickname from his school basketball days) struggles with fidelity, family, fatherhood and changes in American society that threaten to crush him. Rabbit is utterly self-obsessed (he thinks once of that "strange way women have of really caring about someone beyond themselves"). Yet he remains sympathetic and intriguing, even as he sleeps with his daughter-in-law and poisons himself with junk food.

DEFINING MOMENT When he consoles a grieving husband at a funeral by telling him his wife "was a fantastic lay."

CULTURAL IMPACT Bigoted, superficial, selfish, yet not unintelligent, Rabbit is the closest America's postwar fiction has to an everyman. Rabbit's flaws are the flaws of his age and he intrigues because, as **Hermione Lee** notes, inside he is "tender, feminine and empathetic". Obvious echoes can be found, pared down, in **Richard Ford**'s The Sportswriter. Updike, and his hero, have been pilloried as the last of the Great American narcissists (one critic dismissed the author as "a penis with a pen"). Yet Angstrom is one of America's great male fictional heroes, an icon for those who feel trapped emotionally, intellectually or professionally.

IN HIS OWN WORDS **"There was this thing that wasn't there"**

———

CULT FICTION

MOLLY BLOOM

APPEARS IN Ulysses by **James Joyce**.

PERSONA Based on Joyce's wife, **Nora**, Molly Bloom is the supremely sensual spouse of wandering Leopold Bloom, a cabaret singer, earthy and animalistic with an honesty that is rarely found in 'serious' fiction.

DEFINING MOMENT Her raw, passionate soliloquy at the end of the book.

CULTURAL IMPACT For many critics, Molly Bloom is an icon, a real woman with faults and desires who stands out from the pack of sterile female heroines. The stream of consciousness finale in which Molly trawls through her thoughts, base and beautiful, omitting all punctuation, was banned in Britain until the 1950s. She has inspired artists, including **Kate Bush** who used Molly's words in her song The Sensual World. There's even a musical interpretation of the soliloquy by jazz singer **Anna Zapparoli** and composer **Mario Borciani**.

IN HER OWN WORDS *"... yes I said yes I will yes"*

JAMES BOND

APPEARS IN Twelve secret-agent novels and two short-story compilations by former UK Naval Intelligence officer-turned-journalist **Ian Fleming**.

PERSONA The Bond that made his debut in 1953's Casino Royale was only a shadow of the man who became, as **Raymond Chandler** said, "what every man would like to be and what every woman would like to have between her sheets." Despite calling his creation a cardboard dummy, Fleming gradually gave him greater depth. While celluloid Bond is almost a caricature, the books portray a straighter, more vulnerable side (**Roger Moore**'s Bond is probably closest to Fleming's ideal). He is principled; never kills a man in cold blood; is prone to fear and injury; and his penchant for the ladies is seen almost as a weakness. Since Fleming's death in 1964, **Kingsley Amis**, **John Gardner** and **Raymond Benson** have taken up the mantle of James Bond storyteller, not always to good purpose.

DEFINING MOMENT The opening of the very first novel, where, basking in the French sunshine, he orders a dry martini.

CULTURAL IMPACT Fleming was a dream come true for advertisers: rarely a page turned where product placement didn't feature. Vermouth sales doubled, despite its absence in a Bond martini, as did sales of the tuxedo and the Aston Martin.

IN HIS OWN WORDS *"Bond, James Bond"*

SALLY BOWLES

APPEARS IN **Christopher Isherwood**'s Goodbye To Berlin, the source for Cabaret, in which Bowles was fetchingly portrayed by **Liza Minnelli**.

PERSONA Like many self-dramatists, Bowles suspects she is all too easily taken in and is not as interesting as she would like to be. The model for Bowles was **Jean Ross**, a promiscuous nightclub singer who shared a flat with the author in Berlin. Isherwood took her name from novelist **Paul Bowles**.

DEFINING MOMENT On the hero's first visit to Sally's flat for tea, he experiences the full-on Bowles effect. "There was something extraordinarily comic in Sally's appearance. She was really beautiful, with her little dark head, big eyes and finely arched nose – and so absurdly conscious of all these features."

CULTURAL IMPACT The novel became a stage play – I Am A Camera – in 1950 (filmed five years later with **Julie Harris** as Bowles) and then a smash Broadway musical in the 1960s, the source for **Bob Fosse**'s Oscar-winning movie. The relationship between Bowles and Nazism has often been reinterpreted, with some citing the decadence of **Weimar** – and Bowles – as cause for the rise of the Nazis, not a view shared by Isherwood. In **Jay McInerney**'s novel Model Behaviour, a writer suggests, "No question, Holly [Golightly, of **Truman Capote**'s Breakfast At Tiffany's] is an American clone of Sally Bowles, right down to the unconvincingly heterosexual pal. A total rip-off."

309

IN HER OWN WORDS "I feel all marvellous and ethereal as if I was a kind of most wonderful saint or something"

PEPE CARVALHO

APPEARS IN The series of detective novels created by **Manuel Vazquez Montalban**, who died in 2003 aged 64.

PERSONA Carvalho is fat, cynical, silver-tongued, mysteriously irresistible to women, has an epicurean appetite for meat and drink and a past that includes service to the CIA and membership of the Communist Party. His patch is Barcelona (though he does have an extended sojourn in Buenos Aires).

DEFINING MOMENT When Carvalho solves crimes, he does so in the manner of someone cracking an intriguing intellectual puzzle, rather than as a lone hero defending civilisation against criminals. Often he'll put a case on ice to cook an expensive, therapeutic meal – the recipe for which is usually included in the books. Carvalho has an odd habit of burning books – not in a frenzied Nazi sense, but in a casual, keep the fire going and create some space kind of way.

CULTURAL IMPACT The Carvalho novels have styled Barcelona as one of the world's great noir cities. The novels have inspired three films (most effectively

NEAL CASSADY, MUSE TO THE BEATS

A muse more than a writer, **Neal Cassady** was called The Fastest Man Alive. The creative force behind the 1950s Beat Generation movement and **Ken Kesey**'s original hippies, he was an inspiration for numerous literary works – most famously, **Jack Kerouac**'s On The Road and Visions Of Cody – but also **John Clellon Holmes**'s Go, **Tom Wolfe**'s The Electric Kool-Aid Acid Test and Kesey's The Further Inquiry, as well as **Allen Ginsberg**'s Howl and several other poems.

Cassady (1926-1968) was born in Salt Lake City, Utah, but lived in Hollywood until he was six, then moved to Denver with his father, where they shared a condemned building with a group of alcoholics. He lost his virginity at nine and by 12 was having sex in exchange for food. By 21, he had stolen 500 cars and done time in reform schools and juvenile prisons, although he'd also begun to educate himself in philosophy and literature.

In 1946 Cassady travelled to New York to visit a friend at Columbia University, where he met and entranced Jack Kerouac and Allen Ginsberg. A sexual chameleon, he began an affair with Ginsberg and soon afterwards embarked with Kerouac on the first of the aimless cross-country adventures that provided the material for On The Road – Kerouac becoming Sal Paradise, Cassady Dean Moriarty. Although Kerouac wrote a lot at the time, it was only in the ecstatic, unselfconscious rush of Cassady's letters and conversation that he truly found his voice: as Cassady put it, a "continuous chain of undisciplined thought."

Cassady married his second wife **Carolyn** in 1948 and worked as a brakeman on the Southern Pacific Railroad for much of the 1950s. In 1958, however, he was arrested for possession of marijuana and spent two years in San Quentin prison. He met Kesey in 1962, and with Kerouac now an alcoholic recluse, he set off on another great road-trip with Kesey's **Merry Pranksters**, driving a psychedelic bus named Furthur across the continent to New York. Dependent on amphetamines but as wild and sexually active as ever, Cassady seemed to the Pranksters to exude an irresistible magnetism – **Grateful Dead** guitarist **Jerry Garcia** described him as "a tool of the cosmos" – and throughout this period they recorded, transcribed and annotated a number of his "raps" (spontaneous monologues) that make for fascinating reading.

In 1968, after a wedding party in San Miguel, Mexico, Cassady set out to walk 15 miles to the nearest town, but fell asleep on the way and was found in a coma the following morning. He died four days before his 43rd birthday.

Although he published nothing during his lifetime, his unfinished autobiography The First Third describes his childhood in a chaotic, free-flowing style, while his Collected Letters, 1944-67 demonstrate where all that Beatnik fire came from in the first place. Fictionalised, he would later inspire another professional nomad and alcoholic, **Jim Morrison**.

the 1982 movie Murder In The Central Committee) and two Spanish TV series. Caustic about the powerful, but tender to the oppressed, as the **Times Literary Supplement** noted, Carvalho is a thoughtful, left-of-centre contribution to a genre that often stars a quasi-fascist lone hero who is willing to be judge, jury and executioner. Carvalho, at times, owes as much to Don Quixote as to Philip Marlowe, and has a restaurant in Montpelier named in his honour.

IN HIS OWN WORDS **"Do you realise that we private eyes are the barometers of morality?"**

HOLDEN CAULFIELD

APPEARS IN **J.D. Salinger**'s short stories and The Catcher In The Rye.
PERSONA The novel's 16-year-old narrator and principal character, Caulfield is kicked out of school and escapes to New York for a whirlwind three days. The definitive flawed, contradictory, forgivable, alienated adolescent, he hates "phoniness", whether in the show-off piano-playing of a bar-room entertainer or the insincerity his old classmates show towards dates, yet he's desperate to frequent the same bars and meet the same girls. He worries about the fate of ducks in Central Park, yet smokes, drinks and invites a prostitute to his room.
DEFINING MOMENT Caulfield takes his younger sister Phoebe to the zoo and lets her ride the carousel. She over-stretches reaching for the gold ring in the centre of the ride, but he concludes: "If they want to grab for the gold ring, you have to let them do it." It marks a turning point in his attitude to adulthood.
CULTURAL IMPACT Caulfield is the template for the rebellious innocent portrayed by such writers as **John Updike** and **Jack Kerouac**. **Mark Chapman** was carrying The Catcher In The Rye when he shot **John Lennon**.
IN HIS OWN WORDS **"I'm the most terrific liar you ever saw in your life"**

311

ROBINSON CRUSOE

APPEARS IN Robinson Crusoe by **Daniel Defoe**, originally published in 1719 as The Life And Strange Surprising Adventures Of Robinson Crusoe.
PERSONA The son of a respectable German merchant, Crusoe rebels against his upbringing and heads to sea. He craves adventure, but a shipwreck tests him to the limit. He fears solitude, starvation and death, but builds a life on his island, surviving alone for 24 years before Friday joins him.
DEFINING MOMENT Discovering his skill in constructing a raft to rescue provisions: "The hope of furnishing myself with necessaries encouraged me to go beyond what I should have been able to have done upon another occasion."
CULTURAL IMPACT Some critics denounce Crusoe as a bourgeois colonialist

(refusing to treat Friday as an equal), but most respond to the ripping yarn of his struggle. Later castaways, from the Swiss Family Robinson to **Tom Hanks** to the guests on **Desert Island Discs**, owe everything to the original shipwrecked icon. **Luis Buñuel** made an intriguing movie of his story in Mexico in the 1950s and there was even a 1964 sci-fi movie Robinson Crusoe On Mars (co-starring **Adam** 'Batman' **West**) that saw him stranded on the Red Planet with a monkey.

IN HIS OWN WORDS **"I never saw them [his shipmates] afterwards... neither did I see any prospect before me, but that of perishing with hunger or being devoured by wild beasts"**

DRACULA

APPEARS IN Dracula by **Bram Stoker**.

PERSONA Hapless solicitor Jonathan Harker describes the unsettling Count, saying, "his mouth, so far as I could see it under the heavy moustache, was fixed and rather cruel looking with peculiarly sharp white teeth; these protruded over the lips, whose remarkable ruddiness showed astonishing vitality in a man of his years." Through the journals, letters and diaries of the main characters, we learn that Dracula aims to create a race of vampires in London. He drinks human blood, cannot move in the day, has no reflection and can only rest on soil from Transylvania – a fact that provides hope for his downfall.

DEFINING MOMENT Biting Lucy Westenra, transforming her into a vampire.

CULTURAL IMPACT This devilish, seductive vampire has inspired an array of novels, tributes and spoofs. **Anne Rice**'s popular tales of Vampire L'Estat owe an enormous debt to the original Dracula. His image is everywhere – at every Halloween party, on boxes of Count Chocula breakfast cereal and even on Sesame Street, where the Count helps kids learn maths.

IN HIS OWN WORDS On hearing wolves howl: **"Listen to them – children of the night. What music they make!"**

FANTOMAS

APPEARS IN A novel of the same name, but made his debut in short stories also by **Marcel Allain** and **Pierre Souvestre**, many published in French magazines in 1911. Then made immortal in **Louis Feuillade**'s 1913 films.

PERSONA Fantomas, the self-proclaimed lord of terror, is a villain with no redeeming features. His aim is not to rule the world, just to make it suffer – putting sulphuric acid into perfumes, or setting plague-carrying rats loose.

DEFINING MOMENT Punishing a rebellious henchman by forcing him to act as a human clapper in a bell. Eat your heart out, Goldfinger!

CULTURAL IMPACT "Enfantomastic!" crowed the author of Ulysses when these stories first appeared. **James Joyce**'s enthusiasm was shared with **Guillaume Apollinaire** (who wrote a prose poem to the villain) and the surrealist artist **René Magritte**. In the 1960s there were three French-language Fantomas films, all box-office smashes in Cuba. The phenomenon took a stranger turn when Mexican comic writers turned him into their own **Robin Hood**. In Paris, the exiled Argentinian writer **Julio Cortazar** wrote a story called Fantomas Versus The Multinational Vampires, in which our anti-hero

finds his books are being removed from the world's libraries by the same political conspiracy responsible for the repression of human rights in South America.

IN HIS VICTIM'S OWN WORDS Parisians are told Fantomas is no one and yet someone. "What does that someone do?" asks one, to be told: "**Spreads terror!**"

HUCKLEBERRY FINN

APPEARS IN The Adventures Of Tom Sawyer and The Adventures Of Huckleberry Finn by **Mark Twain**.

PERSONA Huck first appears as comrade to Tom Sawyer, a comical figure wearing oversize cast-offs. He's the rootless, swearing, smoking son of the town drunk and is branded "idle and lawless and vulgar and bad" by local mums. In Huckleberry Finn, his character deepens. When he escapes smothering Widow Douglas, he embarks on a journey down the Mississippi with Jim, a runaway slave. Even as he learns about the world, Huck stays true to himself, and it's this – his enthusiasm and self-belief – that give him such appeal.

DEFINING MOMENT When Huck decides to save Jim from the authorities, and that he'll "go to Hell" before giving him up.

CULTURAL IMPACT Huckleberry Finn has been repeatedly banned, initially because parents felt a hero who lied, drank, smoked and swore would corrupt their kids. Later the book was removed from school reading lists (including the **Mark Twain Intermediate School**'s in Virginia) and accused of racism. Some of the language makes uncomfortable reading, leading **Toni Morrison** to write a thought-provoking essay on it, This Amazing, Troubling Book. Yet Huck is a free spirit, an iconoclastic hero, who had a huge influence on later fiction and his ride down the Mississippi is one of the greatest journeys in American literature.

IN HIS OWN WORDS "It's awful to be tied up so"

BILLY FISHER

APPEARS IN Billy Liar, the second novel by **Keith Waterhouse**, and its lesser-known sequel Billy Liar On The Moon.

PERSONA Billy is an undertaker's clerk in a dull industrial northern town, who retreats from boredom into the elaborate fantasy world of Ambrosia, where he is prime minister, a great lover and hero. This wouldn't be a problem except his fantasies spill into real life and he is soon boxed in by a stack of tall tales, engaged to two girls and in love with a third, while suspected of pilfering with each. An obsessive hypochondriac, he has a touchingly unfounded optimism about life.

DEFINING MOMENT When his family find the letter from Danny Boon, who they had all thought was another figment of Billy's imagination.

CULTURAL IMPACT Billy Liar quickly became shorthand for a fantasist of the highest order (see also Walter Mitty, page 322). The book has been adapted into a play and a film, which clearly had a profound effect on **Morrissey**: The Queen Is Dead, Frankly Mr Shankly, and William It Was Really Nothing all allude to it. The book, never out of print in Britain, is often on school reading lists, something his creator lamented: "Billy… was destined, or doomed, to become a school textbook when plodding 'study aids'… were written about it, learnedly explaining the text: 'Shags like a rattlesnake – sexually promiscuous'."

IN HIS OWN WORDS When told he should be glad he has an office job, Billy says: **"I've to be grateful to Shadrack and flaming Duxbury for sitting at a stinking desk all day?"**

314

HARRY FLASHMAN

APPEARS IN Tom Brown's Schooldays by **Thomas Hughes**.

PERSONA Flashman is the older boy, a bully and a coward, who makes Tom's life a misery – "that blackguard Flashman, who never speaks to one without a kick or an oath." His crimes include taunting, fighting and forcing new boys to be thrown in the air on blankets until they are sick, all par for the course in Victorian public schools. He is not bright, but relies on physical strength and sheer malevolence – "Flashman was adept in all ways, but above all in the power of saying cutting and cruel things, and could often bring tears to the eyes of boys, which all the thrashings in the world wouldn't have wrung from them." As the novel verges on sentimentality, Flashman stands out as an unapologetic, unreformed, nasty piece of work.

DEFINING MOMENT Attempting to roast Tom over an open fire.

CULTURAL IMPACT Thanks to Flashman, brutality and public schools became synonymous. Over a century later **George MacDonald Fraser** wrote a series of novels, The Flashman Papers, imagining Flashman's life after school. (He never reformed and remained a bullying, womanising cad, if more likeable.)

IN HIS OWN WORDS **"Here, lend a hand, one of you, and help me pull out this young howling brute. Hold your tongue, sir, or I'll kill you"**

FRANKENSTEIN'S MONSTER

APPEARS IN Frankenstein by **Mary Shelley**.

PERSONA Dr Frankenstein's monster, the "daemon" fashioned from body parts in morgues and cemeteries and brought to life by a mysterious electrical process, appals even his creator: "I saw the dull yellow eye of the creature open… his watery eyes that seemed almost of the same colour as the dun-white sockets in which they were set, his shrivelled complexion and straight black lips." Those who have only seen the films will be surprised by the original's articulate torment (and that there's no mention of any bolts through the neck). Feared and shunned by all, the creature's life unfolds into a powerful tragedy and 'monster' and creator find they are inextricably bound to each other.

DEFINING MOMENT Hoping that Dr Frankenstein's young brother William might accept him, but killing him when the boy recoils from his touch.

CULTURAL IMPACT Frankenstein has become a byword for anything deemed to be against the laws of nature, as when the genetic modification debate gave rise to 'Frankenstein food'. The creature (admittedly the **Boris Karloff** version) has inspired many imitations and spoofs, from **Mel Brooks** to Herman Munster. In all this hilarity, Shelley's "hideous phantasm of man" has sadly lost the sensitivity that makes the disturbing character in the novel so remarkable.

IN ITS OWN WORDS **"You hate me, but your abhorrence cannot equal that with which I regard myself"**

DOROTHY GALE

APPEARS IN **Frank Baum**'s The Wonderful Wizard Of Oz and other works in the series of 14 novels he wrote about his magical kingdom.

PERSONA Dorothy has no surname in the novel but gets one (Gale) in Baum's stage version. Orphaned, she lives with an uncle, aunt and dog Toto (after whom, the balance of evidence suggests, the 1980s rock band were named). In the book her magic slippers are silver, becoming ruby to exploit Technicolor in the film.

DEFINING MOMENT When she faces down the Wiz. She may have just blown in from Kansas's dullest farm, but she won't be fobbed off by some charlatan.

CULTURAL IMPACT The Wizard Of Oz is a children's classic, which, especially in its 1939 film version (watched by 45 million Americans on its first TV screening), has been celebrated by intellectuals and writers, including **Salman**

315

Judy with the first 'friend of Dorothy'

Rushdie. A 16-year-old **Judy Garland** played Dorothy and has become a gay icon, partly due to the message of Dorothy's quest – you can find what you're looking for inside yourself. There was a time when gay men referred to each other in code as "friends of Dorothy". Five days after Garland was found dead (on 22 June 1969, from an overdose in her London home), some gay fans staged a wake at a bar called the **Stonewall Inn** in New York. Some reports suggest Over The Rainbow was playing as police raided the bar. There was a mini-riot, subsequent protests against police harassment and the next month the **Gay Liberation Front** was born. This story may explain why the rainbow is a gay symbol and the song a camp anthem.

The movie inspired various sequels and spin-offs, including the animated Journey Back To Oz (in which Garland's daughter **Liza Minnelli** voices Dorothy) and the surprisingly dark Return To Oz, in which our heroine is saved from a psychological experiment. The phrase "Surrender, Dorothy" became the title for a drama about a heroin addict who'll do anything to get his next dose and, in **Martin Scorsese**'s After Hours, it was the off-putting phrase **Rosanna Arquette**'s ex-lover shouted during sex.

IN HER OWN WORDS **"I won't have any quarrelling in the land of Oz!"**

SHERLOCK HOLMES

APPEARS IN A total of 56 short stories and three novels including The Hound Of The Baskervilles by **Sir Arthur Conan Doyle**.

PERSONA Holmes is "a consulting detective" who regards the human race as of interest only in as much as they help – or hinder – him to solve the conundrums presented by an endless stream of callers to 221B Baker Street. His only vice is occasional cocaine and morphine use. Some have put forward the theory that his behaviour suggests he suffers from bipolar depression, while Raymond Chandler once said Holmes is only an attitude toward life and half a dozen lines of great dialogue. Holmes would, however, be an immense asset in any quiz team, with his "trifling monograph" on ciphers, his knowledge of the Japanese wrestling system called baritsu, his familiarity with the Bible, **Shakespeare** and **Goethe** and his encyclopaedic knowledge of the worst crimes of the century.

DEFINING MOMENT His amazing deductions. Such as glancing at Dr Watson's shoes and telling him that he has been out in vile weather and is employing a careless servant girl.

CULTURAL IMPACT His powers of deduction became known as Sherlockian and inspired the sarcastic phrase, "No shit, Sherlock." Holmes has the unique distinction of being the only fictional character to be made an honorary fellow of the Royal Society of Chemistry. His method of solving crimes – looking for clues, not motivation – has shaped our expectations of police procedure. There have been countless film and TV adaptations, while writers as diverse as **Michael Dibdin**, **Isaac Asimov** and **Stephen King** have penned stories about the character, and the Japanese anime magazine Detective Conan, the movie Star Trek: The Next Generation and **Alan Moore**'s graphic novel The League Of Extraordinary Gentleman have all paid homage to him.

IN HIS OWN WORDS **"How often have I said to you that when you have eliminated the impossible, whatever remains, however improbable, must be the truth?"**

JESUS

APPEARS IN The Bible obviously, but novels like **Robert Graves**'s King Jesus, The Gospel According To The Son by **Norman Mailer** and Quarantine by **Jim Crace** use the character of Jesus and the events of his life as central parts of their stories. In Christ Recrucified by **Nikos Kazantzakis** (who also wrote The Last Temptation Of Christ), a Greek village's Passion play is the backdrop for an exploration of what it was like to be Christ.

PERSONA Physical descriptions of Jesus don't stray much from the gentle, suffering hippy archetype. In Quarantine, the fasting Jesus is: "bare-footed and without a staff. No water skin or bag of clothes. No food. A slow, painstaking figure, made thin and watery by the rising mirage heat." In Christ Recrucified, **Manolios** is chosen to play Jesus and gradually assumes a Christ-like persona, prompting both devotion and scepticism from others. With his final speech, "Arise, starving brothers, my persecuted fellow-beings; how long are we to remain slaves?" Manolios becomes the passionate, charismatic leader featured in the other novels. Even Mailer's Jesus, often full of self-doubt, ridicules the Gospel writers for describing him as "gentle when I was pale with rage." These books are about Christ the man not Christ the God, and have real emotional impact.

DEFINING MOMENT Invariably, the Crucifixion.

CULTURAL IMPACT Christ as a character in a novel can hardly be expected to create the same fuss as the biblical figure, but the very act of putting him in a story can cause controversy. **Anthony Burgess**'s The Kingdom Of The Wicked, in which Jesus features briefly at the beginning, suggests the resurrection may have been Jesus simply fainting from pain and coming round three days later. Jesus's mysterious life also lies at the root of The Da Vinci Code.

IN HIS OWN WORDS (From The Gospel According To The Son) **"If you swear by the gold of the Temple, you will become a debtor to the Lord!"**

JFK

APPEARS IN **D.M. Thomas**'s Flying In To Love most notably; also in **Mark Lane**'s Executive Action, **Don DeLillo**'s Libra and **Norman Mailer**'s spy novel Harlot's Ghost (and namechecked in the same author's An American Dream). Appears lightly disguised in **Richard Condon**'s entertaining, insightful riff on the assassination Winter Kills and in **Gore Vidal**'s Washington DC.

PERSONA JFK's biggest crime, as far as Vidal was concerned, was to be elected president, something Vidal had always aspired to. Kennedy is most credible, as a character, in Thomas's Flying In To Love – Love Field being the airport JFK flew into on the day of his death – and he has an intriguing cameo in Harlot's Ghost.

318

Mailer had met JFK and written a piece called Superman Comes To The Supermarket for **Esquire** magazine, which he felt helped Kennedy get elected. Though Mailer's narrator relies mostly on hearsay from Kennedy's casual lovers, a portrait of an intelligent, charismatic yet flawed individual emerges. (Mailer also wrote Oswald's Tale, in which he insisted that **Lee Harvey Oswald**, JFK's alleged assassin, acted alone.) Vidal's essay about the time he introduced Kennedy to **Tennessee Williams** – only for the playwright to remark what a great ass Kennedy had – is an entertaining insight into pre-presidential JFK.

DEFINING MOMENT His death, the grassy knoll, etc have

JFK, controversial in life, death and fiction

overshadowed one of the 20th century's most remarkable and controversial lives. **Marilyn Monroe**'s breathless rendition of Happy Birthday, Mr President in a skin-tight dress is one of the truly great pop cultural moments – a powerful collision of sex, politics, secrets, charisma and lies.

CULTURAL IMPACT **Esquire** recently picked JFK as the man who brought politics into popular culture. His assassination sparked novels, two short stories (**John Royal**'s Dutch Treat and **Edward J. Delaney**'s Conspiracy Buffs are both worth reading) and films including the chilling Executive Action, from Lane's novel. Kennedy, the barely disguised inspiration for The West Wing's President Bartlett, is the standard by which his successors in the Oval Office are judged.

IN HIS WORDS (From Flying In To Love) **"There's an exceptionally beautiful Democrat nun in Dallas"**

JOSEF K

APPEARS IN The Trial by **Franz Kafka**.

PERSONA One day two men turn up at Josef K's room and tell him he is under arrest. So begins a nightmarish journey through a cloaked legal system where his accuser is unknown and offers of help can't be trusted. Bland sinister figures like the inspector and usher say things like: "Proceedings have been instituted against you, and you will be informed of everything in due course." But K is never informed. He is the alienated everyman, doomed to be crushed by his oppressors.

DEFINING MOMENT His realisation that his arrest is not some elaborate joke by his colleagues at the bank and not a mistake that will easily be rectified.

CULTURAL IMPACT Josef K's creator inspired the word "Kafkaesque", used to describe unhelpful, labyrinthine bureaucracy and any futile struggle against it, as in trying to appeal against a wrongly issued parking ticket or filling in a form at the Post Office. Josef K was the name of an intelligent 1980s band in the vein of **Orange Juice**. His plight has moved many film directors. **Orson Welles** cast Anthony Perkins as Josef K in La Procès, exploiting the actor's fear of being exposed as a homosexual to get the performance he wanted.

IN HIS OWN WORDS **"You made the assertion earlier that the court is impervious to proof, later you qualified that assertion by confining it to the public sessions of the court, and now you actually say that an innocent man requires no help before the court"**

LOLITA

APPEARS IN Lolita by **Vladimir Nabokov**. The character, but not the name, first appeared in his story The Enchanter, published in 1986, after his death.

Nabokov's temptress in her innocent, daisy-fresh days

PERSONA Lolita is the pet name given to 12-year-old Dolores Haze, who is the object of 37-year-old narrator Humbert Humbert's deviant obsession. Humbert is a cultured European paedophile, who yearns for the innocence he felt as a 13-year-old when he had his first romance. He moves to the US, rents a room in Dolores's mum's house, but when she dies in an accident (fleeing the house after discovering his perversion) he takes to the road with the daughter. He claims Lolita initiated their sexual relationship, but, as they tour US motels, admits she cries herself to sleep. She learns to please men sexually, but what Lolita really seeks is the love of a father. She soon tires of Humbert and, at the age of 14, is willingly abducted by another paedophile, Clare Quilty. It's no accident the novel is called Lolita – and not Dolores. She remains an enigma, as we see her refracted through Humbert's warped vision.

DEFINING MOMENT In the hotel after Dolores's mother has died, she kisses Humbert and begins telling him of a sexual game she learned while at camp: "'You mean,' she persisted, now kneeling above me, 'you never did it when you were a kid?' 'Never,' I answered quite truthfully. 'Okay… here is where we start.'"

CULTURAL IMPACT The term Lolita is now a noun for a seductive adolescent. In 1992, an American girl **Amy Fisher** was dubbed the 'Long Island Lolita' after a scandal in which she shot the wife of a local man who had been charged with statutory rape against Fisher. In 2004, **Azar Nafisi** published Reading Lolita In Tehran, a mix of memoir and literary criticism as a group of women read books in the secret of a private living room as a means to escape oppression. In the film American Beauty, **Kevin Spacey**'s character, who is tempted by – but resists – a virgin Lolita, is called Lester Burnham – an anagram of 'Humbert learns'.

IN HER OWN WORDS **"I was a daisy-fresh girl, and look what you've done to me. I ought to call the police and tell them you raped me"**

PHILIP MARLOWE

APPEARS IN **Raymond Chandler**'s The Big Sleep, Farewell My Lovely, The Lady In The Lake, The Little Sister, The Long Goodbye, Payback and Goldfish – the best of the short stories in which he starred.

PERSONA Tarnished idealist, chess-playing tough guy, hard-bitten loner, alert to feminine charm ("he might seduce a countess; he would not despoil a virgin"), cynical, yet romantic – Marlowe is all these. The novels were lauded by **Graham Greene**, **Evelyn Waugh** (who called Chandler "America's greatest living novelist") and **W.H. Auden**, but **Jorge Luis Borges** sniffed: "the atmosphere in these stories is disagreeable."

DEFINING MOMENT Alone, in his office, angrily debating whether to take the bottle of whiskey out of the drawer and pour himself a slug.

CULTURAL IMPACT Many of the genre's clichés – like the private eye who used to be a cop but couldn't stand the corruption – were perfected in Marlowe and personified by **Humphrey Bogart** in The Big Sleep. He was a role model for **Ross Macdonald**'s Lew Archer, **Jack Nicholson**'s Jake Gittes in Chinatown and, worst of all, Spenser, a parodic clone created by **Robert B. Parker**, who further outraged fans by completing Chandler's unfinished Marlowe novel, Poodle Springs,

Like the blurb said: "Marlowe's toughest case. Chandler's greatest book"

321

and writing one of his own. **Dennis Potter** paid homage to Marlowe in The Singing Detective, in which his 'hero' is Philip Marlow.

IN HIS OWN WORDS "I don't mind if you don't like my manners. I don't like them myself – I grieve over them on long winter evenings"

MERLIN

APPEARS IN **Mallory**'s Morte D'Arthur, **T.H. White**'s series The Once And Future King, **Mark Twain**'s A Connecticut Yankee In The Court Of King Arthur, a veritable galaxy of fantasy novels and many tales of Arthurian fiction, the best of which may be **Bernard Cornwell**'s trilogy, The Warlord Chronicles.

PERSONA White's Merlyn is pretty much your classic wizard, "dressed in a

flowing gown with fur tippets and the signs of the zodiac embroidered over it... a pointed hat... a wand of lignum vitae... and a pair of horn-rimmed spectacles." His eccentric references to **Freud** and electricity are a reminder he is living backwards through time. He intervenes in the affairs of men, but allows them their triumphs and errors. Fallible, Merlin is not always respected. Twain's hero groans: "Merlin has wrought a spell! ... That cheap old humbug, that maundering old ass..." In **Nikolai Tolstoy**'s trilogy on Merlin's life (starting with The Coming Of The King) he is an OTT comic force.

322

DEFINING MOMENT Warning Arthur about Guinevere's affair with Lancelot.

CULTURAL IMPACT Merlin is the wizard's wizard, a key figure in British mythology, a magical being embodying the moment society turned from superstition to Christ. Without him, would we have Gandalf or Harry Potter? The Order of Merlin is an honour given to wizards in **J.K. Rowling**'s novels. He appears, as "French enchanter Merlin", in Don Quixote as "someone who knew more than the devil", and has an asteroid, **Merlin 2598**, named after him.

IN HIS OWN WORDS (From The Once And Future King) "I have said about Excalibur and how you must be careful of the sheath? What is confounding me is that I can't remember whether it is in the future or in the past"

WALTER MITTY

APPEARS IN **James Thurber**'s short story The Secret Life Of Walter Mitty.

PERSONA In the course of a short visit to town for his wife to have her hair done, Mitty's wandering imagination has him save a patient from coreopsis, defend himself against a charge of murder (during which a lovely dark-haired girl falls into his arms) and set off cheerily on a walk through hell in the murderous heat of war.

DEFINING MOMENT The opening scene in which Mitty imagines steering a Navy plane through the eye of a hurricane.

CULTURAL IMPACT Thurber published his short story in **The New Yorker** in 1939. A film, starring **Danny Kaye**, followed in 1947 and, ever since, any man accused of having an active fantasy life – or tendency towards self-delusion – has been described as having "a Walter Mitty complex" – be they **David Kelly**, the British government scientist who committed suicide after a BBC story about arms in Iraq; **Howard Dean**, liberal shoe-in for the Democratic presidential nomination – until he lost; or **Robert Hendy-Feegard**, a car salesman whose imaginary life as a secret agent was so convincing he conned thousands of pounds from people. Snoopy was not, as is often said, inspired by Mitty, but the Peanuts website notes that he is "an extroverted beagle with a Walter Mitty complex". On a typical day, you can find Mitty namechecked in 30 news stories on **Google** – not bad for a guy who first appeared in a short story 65 years ago.

But then Thurber was an old hand at spinning such fantasies. Working as a reporter for an American newspaper on the French Riviera, he filed such stories as: "The Hon. Mr Stephen H.L. Atterbury, charge d'affaires of the American legation in Peru, and Mrs Atterbury, the former Princess Ti Ling of Tibet, are

A WHALE OF A TIME WITH MOBY, ELVIS, STAR TREK

In 1968, clad in black leather in the middle of a concert that would revive his career, **Elvis Presley** suddenly grabbed the microphone, brandished it like a spear and shouted "Moby Dick!"

Presley, as a boy, was a genuine fan of the great white whale, whose symbolic significance has kept academics in papers and conference sessions for most of the last century.

Led Zeppelin named an instrumental track after the whale, **Laurie Anderson** did a multimedia stage presentation called Songs And Stories Of Moby Dick, while one Star Trek episode (The Doomsday Machine) and movie (Star Trek II: The Wrath Of Khan) owe an ocean-sized debt to the beast. Sci-fi buffs are almost as mad about Moby as rock stars. **Bruce Sterling**'s novel Involution Ocean is a sci-fi pastiche of Melville's work.

Seaman Thomas Nickerson didn't know what he was getting the world into when he wrote his real account of how, in 1820, his ship **Essex** was attacked – and effectively sunk – by an 80-ton sperm whale. This inspired **Melville**, who published his novel in 1851 to, at the time, very little acclaim.

The key issue with Moby is: to hyphenate or not to hyphenate? The answer, of course, is both – Melville didn't in the novel itself but did in its title.

motoring to Monte Carlo from Aix-le-Provence... Mr Stephen Atterbury is the breeder of the famous Schnauzer-Pincher."

IN HIS OWN WORDS **"Does it ever occur to you that sometimes I am thinking?"**

CAPTAIN NEMO

APPEARS IN 20,000 Leagues Under The Sea by **Jules Verne**, and his later novel Mysterious Island, which has a passage expanding Nemo's background.

PERSONA Born an Indian prince yet educated across the globe, Captain Nemo was the great hope for India's future. After the failure of the 1857 **Indian Mutiny**, he channelled his disappointment into creating the Nautilus, a submarine that allowed him to sink beneath the waves, leaving the 'civilised' world for ever. Arronax, a scientist, says of Nemo: "He was tall, had a large forehead, straight nose, a clearly cut mouth, beautiful teeth, with fine taper hands, indicative of a highly nervous temperament... certainly the most admirable specimen I had ever met." His mind is no less impressive, his brilliant inventions reflecting Verne's fascination with emerging technology. Nemo (Latin for 'no one') is a man who hates war, but will sink a warship; an engineer with the persona of a sorcerer.

DEFINING MOMENT When Nemo ruthlessly orders the Nautilus to massacre a group of cachalots who are attacking whales.

CULTURAL IMPACT Nemo, memorably portrayed by **James Mason** in the 1954 Disney film, is the obvious inspiration for **H.G. Wells**'s Dr Moreau and, as depicted by Mason, a blueprint for the archetypal suave Bond villain, the Blofeld-style evil geniuses who, disappointed by the world's refusal to recognise their greatness, hide from it in a secret high-tech lair and/or try to destroy it.

IN HIS OWN WORDS On sighting a warship: **"I am the law, I am the judge! I am the oppressed, and there is the oppressor! All that I hate is there!"**

SCARLETT O'HARA

APPEARS IN **Margaret Mitchell**'s **American Civil War** epic Gone With The Wind, and an official 1992 sequel by **Alexandra Ripley** catchily entitled Scarlett: The Sequel To Margaret Mitchell's Gone With The Wind, in which Scarlett goes to Ireland. A parody, The Wind Done Gone by **Alice Randall**, narrated by Scarlett O'Hara's illegitimate half-black half-sister, was published in 2002 after an unsuccessful attempt by Mitchell's heirs to ban it.

PERSONA Flirt, businesswoman, romantic, farm help, murderer. This feisty southern belle had the wits, guts and strong will needed to face the Civil War and come out on top. The only thing she doesn't get is her own way with neighbour

Ashley Wilkes, though she does marry three other men, including her sister's beau and dandy scallywag Rhett Butler.

DEFINING MOMENT As the Confederate army abandons Atlanta to the Yankees, Scarlett stays to help deliver the baby of her sister-in-law (and one-time love rival) Melanie. As Atlanta burns, Rhett steals a wagon and rescues them, before abandoning Scarlett when she announces her plan to ride through the Yankees and return home. He kisses her, she slaps him and they insult each other. He walks away chuckling, she takes the reins and with infant son, unconscious new mother and newborn baby onboard, heads home to Tara anyway.

CULTURAL IMPACT The film rights to Gone With The Wind were snapped up by **David O. Selznick** a month after the book was published. In 1939 it was the film everyone wanted to be in – 1,400 actresses, including **Katharine Hepburn** and **Lucille Ball** (!) tested for the heroine before **Vivien Leigh** won the part. The film is the highest-grossing ever, adjusted for inflation, and helped spawn a range of collectible dolls. In 1941 a Louisiana businessman, **George Palmer**, had an exact replica of Tara built in **St Charles Avenue**, New Orleans – number 5705, if you're passing. In 1989 **Helen Taylor** wrote Scarlett's Women: Gone With The Wind And Its Female Fans, in which hundreds of British women discuss their love-hate relationship with Scarlett.

IN HER OWN WORDS "I'm glad Georgia waited till after Christmas before it seceded or it would have ruined the Christmas parties, too"

PORFIRY PETROVICH

APPEARS IN **Fyodor Dostoevsky's** Crime And Punishment.

PERSONA Petrovich is a polite, bumbling, good-humoured detective investigating the murder of an elderly Russian pawnbroker and her younger sister. Beneath the jovial, ineffectual persona is a hard-nosed, intuitive cop. Petrovich's interest lies in making the suspect confess and repent, to which ends he embarks on a psychological battle of wills with Raskolnikov.

DEFINING MOMENT Petrovich, questioning Raskolnikov for the second time, explains his method of treating a suspect – "like a butterfly round a candle" – until the suspect worries himself to death. Raskolnikov, realising he is suspected of the murder, falls for Petrovich's ploy and begins to show his guilt.

CULTURAL IMPACT Petrovich became a role model for detectives in fiction and on screen. From his smoking and bumbling friendliness to his habit of never leaving a room without remembering "just one other thing", the 1970s TV detective Columbo, played by **Peter Falk**, was a particularly close incarnation.

IN HIS OWN WORDS "Good heavens! Why, I learnt it all from you yourself!"

There ain't nothing like a Don: Cervantes's knight errant lives on

DON QUIXOTE

APPEARS IN Don Quixote by **Miguel de Cervantes Saavedra** and in a spurious work by an unknown Spanish writer under the pen name **Alonso Fernandez de Avellaneda**. This fake sequel to part one of Cervantes's Don Quixote (1605) appeared one year before the author's real part two (1615), which contains several references to this impostor and his false tales. Also appears in a pornographic pastiche by **Kathy Acker**.

PERSONA Obsessed by stories of knights errant, Don Quixote sets out on his trusty steed (the aged Rocinante) to roam Spain in search of heroic adventure, damsels in distress and righting wrongs. Quixote's misplaced gallantry (freeing 'kidnapped' criminals, for example) receives little thanks, especially from Sancho Panza, his faithful, put-upon squire who bears the painful brunt of Quixote's delusions. The book is variously seen as social commentary, the first modern novel, slapstick comedy and, by **Vladimir Nabokov**, as "a veritable encyclopedia of cruelty... one of the most bitter barbarous books ever penned."

DEFINING MOMENT Don Quixote spies "thirty monstrous giants" across the plain, each with "more arms than the giant Briareus". Chiding Sancho Panza for his cowardice when he tries to explain that the giants are actually windmills, Quixote, mounted on Rocinante, charges into attack.

THE CHARACTERS

CULTURAL IMPACT As well as the term 'tilting at windmills' (to fight imaginary enemies), 'quixotic' has entered the dictionary to mean impractically idealistic. Tourism in Spain's **La Mancha** thrives on its local hero, one of literature's most enduring characters. His impact extended to outer space in 1983 when a small asteroid belt was named **3552 Don Quixote**. The tale has inspired moviemakers such as **Terry Gilliam** and **Orson Welles** – neither of whom got to finish their film adaptations – and the musical Man Of La Mancha, with its heroic anthem The Impossible Dream. **Graham Greene** penned a knowing tribute Monsignor Quixote, while **Jorge Louis Borges**'s Pierre Menard, Author Of The Don Quixote tells the story of a writer who rewrites the classic work without notes, only to find his finished book matches Cervantes's original word for word.

IN HIS OWN WORDS **"A knight errant who turns mad for a reason deserves neither merit nor thanks. The thing is to do it without cause"**

EASY RAWLINS

APPEARS IN Eight **Walter Mosley** detective novels.

PERSONA Ezekiel Rawlins is not a private eye, yet somehow spends a lot of time sorting out other people's mysteries. He spends his life in the almost entirely black-inhabited Watts area of Los Angeles and the books span World War II to JFK's presidency, with all the changing racial attitudes of the time. He is a war veteran. What he saw in Europe affected him deeply: "I killed enough blue-eyed young men to know that they were just as afraid to die as I was," which helps explain his attachment to his house and garden with its avocado tree – a touchingly domestic dream for a man often embroiled in life's seedier side.

DEFINING MOMENT Easy's bid for a quiet life in A Red Death is scuppered by a racist tax inspector, forcing him back into "the hurting business".

CULTURAL IMPACT Apart from providing a rare leading character (**Denzel Washington** in the film of Devil In A Blue Dress) that black Americans could recognise as reflecting the complexity and variety of their own lives, Rawlins documents an unsung period of US society – the emergence of an affluent black class following their migration to the nation's ports and arms factories in the war effort. In a neat footnote, Mosley appears as Congressman Rawlins in the 2004 remake of **Richard Condon**'s The Manchurian Candidate.

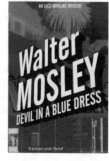

IN HIS OWN WORDS **"Life was hard back then and you just had to take the bad along with the worse if you wanted to survive"**

SATAN

APPEARS IN Classics like **Dante**'s Divine Comedy and **Milton**'s Paradise Lost (where he declared it was better to reign in hell than to serve in heaven) and such thought-provoking fiction as **Mikhail Bulgakov**'s The Master And Margarita. Satanic characteristics have been ascribed to literary characters as diverse as Captain Ahab and the pitchfork-wielding seducer Alec D'Urbeville in **Thomas Hardy**'s Tess Of The D'Urbevilles. In **Ira Levin**'s chilling thriller Rosemary's Baby, Rosemary suspects she's having Satan's child. In his novel The Exorcist, **William Peter Blatty** used ultimate evil to remind us of the need for God. All things devilish were a key 1970s pop cultural motif, a fact that may or may not have had anything to do with **Richard Nixon**'s presence in the White House.

PERSONA In Bulgakov's book the Devil comes to Moscow as a man, menacing in some ways but curiously bland in others. "As for his teeth, he had platinum crowns on the left side and gold on the right. He was wearing an expensive grey suit and imported shoes of a matching colour… under his arm he carried a stick with a black knob shaped like a poodle's head." He goes on to meddle in the lives of those around him, but since his actions are both evil and compassionate, this Satan is an ambiguous figure, a contrast to the fire and brimstone character of popular imagination. In literature, Satan is allowed many guises, from Mocata's demons in **Dennis Wheatley**'s The Devil Rides Out to the urbane Louis Cyphre (geddit?) in Falling Angel by **William Hjortsberg**.

DEFINING MOMENT In a stunning diabolical moment in The Master And Margarita, **Woland** (Satan) predicts the bizarre death of Berlioz, from slipping on sunflower oil, falling and being decapitated by a passing tram.

CULTURAL IMPACT The Devil as a smooth-talking businessman has almost replaced the horns-and-tail version in the popular consciousness. With so many identities, Satan can be seen as all pervasive in modern life, while fictionally, evil is more intriguing and varied than good. Lucifer doesn't just have the best tunes.

IN HIS OWN WORDS (From The Master And Margarita) **"What would your good do if evil did not exist?"**

328

SHANE

APPEARS IN Jack Schaefer's novel Shane.

PERSONA Shane is the stranger with a mysterious past who rides into a valley in Wyoming. As a temporary farmhand and maestro with a gun, Shane is drawn into a squabble over land on the side of the Starrett family, whose son Bob idolises him. The gunslinger trying to escape from his past is something of a cliché, but Schaefer's variation is fresh and his hero strikes deeper chords – struggling with his own character, chaos and destiny and discovering he is only fully himself when doing a thing he consciously hates – gunfighting.

DEFINING MOMENT His arrival, when Bob senses "the easiness of a coiled spring, a trap set", and his final glory, when he shoots the last bad guy with such a rare blend of panache and speed that, to the boy, his motion is almost beautiful.

CULTURAL IMPACT The novel has now sold over 12 million copies in over 30 languages. In Shane, Schaefer created such a powerful character that within four years his novel had been translated for the screen and, forever after, his creation would be in every reader's imagination the golden-buckskinned, worldly-wise **Alan Ladd**. **David Carradine**, of Kung Fu fame, starred as the hero in a 1960s TV series, **Clint Eastwood** pays homage to the novel – and film – in Pale Rider, while in The Negotiator, **Kevin Spacey** and **Samuel L. Jackson** argue over whether Shane is dying as he rides into the next valley. (You wonder when the Schaefer estate will license a sequel.) In Taxi Driver, the scene where **Robert De Niro** stands in front of the mirror and says, "Are you talking to me?" was allegedly improvised, yet the line is a quotation, conscious or not, from a bar-room scene where Shane squares up to a villain.

IN HIS OWN WORDS **"A man is what he is and there's no sense breaking that mould"**

329

JOSEF SVEJK

APPEARS IN The Good Soldier Svejk by **Jaroslav Hasek**. Some aficionados say the e-book The Fateful Adventures Of The Good Soldier Svejk, translated from the Czech by **Zenny K. Sadlon**, is more fluent than the first translation (available in Penguin and Everyman), but it doesn't cover as many stories.

PERSONA Officially declared an imbecile, Svejk (pronounced to rhyme with bake) is the literary ancestor of Catch-22's Yossarian. But beneath his blue, trusting eyes, blank moonface and benign smile, Hasek's idiot savant is more elusive than Heller's anti-hero. Svejk, eventually drafted to fight for the Austro-Hungarian empire in World War I, doesn't rebel outright. He says yes but, to the fury of his superiors, does the exact opposite – and does it in such a way that they can't be sure if he's deliberately flouting their orders.

DEFINING MOMENT As the book opens, Svejk is told about the assassination of someone called **Ferdinand** but pretends to think the victim is not the archduke, but either a local messenger who once drank a bottle of hair oil or a dog-manure collector.

CULTURAL IMPACT This is the grand-daddy of anti-war novels. Svejk is a far more accurate – if at times unflattering – national stereotype for the Czechs than, say, **John Bull** is for England. His evasive stoicism – and knack of averting disaster at the eleventh hour – set the tone for his country's attempt to survive the horrors of Stalinism and what followed. In the 1970s, the hardline Communist leader **Gustav Husak** scolded the nation: "Stop Svejking!" – the term "to Svejk" is almost a recognised verb in Czech. Hasek's good soldier has been the subject of an opera, a **Bertolt Brecht** play, a musical, a slew of films, an Austrian television series, a cartoon and a frighteningly detailed website (SvejkCentral.com). He even has a pub named after him in Stockholm.

IN HIS OWN WORDS "Humbly report sir, I'm a half-wit"

YOUNG WERTHER

APPEARS IN The Sorrows Of Young Werther by **J.W. von Goethe**.

PERSONA If you're looking for a cheery trip through 18th-century Germany, Young Werther is not your best guide. Talented but unstable, he's given to extremes of emotion and his passion and despair are his downfall. His story unfolds in a series of letters detailing his fragile state of mind and his existentialist angst as he ponders the great questions of life, love, death and man's reason for being.

DEFINING MOMENT Falling in love at first sight with already-engaged Charlotte S. "My entire soul was transfixed by her figure, her tone, her manner."

CULTURAL IMPACT The novel was such a spectacular success that a flood of parodies, poems, operas and even Werther perfume followed. In Fleet Street, Mrs Salmon's Royal-Historical Wax-Work offered a tableau of Werther and Charlotte. Young men even dressed in Werther's style of blue frock coat and buff waistcoat. Reports that Werther inspired an epidemic of suicides now appear to be unfounded, although there were cases like that of **Christine Von Lassberg** who was found dead with a copy in her pocket. The Sorrows Of Young Werther is one of the books Frankenstein's monster finds in a sack in **Mary Shelley**'s novel.

IN HIS OWN WORDS "And what is man – that boasted demigod?"

AURELIO ZEN

APPEARS IN **Michael Dibdin**'s atmospheric detective novels set in Italy.

PERSONA Zen is from Venice, but the novels deal with seedy and brutal crime all over Italy. He reads thrillers on a long train journey because they offer "the prospect of a tightly organised guided tour through a theme park of reassuringly foreign unpleasantness." His adventures are a loosely disorganised guide through some – if you're not Italian – reassuringly foreign unpleasantness. Zen remains a

There was nothing camp or overstated about McCulley's creation Zorro

determinedly shadowy figure, part Clouseau, part super-sleuth who may solve cases with his wry understanding of human nature, or the the aid of mysterious patrons who help him avoid retaliation from other éminences grises. Despite the name, Zen is no idealist (he's not above the occasional unethical deal) but he has his own morality and is rarely deflected, even by corruption or terrorism.

DEFINING MOMENT When he discovers a case is hidden beneath layers of intrigue, deception, grudges and modern bureaucracy – the point of no return.

CULTURAL IMPACT Dibdin was groomed by his publisher, Faber, as the new **P.D. James**, but Zen's Italian locales have precluded the usual TV dramatisations. Zen's tales, taken serially, form a secret history of postwar Italy, alluding to countless political conspiracies. Intelligent, not entirely in control of his destiny, a cog caught in conflicting agendas, Zen is the perfect postmodern detective.

IN HIS OWN WORDS "They did ugly things in those days too, they just didn't make ugly things, they didn't know how"

ZORRO

APPEARS IN First, a magazine serialisation in 1919, The Curse Of Capistrano by **Johnston McCulley**. After **Douglas Fairbanks** made his successful screen version The Mark Of Zorro the serial became a novel and the film title was adopted. McCulley continued to write Zorro stories until his death in 1969.

PERSONA Zorro (Spanish for fox) owes something to Robin Hood and The Scarlet Pimpernel, but is a vital character in his own right. A masked avenger who rides El Camino Real in the 1820s to protect the downtrodden of southern California, he cuts a glamorous figure. "The man who stood straight before them had a black mask over his face that effectually concealed his features, and through the two slits in it, his eyes glittered ominously." Yet in his alter ego, as aristocratic Don Diego, he is a bit of a fop and a lot of a snob – he tells his sergeant he's happy to ignore the gap in their social status as long as his pal isn't too cheeky. Those who cross Zorro end up marked by him, a perfect Z carved delicately into their flesh.

DEFINING MOMENT Saving Señorita Pulido from a fate worse than death when Captain Ramon forces himself upon her.

CULTURAL IMPACT The masked do-gooder is a much-copied archetype in romance novels and superhero comics, spawning several films (in which Zorro has been played by **Tyrone Power**, **Alain Delon**, **George Hamilton**, **Anthony Hopkins**, **Antonio Banderas**) and a Disney TV series. Batman is an obvious homage to the gay blade. In comic books Zorro has faced such foes as Dracula.

IN HIS OWN WORDS "I am the friend of the oppressed, Señor, and I have come to punish you"

READERS' DIGEST

THEY ARE A PARTICULAR BREED, AUTHORS.
SOME CAN ONLY WRITE STANDING UP, OTHERS
CAN'T SLEEP IF THE BED ISN'T FACING NORTH

"The ratio of literacy to illiteracy is constant,
but nowadays the illiterates can read"

Alberto Moravia

READERS' DIGEST

What authors did when not writing

William Burroughs was a **pest controller** and a **private detective**.

Philip K. Dick worked as a **disc jockey**.

James Ellroy was a **caddie**.

William Faulkner worked as a **postmaster** at the University of Mississippi, but would ignore customers, throw away mail and spend much of the time writing or playing bridge and mah-jong with friends he had made part-time clerks.

Mary Gaitskill became a **stripper**.

Zane Grey was a **dentist**.

Franz Kafka worked in the **insurance** business.

W.P. Kinsella sold **adverts** for the Yellow Pages, drove **taxis**, ran his own **pizzeria**.

Haruki Murakami ran a **jazz bar**.

Damon Runyon tried – but failed – to organise a Colorado minor **baseball** league.

Colin Wilson worked in a **wool factory**, then as a civil servant in a **tax office**. After the war, he took brief jobs as a **farmhand** and then a **ditch-digger**.

Yevgeny Zamyatin was a **naval engineer** and spent time in Newcastle supervising the construction of ice-breakers for the Russian Navy.

———

Comets, coffee and chills: strange literary deaths

Honoré de Balzac Was so addicted to coffee that he used to eat it. He's thought to have died of caffeine poisoning.

Roland Barthes Run over by a laundry truck.

Arnold Bennett After drinking a glass of local water in Paris to prove it was safe, he contracted typhoid and died.

Maxwell Bodenheim Shot with a .22 rifle after challenging a dish washer who was having sex with his wife. The dish washer then stabbed the wife to death.

Anton Chekhov His body was delivered home to Moscow in a refrigerated railway car marked 'oysters'.

Randall Jarrell In hospital for therapy after slashing his wrists, the poet and novelist went for a walk and was run over by a car. To this day, family and friends cannot decide if he committed suicide or died in an accident.

Seth Morgan Rode a motorcycle off the Golden Gate Bridge into San Francisco Bay.

Rainer Maria Rilke Died of blood poisoning after being cut by the thorn of a rose he picked for a young woman.

CULT FICTION

Mark Twain Predicted he would die the year Halley's Comet visited (1910), and did.

Virginia Woolf Weighed herself down with stones and walked into the River Ouse in Sussex.

Characters inspired by authors

Mark Rampion in Point Counter Point Aldous Huxley modelled the character on D.H. Lawrence.

W.P. Mayhew in Barton Fink Based on William Faulkner. There is some dispute whether the film's titular hero is based on the left-wing playwright Clifford Odets.

Bull Hubbard in Desolation Angels, Book Of Dreams William Burroughs was Jack Kerouac's inspiration.

Terence Mann in Field of Dreams Based on J.D. Salinger. In W.P. Kinsella's original, Shoeless Joe, Salinger is mentioned, but the author wasn't happy with the reference and threatened to sue, so the producers of the movie changed the name.

Peter Mir in The Green Knight Based on Elias Canetti. Canetti was Iris Murdoch's lover, and aspects of his character are present in many of the charismatic older men to be found in her books.

Carlo Marx in On The Road Allen Ginsberg provided the inspiration for Kerouac's character. He was also the inspiration for Alvah Goldbook in The Dharma Bums and Irwin Garden in Desolation Angels.

Arial Lavalina in The Subterraneans Gore Vidal was Kerouac's muse this time.

Dil in To Kill A Mockingbird Believed to be based on Truman Capote.

HJ Heidler in Quartet Based on Jean Rhys's lover Ford Madox Ford.

Truman Capote's top 11 could have beens...
People the writer would like to have been in past incarnations

Caligula

Catherine the Great

Stalin

Sigmund Freud

Rasputin

Cleopatra

Henry VIII

Madame de Pompadour

Alcibiades (Military commander who led both Athenians and Spartans to victory)

J. Edgar Hoover and Clyde Tolson (Hoover's long-time companion and assistant)

From The People's Almanac presents the Book Of Lists 2

Manuscripts lost and found

Nikolai Gogol deliberately destroyed the second volume of his great novel **Dead Souls** in a fit of religious zeal. A few fragments survived.

Albert Camus The manuscript of **The First Man** was found in the wreckage of the car he was killed in, in 1960, but wasn't published until 1994.

Arthur Conan Doyle Was relieved when his first novel, **The Narrative Of John Smith**, got lost in the post. In hindsight he realised much of it was libellous.

Jean Genet Started writing **Our Lady Of The Flowers** in prison, but the manuscript was discovered and destroyed. He rewrote it from memory and had it smuggled out.

Ernest Hemingway Virtually all of his early stories and a novel-in-progress were stolen from a train in Paris when his first wife Hadley left her seat to get a drink.

Malcolm Lowry In 1932 a publisher left the manuscript of **Ultramarine** in his car when he went to make a phone call and it was stolen. Luckily a friend of Lowry's unearthed copies of the work-in-progress from a wastepaper basket.

Jules Verne His early novel, **Paris In The Twentieth Century**, was found in a rusting safe by his great-grandson, having been rejected by Verne's publisher as too gloomy. The dystopian diatribe was published in 1996.

Authors who used little or no punctuation

Jerzy Andrzejewski Having taken up Catholicism and Communism, Andrzejewski later took on a literary cause, disdaining punctuation. In 1962 he published **Gates Of Paradise**, a novel written in one single sentence.

Timothy Dexter After criticism, in the second edition of his early punctuation-free autobiography he added a page of punctuation – rows of colons, commas, question marks etc – for the reader to drop in where they pleased.

Rev. John Dobson His 1815 book, **The Elements Of Geometry**, offered no punctuation except a full stop at the end of each paragraph.

Gertrude Stein Most of Stein's writings avoided all punctuation except full stops, her reasoning being that "they had a life of their own." She found commas "servile" and question marks and exclamation points "positively revolting".

From The People's Almanac presents the Book Of Lists 2

The FBI files: writers under investigation

Pearl S. Buck On the list because she opposed racism, adopted a black Japanese child and belonged to the American Civil Liberties Union.

Allen Ginsberg Though he was ejected from Cuba and Prague for anti-Communist remarks, the FBI deemed him "potentially dangerous" with "emotional instability".

Lillian Hellman A member of the League of Women Shoppers, she attended a dinner for **Theodore Dreiser** and travelled with a copy of the **Little Oxford Dictionary**.

Ernest Hemingway J. Edgar Hoover was obsessed with outing Hemingway as a communist. His file cited his support of the Loyalist cause in the Spanish Civil War, writing an article against war for **Esquire**, and even his arguments with his wife.

CULT FICTION

Sinclair Lewis His un-American activities included not living with his wife, being a member of the American Birth Control League and writing a novel, **Kingsblood Royal**, which the FBI called "propaganda for the white man's acceptance of the Negro as a social equal."

Archibald Macleish Hoover deemed the poet "prematurely anti-Fascist".

Dorothy Parker Investigated by FBI, as a suspected Communist, in 1950s Hollywood.

Strangest movies novelists have worked on

Martin Amis As well as having a scripting credit on the schlocky Hollywood sci-fi movie **Saturn 3** (starring **Farrah Fawcett**, **Kirk Douglas** and **Harvey Keitel**), Amis was also a child actor in **A High Wind In Jamaica**.

John Fante The novelist who inspired Charles Bukowski wrote the script for the **Debbie Reynolds** comedy **My Six Loves**, in which she plays a Broadway star ordered to rest for her health. The movie slogan was "It's Debbie in the funniest fix a girl ever got into."

Raymond Chandler The crime writer was responsible for the screenplay of **Strangers On A Train**, adapted from Patricia Highsmith's first novel.

Gavin Lambert The author of the great Hollywood novel **Inside Daisy Clover** wasn't too proud to write the screenplay for **Liberace: Behind The Music**.

John O'Hara Writer of **Butterfield 8** and **Pal Joey** helped bring to the screen one of **Erich von Stroheim**'s lesser works, the comedy/crime/caper **I Was An Adventuress**.

Budd Schulberg Most famous for **On The Waterfront**, Schulberg also penned **Little Orphan Annie** under the name Budd Wilson Schulberg.

Gore Vidal As well as helping out on **Ben-Hur**, Vidal lent his services to **Mario Puzo** when the author was struggling to adapt his novel **The Sicilian** for the screen.

Writers who died before they reached 40

Anne Brontë 29, of tuberculosis.

Charlotte Brontë 38, from complications during pregnancy.

Emily Brontë 30, of tuberculosis, having caught a cold at her brother's funeral.

Keith Douglas 24, in World War II when a mortar shell exploded above his head.

Mikhail Lermontov 26, following a duel with family friend Major Martynov.

Raymond Radiguet 20, from typhoid fever.

Arthur Rimbaud 37, from synovitis, after having his right leg amputated.

Denton Welch 33, after he was knocked off a bicycle aged 19; his injuries eventually killed him.

Nathanael West 37, distraught at his friend **F. Scott Fitzgerald**'s death, he ignored a stop sign and crashed his car, killing himself and his wife.

Boris Vian 39, from a heart attack during a private screening of a film version of his novel **I Will Spit On Your Graves**.

The fatal forties: only the good die middle-aged

At 40 **Edgar Allen Poe** Mysterious circumstances, after being found in someone else's clothes; **Jack London** Kidney disease; **B.S. Johnson** Suicide; **Franz Kafka** Tuberculosis; **Ronald Firbank** Pneumonia related to acute alcoholism.

At 41 **Brendan Behan** A battle with the bottle; **Cesar Pavese** Suicide.

At 44 **F. Scott Fitzgerald** Heart attack; **J.G. Farrell** While fishing off Bantry Bay, Ireland, he was washed out to sea by a freak wave. Partially crippled by polio, he had no chance of survival in such conditions; **D.H. Lawrence** Tuberculosis.

At 45 **Joseph Roth** Collapsed in a Paris café.

At 46 **George Orwell** Tuberculosis; **Oscar Wilde** Caught meningitis after an ear infection; **Charles Baudelaire** Died in mother's arms of aphasia and hemiplegia; **Albert Camus** Car crash.

At 47 **Jack Kerouac** Abdominal haemorrhage while vomiting in his toilet.

At 48 **Karel Capek** Pneumonia; **Malcolm Lowry** Overdose of sleeping pills.

Novels and their original titles

1984 1948
This Side Of Paradise The Romantic Egoist
Gone With The Wind Tomorrow Is Another Day (also Ba! Ba! Black Sheep)
The Postman Always Rings Twice Bar-B-Q
The Heart Is A Lonely Hunter The Mute
The Time Machine The Chronic Astronauts
War And Peace All's Well That Ends Well

339

Books that never existed

The Curious Incident Of The Patterson Family On The Island Of Uffa, by John H. Watson, MD Mentioned by Watson in Sherlock Holmes.

Mad Trist, by Sir Launcelot Canning One of the books mentioned to build up mystery and atmosphere in Fall Of The House Of Usher by Edgar Allen Poe.

Memoirs, by the Hon. Galahad Threepwood Non-existent autobiography of a character who appears in numerous novels by P.G. Wodehouse.

Necronomicon, by Abdul Alhazred A blasphemous and forbidden work often referred to in the fantasy and horror tales of H.P. Lovecraft, as "the ghastly soul symbol of the forbidden corpse-eating cult of inaccessible Leng in central Asia".

The Seven Minutes, by J.J. Jadway This "171-page most-banned novel in history" was created by Irving Wallace in his real book, also called The Seven Minutes. The contents, according to Wallace, consisted of "the thoughts in one woman's head during seven minutes of copulation with an unnamed man".

From The People's Almanac presents the Book Of Lists

CULT FICTION

Famous people who branched out into fiction

Sarah Bernhardt **In The Clouds** is based on a hot-air balloon trip and shows the actress's imagination in overdrive: "The swans clapped their wings with fright, the lake gathered its brow in a frown."

Winston Churchill **Savrola**, the future prime minister's homage to/rip off of the smash adventure novel **The Prisoner Of Zenda** by **Sir Anthony Hope**. The hero, Savrola, is a surrogate Winston, lovingly described by an author who told **Violet Asquith** once: "We are all worms, but I do believe I am a glow-worm."

Joseph Goebbels **Michael: A German Destiny In Diary Pages**, a fanciful and sentimental autobiographical novel.

Jean Harlow **Today Is Tonight**, a novel of beautiful people, in which the husband is blinded. To earn money, Judy poses as a nude, masked **Lady Godiva** in a club.

Saddam Hussein **Zabibah wal Malik** and **al-Qala'ah al-Hasinah**. His books were released anonymously as **A Novel By Its Author**.

Benito Mussolini **The Cardinal's Mistress**. The future dictator had a somewhat macabre style: "The acrid odour of decomposing human flesh compelled us to draw back a few paces… Then Antonio wished to see the woman whom he had so loved, so desired. The body was recognisable by the golden hair which fell over the pure forehead, and by the eyes not yet contaminated. But from the lips, decomposed into a ferocious grin, oozed a dense, whitish liquid."

340

Writers who have disappeared

Ambrose Bierce On 26 December 1913, when he crossed the Rio Grande into Mexico to join **Pancho Villa**'s revolutionaries. Some consider it an act of suicide. **Carlos Fuentes** wrote the novel, **The Old Gringo** about his disappearance.

Agatha Christie On 3 December 1926, when her mother had recently died and her husband was having an affair. She wrote a series of confusing letters to friends and relatives and her car was found abandoned near a lake. People suspected suicide but Christie turned up after ten days at a Yorkshire health spa.

Weldon Kees His work wasn't widely read until after his disappearance in 1955, when his car was found abandoned near the Golden Gate Bridge. As well as suicide, there is also a theory that he faked his death and fled to Mexico.

Rimbaud Presumed dead when he was 26 – he was gun-running in Africa.

B. Traven The author of **The Treasure Of The Sierra Madre** disappeared from a London prison, only to crop up sending manuscripts to a German publisher.

Lords of the ring

Several literary giants have also had experience of the noble art of boxing

Lord Byron Sparred with **John 'Gentleman' Jackson**, the former bare-knuckled champion. Byron boxed in a dressing gown, Jackson in knee breeches and a shirt.

Arthur Conan Doyle During a stint as a ship's surgeon on a Greenland whaler, **Jack Lamb**, the ship's steward, challenged Conan Doyle to a bout. After the match Lamb said, "So help me, he's the best surgeon we've had! He's blackened my eye."

Arthur Cravan The Dadaist author who claimed to be **Oscar Wilde**'s nephew challenged world champion **Jack Johnson** in 1916. He was knocked out within one round, having turned up blind drunk.

Paul Gallico As a cub reporter, the author of **The Poseidon Adventure** was assigned to **Jack Dempsey**'s camp before a big fight, and asked Dempsey to spar with him for one round. He never saw the punch that flattened him.

Ernest Hemingway After sharing a thermos of frozen daiquiris at Hemingway's Havana home, former heavyweight champ **Gene Tunney** would often spar bare-fisted with the writer. Fellow writer **Morley Callaghan** once fought, and beat, Hemingway while **F. Scott Fitzgerald** timed the rounds. On learning that his friend Fitzgerald had accidentally let the round go on a minute too long, Hemingway cried: "Christ! If you want to see me getting the shit knocked out of me, just say so."

Thom Jones The author of **Sonny Liston Was A Friend Of Mine** was an amateur boxer. Unfortunately he also suffered epilepsy and the bouts worsened his condition.

George Plimpton One of Plimpton's early experiments in 'participatory journalism' was taking on **Archie Moore**, the former light-heavyweight champ. Plimpton asked Moore how long it would take him to polish him off: "'Bout the time it would take a tree to fall on you, or for you to feel the nip of the guillotine."

Albert Payson Terhune An excellent amateur boxer and author of several books about dogs, Terhune was once a reporter for the **New York Evening World**. Assigned to fight six boxing greats (**Jim Corbett**, **Kid McCoy**, **Gus Ruhlin**, **Jim Jeffries**, **Bob Fitzsimmons** and **Tom Sharkey**), Terhune didn't know the editor had offered a first-page feature to whichever fighter knocked him out first. Terhune suffered a broken hand and lost two teeth, but none of the six knocked him out.

341

F.X. Toole The author of **Rope Burns** wasn't a fighter, but a noted corner-man under his real name, **Jerry Boyd**.

Virgil Book Five of the **Aeneid** describes a boxing match between a Trojan and a Sicilian.

A dozen authors who wrote standing up

Lewis Carroll
Benjamin Disraeli
Frederic William Farrar
Ernest Hemingway
Malcolm Lowry
Horace McCoy
Vladimir Nabokov
William Saroyan
Thomas Wolfe
Virginia Woolf

From The People's Almanac presents the Book Of Lists 2

CULT FICTION

Strange things people have asked librarians

"**Do you** have that book by Salman Rushdie, Satanic Nurses?"

"**Do you** have books here?"

"**Do you** have any books with photographs of dinosaurs?"

"**Why don't you** have any books by Ibid? He's written a lot of important stuff."

"**Why were** so many famous Civil War battles fought on National Park sites?"

Notorious literary insomniacs

Charles Dickens The head of his bed had to be pointing north, and he had to place himself exactly in the centre of the bed.

Alexandre Dumas On doctor's orders, he ate an apple every day at 7am under the Arc de Triomphe, in the hope that it would force him into a regular pattern of rising and retiring.

Franz Kafka Unable to sleep in the middle of a novel. His favourite technique for dropping off was to "make myself as heavy as possible", as described in his diary.

Marcel Proust Took Veronal for sleeplessness and lined his room with cork to reduce noise and prevent dust that aggravated his asthma.

James Thurber Often woke at 3am. Went back to sleep by "tinkering with words and letters of the alphabet and spelling words backwards". His favourite sleeping aid was rewriting **Poe**'s **The Raven** from the viewpoint of the bird.

Mark Twain Broke a glass bookcase with a pillow because he couldn't sleep.

And one more thing: famous last words

Lord Byron "Now I shall go to sleep."

Johann Wolfgang von Goethe "Open the second shutter so that more light may come in."

Aldous Huxley On his deathbed, unable to speak, he made a written request to his wife for "LSD, 100µg [micrograms], i.m [intramuscular injection]."

James Joyce "Does nobody understand me?"

Wyndham Lewis "Mind your own business" – after a nurse asked him about the state of his bowels on his deathbed.

Cesare Pavese "I shall write no more" – the last line of his suicide note.

Damon Runyon "You can keep the things of bronze and stone and give me just one man to remember me once a year."

George Bernard Shaw "Sister, you're trying to keep me alive as an old curiosity, but I'm done, I'm finished, I'm going to die."

Dylan Thomas "Eighteen straight whiskies... I think that's the record."

H.G. Wells "Go away, I'm alright."

MOSTLY FACTUAL

TRIPS ON ROADS OR DRUGS; BONGO-PLAYING PHYSICISTS;
DIARIES THAT DISH DIRT AND A WOMAN WHO WAKES
FROM A COMA SPEAKING PERFECT FRENCH: THE SECTION
THAT PROVES TRUTH CAN BE WEIRDER THAN FICTION

"Jorge Luis Borges is another blind man I don't particularly like. There's no question that he's a very good writer, but the world is full of good writers and just because someone writes well doesn't mean you have to like him"

Luis Buñuel tells it like it is in My Last Breath

Che's tales of life on the road are as readable as Jack Kerouac's

MOSTLY FACTUAL

Why does a book called the Rough Guide To Cult Fiction include a section on books that aren't fiction? For the simple reason that not all the cult books we return to again and again are novels. Only **Hunter S. Thompson** – or possibly **Ralph Steadman** – knows how much a book like Fear And Loathing In Las Vegas is true, which is why, arbitrarily, we have consigned Hunter to the authors' section. Certain definitive accounts of some of the horrors of the last century (notably **Primo Levi**'s harrowing recollections of the Holocaust) are listed in our gulags story (see **Danilo Kis** in Authors). What follows is a flawed, idio-syncratic, intriguing selection of cult tomes from across the spectrum.

———

AUTOBIOGRAPHY OF A SUPERTRAMP
W.H. Davies 1908
Nobody could call this iron-moulder's son from the back streets of Newport a stick-in-the-mud. Birched for stealing perfume as a teenager, **Davies** begged his way across America, lost his leg under an express train, married a prostitute 30 years his junior and died, in 1940, at the age of 69. He left behind this autobiography, a memoir of his marriage (Young Emma), and the immortal lines: "What is this life if, full of care, We have no time to stand and stare?" This book is a classic account of America in the Depression, as revealing, in its way, as The Grapes Of Wrath and full of incidental delights, like the impromptu supertramps summit at a camp in Pittsburgh, in which the beggars separate to raise money for whiskey and one returns with a bloody nose, a dollar bill and a new suit.
NOW READ ON Luis Alberto Urrea's The Devil's Highway is an epic, poetic, highly moving tale of a fatal walk across the Mexican-American border.

BLUE HIGHWAYS William Least Heat-Moon 1983
Having lost his job and his wife, **Least Heat-Moon** decided that "a man who couldn't make things go right could at least go." So, in a truck he names Ghost

Dancing after a life-affirming ritual of his Native American ancestors, he takes off on a three-month, 38-state road trip on America's blue highways – the back roads so coloured on old maps. The sights, smells and conversations of forgotten, unknown and isolated places in small-town America with suitable names like Nameless ("I was heading east, and Nameless lay forty-five miles west. I decided to go anyway") are brought to life in his beautifully written folksy travelogue, accompanied by his own photographs of the places and characters he encounters plus charming sketches of the half-ton Ford van he journeyed in. Novelist **Robert Penn Warren** said this book "makes America seem new in a very special way."

NOW READ ON Least Heat-Moon's **PrairyErth** is a microscopically detailed portrait of a rural county in Kansas.

BRILLIANT ORANGE
David Winner 2000

The brilliance on display here isn't just about the greats of Dutch football. As **Winner** celebrates the neurotic genius of the beautiful game in Holland, he explores Dutch culture as a whole, nominating **Johan Cruyff** as the Dutch **John Lennon** and drawing parallels between the way space is used on the pitch with how space is used in Dutch society and architecture. Brilliant as Winner's prose is, the quirky intelligence of the players and coaches talking here, helps. The book's spell never wears off because, unlike many, possibly most, football books, there's not a trace of padding.

NOW READ ON David Edmonds and **John Eidinow's** Bobby Fischer Goes To War, an extraordinary account of the triumph of a genius close to madness.

CONFESSIONS OF AN ENGLISH OPIUM EATER
Thomas De Quincey 1821

A brilliant child and a precocious classics scholar, **De Quincey** was only a moderately successful author until this was published in 1821. Instant fame and notoriety followed, not least because the book never apologises for its author's drug use. Opium was not then an illegal substance and when it was recommended to De Quincey to ease a headache, he was able to buy it over the counter from a pharmacist. Taking it as a tincture (known as laudanum), he was immediately thrilled by "the abyss of divine enjoyment thus suddenly revealed." Then followed eight years of highly pleasurable, but controlled, indulgence. It only started to go wrong when he began taking opium to combat the recurrence of a severe stomach ailment. As his intake grew his dreams turned to nightmares and the heightened state of perception that he'd previously enjoyed turned murky and dull. In a way that anticipates **Freud**, De Quincey scrutinises his own consciousness, analysing the pleasures and pains of his dreamworld and imaginatively exploring its links with childhood privations. The one drawback is the author's occasionally pompous and long-winded style.

NOW READ ON Decadent French poet **Charles Baudelaire** modelled his On Wine And Hashish on De Quincey's book.

THE DEMONIC COMEDY Paul William Roberts 1998

Hideously hungover after too little sleep and too much home-produced Iraqi spirits, the narrator is awoken in his hotel room by a fierce banging on the door and the news that, finally, his request for an interview with **Saddam Hussein** has been granted and he must come immediately. The fear and loathing in Baghdad shtick continues during the interview from which shattering revelations emerge, including the fact that Saddam looked like a man who had consumed most of the world's brandy, had a seriously flawed taste in neckties and when asked to pick his favourite film mumbled: "I very mudge like Godfather moofy." There aren't many books about Hussein's Iraq that make you laugh out loud, but this will. There's meat here too: the author's account of why Hussein thought the Americans would let him annex Kuwait would be an amusing tale of shambling incompetence if it hadn't had such appalling consequences.

NOW READ ON Li Zhisui was Mao's doctor and his The Private Life Of Chairman Mao is a compelling, appalling yet not unsympathetic portrait of the leader.

THE DIARIES OF KENNETH TYNAN
John Lahr (ed) 2001

Rude, vicious, hilarious, intelligent – you can't ask much more from a diary. Critic, writer and creator of Oh! Calcutta! Tynan's diaries are packed with amusing tales, such as the time he inadvertently watched a pornographic movie with **Princess Margaret** (a disaster salvaged by **Peter Cook**). Tynan is an acute observer of British mores and prejudices. The riff on how the **Lord Lucan** case would have been handled if the villain had been a working-class oaf from Streatham called Ginger Noakes is a tour de force. Be warned: there's lashings of S&M sex.

NOW READ ON Alan Clark Diaries – the incorrect, indiscreet, thoughts of a man who was a far better diarist than politician.

THE DIRT Mötley Crüe and Neil Strauss 2002

If **Mötley Crüe** were among the most meretricious and worthless bands of the 1980s, their autobiography – put together by **New York Times** rock critic **Strauss** – reveals them to be among the most appalling people of that or any other decade. It is also the most compelling book about the rock'n'roll lifestyle ever written. Everything you can imagine about rock stars behaving badly is in The Dirt – prostitutes, overdoses, foreign objects introduced into female orifices, more overdoses, deaths by drunk driving, yet more overdoses – along with stuff you never would have imagined – snorting a line of ants from the pavement in the absence of cocaine, for example. What makes the book so compelling is not so much the Caligula-like decadence, but the utter awfulness of the main characters. It gives some idea of their moral fibre that the most sympathetic member of the band is **Tommy Lee**, a convicted wifebeater.

NOW READ ON Please Kill Me, an oral history of punk by **Legs McNeil** and **Gillian McCain**, which proves that bands you loved dearly can be full of people you'd hate.

DISPATCHES Michael Herr 1977

John Le Carré noted that **Herr** brings a musician's ear and a painter's eye to the Vietnam war. Herr, who co-wrote the script of Full Metal Jacket and the narration of Apocalypse Now, covered the war for **Esquire** magazine and pulled his notes together to create this classic of **New Journalism** – fact presented using the techniques of fiction. Reading almost like a long prose-poem, this summons up what novelist **Robert Stone** called "the very essence of the Vietnam war – its space diction, surreal psychology, bitter humour – the dope, the Dexedrine, the body bags, the rot." Herr's only crime is that he writes so well, you almost wish you'd been there.

PICADOR

Dispatches
Michael Herr

'The best book I have ever read on men and war in our time.'
JOHN LE CARRÉ

NOW READ ON Son Of The Morning Star, a meandering, revelatory, chilling account of another famous U.S. military disaster, **Little Big Horn**, by the acclaimed novelist **Evan S. Connell**.

EASY RIDER, RAGING BULLS Peter Biskind 1998

The 1970s was a great decade for Hollywood's gifted mavericks whose creative juices flowed with the aid of copious drugs and alcohol. On the set of the film Five Easy Pieces, director **Bob Rafelson** rolled joints for his star **Jack Nicholson** to slow the actor's performance down. **Biskind**'s tale of sex, drugs and Tinseltown egos, based on hundreds of interviews with the likes of **Warren Beatty**, **Robert Altman** and **Robert Evans**, has many incidental delights – blind movie directors, **Steven Spielberg** seeing women bathing topless for the first time for example. The pace of the narrative matches the subject perfectly, Biskind hurtling from **Dennis Hopper**'s half-gallon of rum, 28 beers and three grams of coke a day to **Faye Dunaway** throwing a cup of urine in **Roman Polanski**'s face. A gossip-monger's dream.

NOW READ ON City Of Nets, **Otto Freidrich**'s fantastic noirish tale of Hollywood in the 1940s.

THE EMPEROR Ryszard Kapuscinski *1983*

Polish journalist **Kapuscinski** is most famous for The Soccer War, a collection headlined by his entertaining insight into the moment a World Cup qualifying match spilled into war in Central America, but this goes beyond the realms of great reportage. Here he weaves together the testimony of courtiers, servants and ministers to create a grotesque, funny, composite portrait of the last days of **Haile Selassie**'s Ethiopian monarchy. This was a court that employed a man to wipe dog's wee off dignitaries' shoes (the dog, belonging to the monarch, could not be disciplined). Kapuscinski tellingly traces this particular downfall while offering wider truths about autocracies and dictatorships.

NOW READ ON Kapuscinski's Another Day Of Life perfectly captures the chaos, destruction and random violence of Angola's civil war.

A HEARTBREAKING WORK OF STAGGERING GENIUS Dave Eggers *2000*

A memoir that tries to avoid being such, **Eggers**'s dazzling prose puts the 'postmodern' into fiction writing. It's a kind of self-conscious meta-narrative that is painful and playful in its anxiety to avoid sentimentality. How else to write about the staggering poignancy of a 21-year-old seeing both parents die of cancer inside a month and still retain a kind of cool? Left to bring up his eight-year-old brother in semi-squalor (his sister goes to college and his older brother works), Eggers jumps out of the narrative constantly to remind us he is resisting the pathos of the story. The editor of a literary magazine and the creator of a satirical fanzine, Eggers knows all about the book's "self-consciousness aspect" but is using the gimmick as "a device… to obscure the black, blinding, murderous rage and sorrow at the heart of this whole story." The reader is left in no doubt that any worries he/she may have about possible sentimentality have already occurred to the author. As Eggers says, we can always "pretend it's fiction".

NOW READ ON Augusten Burroughs's funny twisted memoir Running With Scissors is probably the best book ever written about a boy whose mum gives him away to a strange shrink who looks like **Santa Claus**.

HIROSHIMA John Hersey *1946*

Hersey does the seemingly impossible here, taking one of the most terrible events in the history of mankind and writing a book, which in retelling the accounts of six survivors, offers a strange kind of hope. The existence and use of the atom bomb is up there with the Holocaust as ultimate proof of man's inhumanity to man. But among the death and destruction, what lingers in the memory are the stories of ordinary people trying to help each other survive an extraordinary evil.

NOW READ ON Masuji Ibuse's Black Rain is probably the greatest Japanese historical novel on the bombing.

HOLIDAYS IN HELL
P.J. O'Rourke 1988

When travel writing includes descriptions of looking down the barrel of a gun in war-torn Lebanon and being pepper-sprayed in Korea, you know you've not picked up the latest **Michael Palin**. **O'Rourke** takes on politics, cultures and sub-cultures in this fast-paced, cynical guide to the world's hellholes, offering – in his flippant, sarcastic and non-PC way – memorable descriptions of the people he meets (the Koreans are "hardheaded, hard-drinking tough little bastards – the Irish of Asia") and the pleasures of modern transport ("If Christ came back tomorrow he'd have to change planes at Frankfurt").

NOW READ ON His Republican Party Reptile: fun, even if you detest his politics.

HOMICIDE David Simon 1993

This real-life account of a year in the Baltimore police inspired the cult TV series Homicide: Life On The Streets. As **Simon** follows 15 detectives trying to solve 234 murders, he traces their routines, obsessions, procedures, success rate and safety-valve humour as they deal with the unspeakable. All human life is here, so it's by turns chilling, funny, mundane and sad.

NOW READ ON Robert Fisk's Pity The Nation is an immense, anguished, moving book that tells the story of Lebanon at war, in hard-bitten, intriguing prose.

IN COLD BLOOD Truman Capote 1965

With this book, **Capote** claimed to have created the first 'non-fiction novel'. The story of the real-life murders of Kansas farmer **Herb Clutter**, his wife and their two children in 1959 by a pair of misfit drifters (**Perry Smith** and **Dick Hickock**) reads like a noir thriller. The dialogue is sublimely caught and the writing pitch-dark yet compelling, given further resonance by Capote's subtle empathy with Smith. Smith's line on Herb's death – "I really admired Mr Clutter, right up to the moment I slit his throat" – chills like fiction never could.

NOW READ ON The Family is a disturbing, rambling insight into the **Charles Manson** case by **Ed Sanders**, hippie poet and founder of satirical folk-rock group **The Fugs** that spotlights in his words, "The horror of what those creeps did."

THE MAN WHO MISTOOK HIS WIFE FOR A HAT
Oliver Sacks *1986*

Psychologist **Sacks** couldn't understand why a particular patient had come to see him until, as their meeting ended, the man tried to put his wife's head on his. Invited to see his patient's paintings, Sacks realised the man was losing the ability to process visual information. These wonderfully narrated case histories, including the man stuck in 1945 and the woman who emerged from a coma speaking perfect French, are funny, heartbreaking, inspiring and unforgettable.

NOW READ ON Sacks's Awakenings in which a group of patients regain consciousness and lose it again, is even more heartbreaking than the film version.

MEMOIRS OF AN ITALIAN TERRORIST Giorgio *2003*

An unrepentant and unapprehended terrorist, **Giorgio** reveals what it was like to work for the Red Brigades, the left-wing Italian terror group, in the 1970s. This is a peculiarly Italian take on this well-publicised, and little understood, phenomenon, focusing not on gore but on the day-to-day dilemmas the narrator faces in his secret life. The discourse on how a terrorist selects the right trattoria is one of many incidental highlights. If you got The Sopranos, you'll like this.

351

NOW READ ON Peter Dale Scott's Deep Politics And The Death Of JFK is essential reading for conspiracy theorists or anyone curious about how American democracy has become what it is today.

MINOR CHARACTERS Joyce Johnson *1983*

Scandalously neglected, this minor classic is an enchanting, revelatory memoir of the Beats as seen by one of **Jack Kerouac**'s long-term lovers. **Johnson** (who was Joyce Glassman when she first knew Kerouac) captures the mystique, the evasions, the betrayals, the inspiration and the chauvinism of Kerouac and co and sets them beautifully in the context of the stifling society of the 1950s. More telling, and better written, than much of the stuff by the Beats themselves.

NOW READ ON Eileen Simpson's Poets In Their Youth is almost as good: a moving memoir of John Berryman, Delmore Schwartz and Randall Jarrell.

THE MOTORCYCLE DIARIES
Ernesto 'Che' Guevara *1995*

Take the diary of two young guys on a motorbike journey through Latin America in 1952 and you've got the essentials of a great road trip. Make one of those guys a

23-year-old **Che Guevara** (eight years before the Cuban Revolution) and you've got a road trip with a difference. Actually, the motorbike dies after the first few chapters; their journey continues in the back of many and varied cargo lorries. Che's often poetic descriptions paint vivid portraits of deserts, mountains and local characters. There are tales of visits to leprosy hospitals, blagging free meals, and many impromptu games of football (Che was once a goalie for a first division team in Buenos Aires). The 2004 film adaptation kept close to the book but sacrificed some laddish moments to focus on the political awakening.

NOW READ ON Nicholas Mosley's The Assassination Of Trotsky on the twilight of another revolutionary icon, is just as gripping. The biggest let down: Mosley says Trotsky had a theory on the correct Marxist-Leninist way of washing up, but sadly didn't reveal it.

MY HAPPY DAYS IN HELL George Faludy *1962*

Picaresque reminiscences of a Hungarian poet who was offered 25 sheep as an incentive to marry the daughter of an admirer, and who escaped the Nazis only to be incarcerated in a Communist labour camp. For a book in which a lifelong friend is beaten to death after going mad, a girlfriend is killed when her ship explodes and the hero only avoids torture by confessing to being an American spy, **Faludy**'s memoir is a fantastically invigorating read. Florid, idiosyncratic, unapologetic, this is a full book, written with the power to haunt.

NOW READ ON No Particular Place To Go, a title nicked from a **Chuck Berry** song and a persona out of **Evelyn Waugh** and **Jack Kerouac**, **Hugo Williams**'s book is a tale of a poet at sea in America, coming to grips with the horrors of the first silicon breasts. Williams later said he made most of it up.

MY LAST BREATH Luis Buñuel *1983*

"Sex without religion is like cooking an egg without salt." The autobiography of **Buñuel** – maverick director, artist, provocateur and wit – written as he awaited "the final amnesia" of death, is utterly charming. Meditating on the recipe for a perfect martini: "I never miss my daily cocktail: where certain things are concerned, I plan ahead"; defining the perfect bar: "quiet, dark, very comfortable, no music of any kind" or just name dropping, he is captivating. Line selected at random: "Children and dwarves make the best actors."

NOW READ ON Ruth Brandon's Surreal Lives (2000) is a fascinating collective biography of the likes of Buñuel, **Duchamp**, **Breton**, **Dalí** and **Aragon**.

352

FIVE PILLARS OF LUIS BUÑUEL'S WISDOM

"God and Country are an unbeatable team; they break all records for oppression and bloodshed."

"Frankly, despite my horror of the press, I'd love to rise from the grave every ten years or so and go buy a few newspapers."

"All my life I've been harassed by questions: why is something this way and not another? How do you account for that? This rage to understand, to fill in the blanks, only makes life more banal."

"Age is something that doesn't matter, unless you are a cheese."

"The decline of the aperitif may well be one of the most depressing phenomena of our time."

PAPER LION George Plimpton 1966

'Dilettante' was the adjective most often attached to **Plimpton**: writer, actor, firework enthusiast and lover of sports from gridiron to grape-catching (the subject of one of his funniest magazine pieces). In 1963 Plimpton – tall, patrician, reed-thin – made the unlikeliest third-string quarter-back in the history of the **Detroit Lions**. Getting into training and into the team for a humiliating practice game in which he lost them 30 yards on one play was merely his cover. Once inside, Plimpton opened up the world of pro sports for the first time. He sketched the players not as superstars, but as ordinary men doing the best they could not to be dropped, injured or disgraced.

NOW READ ON Eamon Dunphy's Only A Game? does the same job, albeit in less elegant prose, for journeymen footballers in the English First Division.

THE RECKONING Charles Nicholl 1994

Unfolding with the ominous rhythm of a difficult murder investigation, this is an unsettling account of a drinking session in 16th-century Deptford, which ended in the mysterious death of the poet and playwright **Christopher Marlowe**. **Nicholl** goes beyond the Elizabethan clichés to expose a treacherous, constantly shifting world of espionage, murder and torture, in which even a writer as prominent and public as Marlowe can be killed in the pursuit of political ambition.

NOW READ ON John Bossy's Giordano Bruno And The Embassy Affair, is an intriguing tale in which the wandering scholar is embroiled in Le Carré-style espionage orchestrated by Queen Elizabeth I's spymaster, Francis Walsingham.

STALIN Edvard Radzinsky 1996

Political biographies aren't usually famed for their narrative tension, but this book is almost as fast-paced as **Mario Puzo**'s The Godfather. **Radzinsky** draws on secret state archives to create a chilling portrait of the Communist dictator as a paranoid, psychotic Don Corleone who served as a double agent for the Tsarist secret police, may have plotted (or expedited) Lenin's demise and, having presided over the death of millions, was scheming to start World War III when he died in 1953. Once read, the account of his death – in which he was left to die by his own guards and henchmen after suffering a stroke – will never be forgotten.

NOW READ ON The Last Tsar by **Radzinsky** is a gripping re-evaluation of **Nicholas II**'s reign, told in a similar fast-moving style.

SURELY YOU'RE JOKING, MR FEYNMAN!
Richard P. Feynman 1985

Proof, says the **New York Times**, that you can laugh out loud and scratch your head at the same time. Nobel Prize-winning physicist **Feynman** is probably the only man in his field since **Einstein** to have huge popular appeal. This book is a series of anecdotes passing itself off as an autobiography, that elegantly makes important points about the acquisition of knowledge. As entertaining, thought-provoking and idiosyncratic as you would expect from this scientist who was as happy accompanying a ballet on bongos (he was taught by the leader of a Congolese drumming group) or discussing gambling with **Nick the Greek** as he was trading theories with Einstein.

NOW READ ON In **James McManus**'s Positively Fifth Street: Murderers, Cheetahs And Binion's World Series Of Poker the narrator, a poet and poker fan, risks all for a story in a high-stakes adventure Feynman would adore.

THE TEACHINGS OF DON JUAN
Carlos Castaneda 1968

Life-changing, earth-shattering – this book has received all the clichéd plaudits. But some of them are true. **Castaneda**'s account of his initiation into the teachings of **Don Juan Matus**, a Native American sorcerer, is gripping, even if some critics now doubt the tutor existed. Skip the anthropology (which has since been disputed) and the journals are truly revelatory. You can take this as a spiritual guide (as millions have), an invitation to re-evaluate the world and your place in it, or a chance to play literary detective – trying to guess what's true, what's invented and what was hallucinated under the influence of cactus, mushrooms or datura plants. You might be disappointed when, at the end, Castaneda refrains from seeking any more advice from his guru, which, given the life-changing, earth-shattering stuff that has gone before, seems a bit of a cop-out.

NOW READ ON **Mitch Albom**'s Five People You Meet In Heaven, a moving, inspirational and brief novel with a theme not dissimilar to **Frank**

Nobel deeds: Mr and Mrs Feynman celebrate his prize with a quickstep

Capra's movie It's A Wonderful Life, in which Eddie, the fairground worker, meets five people in heaven who lead him to reappraise his life.

TRUE TALES OF AMERICAN LIFE
Paul Auster (ed) 2002

When novelist **Auster** asked listeners to **National Public Radio** in America to send him written stories, he received 4,000, of which the best 179 are published here. The only constraints on the tales, which are split into categories ranging from Animals and Slapstick to Dreams and Death, were that they had to be short (the opening one is just six sentences long) and true. The collection, as Auster notes in his introduction, includes "hilarious blunders, wrenching coincidences, brushes with death, miraculous encounters, improbable ironies, premonitions, sorrows, pains, [and] dreams." Contributors include: a postman, a crime-scene cleaner, several doctors and assorted housewives. These sparsely told tales – the story in which a boy in a poor family ensures his family have presents to open on Christmas day is especially moving – offer a poignant glimpse into the lives and loves of 20th-century Americans.

NOW READ ON Maya Angelou's I Know Why The Caged Bird Sings is a raw, scathing, beautiful account of growing up in the American South in the 1930s.

356

THE UNABRIDGED DEVIL'S DICTIONARY
Ambrose Bierce 2000

To aficionados, this book is a tour de force. To spoilsport **Paul Theroux**, 19th-century US satirist **Bierce** was a **Jonathan Swift** wannabe without the learning or necessary madness to carry it off. Bierce served in the American Civil War (his war stories at times match **Ernest Hemingway**'s or **Stephen Crane**'s) and he later worked for press baron **William Randolph Hearst** for 20 years. Embittered by his son's suicide and the collapse of his marriage, he compiled The Cynics Word Book, which became *The Devil's Dictionary*. A collection of 1,600 bitingly clever insights, this extensively annotated edition is a treasure to be savoured a few gems at a time. Bierce was last seen crossing the Mexican border in 1913 and is presumed to have died in battle alongside the troops of **Pancho Villa**. **Gerald Kersh** wrote a short story, The Mystery Of The Bottle, about his disappearance.

3 DEVILISH DEFINITIONS

Acquaintance A person whom we know well enough to borrow from, but not well enough to lend to.

Cabbage A familiar kitchen-garden vegetable about as large and wise as a man's head.

Noise A stench in the ear. The chief product and authenticating sign of civilisation.

NOW READ ON Brewer's Rogues, Villains & Eccentrics by **William Donaldson** is simply irresistible and deservedly cherished for such fantastic cross-reference gems as: "Goat's rectum, customs officers shining a torch up a."

ZEN AND THE ART OF MOTORCYCLE MAINTENANCE
Robert M. Pirsig 1974

When a 46-year-old technical writer and former philosophy teacher decided to set out on a motorcycle ride from Minnesota to California with his young son, he thought the trip might make good material for a philosophical essay. Four-and-a-half years later, the result was an autobiographical tale of a spiritual journey that was rejected by 121 publishers before finally being printed to such acclaim as "profoundly important" and with the subtitle An Inquiry Into Values. Intellectual it may be, but it is also inspired, original and exceptionally readable (though useless if you're trying to mend a motorcycle). Through a series of on-the-road lectures dipping into 2,000 years of philosophy and plenty of motorcycle metaphors, **Pirsig** searches for the meaning of quality in life, and the truth about his own past and mental breakdown, related as fragmentary flashbacks to a character he calls Phaedrus. The book put forward what Pirsig called his "metaphysics of quality", an idea he expanded, 20 years later in his subsequent work, Lila: An Inquiry Into Morals.

357

NOW READ ON Tom Wolfe's kaleidoscopic non-fiction novel The Electric Kool-Aid Acid Test has no life-changing quality, but Wolfe is on fine form retelling the tale of **Ken Kesey** and his Merry Pranksters, precursors of the 1960's hippie movement.

INDEX OF AUTHOR ENTRIES

PICTURE CREDITS FOR THE AUTHORS SECTION:
Keystone/Getty Images; Erich Auerbach/Getty Images; Jill Furmanovsky/DNA Press Photos; Jerry Bauer/Dalkey Archive Press; Marion Ettlin; Chris Saunder; David Levenson/Getty Images; CSU Archive/Everett/Rex Features; Gene Shaw/Time Life/Getty Images; Vintage Books; Canongate Books; Penguin Books; New Direction Publishing

Marcel Proust tries to get a grip

ROUGH GUIDES
REFERENCE SERIES

"The Rough Guides are near-perfect reference works"
Philadelphia Enquirer

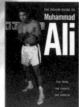

History · Internet · Music · Restaurants · Football
Weather · Astronomy · Health
Movies · Videogaming · TV

DON'T JUST TRAVEL